HUMAN BONDING

Human Bonding

The Science of Affectional Ties

Edited by
Cindy Hazan
Mary I. Campa

THE GUILFORD PRESS
New York   London

© 2013 The Guilford Press
A Division of Guilford Publications, Inc.
72 Spring Street, New York, NY 10012
www.guilford.com

Printed in the United States of America

This book is printed on acid-free paper.

Last digit is print number: 9 8 7 6 5 4 3 2 1

Library of Congress Cataloging-in-Publication Data

Human bonding : the science of affectional ties / edited by Cindy Hazan
and Mary I. Campa.
    pages cm
 Includes bibliographical references and index.
 ISBN 978-1-4625-1067-2 (hardcover : alk. paper)
 1. Friendship. 2. Interpersonal relations. I. Hazan, Cindy. II. Campa, Mary I.
 BF575.F66H84 2013
 158.2—dc23
                                                              2013009746

About the Editors

Cindy Hazan, PhD, is Associate Professor in the Department of Human Development at Cornell University. Dr. Hazan is an internationally recognized scholar whose seminal work on affectional bonds helped define a new field of study in social and personality psychology. Her 1987 article (coauthored with Phillip R. Shaver) "Romantic Love Conceptualized as an Attachment Process" provided a theory, a methodology, and an empirical foundation for an approach to understanding the thoughts, behaviors, and emotions that humans call "love." The attachment approach proved a valuable tool for scientists studying all aspects of adult relationships, making the 1987 article one of the ten most-cited articles published in the *Journal of Personality and Social Psychology*. In 2012, Drs. Hazan and Shaver were awarded the Scientific Impact Award from the Society of Experimental Social Psychology in recognition of the profound influence of their work. While continuing to engage in original theoretical and empirical work, Dr. Hazan designed the course "Human Bonding," which she has developed and taught for 25 years at Cornell. The thesis of the 1987 love-as-attachment article, now elaborated by the work of hundreds of researchers, is the thread that runs through the course and this book.

Mary I. Campa, PhD, is Assistant Professor in the Department of Psychology at Skidmore College in Saratoga Springs, New York, where she teaches courses in introductory psychology, adolescent development, and interpersonal relationships. Dr. Campa's research focuses on adolescent and adult development with an emphasis on close relationships. Her current work is aimed at understanding the reasons why attachment relationships (our closest relationships) are unique and enduring.

Contributors

John T. Cacioppo, PhD, Department of Psychology, University of Chicago, Chicago, Illinois

Mary I. Campa, PhD, Department of Psychology, Skidmore College, Saratoga Springs, New York

Jude Cassidy, PhD, Department of Psychology, University of Maryland, College Park, Maryland

J. Thomas Curtis, PhD, Department of Pharmacology and Physiology, Oklahoma State University Center for Health Sciences, Tulsa, Oklahoma

Lisa M. Diamond, PhD, Department of Psychology, University of Utah, Salt Lake City, Utah

Matthew J. Dykas, PhD, Department of Psychology, State University of New York at Oswego, Oswego, New York

Paul W. Eastwick, PhD, Department of Human Development and Family Sciences, University of Texas at Austin, Austin, Texas

Gül Günaydin, PhD, Department of Psychology, Cornell University, Ithaca, New York

Louise C. Hawkley, PhD, Department of Psychology, University of Chicago, Chicago, Illinois

Cindy Hazan, PhD, Department of Human Development, Cornell University, Ithaca, New York

Lauren A. Lee, MA, Department of Psychology, University of Arizona, Tucson, Arizona

Sandra Metts, PhD, School of Communication, Illinois State University, Normal, Illinois

Mario Mikulincer, PhD, Interdisciplinary Center (IDC) School of Psychology, Herzliya, Israel

Harry T. Reis, PhD, Department of Clinical and Social Sciences in Psychology, University of Rochester, Rochester, New York

David A. Sbarra, PhD, Department of Psychology, University of Arizona, Tucson, Arizona

Emre Selcuk, PhD, Department of Human Development, Cornell University, Ithaca, New York

Phillip R. Shaver, PhD, Department of Psychology, University of California, Davis, Davis, California

Susan Sprecher, PhD, Department of Sociology and Anthropology, Illinois State University, Normal, Illinois

Natasha D. Tidwell, BA, Department of Psychology, Texas A&M University, College Station, Texas

Debra M. Zeifman, PhD, Department of Psychology, Vassar College, Poughkeepsie, New York

Reflections on "Human Bonding"

LISA M. DIAMOND, PhD

It is no exaggeration to say that Cindy Hazan's "Human Bonding" course significantly changed the path of my career. When I served as a teaching assistant for the course in graduate school, I primarily thought of myself as a sexuality researcher who was, by extension, interested in intimate relationships. By the end of the course, I was completely besotted with the science of intimate relationships, and especially with the emerging body of research on the psychobiological underpinnings of romantic attachments and their long-term health implications. Intimate relationships ended up becoming the topic of my dissertation and a core part of my overall research program. Quite simply, "Human Bonding" transformed me from a relatively narrow sexuality researcher to a much broader sexuality-and-relationships researcher. The course also gave me a much deeper appreciation for theory—especially evolutionary theory and attachment theory—than I had previously held. It was not only the comprehensive, sweeping, fascinating range of material in "Human Bonding" that was so influential, but also Cindy Hazan's effective way of organizing and presenting the material. Attending her lectures was like watching an exciting miniseries unfold, installment by installment. The scope of her knowledge was dazzling, and she managed to convey not only an abiding and infectious scientific curiosity, but also a compelling sense of basic human wonder.

PAUL W. EASTWICK, PhD

My most vivid memory of Cindy Hazan's "Human Boding" course probably came about a year after I took it. I had just finished my undergraduate work, I was living in New York City, and I had no idea what I wanted to do with my life. I was trying to make it as a musician in a band, and I was working as a computer consultant. Yet I still had this vague idea that I might eventually pursue a career in psychology. Toward that end, I had e-mailed Dr. Niall Bolger at New York University to learn more about his research on support processes in couples, and he invited me to attend one of his lab meetings. I arrived about 20 minutes early for the meeting and took that time to review my notes from "Human Bonding" just to reacquaint myself with the material. Sitting outside his office with my notes, I thought over and over again: "Oh yeah, I loved this stuff! I really want to study this!" There was something about re-encountering the material once I was out of college—and wasn't worried about tests and GPAs anymore—and I realized that making new discoveries about human relationships was the best career anyone could ever hope for. And I have never looked back!

DAVID A. SBARRA, PhD

In the fall of my sophomore year at Cornell University, I had the opportunity to read some of Urie Bronfenbrenner's influential work on ecological systems theory. I was thrilled with the way he explained human development and his model of nested systems, and I started wondering about the implications of his model for mental health. When I took Cindy Hazan's "Human Bonding" course the next semester, I was entirely receptive to the idea that our closest social relationships—that is, our experiences within Bronfebrenner's microsystem—could set the stage for much of life's happiness and, to a large degree, emotional pain. "Human Bonding" introduced me to ideas that remain foundational to the research I do now, nearly 15 years later. When I took the course, the science of close relationships did not hold the wide appeal it does today; it was still considered a marginal enterprise. Its novelty is precisely what sparked my interest in the field, and I felt it would be incredibly exciting to combine research in close relationships with the study of mental health and psychological well-being. This book is a terrific starting point for anyone hoping to learn about or enter the vibrant field of close relationship research.

GÜL GÜNAYDIN, PhD

I was a teaching assistant for Cindy Hazan's "Human Bonding" course 2 years ago. I took notes as Professor Hazan lectured so that I could check them if students had any questions about the material. But my note-taking efforts were not always completely successful. The course included so many interesting empirical findings that were organized into rich theoretical frameworks, and Cindy Hazan, being the great lecturer she is, made the material seem so captivating and intuitive with great examples and anecdotes that I often got carried away and found myself jotting down research ideas instead of lecture notes. Many of the ideas that I jotted down during those lectures shaped my research, and the concepts I learned in "Human Bonding" changed the way I think about relationship science.

EMRE SELCUK, PhD

Cindy Hazan's "Human Bonding" course has a special place in my graduate career. When I arrived at Cornell University as a new graduate student deeply interested in relationship science, "Human Bonding" proved to be an invaluable resource. It provided a thorough review of modern relationship science, and its theoretical framework served as the building blocks for my own program of research. Years later, I had the pleasure of teaching the class myself at Cornell. Having the opportunity of discussing with young adults the processes "that lie at the core of human existence," as social psychologist Ellen Berscheid wrote, was truly fascinating. The memories from teaching the class are definitely among the most cherished of my graduate training as a relationship scientist.

DEBRA M. ZEIFMAN, PhD

I've taught a relationships course, modeled on Cindy Hazan's "Human Bonding" course at Cornell, ever since I arrived as a new faculty member at Vassar College. Students typically begin the semester skeptical about taking an empirical, evidence-based approach to something as complicated as close relationships. They especially resist the idea that we can learn something about the nature of emotional bonds in humans by examining the same processes in rats, voles, or monkeys, to name a few of the species we analyze as models for human bonding. By the end of the semester, even the most resistant students come around to the view that the scientific method can be fruitfully applied to relationships, despite some inherent limitations. And although research doesn't always guide personal choices, many students report gaining insight into their own personal behavior through the course content. Watching students gain these insights about themselves and appreciate the relevance of this research to their own lives has been one of the most rewarding aspects of my teaching career.

MARY I. CAMPA, PhD

I have fond memories of Cindy Hazan's "Human Bonding" course as a graduate student, a teaching assistant, and a professor. The graduate seminar I attended had two components, the undergraduate lecture and the graduate discussion. These classes were my favorite part of the week. We would go from the undergraduate lecture in which Professor Hazan provided background to the graduate discussion in which we would hash out the details of each topic, from concepts like good-enough parenting to the similarities and differences in same-sex and opposite-sex relationships. The next year, as a teaching assistant for the class, I had the joy of grading 500 essays on the pros and cons of sexual strategies theory. Several years later, I would get the opportunity to teach "Human Bonding" at Cornell University to a class of 250 students. My first class was twice the intended size, but so many students heard great things about the course and wanted to be included that I could not turn them away. I later taught the class to 500 students and then, as I transitioned to Skidmore College, to a group of just 11! Amazingly, regardless of size, each time I taught the course the enthusiasm students brought to the discussions was always evident. The course material is exciting for students because it speaks to them about the most valuable part of their lives—their relationships with others. Although I have shared "Human Bonding" with hundreds of people since that first day of graduate school, my fondest memories of the class are the days I spent with Professor Hazan. In preparation for teaching, Professor Hazan walked me through each lecture, in which I learned not just the science of human bonding but also the passion behind the science. Since then, we have had countless discussions about close relationships, what they mean, and how we can best understand and study them. There are many ways to present this material, but I will be forever grateful to my dear friend and mentor for sharing with me her vision of human bonding. In my newest role as coeditor of *Human Bonding*, it is my great privilege to join her in sharing this vision with a wider world.

Contents

Introduction

CINDY HAZAN
MARY I. CAMPA

*I*t is amply documented that day-to-day well-being, overall happiness and psychological adjustment, physical health, and even the length of life itself are all significantly influenced by the quality of our closest relationships. Indeed, our continuation as a species depends on the formation and maintenance of social bonds. As helpless infants, we require nurturance and protection for our very survival; as adults, we must find and retain mates long enough to reproduce; and as parents, we must provide adequate care to our offspring so that they too survive to reproductive age. Dependence on and interdependence with our conspecifics is a fundamental fact of the human condition.

The central aim of this book is to provide an integrative, science-based overview of human bonding across the lifespan. To achieve this goal, we draw from the large, heterogeneous and multidisciplinary field of theory and research that defines contemporary relationship science. Topics include infant–caregiver attachment, human social nature, child and adolescent social development, mate selection, love and sexual desire, "hooking up" and online dating, keys to relationship success, predictors and consequences of relationship dissolution, and the role of social connectedness in morbidity and mortality. Together, the chapters tell the fascinating story of how and why humans bond with each other and how they enable, enrich, and, yes, complicate the unique experience of being human.

The book is organized into four major parts. Part I covers early bonding experiences from infancy through adolescence. The chapters in this part address the basics of ethological attachment theory, the coevolution of infant–caregiver behavior systems, and the normative developmental transition from parental to peer to partner attachment. Part II addresses three different perspectives on mating phenomena. The chapters in this part examine mating through the lenses of social psychological processes, evolutionary trade-offs, and animal models. Part III highlights new topics, ideas, and developments in the relationship field. The chapters in this part explore the changing nature of romantic relationship initiation via hooking up and online dating, links and distinctions between love and lust and their implications for same-sex sexuality, and the latest findings on the conceptualization and measurement of adult attachment styles. Part IV emphasizes the profound and pervasive impact of interpersonal relationships in everyday life. The chapters discuss the key role of perceived partner responsiveness in relationship well-being, the predictors and consequences of relationship dissolution, and the effects of social connectedness on morbidity and mortality.

BONDING PHENOMENA FROM INFANCY THROUGH ADOLESCENCE

The book begins with babies for two reasons. First, there is overwhelming evidence that the quality of relationships with primary caregivers during infancy can have lasting effects on how one subsequently relates to others. Second, in terms of their functions and dynamics, infant–caregiver attachments and adult pair bonds have much in common.

The first chapter of Part I (by Dykas and Cassidy) provides a detailed overview of John Bowlby's ethological attachment theory, which grew out of his attempts to explain the distress of infants and young children in response to separation from their primary caregivers. A central concept of the theory is that attachment is regulated by an innate behavioral system designed to ensure that helpless and vulnerable infants will maintain proximity to and resist separations from the adults who care for and protect them. All normal human infants, provided the opportunity, form an emotional bond with at least one person before their first birthday. This predisposition to bond is one of several basic, hardwired human universals. Many animal species are capable of walking within hours after birth, and some of our closest primate relatives reach sexual maturity by age 4. In stark contrast, human infants are completely helpless at birth. It takes weeks just to develop the strength to hold up our own relatively large heads, a year or more to walk, and another decade beyond that to reach sexual maturation. Simply stated, we would not survive if we did not form close ties with adult caregivers and protectors.

While forming such bonds is the norm, there are nonetheless differences in the quality of these relationships. In testing Bowlby's normative theory, Mary Ainsworth and her colleagues observed distinct patterns of individual differences in infant–caregiver attachments. Specifically, the patterns they identified—one secure and two insecure—reflect systematic variation in how infants feel and behave in relation to their primary caregivers. Further, the different patterns were found to be systematically related to the quality of care the infants had received in the first few months of life. Subsequent studies have shown these patterns of attachment to be related to a wide variety of developmental outcomes.

The attachment system is one evolved mechanism that serves to bring infants and adults into bond-promoting contact. Chapter 2 (by Zeifman) describes the role played by other coevolved characteristics (i.e., features of one individual that evoke a particular response in another individual). For example, infant faces are typified by bulging foreheads, large eyes, and receding chins, and these features elicit caregiving responses from adults. Another example is that in interacting with infants adults spontaneously modify the pitch and intonation of their speech in a manner that the infants find appealing. Chapter 2 addresses additional coevolved characteristics as well as the many ways in which early brain development is shaped by infant–caregiver interactions.

Chapter 3 (by Campa) serves as a bridge between infant–caregiver attachment and adult romantic attachments, which are the focus of subsequent chapters. Among the many developments between infancy and adolescence, two have special significance for bonding. The first is a steady increase in the balance of time spent with peers versus parents. The second is the physical transformation associated with puberty. Both developments enhance the salience of gender. Children self-segregate on the basis of sex, boys and girls have distinctly different patterns of peer play, and physical changes associated with puberty serve to differentiate male from female.

CONTEMPORARY APPROACHES TO MATING

Part II offers three distinct perspectives on mating. The first—introduced in Chapter 4 (by Günaydin, Selcuk, and Hazan)—is a social-psychological approach to the factors that influence mate selection. In essence, it is a process of narrowing a large pool of potential mates down to "the one." Factors such as propinquity and similarity reduce the pool significantly. Within this smaller pool, some people are judged more appealing than others on the basis of such characteristics as physical appearance, personality, and social status. As a result of an inherent aversion to social rejection, the pool is narrowed still further to those individuals who are judged to be responsive or attainable. Perceived reciprocal liking on the part of an appealing other is a common trigger for romantic infatuation whereby one individual becomes the sole focus of attention.

The second perspective is based in evolutionary psychology and, more specifically, the question of whether to adopt a long-term, pair-bonding mating strategy or not. Traditionally, evolutionary models of human mating emphasized sex differences, especially the differential costs of reproduction for men versus women. The typical woman produces an average of one egg per month from puberty to menopause. In contrast, a typical man produces 500 million sperm cells per day, and for many more years. Additionally, including gestation, lactation, and offspring care, the reproductive cost for women is years of investment, whereas the minimal investment for men is a few minutes. This asymmetry is hypothesized to affect every aspect of mating psychology, including interest in long- versus short-term mating, what qualities are most desired in a potential mate, and the strategies one employs to attract and retain mates. Chapter 5 (by Eastwick and Tidwell) summarizes the multiple evolutionary forces that have shaped the extent to which individuals invest in parenting effort versus mating effort. Importantly, the chapter includes more recent advances in evolutionary models of human mating. The newest findings underscore the value of hormonal and physiological evidence (compared with self-reports) and the magnitude of within-sex (compared with between-sex) differences.

The third contemporary approach looks to animal models for potential clues and fruitful avenues of research on the underlying mechanisms of human bonding. For example, monogamy is exceedingly rare in the animal kingdom. Humans typically equate monogamy with sexual exclusivity, whereas ethologists use a variety of behavioral and physical features to determine the mating pattern of a species (e.g., whether ovulation is overt or covert, the degree of sexual dimorphism, the extent of paternal offspring care, and especially the presence or absence of a pair bond between reproductive partners). As noted in Chapter 6 (by Curtis), it is exceptional for two unrelated adult animals to form a close, enduring bond. However, much has been learned from studying the tiny proportion of species in which pair bonding is the norm. Specifically, there is strong evidence that social bonding—whether between parents and offspring or between reproductive partners—involves essentially the same mechanisms and the same neurobiological and neurochemical underpinnings.

NEW TOPICS, IDEAS, AND DEVELOPMENTS

Part III is devoted to new topics of study, new ways of thinking about some old topics, and new developments in an established but evolving area of research. Chapter 7 (by Sprecher and Metts) addresses two new ways of initiating interpersonal relationships or meeting potential mates: online dating and hooking up. In Western cultures, the average age at marriage continues to go up, which often translates into more years of uncommitted relationships. Technological advances have made it easy to meet lots of people with whom encounters would otherwise be unlikely, thus expanding the pool of potential mates. New terms for these new arrangements have entered the lexicon, like *booty calls* and *friends with benefits*. Researchers have begun to investigate these changes, but more work is needed to understand their full impact on relationship trajectories and outcomes. In the meantime, it appears that romantic attraction is still a key factor in relationship initiation.

Love, desire, and sexual orientation are not new topics, but the perspective on them that is offered in Chapter 8 (by Diamond) is significantly new. Kinsey advanced our understanding of sexual orientation by viewing it as a continuum rather than a discrete category. More recent research has shown that sexual orientation can and should be conceptualized in terms of multiple dimensions and that individuals may vary independently on these dimensions. Specifically, a person can be sexually attracted to one gender yet romantically attracted to the other. What is new here is the hypothesis that a key to understanding sexual orientation is to view it through the lens of distinct social behavioral systems. If romantic love and sexual desire are rooted in different systems, their targets (whether same sex or other sex) need not correspond. Additionally, each system serves a unique function, but they can and often do influence the activation of other systems. For example, the close interpersonal proximity inherent to the attachment system can trigger the activation of the sexual mating system, or vice versa. Sexual desire can lead to romantic love or follow from it. Further, differences in the likelihood of one system acting as a trigger for another might also help explain important differences between female and male sexuality.

Chapter 9 (by Shaver and Mikulincer) reviews the latest developments in the measurement of adult attachment. The initial measure was simply a translation of Ainsworth's three patterns of infant–caregiver attachment into terms appropriate for adult romantic relationships. In the 25 years since, countless studies have found systematic associations between attachment styles and the way people think, feel, and behave and in their closest social relationships. What is new in the area of adult attachment is how individual differences are conceptualized and measured. Based on the results of taxometric analyses, the three-category model of attachment styles was replaced with a two-dimensional model. One dimension is attachment anxiety, the core of which is fear of abandonment; the other dimension is attachment avoidance, which is essentially avoidance of interpersonal closeness. Chapter 9 details these developments in the conceptualization and measurement of adult attachment as well as the theoretical implications. In addition, it sheds considerable light on why some romantic relationships endure and others do not.

RELATIONSHIP EFFECTS ON MORBIDITY AND MORTALITY

Long before there was a field of relationship science there was awareness and even empirical evidence of powerful links between relationships and health. The famous Hammond report on the health effects of cigarette smoking is a great example. During the multiyear study, smokers were twice as likely to die as nonsmokers. However, the rate of death was also associated with relationship status. Even though in every relationship category—married, single, widowed, divorced—the death rate for smokers was double the rate for nonsmokers, the death rate for married smokers was not different from the death rate for divorced nonsmokers. Part IV is devoted to three very different but equally important ways in which relationships impact psychological and physical health.

Chapter 10 (by Reis) tackles the big question of what makes relationships happy and satisfying. Rather than simply reviewing the many research findings and theories about relationship well-being, it offers an integration of the various conceptualizations. Most important, it identifies the common core. What is it that concepts like felt security, belonging, connectedness, and social support share? It turns out that the key to relationship well-being is the perception that a partner is responsive to one's most important needs, goals, and values. We want to be understood and accepted and, as Victor Hugo put it, "loved not just for but in spite of ourselves."

Another angle on understanding the importance of relationships is to examine the effects of and reactions to relationship dissolution. From an outsider's perspective, the dissolution of a romantic relationship appears to be a sudden event. "I just heard that so and so broke up!" However, it is usually the culmination of an extended process of uncoupling, and it is typically unilateral. That is, one member of the couple wants the breakup and the other does not. Moreover, the initiator begins working through the process long before the partner has any real inkling that anything serious is going on. Likewise, there is evidence that reactions to breakups can also be characterized in terms of a process that unfolds over time, and includes systematic variations in emotional valence and intensity as well as differences in adjustment to the loss. Chapter 11 (by Lee and Sbarra) makes the case that relationship scientists have identified, on the one hand, the predictors of breakup and, on the other, successful and unsuccessful patterns of coping, but thus far have failed to integrate the two. A theoretical framework is offered that spans predictors and consequences of breakup and suggests promising directions for future research.

It is a well-documented fact that highly socially integrated people are happier, healthier, and longer lived! It is also now established that the morbidity and mortality costs of social isolation are equal to those of smoking. Chapter 12 (by Hawkley and Cacioppo) provides a detailed overview of the psychological and physiological pathways by which relationships influence health and well-being. It also underscores the importance of perceptions. It is not the quantity but rather the quality of social relationships that matters most, and quality boils down to perceptions of the responsiveness of others. When we feel hungry, we drop what we are doing and look for something to eat. When we are thirsty, we orient our attention to finding something to drink. Imagine what would happen if we became so engaged in other activities that we completely forgot to eat or drink. Social bonding is as vital to our survival as food and drink, and it is why when our relationship needs are unmet we get such a strong feeling that something is wrong. Social bonding is a fundamental fact of the human condition.

Part I

BONDING PHENOMENA FROM INFANCY THROUGH ADOLESCENCE

Chapter 1

The First Bonding Experience

The Basics of Infant–Caregiver Attachment

MATTHEW J. DYKAS
JUDE CASSIDY

Can any of us picture an infant without his or her parents? Probably not, because much of an infant's daily life is spent in the company of these persons. Bonding to mothers, fathers, and other caregivers is simply what infants do; regardless of gender, race, ethnicity, culture, or history, the bonding of infants is part of the basic human experience. Although many scholars have debated the conceptual nature of these bonds and have proposed various theories to explain them (e.g., Erickson, 1950; Freud, 1909/1999; Klein, 1932), mounting theory and research suggest that the infant–caregiver bond can best be conceptualized as most centrally an *attachment bond* (Ainsworth, 1989; Bowlby, 1969/1982, 1973; see also Cassidy, 1999, 2008; Thompson, 2006). In this chapter, our principal aim is to provide a brief overview of the nature of the infant–parent attachment bond. In the first part of this chapter, we describe the evolutionary basis of this bond, and discuss the normative features that constitute nearly all human infant–caregiver attachments. In the second part, we describe individual differences in the quality of these bonds, the precursors and outcomes of these individual differences, and the mechanisms through which these individual differences contribute to human social and emotional functioning.

INFANT–PARENT ATTACHMENT BONDS: NORMATIVE PROCESSES AND DEVELOPMENT

Defining Features

Infants—with very few exceptions—form attachments to their principal caregivers (e.g., a mother, a father, or another consistent caregiver to whom they may or may not be biologically related). The protection that caregivers provide is an important element of attachment bonds, even though the precise feelings and beliefs that might constitute a sense of intrapersonal security can vary significantly across infants, contexts, and developmental periods (see Waters & Cummings, 2000; see also Goldberg, Grusec, & Jenkins, 1999). For example, a caregiver is thought to serve as a haven of safety (i.e., a *safe haven*), providing an infant with a basic sense that he or she is (or will be) protected physically and/or psychologically when needed (Bowlby, 1973; Cassidy, 1999, 2008; Goldberg et al., 1999). Parents—and all other persons to whom infants are attached—are referred to as *attachment figures.* Ainsworth (1985) characterized an attachment bond as similar to other affectional bonds in that "it is a relatively long-lived tie in which the partner is important as a unique individual, interchangeable with none other, from whom inexplicable, involuntary separation would cause distress, and whose loss would occasion grief" (p. 799); she then added the essential characteristic that specifies an affectional bond as an attachment: "seeking to find comfort and security in the other" (p. 800).

Parents (or any other attachment figure), although bonded to the infant in the context of a caregiving role and invested in his or her survival, are not considered to be attached to the infant because parents do not typically attempt to derive security from the infant (e.g., parents do not seek the infant for physical and/or psychological protection and do not rely on the infant as an older, stronger, and wiser safe haven). Thus, the infant's attachment bond to his or her parent is both unidirectional (i.e., nonreciprocated) and categorically different from the caregiving bond that parents establish to the infant, although both types of bonds contribute correspondingly to the reciprocal attachment–caregiving relationship (see Solomon & George, 2008). Also, an infant will develop many relationships with individuals over the course of the first few years of life, but only a handful of these relationships will likely meet the criteria for being an attachment bond.

An Evolutionary Perspective

British psychiatrist John Bowlby (1969/1982, 1973, 1980, 1988) originally formulated the idea that infants' bonds to their parents are attachments. On the basis of his extensive clinical work with children and adolescents in the United Kingdom after World War II, as well his training in psycho-analytic theory (see Bretherton, 1992, for a biography), Bowlby developed a way of thinking about the nature of the child–parent bond that differed fundamentally from all previous conceptualizations. For example, Bowlby was intrigued by the fact that many of the children orphaned during the war continued to mourn and pine for their parents for months (and some-times years) after being separated from them. These children also tended to suffer from considerable despair and malaise, to be inconsolable, and to reject the notion that "new" caregivers could assume their parents' role.

These observations were noteworthy because they did not appear to correspond to the prevailing psychoanalytic theory in which Bowlby had been trained. According to psychoanalytic theory, a child's emotional bond to the parent emerged and persisted only because the parent satisfied the child's "primary drive" for obtaining physical necessities (e.g., food and shelter). Thus, the emotional bond that a child developed to the parent essentially reflected a "secondary drive," which suggested that there was nothing inherently extraordinary about the relationship of a child to a par-ent. Instead, according to this traditional view, the emotional bond a child formed to a parent could be conceived of as the necessary by-product of the person meeting the child's physical needs, and such a bond could be devel-oped to anyone who met the child's basic physiological needs. However, when Bowlby observed children longing for their deceased parents, who could no longer satisfy their children's basic physiological needs, while also failing to form new bonds to adults who did attend to these needs (e.g., orphanage caretakers), he began to believe that perhaps the child–parent bond did not emerge as a result of a secondary drive process and that chil-dren bonded to their parents for other reasons.

Bowlby (1969/1982, 1973) drew on Harry Harlow's comparative psychology research with rhesus monkeys when formulating his thinking (Harlow, 1961; Harlow & Harlow, 1962; Harlow & Zimmermann, 1959). In these now well-known studies, Harlow observed that monkey infants reared with both a wire mesh, food-providing "mother" and a terry cloth, non-food-providing "mother" did not always prefer the former. When frightened, for example, these infant monkeys sought contact with the terry cloth mother and not the wire mesh mother. Moreover, even during non-stressful periods, these infant monkeys spent the majority of their time in the presence of the terry cloth mother and typically visited the wire mesh mother only to nurse. These studies (as well as ethological studies, especially Konrad Lorenz's, 1935, imprinting studies) corroborated Bowlby's (1969/1982) ideas that an infant's bond to the mother was not based on the physical provisions of food, shelter, and other necessities. At the same time, the first systematic observations of human infants and parents indicated that infants become attached to fathers and other caregivers who never feed them (Ainsworth, 1967; Schaffer & Emerson, 1964); moreover, indications that infants become attached to abusive parents suggest that the attachment system is not driven by simple pleasurable associations (Bowlby, 1956). This body of emerging data led Bowlby to speculate that infant–caregiver attachment might be based on something other than associations with food or pleasure, perhaps on the provision of *security*.

To build the case for the importance of security in the formation of attachment bonds, Bowlby (1969/1982) formulated a revolutionary theory proposing how such bonds could have emerged in humans. Bowlby (1969/1982) based his theory on the concept of "biologically based behavioral systems" (borrowed from ethologists) to describe a species-specific system of behaviors that leads to certain predictable outcomes, at least one of which contributes to reproductive fitness. According to Bowlby (1969/1982), behaviors that increase infant proximity to or contact with an attachment figure, either through the infant's active behavior or by drawing the attachment figure to the infant, are *attachment behaviors* (e.g., crying, clinging, calling, following). These behaviors are organized within the *attachment behavioral system*. Two central characteristics of infant attachment relate to *proximity/contact maintenance* and *separation protest*. The infant attempts to maintain proximity to the attachment figure (the extent of the attempt varies as a function of the state of the infant, the whereabouts and likely responsiveness of the attachment figure, and the nature of the environment) and, to this end, protests unwanted separation. Through the process of natural selection (and in the setting Bowlby referred to as the *environment of evolutionary adaptedness*), all humans acquired an attachment behavioral system because it enhanced reproductive fitness. The concept of the behavioral system involves inherent motivation; there is no need to view behavior (e.g., attachment behavior) as the by-product of any more fundamental process or "drive." This conceptual notion is compatible with the data, described previously, that infants become attached to caregivers who are not associated with feeding (Ainsworth, 1967; Harlow & Harlow, 1962).

Bowlby speculated that for infants, maintaining proximity to an attachment figure who could protect them from danger—and protesting physical separation from this figure—increased their chances of survival and reproductive success. Indeed, whereas other mammals may protect themselves using physical safe havens without relying on conspecifics for survival (e.g., by retreating to a den), human infants are largely incapable of manipulating their environments to find a nonhuman safe haven. Thus, over time and through the process of natural selection, infant behaviors that decreased separation from a caregiver and increased the proximity of the caregiver to the infant in times of danger were selected (perhaps because infants who did not engage in such behaviors perished), and the genes promoting such behavioral strategies were propagated across subsequent generations. As a result, infants are biologically predisposed through human evolutionary processes to use their caregivers as safe havens in times of need and/or distress.

Drawing on control systems theory, Bowlby (1969/1982) further claimed that the attachment behavioral system, while continually activated, is stimulated at different levels as a function of immediate circumstances. The "thermostat" that controls the attachment system's level of activation relates to (1) the presence of danger and, perhaps more important, (2) the presence of or access to an attachment figure. Thus, the attachment system is relatively highly activated when the infant is in the presence of immediate threat or when the infant is separated from an attachment figure. According to Bowlby (1973), even the possibility of separation from an attachment figure can be frightening. He wrote, "Of the many fear arousing situations that a child, or older person, can foresee, none is likely more frightening than the possibility that an attachment figure will be absent or . . . unavailable when wanted" (p. 201). On the basis of his understanding of reflexes and fixed-action patterns, Bowlby (1969/1982) further proposed that attachment behavior, once instigated by the attachment behavioral system, is unlikely to be extinguished until the goal of attaining proximity to the attachment figure is met (e.g., Bowlby, 1969/1982, noted that like a missile seeking a target, a child seeking contact with an attachment figure continues until the point of impact).

Although infants are usually not separated from their attachment figures for an extended period of time, there are circumstances when longer separations (a few days or more) do occur. Relying on both his clinical observations and a seminal collaboration with James Robertson (documented in numerous films, including *A Two-Year-Old Goes to Hospital* [Robertson, 1953a]; see also Robertson, 1953b; Robertson & Bowlby, 1952), Bowlby proposed that relatively long-term separations are accompanied by a typical sequence of protest, despair, and detachment. At first, infants protest separation, engaging in the attachment behaviors described previously to end the separation and to regain proximity to the attachment figure; these behaviors may also reduce the likelihood of such a separation recurrence. If the separation endures, despair typically overtakes the infant. During this period, infants may appear listless and depressed or agitated, and psychological and physiological functioning is hampered (see Bowlby, 1973). Finally, when the infant no longer foresees that a reunion with the attachment figure will take place, the infant undergoes what Bowlby labeled *detachment*. During this period, the infant behaves as if he or she is uninterested in the attachment figure, protest and despair cease, and behavior appears to "return to normal." Bowlby, however, described this behavior as a defensive stance that helps the infant cope with the psychological pain associated with the loss of the attachment figure. Bowlby considered the fact that on reunion with the attachment figure the defensive "detachment" typically soon gives way to heightened attachment behaviors, evidence of the defensive nature of infant behavior during this phase.

The Secure-Base Phenomenon

Within the conceptual framework of attachment theory, the attachment figure serves not only as a safe haven to whom the child can return for comfort when distressed but also as a *secure base* from which to safely explore with confidence (Ainsworth, 1967). For Bowlby (1988), the concept of the attachment figure serving as a secure base for the child is at the heart of attachment theory: "No concept within the attachment framework is more central to developmental psychiatry than that of the secure base" (pp. 163–164). Parents provide a secure base when children, based on prior experiences with the parents, feel confident to explore, with an expectation that the parent will be available and sensitively responsive when needed. The use of a parent as a secure base may have evolved because it enhanced the child's survival by reducing the threat of predators and other dangers while at the same time fostering the exploration that would provide the child with skills to navigate the environment successfully.

Bowlby (1973) noted that his perspective differed from one in which attachment was considered to hinder exploration. According to Bowlby, it is not the case that attachment promotes dependency and limits exploration, nor is it the case that infants and children who are playing are both physically and psychologically "disconnected" from their parents. Instead, it is precisely when infants have confidence in the caregiver's availability if needed that exploration is enhanced; infants are viewed as capable of engaging fully in such activities largely *because* they are confident of their attachment figures' availability when needed. Without such confidence, infants' exploratory behavior diminishes. Thus, attachment, far from interfering with exploration, is viewed as fostering exploration. Most infants respond flexibly to a specific situation after assessing both the environment's characteristics and the caregiver's availability and likely behavior (Ainsworth, Bell, & Stayton, 1971). For instance, when the infant experiences the environment as dangerous, exploration is unlikely. Furthermore, when the attachment system is activated (perhaps by separation from the attachment figure, illness, fatigue, or unfamiliar people and surroundings), infant exploration and play decline. Conversely, when the attachment system is not activated (e.g., when a healthy, well-rested infant is in a comfortable setting with an attachment figure nearby), exploration is enhanced. Bowlby (1973) described as important not only the physical presence of an attachment figure but also the infant's belief that the attachment figure will be available if needed. A converging body of empirical work, in which maternal physical or psychological presence was experimentally manipulated, has provided compelling evidence of the theoretically predicted associations between maternal availability and infant exploration (Ainsworth & Wittig, 1969; Carr, Dabbs, & Carr, 1975; Rheingold, 1969; Sorce & Emde, 1981; see Grossmann, Grossmann, Kindler, & Zimmermann, 2008, for a review of infant exploration in the context of child–parent attachment relationships).

Phases of the Development of Attachment

Developing an attachment to a specific caregiver is not a rapid event, but occurs over a relatively long period of time that spans many months. This process is thought to occur during four distinct developmental phases (Bowlby, 1969/1982; see also Marvin & Britner, 2008). During the first phase—from birth to approximately 10 weeks of age—newborn attachment behavior (like all behavior) is largely reflexive and is not directed toward any specific person. Instead, infants seek out contact with any available individual nondiscriminantly and can be comforted by a variety of individuals. However, in the second phase—from approximately 10 weeks to 6 months—infants develop higher order social-cognitive capacities to discriminate persons based on their physical attributes; they also gain greater control over their gross motor skills (as a result of simple behavior systems elaborating into more complex ones; see Marvin & Britner, 2008).

As such, during this period, an infant acquires the capacity to orient attachment signals toward their consistent caregivers (most often mothers and fathers) in preference to other persons.

Yet the shifts that occur at approximately 6 to 7 months of age demarcate what Bowlby (1969/1982) viewed as the "clear cut" formation of an attachment to a caregiver. At this point, labeled Phase 3, attachments to mothers, fathers, and other principal caregivers (e.g., a nonbiologically related adoptive parent) are fully evident. Bowlby noted that in Phase 1 infants are not attached to their caregivers, and yet by Phase 3 they are "plainly so"; Phase 2 was considered a transition phase: "Whether and to what extent a child can be considered to be attached during Phase 2 is a matter of how we define attachment" (1969/1982, p. 268). One of the new capacities that render attachment so clear cut is the capacity to crawl (and later walk), which gives infants self-initiated, voluntary control over establishing and maintaining contact with their caregivers, and also enables them to actively seek out their caregivers when upset, distressed, and/or in need of protection (Marvin & Britner, 2008). By no longer having to rely solely on a caregiver to respond to their attachment-related needs, infants at this age can express their attachment behaviors toward particular caregivers more actively; such active expression typically evokes responses from these caregivers, thereby contributing to the forging of powerful connections with them. Indeed, the formation of these attachment bonds is thought to be a critical developmental milestone because once formed, these bonds will persist over the course of the lifespan and will contribute to other key areas of development (a point we discuss later). Infants' attachments to multiple caregivers typically form hierarchically, such that infants will tend to prefer one attachment figure over another (e.g., an infant may desire to use a mother, rather than a father, as a safe haven to return to in times of need and/or distress; Bowlby, 1969/1982, referred to this phenomenon as *monotropy*).

Finally, during the fourth phase of attachment development—commencing at approximately 30 months—infants begin to learn how to cope adaptively with typically occurring separations from their attachment figures. By gaining more sophisticated social-cognitive capacities, infants can begin to modify the attachment behavioral system's goal of maintaining proximity to the attachment figure, which will cause infants to scale back the rate at which they engage in attachment behavior (most notably contact- and proximity-seeking behavior) during the context of everyday living. For example, prolonged separations that were distressing for infants earlier in development are managed more effectively because the goal of maintaining immediate physical proximity to the caretaker is corrected through miti-gating psychological processes (e.g., the capacity to understand that a care-giver will be back after a few hours away; that being separated from a parent in certain contexts is not a dangerous event).

Formation of Attachment Bonds: Internal Working Models of Attachment and Hidden Regulators

In order to use a specific person as a safe haven and secure base, infants are required to identify persons who might serve in these capacities and to men-tally store information about them. How is it that infants become attached to some people and not others? This process is not completely understood. Two factors are likely to play a role: what Bowlby (1969/1982) called *inter-nal working models of attachment* (he also called these *representational models*) and what Hofer (1994) called *hidden regulators*. We describe each of these briefly.

Drawing on cognitive theory, Bowlby (1969/1982, 1973) proposed that the organization of the attachment behavioral system involves cogni-tive components—specifically, mental models of the attachment figure, the self, and the environment, all of which are largely based on experiences. Bretherton (1991) suggested that repeated attachment-related experiences could become organized as scripts, which would in turn become the build-ing blocks of broader working models (see also Vaughn et al., 2006). Of note, the proposition that infants mentally internalize their relationships with parents on the basis of real-life experiences with them is a key feature of attachment theory and is congruent with other theories purporting that humans internalize relational experiences (e.g., Baldwin, 1995; Heider, 1958; Lewin, 1933; Mead, 1934; Piaget, 1954). It also sets the theory apart from earlier theories suggesting that infants mentalize their experiences with parents through fantasy and other non-reality-based processes (Freud, 1909/1999; Klein, 1932).

According to Bowlby, these models allow individuals to anticipate the future and make plans, thereby operating most efficiently (see also Breth-erton & Munholland, 2008; Main, Kaplan, & Cassidy, 1985). The child is thought to rely on these models, for instance, when making decisions about which specific attachment behavior(s) to use in a specific situation with a specific person, and as such may play a particular role in attach-ment formation (see Sherman & Cassidy, 2013, for a discussion of infant cognitive capacities related to the formation of internal working models and empirical evidence of these capacities). Moreover, because infants' attachment-related experiences with parents vary, these models (and the behavioral decision-making patterns associated with them) will also vary across specific infant–parent dyads. Later in this chapter, we more thoroughly discuss these individual differences in attachment models.

In addition to the formation of internal working models of attachment, which are thought to develop and function at a social-cognitive level within the infant, emerging theory and animal-based research suggest that hidden regulators within infants' interactions with their caregivers might contribute independently to infant attachment formation (Polan & Hofer, 2008). A hidden regulator is conceived of as a physiologically (rather than psychologically) based component of an infant's interaction with a caregiver that might contribute both to the infant's attachment and to the quality of the infant's internal neuroregulatory functioning. Such regulators are referred to as "hidden" because they are discretely present—but not directly observable—in infants' social interactions with their caregivers. For example, a hidden regulator might be the smell, the touch, and/or the body temperature of a caregiver.

Although the notion that hidden regulators exist and contribute to attachment formation has not yet been examined empirically in humans, evidence in support of the existence of such regulatory mechanisms comes from Hofer's examination of rat pups over the past 30 years (for a review, see Polan & Hofer, 2008). Through a series of carefully designed experiments, Hofer's data suggest that these regulators may affect a variety of systems and emotional states in rat pups that are closely linked to attachment (e.g., behavioral, autonomic, endocrine systems; sleep–wake states). Maternal rat behaviors such as licking and grooming have been linked to positive physiological responses in infant rats, such as decreases in the production of the stress hormone corticotropin-releasing factor (i.e., CRF). These maternal behaviors may, for example, promote systems within infants that inhibit the production of CRF, which target glucocorticoid receptors in the hippocampus and gamma-aminobutyric acid receptors in the amygdala. Moreover, the extensive work of Levine and colleagues identified ways in which mothers serve as regulators of infants' pituitary–adrenal stress response system (for a review, see Levine, 2005), and the research of Meaney and colleagues identified the ways in which maternal behavior contributes to gene expression (e.g., Meaney, 2001, 2010).

These intriguing animal studies suggest that hidden regulators may exist in human infant-parent bonds, and future studies will undoubtedly shed light on what these specific regulators are and how they may contribute (independently or interactively) to infant–caregiver attachment formation (Cassidy, Ehrlich, & Sherman, in press; Main, 1999). On the basis of the available evidence, it seems plausible that some hidden regulators of infant stress reactivity may be touch, close body contact, and eye gazes. For example, recent data indicate that a mother's touching of her infant attenuates the infant's physiological response to stress (Feldman, Singer, & Zagoory, 2010). Through different hidden regulatory mechanisms, the repeated reduction of stress in the presence of a specific caregiver could potentially lead an infant to become attached to that caregiver and use him or her as a safe haven and secure base.

INDIVIDUAL DIFFERENCES: SECURE VERSUS INSECURE INFANT ATTACHMENT

Defining Features

Although nearly all infants develop attachments to their principal caregivers (i.e., caregivers who are physically present to the infant on a regular basis), the *quality* of these early attachments varies (van IJzendoorn & Sagi-Schwartz, 2008). Some infants derive a stable sense of security from their caregivers and use these individuals as a safe haven and secure base; these infants are considered to be securely attached to such caregivers. Other infants, in contrast, may have difficulties deriving security from their caregivers and may not perceive their caregivers as providing a necessary safe haven or secure base; these infants are considered to be insecurely attached to such caregivers. We note that during infancy, attachment security versus insecurity is not considered to be a trait of the infant, but instead reflects the quality of the attachment bond to a particular caregiver (i.e., an infant is more appropriately described as "securely attached to his mother" than as "a securely attached infant"), and indeed data suggest that infants can be securely attached to one parent and insecurely attached to another (see Fox, Kimmerly, & Schafer, 1991).

According to Bowlby, the defining feature of secure attachment is the infant's confidence in the availability and responsiveness of the attachment figure when needed. Although it is likely that some of this confidence involves implicit physiological processes (perhaps those related to hidden regulators that have yet to be examined), Bowlby focused on the affective-cognitive concept of internal working models as important when considering not only the normative development of infant attachment to specific individuals (as described previously) but also whether those attachments will be secure or insecure. Internal working models of attachment are thought to be based on the infant's attachment-related real-life interactions with attachment figures. As noted earlier, Bretherton (1991) proposed that the rudimentary "building blocks" of these models are secure base scripts (see also Waters & Waters, 2006, for a discussion of secure base scripts; see Schank & Abelson, 1977, for general psychological theory about the script construct and how such scripts may enable humans to internalize the sequential events that have occurred in their lives). In infant–parent attachment relationships, infants are believed to develop scripts for how the parent will respond to their attachment-related needs; example scripts could be "When I am distressed, my mother holds me," and "When I am in pain, my father becomes angry at me" (see Johnson, Dweck, & Chen, 2007, for experimental evidence that infants securely attached to their mothers are more likely than insecurely attached infants to possess scripts that mothers will respond sensitively to infant separation distress).

Assessment of Individual Differences in Infant Attachment

Since the mid-1960s, attachment researchers have attempted to gain insight into the quality of infants' attachments to their caregivers using different methodologies (see Solomon & George, 2008, for a review). To date, the most widely used instrument to assess the quality of infant attachment has been the Strange Situation procedure (Ainsworth, Blehar, Waters, & Wall, 1978; Ainsworth & Witting, 1969). The Strange Situation procedure is approximately 20 minutes long and is administered in a novel environment, typically a university laboratory room. During the procedure, an infant undergoes short episodes involving a caregiver and a stranger (typically an adult female research assistant). Twice during the procedure, the caregiver leaves the infant in the room (once with the stranger for 3 minutes, and once alone and then with the stranger for a total of 6 minutes) and returns (see Ainsworth et al., 1978, for a detailed description of the procedure). Infants are classified into one of four groups on the basis of their behavior toward the caregiver upon reunion: *secure, insecure–avoidant, insecure–resistant*, and *insecure–disorganized.*

Infants classified as *secure* seek proximity to their caregivers on reunion (usually through, but not limited to, direct physical contact), are comforted by such proximity, and reengage smoothly in exploration. *Insecure–avoidant* infants do not seek physical proximity to their caregiver (perhaps to minimize contact with the caregiver) and focus almost entirely on continued exploration. *Insecure–resistant* infants, on the other hand, seek proximity to and contact with their caregivers upon reunion, yet do not derive comfort from this contact. These infants also appear to maximize interaction with the caregiver by demonstrating continued distress and yet may resist contact with the caregiver once it is achieved (e.g., by pulling away from a caregiver when held); because of their continued heightened distress, these infants do not successfully reengage in exploration. (For a detailed description of these Strange Situation classifications and additional subclassifications within each of these three principal groups, see Ainsworth et al., 1978; Solomon & George, 2008.)

Although most infants in the Strange Situation procedure demonstrate one of these patterns of attachment, considered to be *organized* patterns (i.e., marked by either secure patterns of contact seeking and exploration or insecure patterns of minimizing or maximizing interaction with the caregiver upon reunion), other infants show an *insecure–disorganized* pattern of attachment behavior. Infants classified as *insecure–disorganized* display relatively odd, overtly conflicted, and/or fearful behaviors in the presence of their parents (see Main & Solomon, 1986, 1990). They may, for example, display anomalous movements and postures (e.g., freezing upon reunion with a parent), engage in sequential or simultaneous displays of contradictory attachment behavior (e.g., strong avoidance from the parent coupled with strong proximity seeking to the parent), and/or show subtle/overt signs of being frightened by the parent (e.g., the classic hand-to-mouth gesture and/or fearful facial expressions). Infants classified as disorganized lack an organized strategy for relating to their attachment figures, and their atypical behaviors run contrary to the notion that their attachment behavioral systems have adapted successfully to manage the infant–caregiver attachment bond (Lyons-Ruth & Jacobvitz, 2008).

Meta-analytic data indicate that the distribution of Strange Situation classifications in low-risk North American community samples of infants is 62% secure, 15% insecure–avoidant, 9% insecure–resistant, and 15% insecure–disorganized (van IJzendoorn, Schuengel, & Bakermans-Kranenburg, 1999). Yet the distribution of these classifications can vary significantly in any population, especially as risks to infant attachment security increase (e.g., infant attachment insecurity and disorganization are much more prevalent in low socioeconomic samples; see van IJzendoorn, Goldberg, Kroonenberg, & Frenkel, 1992, for a review). Moreover, a variety of cross-cultural studies have indicated that although the proportion of secure infants matches that found in North American community samples, the proportions of insecure–avoidant and insecure–resistant infants vary considerably in some cultures. For example, relatively few German infants are classified as insecure–resistant; the majority of insecure infants are classified as insecure–avoidant. In studies conducted in Israel, the reverse has been observed, with most insecure infants being classified as insecure–resistant (see van IJzendoorn & Sagi-Schwartz, 2008, for a review).

Since the initial development of the Strange Situation procedure, a variety of data lends support to its strong psychometric properties. In addition to the considerable validity data presented later in this chapter (e.g., links between Strange Situation classifications and the quality of parent–child interaction and many important developmental outcomes), other data indicate that researchers can reliably code infants' Strange Situation behavior, and that the measure is correlated with home-based measures of security (e.g., the observer-rated Attachment Q-Sort; Waters, 1987/1995; see Solomon & George, 2008, for a detailed description of the Strange Situation's psychometric properties).

Of note, although the psychometric properties of measures are often gauged in terms of its test–retest reliability, gauging the reliability of the Strange Situation is complicated by the fact that attachment is susceptible to change based on the current status of the infant's relationship to the parent. Indeed, it is expected that an infant's Strange Situation classification would remain stable over time in the context of a stable attachment relationship; however, when the relationship changes (e.g., a parent becomes more or less of a secure base and/or safe haven), then there should be some resulting lawful change in the quality of the attachment. Thompson, Lamb, and Estes (1983), for example, reported that changes in maternal employment and consistent nonmaternal care, which could influence mothers' secure base provision, were associated with changes in infant attachment status from ages 12 to 19 months. Thus, if changes in the stability of infant–caregiver attachment security do occur, they are not likely random, but instead are likely linked lawfully to changes in the stability of these relationships (see Belsky, Fish, & Isabella, 1991; Lewis, Feiring, & Rosenthal, 2000).

Precursors of Individual Differences

Attempting to understand why individual differences in infant attachment emerge has arguably been one of the most challenging topics in attachment research, and the possibilities have been widely studied and debated (see Belsky & Fearon, 2008). In his early conceptualizations of attachment theory, Bowlby (1969/1982, 1973, 1988) relied heavily on clinical case studies and a handful of empirical studies to speculate why some children appeared to be securely attached to their mothers and others appeared to be insecurely attached. Bowlby's fundamental belief was that both infant and caregiver make important contributions to infant attachment quality, noting that individual differences "turn partly on the initial biases that infant and mother each bring to their partnership and partly on the way that each affects the other during the course of it" (1969/1982, p. 340). Although Bowlby briefly mentioned ways in which infant characteristics could contribute to these individual differences (and it is interesting to note that these characteristics centered on atypical development such as cognitive delay or minimal brain damage rather than on typically occurring variations of infant temperament), Bowlby's focus was on environmental contributors. Indeed, Bowlby speculated that the origins of attachment security (vs. insecurity) stemmed from the confidence that children have that their attachment figures will be responsive when needed. For example, Bowlby (1973, p. 204) claimed that "confidence that an attachment figure is, apart from being accessible, likely to be responsive can be seen to turn on at least two variables: (a) whether or not the attachment figure is judged to be the sort of person who in general responds to calls for support and protection; (b) whether or not the self is judged to be the sort of person towards whom anyone, and the attachment figure in particular, is likely to respond in a helpful way." In this initial thinking about environmental factors, Bowlby was again largely interested in atypical rearing situations and focused his discussion on the precursors of security versus insecurity largely in terms of nonnormative child-rearing practices (e.g., parental neglect) and extreme family circumstances (e.g., the loss of a parent).

Since Bowlby published his initial ideas about the precursors of security versus insecurity of attachment, attachment researchers have taken a broader approach to understanding how these differences typically emerge across the population (although researchers continue to study the emergence of these differences in clinically at-risk samples as well; see DeKlyen & Greenberg, 2008, for a review). On the basis of Bowlby's ideas that parental behavior contributes to infant attachment quality, Ainsworth and her colleagues (1978) were the first researchers to examine whether patterns of infant attachment to mother observed in the Strange Situation were linked to maternal behavior within the home in a middle-class community sample. The three patterns of organized attachment behavior exhibited in the Strange Situation that existed at the time (the disorganized pattern of attachment had not yet been identified) were linked to the type of caregiving that infants received during daily repeated interactions in their everyday home environments (Ainsworth et al., 1978; see also Vaughn & Waters, 1990). More precisely, a mother's degree of sensitivity (vs. insensitivity) was highly associated with her infant's Strange Situation classification; this dimension tapped the degree to which a mother consistently perceived, accurately interpreted, and appropriately responded to infant behavior (see Ainsworth et al., 1978).

Ainsworth et al.'s (1978) original focus on maternal sensitivity as the precursor of infant attachment quality set the stage for much additional research on sensitivity–attachment links in the following years (Belsky & Fearon, 2008; van IJzendoorn, 1995). Many studies replicated the original finding. For example, in home environments, parents of secure infants provide a sufficient secure base and safe haven (e.g., Posada, Kaloustian, Richmond, & Moreno, 2007), parents of insecure–avoidant infants are more rejecting (e.g., Ainsworth et al., 1978), parents of insecure–ambivalent infants are more inconsistent in their caregiving (see Cassidy & Berlin, 1994, for a review), and parents of disorganized infants are more likely to frighten their children (including increased rates of abuse; see Lyons-Ruth & Jacobvitz, 2008, for a review). However, whereas Ainsworth and her colleagues reported a relatively large effect size between sensitivity and infant–mother attachment, the collective effect sizes gathered from subsequent studies have been modest (van IJzendoorn's, 1995, meta-analyses revealed a modest $r = .22$ effect from 66 studies including 4,176 infant–parent dyads). These modest meta-analytic effect sizes may be attributable to the fact that the sensitivity construct has often been broadly defined, and such broad definitions may have captured behaviors that do not contribute to infant attachment security. There has also been debate regarding whether caregiver sensitivity is a culturally dependent, rather than universally constant, construct (see Rothbaum, Weisz, Pott, Miyake, & Morelli, 2000). As a result, researchers have attempted to lend greater conceptual specificity to the aspects of sensitivity that may be linked to the formation of a secure infant attachment (e.g., Cassidy et al., 2005).

In addition to maternal behavioral sensitivity, other related contextual factors may contribute to individual differences in infant attachment. Considerable data indicate that one key factor may be parents' own attachment security (what attachment theorists refer to as an *attachment organization* or a *state of mind with respect to attachment*, which is typically tapped using the Adult Attachment Interview [AAI; George, Kaplan, & Main, 1996]; see Hesse, 2008, for a description of the AAI and for information about the state-of-mind construct). A wealth of data indicates that mothers who have a secure state of mind with respect to attachment (marked by open and coherent discourse about attachment relationships and attachment-related childhood experiences; see Hesse, 2008) are likely to have secure infants, whereas those possessing an insecure state of mind are likely to have insecure infants; the connection between security in mothers and security in infants is relatively high, with meta-analytic data indicating 75% concordance (van IJzendoorn, 1995; see also Bakermans-Kranenburg & van IJzendoorn, 2009).

Researchers have examined whether behavioral sensitivity is the mediating mechanism through which maternal state of mind with respect to attachment is linked to infant attachment; the available data, however, indicate that behavioral sensitivity only partially accounts for this link and other mediating factors likely exist. (The lack of evidence explaining a link between mother attachment and infant attachment via mothers' behavioral sensitivity has been referred to as the *transmission gap*; van IJzendoorn, 1995.) Thus, researchers have sought to identify other factors that may explain the link between parent and infant attachment and have focused on social-cognitive constructs such as maternal mind-mindedness, maternal reflective functioning, and maternal insightfulness (e.g., Meins, Fernyhough, Fradley, & Tuckey, 2001; Oppenheim & Koren-Karie, 2002; Slade, Grienenberger, Bernbach, Levy, & Locker, 2005; see Dykas, Ehrlich, & Cassidy, 2011, for a review). Behaviorally based mechanisms, such as parental gaze and parent–infant open communication patterns, have also been considered (Beebe et al., 2010; Bretherton, 1990).

Although many important questions remain about how individual differences in infant attachment emerge, researchers have used the available data to construe how infants internalize their experiences with caregivers and how such internalized representations may ultimately become manifested behaviorally in the Strange Situation. Infants' Strange Situation classifications are believed to reflect the quality of their internal working models of attachment, most notably the experience-based social-cognitive forecasts that infants generate according to their preexisting attachment-related knowledge about their caregivers (Ainsworth et al., 1978; Bowlby, 1973; see also Dykas & Cassidy, 2011). Thus, based on infants' behavior in the Strange Situation, inferences can be drawn about how infants may, through their internal working models of attachment, forecast caregiver availability, responsiveness, and sensitivity (see Bretherton & Munholland, 2008), leading to a behaviorally based *strategy* for maintaining the relationship with the attachment figure (Main, 1990). As such, viewing infant Strange Situation behavior as a strategy can be very useful when trying to understand the experiential precursors of individual differences in infant attachment.

Secure infants' attachment behavior in the Strange Situation may reflect a strategy based on knowledge that their caregiver has served as a secure base/safe haven in the past, and will likely continue to serve in these ways in both the present and the future (Ainsworth et al., 1978). The behavior of insecure–avoidant infants, on the other hand, in which attention to the attachment figure is minimized, could serve to protect them from the further rejection and/or insensitivity that they predict will come from the caregiver when the attachment system is activated (Main, 1990). The behavior of insecure–resistant infants, in which attention to and preoccupations with the attachment figure is heightened, may indicate a prediction that the caregiver will be responsive only if the infants maximize their attachment behaviors (Cassidy & Berlin, 1994). Insecure–disorganized infants, who appear frightened of their caregiver and/or disoriented in his or her presence, may have knowledge of being frightened by the caregiver in the past (e.g., these infants may have been maltreated by their caregiver), leading to the prediction that their caregiver could again frighten them. Such predictions lead to "conflict without resolution," such that infants desire to seek proximity to their caregiver when the attachment system is activated, yet cannot do so successfully because they perceive the caregiver as a potential source of danger (Hesse & Main, 2000; see also Lyons-Ruth & Jacobvitz, 2008).

Since Bowlby's original writings, there has been an extensive focus on the ways in which variation within the typical range of infant temperament contributes to individual differences in infant attachment. Decades of research, in which infant temperament (assessed at a variety of ages by observations, experimental and clinical measures, and reports of neonatal nurses, parents, and researchers) failed to emerge as a direct predictor of attachment quality, led Vaughn, Bost, and van IJzendoorn (2008) to characterize the current extensive agreement among most researchers as indicating "that attachment and temperament constitute separate domains of development, and that most constructs from one domain do not explain individual differences in the other" (p. 210). These authors further noted that both constructs of attachment and temperament, and their interaction, have been linked in compelling ways to a variety of domains of infant and child functioning, and that future research containing measures of both constructs remains important.

Developmental Outcomes and Mechanisms of Influence

Decades of developmental theory and research have suggested that a variety of factors contribute to infant well-being (see, e.g., Shonkoff & Phillips, 2000). According to attachment theory, an infant's success in developing a secure attachment to a main caregiver is an important precursor to his or her healthy social and emotional development (Bowlby, 1969/1982, 1973, 1988; see also Sroufe, Egeland, Carlson, & Collins, 2005; Sroufe & Waters, 1977). However, the extent to which researchers believe that infant–caregiver attachment influences different areas of development has varied. Whereas some researchers have suggested that attachment should permeate and influence many parts of an infant's development, others have insisted that attachment should contribute to only a narrow set of individual outcomes (see Belsky & Cassidy, 1994, for an extensive discussion; see also Goldberg et al., 1999; Waters & Cummings, 2000). Although, empirically speaking, the "jury is still out" regarding the extent of the domains to which the infant–caregiver attachment bond contributes, attachment theory makes some compelling arguments regarding *how* the quality of the infant–parent bond sets individuals on a trajectory for positive social and emotional well-being. In this section, we briefly describe theory about two factors—infants' internal working models of attachment and emotion regulation—that could be mechanisms through which attachment affects subsequent development. Following this theoretical review, we provide a brief summary of the existing data on links between infant–caregiver attachment and selected developmental outcomes.

When considering mechanisms whereby early attachment relationships influence later development, the construct on which Bowlby focused was that of internal working models of the self and others. With regard to the self, Bowlby (1973) wrote, "In the working model of the self that anyone builds a key feature is his notion of how acceptable or unacceptable he himself is in the eyes of his attachment figures" (p. 203). According to attachment theory, a person's sense of acceptability (and self-worth) is tied to the manner in which attachment figures have responded to his or her attachment-related needs, such that parents serving as suitable secure bases and safe havens will instill in their infant a growing sense that the infant is valuable and has inherent worth. This notion that the quality of the self-concept is tied to relational experiences is found in other developmental theories (e.g., Mead, 1934; see Harter, 2006, for a review; see also Cassidy, 1988, 1990, for discussion of attachment and self). In relation to working models of others, secure infants, with experience-based representations of access to a parental secure base and safe haven, may come to expect that other persons will treat them similarly (Berlin, Cassidy, & Appleyard, 2008). On the other hand, insecure infants who have lacked a consistent secure base and/or safe haven in their life may expect that others may not be responsive or available in times of need. (Indeed, researchers have theorized that the quality of the infant–caregiver attachment bond could serve as a prototype for how close human bonds—e.g., bonds with siblings, peers, and future romantic partners—should be created and maintained; see Berlin et al., 2008; Waters, Kondo-Ikemura, Posada, Richters, 1991). It is the expectations arising from these working models of the self and others that Bowlby viewed as important mechanisms of development because they lead the infant to develop particular behavioral strategies, which lead to relatively positive versus negative encounters with the social world and individuals found within it (e.g., a child with a working model of the self as one who is ignored may engage in aversive behaviors to gain attention, which could ultimately lead to peer rejection and/or victimization).

An additional mediator of the link between early attachment relationships and later child functioning that has received particular attention since the time of Bowlby's initial writings is emotion regulation (Cassidy, 1994; Kobak & Madsen, 2008; Thompson, 2006). This attention rests on the assumption that the quality of infant–caregiver attachment contributes directly to the ways in which infants learn to cope with both positive and aversive emotional states. Through the experience of having a sensitive parental secure base and safe haven (especially in situations in which parents openly communicate with their infants about the nature of negative as well as positive emotions), secure infants may learn that when negative affect occurs, it can be tolerated and positively resolved (see Bretherton, 1990). Insecure infants, in contrast, may have difficulties dealing with negative affective states because their caregivers minimized the gravity of such emotions by dismissing or neglecting them (in the case of parents of insecure–avoidant infants) or heightened the gravity of such emotions by maximizing their adverse characteristics and/or consequences (in the case of parents of insecure–ambivalent infants). Secure infants' competent emotion regulation capacities, emerging from experiences with sensitive caregivers, are in turn thought to contribute to myriad positive outcomes; capacities to regulate both anger and fear, for instance, would enhance relationships with peers (see Eisenberg, Eggum, Sallquist, & Edwards, 2010, for an extensive review of data linking positive emotion regulation capacities to a variety of positive developmental outcomes).

With these potential mechanisms of influence in mind, we now consider the many empirical studies that have reported that, compared with infants classified as insecure in infancy, infants classified as secure have more favorable developmental outcomes (for detailed reviews, see Thompson, 2006, 2008; Weinfield, Sroufe, Egeland, & Carlson, 2008). Although the studies linking attachment to these outcomes are too numerous to describe here, we note that many longitudinal studies have shown, for example, that compared to their insecure counterparts, infants with secure attachment histories are more open to the processing of a range of social information, more socially competent, and more likely to have better relationships with family members and peers (for reviews, see Berlin et al., 2008; Dykas & Cassidy, 2011; Schneider, Atkinson, & Tardif, 2001). Moreover, although the insecure attachment patterns observed in the Strange Situation are not considered to be pathological in nature (i.e., the insecure–avoidant and insecure–ambivalent attachment patterns are considered conditional behavioral strategies for managing caregiver responsiveness, whereas the insecure–disorganized strategy reflects the lack of such a strategy), several studies have indicated that insecure attachment may place individuals at increased risk for psychopathology (see Lyons-Ruth & Jacobvitz, 2008). Being classified as insecure–disorganized in infancy, for example, has been linked to chronic externalizing behavioral problems and to diagnoses such as conduct disorder and oppositional defiant disorder (for reviews, see DeKlyen & Greenberg, 2008; Lyons-Ruth & Jacobvitz, 2008; van IJzendoorn et al., 1999). Finally, data indicate that individuals classified as secure in infancy will likely be classified as secure in childhood and beyond (for data linking infant attachment security to child, adolescent, and adult attachment security, see Main & Cassidy, 1988; Weinfield, Sroufe, & Egeland, 2000; Waters, Merrick, Treboux, Crowell, & Albersheim, 2000), although lawful discontinuity continues to be possible in the context of unstable family situations (e.g., Van Ryzin, Carlson, & Sroufe, 2011).

Although attachment theory suggests that infant–caregiver attachment bonds likely contribute to different areas of development, it is important to keep in mind that the size of this contribution may range considerably and that other factors besides attachment are likely to influence the same developmental outcomes described previously (see Thompson, 2006). Indeed, in infant–parent relationships, "good things may typically go together" (see Vondra & Belsky, 1993; see also Belsky & Cassidy, 1994). As such, a secure infant may have better developmental outcomes not because of the positive influence of attachment, but because of other caregiver behaviors that promoted those outcomes. For example, a secure infant may grow to have excellent social skills because the caregiver simply gave the infant more opportunities to socialize with age mates, and not because the caregiver's secure base provision affected the infant's internal working models of attachment and/or emotion regulatory capacities.

Deprivation: Failure of Attachment Formation

At the outset of this chapter, we noted that nearly all human infants develop an attachment to their mother, father, and/or other principal caregivers during infancy. However, in unusual situations where a consistent caregiver is not sufficiently physically present, infant–caregiver attachments may fail to develop. This situation differs from situations in which there has been sufficient consistent contact with a neglectful or abusive caregiver for an attachment to form, although such attachments are typically disorganized (see Lyons-Ruth & Jacobvitz, 2008). An infant's failure to form this bond will likely have a host of immediate detrimental effects on infant well-being (see Rutter et al., 2009), and also places the infant on a trajectory for later (and potentially irreparable) social and emotional maladjustment.

One of the most prolific examples of the consequences associated with infants' lack of attachment formation occurred several decades ago in communist Romania under the rule of Nicolae Ceauşescu (1967–1989). After establishing laws barring contraception and abortion, the country witnessed a significant increase in the number of children housed in state-run orphanages, leading to severe overcrowding and a variety of child care-related shortcomings. Most notably, many infants had little or no contact with other persons other than during feeding and changing times. When the poor conditions of these orphanages came to light in 1989 (after the fall of the communist regime), the incidence of lack of attachment formation was staggering. For example, in one noteworthy study, 35% of children (ages 12–31 months) displayed behaviors indicative of nonattachment (i.e., behaviors indicating that a child did not have preference for a familiar caregiver over a stranger); of the 65% who did display such a preference, only 3% displayed a pattern of clear-cut attachment behavior toward that caregiver (Zeanah, Smyke, Koga, Carlson, & Bucharest Early Intervention Project Core Group, 2005). Moreover, after the public became aware of the severe neglect these orphans endured and surrogate caregivers (largely in countries outside of Romania) began adopting them, it has become evident that longer histories of severe deprivation are linked to later difficulties forming organized attachments to adoptive caregivers (see Dozier & Rutter, 2008). Such difficulties developing new organized attachments to caregivers likely stem from a variety of factors, some of which may relate to socioemotional disturbances such as posttraumatic stress disorder (see Hoksbergen et al., 2003; see also Chugani et al., 2001, for evidence of abnormal brain structure and functioning in children who failed to develop an attachment).

CONCLUSION

This chapter provides a concise overview of theory and research on the infant–caregiver attachment bond, describing the evolutionary basis of this bond, the normative features of infant attachment development, and how individual differences in the quality of infants' attachment to their caregivers might emerge and predict later outcomes. Many additional sources can provide readers with more in-depth discussion of these important topics (see chapters in Cassidy & Shaver, 2008, for extensive citation lists of theoretical writings and empirical studies). Although the infant–caregiver attachment bond is only one of the many bonds that individuals will form over the course of their life, this bond is considered a distinct and essential part of human development—one that is likely to influence many subsequent bonds.

ACKNOWLEDGMENT

We thank Katherine George for her assistance with compiling references.

REFERENCES

Ainsworth, M. D. S. (1967). *Infancy in Uganda: Infant care and the growth of love.* Baltimore: Johns Hopkins University Press.

Ainsworth, M. D. S. (1985). Attachments across the lifespan. *Bulletin of the New York Academy of Medicine, 61,* 792–812.

Ainsworth, M. D. S. (1989). Attachments beyond infancy. *American Psychologist, 44,* 709–716.

Ainsworth, M. D. S., Bell, S. M., & Stayton, D. J. (1971). Individual differences in strange-situation behaviour of one-year-olds. In H. R. Schaffer (Ed.), *The origins of human social relations* (pp. 17–58). New York: Academic Press.

Ainsworth, M. D. S., Blehar, M. C., Waters, E., & Wall, S. (1978). *Patterns of attachment: A psychological study of the Strange Situation.* Hillsdale, NJ: Erlbaum.

Ainsworth, M. D. S., & Wittig, B. (1969). Attachment and exploratory behavior of one-year-olds in a strange situation. In B. Foss (Ed.), *Determinants of infant behavior* (Vol. 4, pp. 111–136). London: Methuen.

Bakermans-Kranenburg, M. J., & van IJzendoorn, M. H. (2009). The first 10,000 Adult Attachment Interviews: Distributions of adult attachment representations in clinical and non-clinical groups. *Attachment & Human Development, 11,* 223–263.

Baldwin, M. W. (1995). Relational schemas and cognition in close relationships. *Journal of Social and Personal Relationships, 12,* 547–552.

Beebe, B., Jaffe, J., Markese, S., Buck, K., Chen, H., Cohen, P., et al. (2010). The origins of 12-month attachment: A microanalysis of 4-month mother-infant interaction. *Attachment & Human Development, 12,* 6–141.

Belsky, J., & Cassidy, J. (1994). Attachment: Theory and evidence. In M. Rutter & D. Hay (Eds.), *Development through life: A handbook for clinicians* (pp. 373–402). Oxford, UK: Blackwell.

Belsky, J., & Fearon, R. M. P. (2008). Precursors of attachment security. In J. Cassidy & P. R. Shaver (Eds.), *Handbook of attachment: Theory, research, and clinical applications* (2nd ed., pp. 295–316). New York: Guilford Press.

Belsky, J., Fish, M., & Isabella, R. A. (1991). Continuity and discontinuity in infant negative and positive emotionality: Family antecedents and attachment consequences. *Developmental Psychology, 27,* 421–431.

Berlin, L. J., Cassidy, J., & Appleyard, K. (2008). The influence of early attachments on other relationships. In J. Cassidy & P. R. Shaver (Eds.), *Handbook of attachment: Theory, research, and clinical applications* (2nd ed., pp. 333–347). New York: Guilford Press.

Bowlby, J. (1956). Mother-child separation. In K. Soddy (Ed.), *Mental health and infant development. Vol. I. Papers and discussions* (pp. 117–112). Oxford, UK: Basic Books.

Bowlby, J. (1973). *Attachment and loss: Vol. 2. Separation.* New York: Basic Books.

Bowlby, J. (1980). *Attachment and loss: Vol. 3. Loss.* New York: Basic Books.

Bowlby, J. (1982). *Attachment and loss: Vol. 1. Attachment* (2nd ed.). New York: Basic Books. (Original work published 1969)

Bowlby, J. (1988). *A secure base: Parent–child attachment and healthy human development.* London: Routledge.

Bretherton, I. (1990). Communication patterns, internal working models, and the intergenerational transmission of attachment relationships. *Infant Mental Health Journal, 11,* 237–252.

Bretherton, I. (1991). Pouring new wine into old bottles: The social self as internal working model. In M. Gunnar & L. A. Sroufe (Eds.), *Minnesota symposia in child psychology: Self processes in development* (pp. 1–41). Hillsdale, NJ: Erlbaum.

Bretherton, I. (1992). The origins of attachment theory: John Bowlby and Mary Ainsworth. *Developmental Psychology, 28,* 759–775.

Bretherton, I., & Munholland, K. A. (2008). Internal working models in attachment relationships: Elaborating a central construct in attachment theory. In J. Cassidy & P. R. Shaver (Eds.), *Handbook of attachment: Theory, research, and clinical applications* (2nd ed., pp. 102–127). New York: Guilford Press.

Carr, S., Dabbs, J., & Carr, T. (1975). Mother-infant attachment: The importance of the mother's visual field. *Child Development, 46,* 331–338.

Cassidy, J. (1988). Child-mother attachment and the self in six-year-olds. *Child Development, 59,* 121–134.

Cassidy, J. (1990). Theoretical and methodological considerations in the study of attachment and the self in young children. In M. Greenberg, D. Cicchetti, & E. M. Cummings (Eds.), *Attachment in the preschool years: Theory, research, and intervention* (pp. 87–119). Chicago: University of Chicago Press.

Cassidy, J. (1994). Emotion regulation: Influences of attachment relationships. *Monographs of the Society for Research in Child Development, 59*(2–3), 228–283.

Cassidy, J. (1999). The nature of the child's ties. In J. Cassidy & P. R. Shaver (Eds.), *Handbook of attachment: Theory, research, and clinical applications* (pp. 3–20). New York: Guilford Press.

Cassidy, J. (2008). The nature of the child's ties. In J. Cassidy & P. R. Shaver (Eds.), *Handbook of attachment: Theory, research, and clinical applications* (2nd ed., pp. 3–22). New York: Guilford Press.

Cassidy, J., & Berlin, L. (1994). The insecure/ambivalent pattern of attachment: Theory and research. *Child Development, 65,* 971–981.

Cassidy, J., Ehrlich, K. B., & Sherman, L. J. (in press). Child-parent attachment and response to threat: A move from the level of representation. In M. Mikulincer & P. R Shaver (Eds.), *Nature and development of social connections: From brain to group*. Washington, DC: American Psychological Association.

Cassidy, J., & Shaver, P. R. (Eds.). (2008). *Handbook of attachment: Theory, research, and clinical applications* (2nd ed.). New York: Guilford Press.

Cassidy, J., Woodhouse, S. S., Cooper, G., Hoffman, K., Powell, B., & Rodenberg, M. (2005). Examination of the precursors of infant attachment security: Implications for early intervention and intervention research. In L. J. Berlin, Y. Ziv, L. Amaya-Jackson, & M. T. Greenberg (Eds.), *Enhancing early attachments: Theory, research, intervention, and policy* (pp. 34–60). New York: Guilford Press.

Chugani, H. T., Behen, M. E., Muzik, O., Juhász, C., Nagy F., & Chugani, D. C. (2001). Local brain functional activity following early deprivation: A study of postinstitutionalized Romanian orphans. *NeuroImage, 14*, 1290–1301.

DeKlyen, M., & Greenberg, M. T. (2008). Attachment and psychopathology in childhood. In J. Cassidy & P. R. Shaver (Eds.), *Handbook of attachment: Theory, research, and clinical applications* (2nd ed., pp. 637–665). New York: Guilford Press.

Dozier, M., & Rutter, M. (2008). Challenges to the development of attachment relationships faced by young children in foster and adoptive care. In J. Cassidy & P. R. Shaver (Eds.), *Handbook of attachment: Theory, research, and clinical applications* (2nd ed., pp. 698–717). New York: Guilford Press.

Dykas, M. J., & Cassidy, J. (2011). Attachment and the processing of social information across the life span: Theory and evidence. *Psychological Bulletin, 137*, 19–46.

Dykas, M. J., Ehrlich, K. B., & Cassidy, J. (2011). Perspectives on intergenerational links between attachment and social information processing. In J. B. Benson (Ed.), *Advances in Child Development and Behavior, 40*, 51–94.

Eisenberg, N., Eggum, N. D., Sallquist, J., & Edwards, A. (2010). Relations of self-regulatory/control capacities to maladjustment, social competence, and emotionality. In R. H. Hoyle (Ed.), *Handbook of personality and self-regulation* (pp. 21–46). Malden, MA: Wiley-Blackwell.

Erikson, E. H. (1950). *Childhood and society*. New York: Norton.

Feldman, R., Singer, M., & Zagoory, O. (2010). Touch attenuates infants' physiological reactivity to stress. *Developmental Science, 13*, 271–278.

Fox, N. A., Kimmerly, N. L., & Schafer, W. D. (1991). Attachment to mother/attachment to father: A meta-analysis. *Child Development, 62*, 210–225.

Freud, S. (1999). *The interpretation of dreams* (J. Crick, Trans.). New York: Oxford University Press. (Original work published 1909)

George, C., Kaplan, N., & Main, M. (1996). *Adult Attachment Interview protocol* (3rd ed.). Unpublished manuscript, University of California, Berkeley.

Goldberg, S., Grusec, J. E., & Jenkins, J. M. (1999). Confidence in protection: Arguments for a narrow definition of attachment. *Journal of Family Psychology, 13*, 475–483.

Grossmann, K., Grossmann, K. E., Kindler, H., & Zimmermann, P. (2008). A wider view of attachment and exploration: The influence of mothers and fathers on the development of psychological security from infancy to young adulthood. In J. Cassidy & P. R. Shaver (Eds.), *Handbook of attachment: Theory, research, and clinical applications* (2nd ed., pp. 857–879). New York: Guilford Press.

Harlow, H. F. (1961). The development of affectional patterns in infant monkeys. In B. M. Foss (Ed.), *Determinants of infant behaviour* (pp. 75–88). Oxford, UK: Wiley.

Harlow, H. F., & Harlow, M. K. (1962). Social deprivation in monkeys. *Scientific American, 207,* 136–146.

Harlow, H. F., & Zimmermann, R. R. (1959). Affectional responses in the infant monkey. *Science, 130,* 421–432.

Harter, S. (2006). The self. In N. Eisenberg, W. Damon, & R. M. Lerner (Eds.), *Handbook of child psychology: Vol. 3. Social, emotional, and personality development* (6th ed., pp. 505–570). Hoboken, NJ: Wiley.

Heider, F. (1958). *The psychology of interpersonal relations.* New York: Wiley.

Hesse, E. (2008). The Adult Attachment Interview: Protocol, method of analysis, and empirical studies. In J. Cassidy & P. R. Shaver (Eds.), *Handbook of attachment: Theory, research, and clinical applications* (2nd ed., pp. 552–598). New York: Guilford Press.

Hesse, E., & Main, M. (2000). Disorganized infant, child, and adult attachment: Collapse in behavioral and attentional strategies. *Journal of the American Psychoanalytic Association, 48,* 1097–1127.

Hofer, M. A. (1994). Hidden regulators in attachment, separation, and loss. *Monographs of the Society for Research in Child Development, 59*(2–3), 192–207, 250–283.

Hoksbergen, R. C., Ter Laak, J. J., van Dijkum, C. C., Rijk, S. S., Rijk, K. K., & Stoutjesdijk, F. F. (2003). Posttraumatic stress disorder in adopted children from Romania. *American Journal of Orthopsychiatry, 73,* 255–265.

Johnson, S. C., Dweck, C. S., & Chen, F. S. (2007). Evidence for infants' internal working models of attachment. *Psychological Science, 18,* 501–502.

Klein, M. (1932). *The psycho-analysis of children.* London: Hogarth.

Kobak, R., & Madsen, S. D. (2008). Disruptions in attachment bonds: Implications for theory, research, and clinical intervention. In J. Cassidy & P. R. Shaver (Eds.), *Handbook of attachment: Theory, research, and clinical applications* (2nd ed., pp. 23–47). New York: Guilford Press.

Levine, S. (2005). Developmental determinants of sensitivity and resistance to stress. *Psychoneuroendocrinology, 30,* 939–946.

Lewin, K. (1933). Environmental forces. In C. Murchison (Ed.), *A handbook of child psychology* (2nd ed., pp. 590–625). Worcester, MA: Clark University Press.

Lewis, M., Feiring, C., & Rosenthal, S. (2000). Attachment over time. *Child Development, 71,* 707–720.

Lorenz, K. (1935). Der Kumpan in der Umwelt des Vogels. Der Artgenosse als auslösendes Moment sozialer Verhaltensweisen. *Journal für Ornithologie, 83,* 137–213.

Lyons-Ruth, K., & Jacobvitz, D. (2008). Attachment disorganization: Genetic factors, parenting contexts, and developmental transformation from infancy to adulthood. In J. Cassidy & P. R. Shaver (Eds.), *Handbook of attachment: Theory, research, and clinical applications* (2nd ed., pp. 666–697). New York: Guilford Press.

Main, M. (1990). Cross-cultural studies of attachment organization: Recent studies, changing methodologies, and the concept of conditional strategies. *Human Development, 33*, 48–61.

Main, M. (1999). Attachment theory: Eighteen points with suggestions for future studies. In J. Cassidy & P. R. Shaver (Eds.), *Handbook of attachment: Theory, research, and clinical applications* (pp. 845–887). New York: Guilford Press.

Main, M., & Cassidy, J. (1988). Categories of response to reunion with the parent at age six: Predictable from infant attachment classifications and stable over a 1-month period. *Developmental Psychology, 24*, 415–426.

Main, M., Kaplan, N., & Cassidy, J. (1985). Security in infancy, childhood, and adulthood: A move to the level of representation. In I. Bretherton & E. Waters (Eds.), Growing points in attachment theory and research. *Monographs of the Society for Research in Child Development, 50*(1–2, Serial No. 209), 66–106.

Main, M., & Solomon, J. (1986). Discovery of an insecure-disorganized/disoriented attachment pattern. In T. B. Brazelton & M. W. Yogman (Eds.), *Affective development in infancy* (pp. 95–124). Westport, CT: Ablex.

Main, M., & Solomon, J. (1990). Procedures for identifying infants as disorganized/disoriented during the Ainsworth Strange Situation. In M. T. Greenberg, D. Cicchetti, & E. M. Cummings (Eds.), *Attachment in the preschool years: Theory, research, and intervention* (pp. 121–160). Chicago: University of Chicago Press.

Marvin, R. S., & Britner, P. A. (2008). Normative development: The ontogeny of attachment. In J. Cassidy & P. R. Shaver (Eds.), *Handbook of attachment: Theory, research, and clinical applications* (2nd ed., pp. 269–294). New York: Guilford Press.

Mead, G. H. (1934). *Mind, self, and society from the standpoint of a social behaviorist.* Chicago: University of Chicago Press.

Meaney, M. J. (2001). Maternal care, gene expression, and the transmission of individual differences in stress reactivity across generations. *Annual Review of Neuroscience, 24*, 1161–1192.

Meaney, M. J. (2010). Epigenetics and the biological definition of gene × environment interactions. *Child Development, 81*, 41–79.

Meins, E., Fernyhough, C., Fradley, E., & Tuckey, M. (2001). Rethinking maternal sensitivity: Mothers' comments on infants' mental processes predict security of attachment at 12 months. *Journal of Child Psychology and Psychiatry, 42*(5), 637–648.

Oppenheim, D., & Koren-Karie, N. (2002). Mothers' insightfulness regarding their children's internal worlds: The capacity underlying secure child-mother relationships. *Infant Mental Health Journal, 23*, 593–605.

Piaget, J. (1954). *The child's construction of reality.* New York: Basic Books.

Polan, H. J., & Hofer, M. A. (2008). Psychobiological origins of infant attachment and its role in development. In J. Cassidy & P. R. Shaver (Eds.), *Handbook of attachment: Theory, research, and clinical applications* (2nd ed., pp. 158–172). New York: Guilford Press.

Posada, G., Kaloustian, G., Richmond, M. K., & Moreno, A. J. (2007). Maternal secure base support and preschoolers' secure base behavior in natural environments. *Attachment & Human Development, 9*, 393–411.

Rheingold, H. (1969). The effect of a strange environment on the behaviour of infants. In B. M. Foss (Ed.), *Determinants of infant behaviour* (Vol. 4, pp. 137–166). London: Methuen.

Robertson, J. (1953a). *A two-year-old goes to hospital* (Film). London: Tavistock Child Development Research Unit.

Robertson, J. (1953b). Some responses of young children to loss of maternal care. *Nursing Care, 49*, 382–386.

Robertson, J., & Bowlby, J. (1952). Responses of young children to separation from their mothers. *Courrier du Centre International de l'Enfance, 2*, 131–142.

Rothbaum, F., Weisz, J., Pott, M., Miyake, K., & Morelli, G. (2000). Attachment and culture: Security in the United States and Japan. *American Psychologist, 55*, 1093–1104.

Rutter, M., Beckett, C., Castle, J., Colvert, E., Kreppner, J., Mehta, M. et al. (2009). Effects of profound early institutional deprivation: An overview of findings from a UK longitudinal study of Romanian adoptees. In G. Wrobel & E. Neil (Eds.), *International advances in adoption research for practice* (pp. 147–167). Malden, MA: Wiley-Blackwell.

Schaffer, H. R., & Emerson P. E. (1964). The development of social attachments in infancy. *Monographs of Social Research in Child Development, 29* (Serial No. 94), 1–77.

Schank, R. C., & Abelson, R. (1977). *Scripts, plans, goals, and understanding: An inquiry into human knowledge structures.* Hillsdale, NJ: Erlbaum.

Schneider, B. H., Atkinson, L., & Tardif, C. (2001). Child–parent attachment and children's peer relations: A quantitative review. *Developmental Psychology, 37*, 86–100.

Sherman, L. J., & Cassidy, J. (2013). *Infant capacities related to building internal working models of attachment figures: A theoretical and empirical review.* Manuscript submitted for publication.

Shonkoff, J., & Phillips, D. (Eds.). (2000). *From neurons to neighborhoods: The science of early childhood development.* Washington, DC: National Academy Press.

Slade, A., Grienenberger, J., Bernbach, E., Levy, D., & Locker, A. (2005). Maternal reflective functioning, attachment, and the transmission gap: A preliminary study. *Attachment & Human Development, 7*, 283–298.

Solomon, J., & George, C. (2008). The measurement of attachment security and related constructs in infancy and early childhood. In J. Cassidy & P. R. Shaver (Eds.), *Handbook of attachment: Theory, research, and clinical applications* (2nd ed., pp. 383–416). New York: Guilford Press.

Sorce, J. F., & Emde, R. N. (1981). Mother's presence is not enough: Effect of emotional availability on infant exploration. *Developmental Psychology, 17*, 737–745.

Sroufe, L. A., Egeland, B., Carlson, E. A., & Collins, W. A. (2005). *The development of the person: The Minnesota study of risk and adaptation from birth to adulthood.* New York: Guilford Press.

Sroufe, L. A., & Waters, E. (1977). Attachment as an organizational construct. *Child Development, 48*, 1184–1199.

Thompson, R. A. (2006). The development of the person: Social understanding, relationships, conscience, self. In N. Eisenberg (Vol. Ed.), W. Damon, & R. M. Lerner (Eds.-in-Chief), *Handbook of child psychology: Volume 3. Social, emotional, and personality development* (6th ed., pp. 24–98). New York: Wiley.

Thompson, R. A. (2008). Early attachment and later development: Familiar questions, new answers. In J. Cassidy & P. R. Shaver (Eds.), *Handbook of attachment: Theory, research, and clinical applications* (2nd ed., pp. 348–365). New York: Guilford Press.

Thompson, R. A., Lamb, M. E., & Estes, D. (1983). Harmonizing discordant notes: A reply to Waters. *Child Development, 54*, 521–524.

van IJzendoorn, M. (1995). Adult attachment representations, parental responsiveness, and infant attachment: A meta-analysis on the predictive validity of the Adult Attachment Interview. *Psychological Bulletin, 117*, 387–403.

van IJzendoorn, M. H., Goldberg, S., Kroonenberg, P. M., & Frenkel, O. J. (1992). The relative effects of maternal and child problems on the quality of attachment: A meta-analysis of attachment in clinical samples. *Child Development, 63*, 840–858.

van IJzendoorn, M. H., & Sagi-Schwartz, A. (2008). Cross-cultural patterns of attachment: Universal and contextual dimensions. In J. Cassidy & P. R. Shaver (Eds.), *Handbook of attachment: Theory, research, and clinical applications* (2nd ed., pp. 840–858). New York: Guilford Press.

van IJzendoorn, M. H., Schuengel, C., & Bakermans-Kranenburg, M. J. (1999). Disorganized attachment in early childhood: Meta-analysis of precursors, concomitants, and sequelae. *Development and Psychopathology, 11*, 225–249.

Van Ryzin, M. J., Carlson, E. A., & Sroufe, L. A. (2011). Attachment discontinuity in a high-risk sample. *Attachment & Human Development, 13*, 381–401.

Vaughn, B. E., Bost, K. K., & van IJzendoorn, M. H. (2008). Attachment and temperament: Additive and interactive influences on behavior, affect, and cognition during infancy and childhood. In J. Cassidy & P. R. Shaver (Eds.), *Handbook of attachment: Theory, research, and clinical applications* (2nd ed., pp. 192–216). New York: Guilford Press.

Vaughn, B. E., & Waters, E. (1990). Attachment behavior at home and in the laboratory: Q-sort observations and Strange Situation classifications of one-year-olds. *Child Development, 61*, 1965–1973.

Vaughn, B. E., Waters, H. S., Coppola, G., Cassidy, J., Bost, K. K., & Veríssimo, M. (2006). Script-like attachment representations and behavior in families and across cultures: Studies of parental secure base narratives. *Attachment & Human Development, 8*, 179–184.

Vondra, J., & Belsky, J. (1993). Developmental origins of parenting: Personality and relationship factors. In T. Luster & L. Okagaki (Eds.), *Parenting: An ecological perspective* (pp. 1–33). Hillsdale, NJ: Erlbaum.

Waters, E. (1995). The attachment Q-set (Version 3). In E. Waters, B. Vaughn, G. Posada, & K. Kondo-Ikemura (Eds.), Caregiving, cultural, and cognitive perspectives on secure-base behavior and working models: New growing points of attachment theory and research. *Monographs of the Society for Research in Child Development, 60*(2–3, Serial No. 244), 234–246. (Original work published 1987)

Waters, E., & Cummings, E. (2000). A secure base from which to explore close relationships. *Child Development, 71*, 164–172.

Waters, E., Kondo-Ikemura, K., Posada, G., & Richters, J. E. (1991). Learning to love: Mechanisms and milestones. In M. R. Gunnar & L. Sroufe (Eds.), *The Minnesota Symposia on Child Psychology: Vol. 23. Self processes and development* (pp. 217–255). Hillsdale, NJ: Erlbaum.

Waters, E., Merrick, S., Treboux, D., Crowell, J., & Albersheim, L. (2000). Attachment security in infancy and early adulthood: A twenty-year longitudinal study. *Child Development, 71*, 684–689.

Waters, H. S., & Waters, E. (2006). The attachment working models concept: Among other things, we build script-like representations of secure base experiences. *Attachment & Human Development, 8*, 185–197.

Weinfield, N., Sroufe, L., & Egeland, B. (2000). Attachment from infancy to early adulthood in a high-risk sample: Continuity, discontinuity, and their correlates. *Child Development, 71*, 695–702.

Weinfield, N. S., Sroufe, L., Egeland, B., & Carlson, E. (2008). Individual differences in infant–caregiver attachment: Conceptual and empirical aspects of security. In J. Cassidy & P. R. Shaver (Eds.), *Handbook of attachment: Theory, research, and clinical applications* (2nd ed., pp. 78–101). New York: Guilford Press.

Zeanah, C. H., Smyke, A. T., Koga, S. F., Carlson, E., & Bucharest Early Intervention Project Core Group (2005). Attachment in institutionalized and community children in Romania. *Child Development, 76*, 1015–1028.

Chapter **2**

Built to Bond

Coevolution, Coregulation, and Plasticity
in Parent–Infant Bonds

DEBRA M. ZEIFMAN

*B*abies are like magnets. We are drawn to them with a powerful force. Our attraction to babies is so strong that it manifests itself even when they are just a figment of our imagination. How many of us have sheepishly asked if we may touch a pregnant woman's bulging belly in the hope that we might feel the baby move or kick? We have a strong desire to touch babies even before we can lay eyes on them, and we violate a fairly firm social prohibition to do so. Can you imagine asking a grown woman who is not your romantic partner or a medical patient in your care if you can just place your hands on her stomach under any other circumstances? Our urge to touch infants is reciprocated with powerful attraction on the part of infants toward potential caregivers. Place your finger in the hand of a newborn infant, and he or she will grasp it with a force that is completely disproportionate to his or her tiny body weight and size. Babies and adults who may potentially care for them are built to bond with one another.

The current chapter reviews a substantial and growing body of evidence suggesting that infants and adults possess reciprocal, coevolved character-istics (i.e., features in one individual that evoke a particular response in another) designed to ensure that a strong emotional bond forms between them. These coevolved characteristics have been selected over the course of human evolution because they promote infant survival as well as parental reproductive fitness. Infant readiness to form an emotional bond is mani-fested in the infant's innate attraction to a wide range of characteristics associated with many different potential caregivers, from adult faces, to scents, to speech sounds. The infant's heightened attention to features pos-sessed by many potential caregivers leads to rapid recognition of the spe-cific features of a particular caregiver from whom the infant has received care, followed by a strong preference for that caregiver in particular, often to the exclusion of others. Although there are notable differences between infant and parent bonding, there are also similarities. Adults are drawn to the neotenous (i.e., baby-like) features of many infants and young children, but following only minimal interaction, they recognize their own infants and typically display a high degree of partiality toward the children they have nurtured.

In addition to describing features of caregivers and infants that are mutually attractive and facilitate emotional bonding, this chapter addresses some of the profound physiological and behavioral effects that social inter-actions between infants and caregivers have on both members of the dyad. Infant–caregiver emotional bonds, in large part, thus reflect the mutual reliance of relationship partners on one another to regulate personal inter-nal physiological states. This process that Hofer (1984, 1994, 1995) termed *coregulation* is most obvious in the case of the infants' reactions to physi-cal separations from caregivers; however, hidden regulatory processes are embedded within many infant–caregiver exchanges. Although infants are far more dependent on adults to achieve physiological homeostasis, coregu-lation is bidirectional. Infant stimuli and infant–caregiver interactions have physiological effects on adults that serve to facilitate parental bonding and may be implicated in experiences of separation and loss. The psychologi-cal connection that children and parents feel toward one another is thus a consequence, at least in part, of coregulation. Infants and caregivers rely on one another to achieve positive transformations of mood and states that are highly rewarding and can even be described as "addictive" in the sense that once a bond is established, both members will typically vehemently resist severing it.

Finally, the chapter touches on aspects of human brain development and plasticity that may underlie emotional bonding in parents and off-spring. Compared with the brains of infants of other species, the human infant's brain, including speech, vision, and auditory centers, is extremely underdeveloped at birth. Human brains, as a result, are highly malleable in response to environmental input in the first year of life. The unusual degree of plasticity of the human infant's brain enables an infant to form a bond that is both selectively responsive to a specific individual as well as adapted to the environmental context in which the bond is formed. The process of bonding with an attachment figure is thus biologically prepared and experience expectant. Like learning a first language, forming a bond with a primary caregiver is a universal, species-typical experience; if deprived of the opportunity to form such a relationship in early life, an infant will not develop normally. However, just as language is biologically prepared but one's specific language, accent, intonation, vocabulary, and so on depend on the particular neighborhood in which one resides, so too the specific individual to whom an infant bonds and the nature of the bond depend on the local environment. Adults, although less malleable than children, also display remarkable neuroanatomical and endocrine adjustments in response to the experience of being a parent, suggesting an important role of neural plasticity in bonding.

SENSORY, PHYSIOLOGICAL, AND BRAIN BASES OF THE INFANT'S BOND

William James (1890) famously described the newborn's experience of the world as a "blooming, buzzing confusion," and psychoanalyst Margaret Mahler (1974) referred to the first weeks of life as the "normal autistic phase." These psychologists held the view, common in their times, that newborn infants are relatively unaware of their surroundings and incapable of responding in a discriminating fashion to external stimuli. The last four decades have transformed the way we look at the newborn period. We no longer see newborn and young infants as unconscious beings or newborns' perceptions of the world as disorganized. Advances in research methodology have given experimenters tools to demonstrate the cognitive and behavioral capabilities of infants from birth or earlier, during the fetal period. Utilizing these newer methodologies, researchers have revealed that young infants are far more responsive to external stimuli, and that infants' responses to external stimuli are far more organized than was once believed. As a consequence, we now understand that newborns' preferences for particular individuals emerge at an earlier age than psychologists previously recognized.

Modern research designs exploit infants' earliest capacity to discriminate among stimuli through, for example, measurable changes in heart rate or sucking pattern or through head turning and looking in one direction over another. Using such paradigms, researchers have demonstrated that infants as young as 3 months grasp the basic laws of physics (Baillargeon, 2004; Spelke & Kinzler, 2007), understand simple arithmetic (Wynn, 1992), and possess a primitive moral sensibility (Hamlin, Wynn, & Bloom, 2010). Of all of the mental tasks infants must achieve in the first months of life, however, the most crucial task for infant survival is arguably identifying and forming a close bond with a specific caregiver. Human infants' survival depends entirely on their ability to procure nourishment and physical protection from a highly invested, caring adult. Infants' nervous system is, therefore, highly specialized for learning and remembering the characteristics of a specific caregiver, acquiring a preference for that person and his or her qualities, and maintaining proximity to that individual through whatever means possible, given an initially limited behavioral repertoire.

The Infant's Sensory Capacities at Birth: Vision and Faces

The newborn's sensory channels are all fine-tuned to receive input from the individual who provides nurturance. For example, the newborn is extremely nearsighted at birth, with most estimates of the newborn's vision in the range of 20/800, or 40 times worse than that of an adult (Maurer & Lewis, 2001). In spite (or because) of this degree of nearsightedness, a newborn's point of greatest visual acuity is 19 centimeters, or 7.5 inches, roughly the distance between an infant's eyes and a caregiver's face when an infant is held in the typical nursing (or bottle-feeding) position (Salapatek, Bechtold, & Bushnell, 1976). The feeding context places an infant not only in the ideal physical proximity to visualize a caregiver's face but also in the alert-awake state that is optimal for learning (Bushnell, 2001). Because newborns spend more than 16 hours a day sleeping (Thoman & Whitney, 1989) and 1–2.75 hours a day crying (Brazelton, 1985), they are typically awake and alert only a small percentage of time in the first weeks of life. Most of this brief awake and alert time is spent feeding, in close physical contact with the caregiver, often staring into the caregiver's face (Zeifman, Delaney, & Blass, 1996). It may be partly as a result of seeing faces repeatedly in a highly motivated context, such as nursing or feeding, that infants learn faces at a rapid clip.

In addition to being in the optimal focal range and ideal state for learning about faces during feeding, infants have an innate preference for face-like stimuli over other types of visual stimuli (Morton & Johnson, 1991). Within minutes following delivery, newborns prefer faces over other patterned stimuli with similar visual properties (Mondloch et al., 1999;

Valenzà, Simion, Cassi, & Umiltà, 1996). Given a choice, newborns look for longer periods of time at faces with features that are organized in the normal facial schematic (i.e., two eyes in the upper region, nose in the mid-section, and mouth in the lower region) than at upside-down faces (Turati, Simion, Milani, & Umiltà, 2002) or at faces with randomly scrambled features (Goren, Sarty, & Wu, 1975; Johnson, Dziurawiec, Ellis, & Morton, 1991). Since scrambled and normally arranged faces are composed of exactly the same physical elements, infants' preference for normally arranged facial configurations suggests that their attraction to faces is not simply the result of the visual properties of faces, such as areas of high contrast, contours, and angles, but rather a specific attraction to a facial template. Further, infants' attraction to the species-typical facial configuration precedes any experience with actual faces and is thought to be controlled by subcortical structures in the brain that are developed and functional at birth (Morton & Johnson, 1991). Infants' innate attraction to faces is one of many mechanisms that draws them to their caregiver and facilitates bonding.

Infants' attraction to face-like stimuli rapidly progresses into a preference for the face of the particular person with whom the infant has interacted. After only hours of interaction with a caregiver, 4-day-old infants look longer at their own mother's face than at the face of a stranger (Field, Cohen, Garcia, & Greenberg, 1984; Pascalis, de Schonen, Morton, Deruelle, & Fabre-Grenet, 1995). The infant's preference for his or her own mother's face is robust even when olfactory information is blocked by a strong deodorant spray (Bushnell, Sai, & Mullin, 1989) or when the mother's and stranger's faces are presented via video feed rather than live (Walton, Bower, & Bower, 1992). The infant's ability to recognize his or her mother's face in the first days of life following mere hours of exposure is remarkable when contrasted with an adult's capacity to recognize a new face that has been seen only a number of times. While adults can readily identify familiar faces even after many years, they perform notoriously poorly when it comes to recognizing faces of unfamiliar individuals, even when the learning task is simplified in a laboratory situation (Hancock, Bruce, & Burton, 2000). This postnatal period of rapid face learning on the part of the infant is highly adaptive because of the centrality of the caregiver to the infant's very survival and well-being.

Infants' preference for their own caregiver's face becomes generalized to a preference for the mother's facial prototype as their facial recognition skills become more refined. With time, other individuals of the same gender, race, and hair color as the infant's own mother become preferred to those who are different (Pascalis, Scott, Kelly, Shannon, & Nicholson,

2005). By 3 to 4 months of age, infants who have been cared for primarily by a woman prefer women's faces, but the small minority of infants whose primary caregiver is a man prefers male faces (Quinn, Yahr, Kuhn, Slater, & Pascalis, 2002). Similarly, Israeli infants reared in environments with exposure to Ethiopian and Caucasian adults do not show the typical pattern of own-race preference that 3-month-old Israeli infants reared in more segregated environments do (Bar-Haim, Ziv, Lamy, & Hodes, 2006). Infants' progression from an initial attraction to faces to a preference for a particular person's face, and then to a preference for faces that resemble a particular person's face is characteristic of many of infants' sensory systems and developing preferences. The generalization of a preference for a particular person to a prototype or template of the original preferred object is one manifestation of the lasting consequences of the infant–caregiver bond.

Hearing and Infant-Directed Speech

Although hearing continues to improve until approximately 10 years of age (Fernald, 2001), infants recognize and prefer their own mother's voice just hours after birth (DeCasper & Fifer, 1980). In an experiment utilizing a nonnutritive nipple (i.e., a pacifier-like device with sensors that detect sucking rate and intensity), infants altered their rate of sucking to activate a recording of their own mother's voice preferentially over the recorded voice of another woman who had recently given birth. This preference for one's own mother's voice over that of a stranger is thought to result from prenatal learning, because infants are exposed to their mother's voice in utero throughout the prenatal period in the form of sound waves and accompanying vibrations (Lecanuet & Schaal, 2002). Given a choice between the mother's voice as heard ex utero and the mother's voice filtered to simulate how it is heard in utero, newborns prefer the low-pass, filtered version (Fifer & Moon, 1995). Based on these observations, it is assumed that newborns' preferences for features of their own mother begin before birth, during the fetal period.

In addition to preferring their own mother's voice, infants are attracted to spoken language in general and are equipped with the capacity to discriminate phonemes (i.e., the sound parts that are the building blocks of speech) beginning in the fetal period (Lecanuet & Schaal, 2002). Adults universally modify their speech automatically when speaking to young infants (Burnham, Kitamura, & Vollmer-Conna, 2002; Fernald & Kuhl, 1987), and infants prefer "baby talk" or infant-directed speech (IDS) to adult-directed speech (ADS), apparently because it is more melodic, higher in pitch/frequency, and exaggerated in contour and emotion compared with ADS. Given a choice between IDS and ADS, infants will turn their heads in one direction over another to activate recordings of IDS (Fernald, 1985; Fernald & Kuhl, 1987; Kitamura, Thanavishuth, Burnham, & Luksaneeyanawin, 2001). Thus, the impulse shared by adults across a wide range of diverse cultures to speak to infants in high-pitched and exaggerated tones has the function of attracting the attention of and pleasing infants.

Just as infants' attraction to human faces is quickly transformed into a preference for a particular caregiver's face, so too is their preference for IDS quickly transformed into a more refined preference for a specific language to which they have been exposed. While neonates prefer IDS to ADS regardless of the language in which it is spoken (Werker, Pegg, & McLeod, 1994), by 2 days of age, infants prefer to hear IDS spoken in the language they have heard around them. Given a choice between a language they have heard and a foreign language, infants will alter their sucking rate to activate audio recordings of their "mother tongue" (Moon, Cooper, & Fifer, 1993). Thus, much in the same way infants acquire a preference for faces that resemble their mother's face, they also come to prefer speech sounds, intonation, and patterns that resemble their own caregiver's spoken language in the first days of life. By the end of the first year, infants' ability to distinguish between phonemes in languages to which they have not been exposed is greatly diminished (Werker, 1989), presumably through a process of synaptic pruning whereby used synaptic pathways are preserved and unutilized ones are discarded (Webb, Monk, & Nelson, 2001). The overproduction and subsequent honing of synapses in the first several months of life enables infants to adapt to a range of potential qualities in the postnatal environment, including a range of languages encountered.

Taste and Mother's Milk

Compared with vision and hearing, infants' sense of taste is well developed at birth (Mennella & Beauchamp, 1998). Newborn infants show distinct preferences for sweet flavors that resemble the taste of breast milk and make characteristic facial expressions in response to sweet-, sour-, and bitter-tasting substances that are similar to those adults make (Ganchrow, Steiner, & Daher, 1983). For instance, newborns scrunch up their noses and purse their lips when they encounter sour-tasting solutions (Rosenstein & Oster, 1988), and smile and smack their lips with sweet solutions (Ganchrow, Steiner, & Daher, 1983). Infants also consume greater quantities of sweet solutions than plain water, and they slow their sucking rate comparatively when offered sweeter substances in order to savor the taste (Ashmead,

Reilly, & Lipsitt, 1980), presumably indicating a pleasant hedonic experience. Because the most salient characteristic of mother's milk is its sweet taste, newborns' hedonic responses to sweet tastants is yet another manifestation of their biological preparation for becoming attached to caregivers (Mennella & Beauchamp, 1998).

Infants relish breast milk not only because it is sweet tasting but also because it has state-altering and analgesic properties. These pain-relieving and soothing properties of breast milk are believed, based on animal models, to be mediated through the release of endogenous opioids (Shide & Blass, 1989). Small, microliter volumes of sucrose solution administered to vigorously crying 1- to 3-day-old human infants eliminate crying, dampen sympathetic arousal, and result in a period of sustained calm (Smith, Fillion, & Blass, 1990; Zeifman et al., 1996). Infants who are allowed to breast-feed before a painful venipuncture or heel lance show increased pain threshold and reduced crying relative to those who are simply held or allowed to suck on a pacifier (Carbajal, Veerapen, Couderc, Jugie, & Ville, 2003). Similarly, administering small quantities of expressed breast milk to infants before a heel lance procedure reduces signs of distress relative to administering plain water (Upadhyay at al., 2004). Mother's milk is, therefore, favored not only for its unique flavor but also because of the rewarding physiological changes it induces in the infant.

While infants universally prefer sweeter tasting solutions and respond positively to the soothing quality of milk and other sweet solutions, they also respond selectively to the specific chemosensory properties of their own mother's milk. Exposure to maternal diet begins in utero, with flavors ingested by the mother affecting the composition of the amniotic fluid, which the fetus swallows and is capable of tasting by the third trimester (Mennella & Beauchamp, 1998). Infants' preferences for flavors associated with the mother thus begin in the prenatal period. In one experiment, infants whose mothers were randomly assigned to add carrot juice to their diet during the last 3 months of pregnancy had more positive reactions to carrot-flavored cereal than infants in a control group whose mothers did not ingest carrot juice during pregnancy when both groups were tested months later (Mennella, Jagnow, & Beauchamp, 2001). The mother is the medium through which flavors are introduced in utero, and flavors associated with the mother are preferred to less familiar flavors, even when those flavors are reintroduced in an entirely different form such as in solid food.

Distinct flavors, such as garlic, mint, and vanilla, ingested by mothers who are breast-feeding are expressed in breast milk, and these flavors rapidly become preferred by infants who are exposed to them in breast milk (Beauchamp & Mennella, 2011). When flavors are added to commercial infant formula (a more easily controlled medium than breast milk for delivering specific flavors), there appears to be the equivalent of a critical period (i.e., a brief window of opportunity) for acquiring taste preferences in the first months of life (Beauchamp & Mennella, 2011). For example, protein hydrolysate infant formulas (substituted when infants are allergic to soy milk and cow's milk), which are unpleasantly bitter and sour tasting compared with cow milk formulas, are acceptable to infants if they are offered in the first 3–4 months of life. The same foul-tasting formulas introduced for the first time when an infant is 5–6 months of age are disliked and often completely rejected (Beauchamp & Mennella, 2011). The rapid acquisition of preferences for flavors associated with the mother in the first weeks of life and the gradual closing of this window of opportunity for acquiring taste preferences after several months mirror other sensory and perceptual capacities in early infancy. Reduced plasticity in flavor acceptance by the middle of the first year suggests there may be a sensitive period in early infancy for acquiring flavor preferences that is similar to the documented sensitive period for acquiring phonemic distinctions in early language processing (Beauchamp & Mennella, 2011).

Odor and the Caregiver's Signature Scent

Like their sense of taste, infants' sense of smell is well developed at birth (Marlier & Schaal, 2005). Infants are spontaneously attracted to the smell of breast milk, even if they have been exclusively bottle-fed. Given the choice between a cotton pad soaked in breast milk and one soaked in formula, bottle-fed infants who have never been exposed to breast milk turn their head and orient for longer periods of time to the scent of breast milk than to the scent of formula (Marlier & Schall, 2005). By 6 days after birth, infants can discriminate between the scent of their own mother's breast milk and that of another lactating female, and will preferentially turn their head in the direction of their own mother's nursing pad and away from that of another unfamiliar lactating female (MacFarlane, 1975; Russell, 1976). This refined ability to discriminate between the odors of two closely matched conspecifics is unusual for humans, who tend to rely on visual cues for kin recognition, and is suggestive of the possible role of an odor-mediated early-recognition mechanism in human neonates similar to those that operate in more primitive species (Blass, 1990).

Newborns' preference for odors associated with breast feeding extends to artificially applied fragrances. One study of odor learning in newborns took advantage of a local medical practice in a French hospital that encouraged nursing mothers to apply a chamomile-scented balm to their nipples to prevent the chaffing often associated with nursing. Three-day-old infants whose mothers applied the balm were shown to rapidly acquire a preference for the novel chamomile scent (Delaunay-El Allam, Marlier, & Schaal, 2006). Compared with infants who had not been exposed to chamomile, those exposed to chamomile while breast-feeding preferred the chamomile odor at 7 months of age, a preference that persisted into toddlerhood. At 21 months, toddlers who had been exposed to chamomile while breast-feeding as infants preferred toys and bottles scented with chamomile to violet-scented matched control objects. Toddlers for whom the chamomile scent was unfamiliar did not show any preference for chamomile-scented objects and were equally likely to choose chamomile- or violet-scented objects (Delaunay-El Allam, Soussignan, Patris, Marlier, & Schaal, 2010). Exposure to a scent associated with a caregiver and breast feeding in infancy had enduring effects on children's responses to that scent months and even years later.

Infants' attraction to their own caregiver's scent is not limited to odors paired with breast milk. Infants recognize and prefer the unique properties of their own mother's body odor and so-called signature scent, composed of her perspiration and other bodily secretions. For example, by 2 weeks of age, infants discriminate between a gauze pad that has been taped to their own mother's underarm and infused with her personal body odor and a gauze pad that has been taped to the underarm of an unfamiliar lactating woman infused with unfamiliar body odor (Cernoch & Porter, 1985). Given the choice between the two odor-infused pads, infants turn their heads to the direction of their own mother's odor and remain oriented toward their own mother's odor for a longer period of time than to the odor of an unfamiliar woman. Like the other sensory systems in early infancy, infants' olfactory system is primed to recognize and react favorably to the unique qualities of the person who has provided nurturance and care.

The Regulatory Effects of Touch

The normal growth of the human infant depends critically on the caregiver's touch. Infants reared in institutions and in severely emotionally deficient family settings are prone to psychosocial dwarfism (sometimes referred to as affective deprivation) or nonorganic failure to thrive for reasons that are still poorly understood but appear to be related to lack of tactile stimulation (Green, Campbell, & David, 1984; Muñoz-Hoyos et al., 2011). In these two closely related conditions, children fail to gain weight and height on a normal developmental schedule and do not achieve standard developmental milestones although adequate nourishment has been provided and hygienic needs have been met. Further, children suffering from these disorders have abnormal levels of various neuroendocrine markers, including growth hormone (Muñoz-Hoyos et al., 2011). Often, removing children with these conditions from institutional settings and providing therapeutic support restores more normal growth patterns.

Our incomplete understanding of the mechanisms controlling the deleterious effects of maternally impoverished environments on organ development and tissue growth in human infants comes from experiments using lab rats as models. In rats, most maternal tactile stimulation takes the form of the dam (i.e., the rat mother) licking and grooming her rat pups (i.e., rat babies). Rat pups deprived of active tongue licking show abnormally low levels of growth hormone and protein synthesis as well as retarded growth (Schanberg & Field, 1987). Neither administering exogenous growth hormone nor providing nontactile forms of maternal contact reverses the harmful effects of maternal tactile deprivation on growth patterns. Simulating the mother's active tongue licking by stroking her rat pups with a wet paintbrush, however, restores the normal growth curve as well as the normal pattern of organ development (Schanberg & Field, 1987). Thus, it appears that the rat pup's continued physical growth depends directly on a form of tactile stimulation provided exclusively by the dam under normal circumstances.

This insight regarding the importance of tactile stimulation for normal physical growth in infancy has been successfully applied to treatments for premature infants (see Field, 1998; Field, Diego, & Hernandez-Reif, 2010 for reviews). Premature infants given a skin-to-skin massage therapy gain weight more quickly and are discharged from the hospital sooner than infants who receive standard medical care without supplemental massage. In a fairly typical result, preterm infants given three 15-minute massage sessions per day over the course of 10 days gained 21% more weight per day than control infants—despite having the same caloric intake—and were discharged on average 5 days earlier (Scafidi et al., 1990). These types of positive outcomes associated with massage therapy have been replicated by several independent research groups and are so compelling that many hospital neonatal units recruit volunteer "baby cuddlers" to provide skin-to-skin contact for premature infants whose parents cannot provide adequate physical contact in the first months of life.

The role of skin-to-skin, tactile contact in regulating infant behavioral states is not limited to premature infants or other atypical populations. Negative effects of lack of tactile stimulation and positive effects of touch are also well documented for normally developing infants. The most common cause of infant crying is simply being out of physical contact with the caregiver, and crying typically stops when the infant is picked up (Newman, 1985, 2007). Caregiving practices aimed at relieving crying universally involve close physical contact or some simulation of skin-to-skin contact, such as holding the infant to a shoulder or swaddling the infant in cloth (Zeifman, 2001). Numerous experiments demonstrate the effect of touch for transforming an infant's state from distress to calm. In one randomized, controlled trial, supplemental carrying of infants by parents in the first 6 weeks resulted in a 43% reduction in fussing and crying relative to standard rates of carrying (Hunziker & Barr, 1986). These findings suggest that tactile stimulation in the form of additional holding by caregivers may support infant emotional regulation and be protective against infant distress.

Touch is also effective in promoting infant attention and receptivity to social stimuli. In one experiment, researchers compared infants' reactions to adult-initiated eye contact and smiling with and without touch (Peláez-Nogueras, Gewirtz, Field, & Cigales, 1996). Young infants displayed more eye contact, smiling, and cooing and less crying in response to an experimenter when the experimenter rubbed the infants' legs and feet while looking and smiling at them compared with when the experimenter maintained eye contact and smiled but did not provide tactile stimulation (Peláez-Nogueras et al., 1996). The reductions in crying and increases in positive mood that accompany holding, carrying, and touching suggest that infants are predisposed to favor a high level of physical contact with their caregiver. When levels of tactile stimulation are within a normal range, infants' preference for a high degree of contact is discernible through subtle changes in their mood and state. Under more extreme conditions of deprivation, when tactile stimulation drops below a certain threshold level of need, infants' long-term physical condition is severely compromised by the absence a normal component of early caregiving environments.

Protoconversations between Infants and Their Caregivers

Adults and infants have conversation-like exchanges before infants acquire language. Infants and adults take turns looking at each other, touching one another, smiling and making faces at one another, and vocalizing to one another in a contingent, turn-taking fashion that closely resembles conversations between two linguistically capable individuals (Murray & Trevarthen, 1986; Stern, 1977; Tronick, Als, Adamson, Wise, & Brazelton, 1978). Research has shown that infants are exquisitely sensitive to the emotional content and tempo of feedback from their partners in these earliest of conversations beginning in the first days of life (Nagy, 2008). Trevarthen

(2006) and Trevarthen and Aitken (2001) refer to infants' inborn sensitivity to the emotional feedback of partners in face-to-face interaction as *primary intersubjectivity*, to contrast this early innate ability with one that emerges later in infancy, when infants and caregivers refer to objects and events beyond themselves (e.g., as in the case of social referencing, where infants look at a caregiver's facial expression to learn about the safety of objects). In the early stages of infant–parent communication, infants are highly attuned to signs of their parent's emotional availability and contingent responsiveness.

Evidence for infants' inborn sensitivity to the subtle cues and responsive feedback of relationship partners comes from studies in which the rhythmic, turn-taking exchanges of infants and caregivers are disturbed experimentally. In one of the earliest experiments of its kind, investigators set up a double-video link so that 6- to 9-week-old infants and their mothers could see each other on video screens and communicate in real time (Murray & Trevarthen, 1986). Once free-flowing, positive communication was established, researchers replayed a segment of the mother's behavior to the young infant as it had been a minute prior rather than as it was occurring in real time. The time-lagged video that was played back to the infant during this portion of the experiment lacked the contingent responsiveness of normal mother–infant interactions, although it preserved the quality of the mother's behavior in every other way. Young infants almost uniformly became unsettled and upset by the noncontingent feedback and reacted by turning away, frowning, touching their own bodies and clothing (in an attempt to self-soothe), and often crying (Murray & Trevarthen, 1986; Nadel, Carchon, Kervella, Marcelli, & Réserbat-Plantey, 1999).

Another procedure that has been used to demonstrate young infants' sensitivity to contingent feedback as well as their active role in carrying on conversations with a caregiver is Tronick's still-face procedure (Tronick et al., 1978; Tronick & Cohn, 1989). After a period of normal face-to-face interaction, a mother is asked by the experimenter to assume a neutral, nonresponsive facial expression for several minutes. Newborn infants, just hours after birth, react unfavorably to this breech of normal interaction, although they presumably have no experience-based expectation that caregivers will behave in a contingent, responsive fashion. Newborns display their discontent by averting their gaze, closing their eyes, and grimacing at higher rates during the still-face portions of the experiment than during the segments of the experiment in which normal, contingent interaction is maintained (Nagy, 2008). At 2 to 3 months of age, infants react to the mother's lack of responsiveness in the still-face procedure with even more obvious displeasure—turning their faces away, arching their backs, frowning, and often crying (Tronick et al., 1978). By 6 months of age, infants show measurable signs of physiological dysregulation, such as increases in heart rate and decreases in vagal tone, in response to the still-face procedure (Weinberg & Tronick, 1996). Behaviorally, older infants go to great lengths to reengage their frozen-conversation partners: waving their hands and hurling their bodies in their mother's direction, often screaming and actively protesting this unwelcome turn of events. Collectively, these experiments demonstrate that from the earliest age infants are attentive to caregiver cues of availability and responsiveness. Far from being passive recipients of caregivers' ministrations, even young infants play an active role in striking up conversations with caregivers and, once under way, in preserving the quality of communication.

Crying as Communication and Context

Additional evidence that human infants are "built to bond" is found in their tendency to cry whenever in need of attention and adults' tendency to respond to crying with caregiving. Crying has been referred to as an "acoustical umbilical cord" because of its primary role in connecting the infant and caregiver before language develops. The idea that crying is a signal of need designed to elicit care is supported by the fact that distress vocalization in some form or another is typical of all mammalian species requiring maternal care and nursing (Newman, 1985). Among human infants, crying occurs in a predictable fashion in response to maternal separation as well as to physical signs of maternal separation, such as hunger and cool temperature (Stark & Nathanson, 1973). As infants mature and develop the cognitive capacity to anticipate future events, crying occurs in response not only to the physical consequences of separation but also to anticipation of separation as a form of separation protest/anxiety. Crying is, therefore, one of the primary triggers of parent–infant contact in infancy and plays an important role in bonding.

Across diverse cultures, crying typically elicits nurturant responses (Bell & Salter Ainsworth, 1972; Konner, 1972; Kruger & Konner, 2010; Zeifman, 2001). As such, crying brings the infant and caregiver repeatedly into close physical contact in an emotionally charged, highly motivated situation (Zeifman, 2004). For the infant, it is in this salient context that the caregiver repeatedly becomes associated with a rewarding transformation—from a state of emotional distress and discomfort to one of calm and contentment. Based on studies in animal models, it is widely believed that this positive state transformation from crying to calm is mediated by the release of endogenous opioids, substances produced in the brain in response to stress that mimic the pain-relieving qualities of opiate drugs such as heroin (Panksepp, Meeker, & Bean, 1980). Like exogenous opiate drugs, endogenous opioids have powerfully addictive properties (e.g., the euphoric feelings associated with "runner's high"). It is, therefore, predictable that the infant typically becomes dependent on the individual who most reliably responds to his or her cries. Indeed, many biological psychologists suggest a primary role for opioids in promoting attachment and social bonding (Depue & Morrone-Strupinsky, 2005; Panksepp, Siviy, & Normansell, 1985).

Although there is significant cultural and individual variability in how much infants cry, crying is typical of all healthy newborns and peaks at around 6 weeks of age regardless of caregiving context and practices (Barr, 1990). One potential consequence of the early postnatal crying curve is that it precipitates a certain degree of contact between the infant and caregiver in the first weeks of life. Infants cry, and parents find it difficult to ignore crying. Through these initial distress-relief sequences, the infant and caregiver become coordinated with one another and learn to regulate each other's arousal (Zeifman, 2004). It is obvious that, for the infant, being picked up, being held, and being fed reduce the emotional distress preceding these interventions; but distress-relief sequences also attenuate the unpleasant sympathetic arousal parents experience when they are exposed to the aversive sound of crying (Owings & Zeifman, 2004). As a result, parents as well as infants experience a rewarding transition from unpleasant arousal to a neutral or positive emotional state in the context of a crying infant being quieted. Repeated interactions like those surrounding infant crying that are mutually satisfying and mutually regulating predispose the infant and parent to forming a strong and lasting emotional connection.

Plasticity and Coregulation in Bonding

A review of sensory capacities at birth suggests that the human nervous system in the first year of life is specialized for learning about the caregiver. The caregiver, in turn, is the primary source of information for the infant about the broader environment (Meaney, 2001). Compared with other mammals, human infants are exceedingly immature at birth and require a far more protracted period of parental care. The extended dependence of childhood that is characteristic of humans across cultures is widely believed to be advantageous in light of the competitive and socially complex nature of human societies. Because human environments are competitive and highly variable, infants and children are thought to benefit from a longer period of dependence and apprenticeship-style learning from caregivers than is typical of other species. The greater plasticity of the human brain compared with that of other species allows the human infant to develop a behavioral repertoire that can be adapted to particular caregivers and environments.

Evidence that infants adjust their emotional behavior in response to a specific caregiver's emotional availability comes from research on individual differences in attachment styles (Ainsworth, Blehar, Waters, & Wall, 1978). Infants with highly responsive caregivers who attend to their emotional needs promptly develop patterns of coping with distress that involve a relatively greater degree of relying on others for emotional support. In contrast, infants who experience more rejecting caregiving and whose primary caregivers ignore their cries and pleas for attention develop styles of coping with distress that are relatively independent of others. Although infants' styles of coping with distress are influenced by inherited characteristics, including temperament and susceptibility to distress, empirical evidence from intervention studies suggests that infants' attachment and coping style outcomes are driven primarily by the relative availability and responsiveness of primary caregivers (Spangler & Grossmann, 1993; van den Boom, 1994). Furthermore, the availability and responsiveness of a caregiver are not determined solely by a caregiver's own personality or temperament. The nature and quality of caregiving are also influenced by broader environmental influences, such as parents' status within the social group and their access to needed resources (Suomi, 1999).

Environmental effects on caregiving have been demonstrated through experiments in which the foraging demands of bonnet macaque monkey mother–infant dyads were manipulated (Andrews & Rosenblum, 1991). When the foraging demands were increased so that mothers had to spend more time procuring food for survival, the quality of the care they provided to their infants suffered, and there was a greater incidence of emotionally vulnerable and depressed offspring compared with when foraging demands were low and the availability of provisions was predictable. Among humans, the fact that care suffers when caregivers are faced with unpredictable conditions or impoverished resources is supported by a number of studies documenting insensitive parenting, a greater incidence of child abuse and neglect, and higher rates of insecure attachment in economically disadvantaged populations (Crockenberg, 1981; Steinberg, Catalano, & Dooley, 1981). The effects of economic conditions on parenting quality and the consequent effects of parenting quality on child outcomes are indicative of the ways in which infant–parent dyads are interdependent and function as a coregulated unit within the broader context of an environment rather than as independent entities. The finding that infant behavioral outcomes are highly influenced by the demands placed on caregivers demonstrates that the dyad, operating as a unit, makes predictable adjustments to accommodate environmental conditions.

The influence of caregiving context on parenting and child outcomes extends well beyond infancy and early childhood into adolescence and adulthood. For example, children's rates of sexual maturation and reproductive strategies are influenced by the availability of parents, the strength of the parental marital bond, and the extent of conflict in the home (Belsky, Steinberg, & Draper, 1991). Individuals of both sexes who grow up in conflict-ridden, unstable homes are predisposed to early puberty and to adopting sexual attitudes that favor promiscuity over long-term, committed relationships (Ellis, Figueredo, Brumbach & Schlomer, 2009). Girls from divorced, conflict-ridden, and father-absent homes experience earlier onset of menses and have first intercourse at a younger age than girls from more benign homes and homes where fathers are present and involved (Ellis at al., 2003). Although the exact timing of puberty is more difficult to identify in boys, evidence suggests that boys from father-absent homes hold more exploitative sexual attitudes than their peers from intact homes (Barber, 1998) and are more prone to externalizing (i.e., acting out) behavior. Collectively, these studies suggest that parents shape children's sexual attitudes and behavior in childhood. The finding that puberty is achieved at an earlier or later point in development depending on the availability of parental resources in the natal home is further evidence for plasticity in bonding.

THE BASES OF THE CAREGIVER'S BOND

This chapter opened with a description of the strong urge many of us feel to touch babies even when they are hidden from view, tucked away in their mothers' bellies. As primates, we are not unique in this regard. Other primates also show a strong attraction to infants (Hrdy, 2005). Among many species of Old and New World monkeys, there is a "lust" for touching, inspecting, and carrying infants, which is limited only by the mother's tolerance for allowing such contact (Hrdy, 2005). Although young females are particularly avid in their interest in allomothering (i.e., substitute parenting), in the majority of primate species, individuals of all ages and both sexes display heightened interest and protective behavior toward infants in their group (Berman, 1982). The desire to get one's hands on a baby has a conservative evolutionary history. This impulse to take charge of an infant has the obvious evolutionary advantage of enhancing infants' chances of survival while at the same time increasing parents' reproductive success.

Among humans, an inborn predisposition to care for infants begins with a strong attraction to infantile physical features (Lorenz, 1942) and unlearned, stereotyped responses to infant signals such as crying (Bell & Ainsworth, 1972; Bowlby, 1969/1982). Just as the infant's brain and behavior are adapted to forming and solidifying a bond with a caregiver, so too are caregivers' brain and behavior fine-tuned for forming a bond with a specific infant. In addition, although some aspects of caregiving are hormonally primed by pregnancy, human caregiving is largely experience dependent (Greenough, Black, & Wallace, 1987). Many of the profound transformations of the brain and behavior associated with parenthood are activated through social learning and exposure to infants. Naïve, prepubescent females and fathers both routinely demonstrate high levels of interest in caring for infants despite a lack of pregnancy-related hormonal preparation. The thriving practice of adoption and foster care in Western society may be viewed as additional proof that the strong urge of many adults to take care of infants and young children does not depend solely on the hormonal transformations that accompany pregnancy. In fact, recent studies have revealed that fathers' hormones change with parenthood, suggesting that men and women alike are biologically prepared to bond with infants when they are exposed to them.

The Newborn's Physical Appearance

Lorenz (1942) introduced the idea that the young of many species possess infantile physical features that elicit automatic, unlearned caretaking behavior in conspecifics. In humans, infants, compared with adults, have large heads relative to their body size, protruding foreheads, eyes in the midline of the face as opposed to in the upper region, round pudgy cheeks, thick lips, and plump, fleshy bodies (Fullard & Reiling, 1976). According to Lorenz, infantile features make the young of many species appear "cute" and "cuddly" to more mature members of the species, who are then motivated to provide attention, care, and protection to younger members of the species. Lorenz's concept is supported by numerous empirical studies showing that, given a choice between photographs of infant and adult faces, individuals of all ages and both sexes prefer looking at infant faces (Fullard & Reiling, 1976; Maestripieri & Pelka, 2002). Although females, particularly when they are young, show a more pronounced preference for infant faces than males, most studies show that both sexes find infant photos more attractive than those of adults (Berman, Goodman, Sloan, & Fernander, 1978). It is widely believed that the infant's "adorable" appearance is part of what motivates adults to attend to, and nurture, offspring.

A more macabre form of evidence supporting the triggering role of the newborn's physical appearance for eliciting nurturant caregiving behavior comes from cases of infants who are born with physical deformities. Infants who are born with craniofacial anomalies such as cleft lip and palate are subjected to parenting that is less warm and responsive than the parenting that normal-appearing infants receive (Allen, Wasserman, & Seidman, 1990; Barden, Ford, Jensen, Rogers-Salyer, & Salyer, 1989; Field & Vega-Lahr, 1984). Prematurity and other indices of poor infant condition at birth are associated with increased risk for physical abuse and maltreatment (Belsky, 1993; Sherrod, O'Connor, Vietze, & Altemeier, 1984). Even when infants fall within the normal range of physical appearance and health, relatively unattractive infants are subjected to less warm and indulgent treatment by parents than their more attractive counterparts (Langlois et al., 2000) beginning even in the first days of life (Langlois, Ritter, Casey, & Sawin, 1995). The heightened risk of abuse associated with an infant's being abnormal in appearance indirectly implies that the normal appearance of the neonate facilitates development of warm parental feelings.

Receptivity to Infant Cues and Recognition of One's Own Infant

In addition to possessing a species-typical affinity for characteristics of all healthy newborns, parents show rapid learning of—and rapidly acquire preferences for—the specific features of their own infant. Within hours of interacting with their own child, parents can distinguish their own child from someone else's based on relatively impoverished sensory information. This process overcomes a relatively high perceptual/cognitive hurdle because, as a result of neoteny (i.e., baby-like features), most infants look a bit alike. Distinctive facial characteristics that emerge as faces mature are concealed in early infancy (Pagel, 1997). Recognizing the specific features of a particular infant is so difficult, and matching an infant to his or her parents based on physical characteristics so challenging, that modern hospitals are vigilant about branding infants with personal identification bracelets that are checked every time infants are brought from the nursery into their room. Yet parents can recognize their own baby by face, hand, odor, and cries within only minutes of interaction.

In one study demonstrating mothers' ability to recognize their own infant, new mothers were asked to pick out the undershirt worn by their own baby from among a group of three undershirts, which included undershirts worn by two other newborns. The vast majority of mothers (over 90%) recognized their own infant by odor alone, with visual cues blocked, after only 1 hour of exposure to their infant (Kaitz, Good, Rokem, &

Eidelman, 1987, 1988; Porter, Cernoch, & McLaughlin, 1983; Russell, Mendelson, & Peeke, 1983). More remarkably, after approximately 7 hours of routine interactions with their infant in the hospital, mothers were able to distinguish between their own infant's hand and the hands of two unrelated infants by tactile cues alone, with visual and olfactory cues blocked (Kaitz, Lapidot, Bronner, & Eidelman, 1992). Fathers, who typically have less physical contact with their infant than mothers in the first days postpartum, can also recognize their infant by touch and require only slightly more exposure than mothers to do so (Kaitz, Shiri, Danziger, & Hershko, 1994). The sheer alacrity with which parents acquire the ability to discriminate the unique features of their own infant can be contrasted with the ability of nonparents to distinguish between any other two members of the species based on so limited a set of cues. For example, most adults could not reliably recognize the personal scent or tactile "feel" of a person with whom they have only interacted briefly.

Mothers and fathers both can pick out their own infant's photograph from an array of six photographs of infants with the same skin and hair color after interacting with their own infant for less than an hour (Kaitz et al., 1988; Porter, Cernoch, & Balough, 1984). When it comes to recognizing photographs of their own infant after seeing the infant only once, briefly, in the delivery room, fathers are even more proficient than mothers (Kaitz et al., 1988). Compared with adults' poor ability to recall the faces of relatively unfamiliar persons, parents' ability to pick out their own infant's face after so brief a window of exposure suggests a period of heightened attentiveness immediately following birth. Increased attention to infant cues extends to the sounds emitted by infants. Parents can pick out their own infant's cries from among the crying of other similar-age infants after only 48 hours (Formby, 1967) and show different patterns of heart rate arousal to their own infant's cries (Wiesenfeld, Malatesta, & DeLoach, 1981). The speed with which mothers and fathers learn and remember the specific features of their own infant supports the idea that adults are biologically prepared to form a one-on-one bond with an infant after only a brief period of interaction.

The keen ability of parents to recognize the specific sensory cues associated with their own infant appears to be rooted in how the brain responds to these biologically relevant stimuli. Studies utilizing brain-imaging techniques have demonstrated that stimuli associated with infants activate brain regions that are distinct from those activated by other kinds of stimuli (Lorberbaum et al., 2002). Further, parents respond differently than nonparents to a host of infant signals, including smiles (Seifritz et al., 2003; Strathearn, Li, Fonagy, & Montague, 2008) and cries of distress

(Swain, Lorberbaum, Kose, & Strathearn, 2007). Parents also respond differently to a photograph of their own infant compared with the photograph of an unfamiliar same-age infant (Strathearn et al., 2008). Brain regions controlling motivation, memory, emotion processing, and reward circuits in other mammalian species are consistently implicated in human parents' responses to infants. The involvement of specific brain regions in parental responses to their own versus unfamiliar infants provides further support for the existence of evolved mechanisms whereby adults bond specifically with a child.

Hormonal Activation of Parenting and Physiological Coregulation

Parents are also prepared to bond with an infant through changes in hormone levels during pregnancy. Across diverse cultures and species, parents-to-be engage in "nesting" behavior in advance of an infant's arrival. In humans, nesting behaviors are believed to be at least partly driven by the hormone progesterone, and are typically focused on ensuring an infant's safety and comfort in his or her future home (Hahn-Holbrook, Holbrook, & Haselton, 2011). Other changes in women's behavior during pregnancy are also seen by some as precautions to ensure the health of a pregnancy and infant. For example, some pregnant women are reluctant to travel far from home, and it is common for pregnant women to develop aversions to meat and other foods that have a high rate of contamination (Hahn-Holbrook et al., 2011; Pepper & Roberts, 2006). Following an infant's arrival, the vast majority of mothers as well as fathers report experiencing obsessional intrusive thoughts about harm coming to their babies (Abramowitz, Schwartz, & Moore, 2003; Abramowitz, Schwartz, Moore, & Luenzmann, 2003). Television sitcoms often parody the compulsive actions parents engage in to ensure their infant is safe, such as repeatedly checking the infant's breathing or waking their sleeping infant for proof that he or she is still alive. Parental vigilance about keeping infants safe from harm, which begins in pregnancy, is yet another manifestation of the value parents place on preserving the well-being of infants in their care.

In spite of heightened anxiety surrounding parenthood, parents find it intensely rewarding to interact with their infant in the first weeks postpartum (Hahn-Holbrook et al., 2011; Swain et al., 2007). The enjoyment produced by parent–infant interaction is believed to be, at least in part, driven by hormonal shifts, most notably in oxytocin and vasopressin levels (Insel, 1997). Oxytocin, sometimes referred to as the "love hormone" because it produces affiliative feelings, is released by vaginal stimulation during birth and by nursing and skin-to-skin contact with one's infant following birth

(Carter & Altemus, 1997; Nelson & Panksepp, 1998). Oxytocin also intensifies the action of endogenous opiates released during pleasurable social interactions (Depue & Morrone-Strupinsky, 2005), further explaining the profoundly alluring "tug" parents feels toward their infant in the first weeks of life. In at least one animal model, there is evidence that the rewards of parenting are equal to or greater than those of highly addicting narcotics. Given a choice between cocaine and interacting with their rat pups, newly delivered dams choose pups over cocaine in the first 8 days postpartum (Mattson, Williams, Rosenblatt, & Morrell, 2001). The hormone profiles of new parents suggest that hormonal changes during pregnancy as well as contact with their infant contribute to the strong need of parents to be close to and take care of their young children.

Although men do not experience pregnancy per se, there is growing evidence that they experience hormonal changes triggered by their partners' pregnancies and exposure to infant stimuli (Storey, Walsh, Quinton, & Wynne-Edwards, 2000; Fleming, Corter, Stallings, & Steiner, 2002). Men whose wives or partners are pregnant frequently experience pregnancy-like symptoms, including weight gain, morning nausea, and disturbed sleep, commonly referred to as couvade syndrome (Mason & Elwood, 1995). Recent evidence suggests that men's sympathetic pregnancy symptoms are not merely psychosomatic, but rather are caused by actual changes in hormone titers. In one study, the hormone levels of expectant fathers living with pregnant partners were measured before the birth of their child and again after the child was born. Men showed stage-like changes in hormones that mimicked the changes observed in pregnancy, including elevated prolactin levels before and lower testosterone after the birth of a child (Storey et al., 2000). Furthermore, new fathers who showed relatively greater pre- and postnatal increases in prolactin and reductions in testosterone were more alert and sympathetic to cries than fathers with less dramatic hormonal fluctuations (Fleming et al., 2002). Taken together, these findings suggest that for both fathers and mothers parenting is hormonally prepared and activated through exposure to stimuli associated with infants.

Neuroanatomical Effects of Parenting and Brain Plasticity in Adults

The profound effects of parenthood are reflected not only in intended parents' and caregivers' shifting hormone profiles but also in structural changes in the brain (Kim et al., 2010; Leuner, Glasper, & Gould, 2010). In healthy mothers, brain size decreases during pregnancy and then increases for 6–8 weeks after delivery (Fleming, 2005; Oatridge et al., 2002). In one longitudinal study using functional magnetic resonance imaging gray matter was measured in new mothers at 2–4 weeks postpartum and again at

3–4 months postpartum. Comparing gray matter volume at the two points in time indicated that the first few months of motherhood are associated with significant gains in gray matter (and presumably in cognitive function) in key brain regions (Kim et al., 2010). Although specific regions differed in terms of how much gray matter was gained, no brain region lost volume over the period of early motherhood measured. Further, a mother's positive perception of her baby at the first postpartum measurement time predicted the extent of increase in gray matter volume 2–3 months later. Changes in maternal brains following parturition suggest plasticity in adult brains, which appears to be shaped by the experience of motherhood.

Among species in which fathers participate in child care, many of the same brain regions activated by parenthood in mothers are also activated in fathers through early contact with offspring (Leuner et al., 2010). Two specific brain areas displaying adult neurogenesis as a function of parenthood in humans are the hippocampus, an area involved in spatial memory, navigation, and learning, and the prefrontal cortex, an area involved in working memory, judgment, and mood regulation (Leuner et al., 2010). The effects of parenting on human hippocampus and prefrontal cortex correspond meaningfully to documented parenting-related changes in nonhuman species. For example, in female rats, parity is associated with gains in spatial skills, such as an enhanced ability to remember the location of food (Kinsley et al., 1999; Pawluski, Vanderbyl, Ragan, & Galea, 2006). Among marmosets, a species in which fathers are intricately involved in carrying, feeding, and protecting young, fatherhood is associated with increased dendritic spines in the prefrontal cortex (Kozorovitskiy, Hughes, Lee, & Gould, 2006). The fact that increased dendritic growth in the prefrontal cortex is seen in animals living in other kinds of enriched environments (Greenough et al., 1987) suggests that parenting itself is an enriching experience that has the potential to expand animals' minds (Leuner et al., 2010).

CONCLUDING REMARKS

Infants and caregivers possess physical features that have been naturally selected over the course of evolution because they are mutually attractive and promote infant–caregiver proximity. Early forms of infant–parent interaction such as face-to-face communication, skin-to-skin contact, and distress-soothing sequences are highly rewarding for both members of the dyad and, therefore, help to solidify infants' and parents' preferences for their partners in these exchanges. Because many social interactions between infants and the adults who care for them are associated with the release of endogenous opioids, oxytocin, and other neuropeptides that promote positive feelings of calm, contentment, and well-being, repeated interactions between infants and caregivers typically lead to a strong physiological and psychological interdependence and an enduring emotional bond. This bond is apparent in the vigorous efforts of older infants and parents to resist separations from each other once a bond is established.

The bond between infants and their caregivers is also apparent in the transformative effects each has on the other's brain. Infancy is a period of rapid brain development, and the formation of a bond with a primary caregiver is a species-typical, experience-expectant process (Greenough et al., 1987). It is, therefore, not surprising that the quality of parenting and family environment a child experiences has profound and lasting effects on the child's physiological functioning and developmental outcome (Meaney, 2001, 2010). Adult brains are comparatively less malleable than those of infants, but also display significant plasticity in response to the experience of parenthood (Fleming, 2005). Although scientists have only recently begun to appreciate the enriching effects infants have on adults (Kinsley et al., 1999), there is substantial and growing evidence that parenthood has the potential to stimulate adult neurogenesis. Proliferation of dendritic spines in key areas in the brains of new parents suggests that parenting triggers significant brain growth in adults. Thus, the human infant and caregiver both display an extraordinary capacity to be shaped by the relationship that unfolds between them and by the environment in which the relationship takes place.

Anyone who has had the experience of holding a newborn baby knows that evolution could not have selected a more alluring creature. Picture this scene: An infant in your charge wakes from his nap and lets out a blood-curdling cry. Terrified, your blood pressure soars and your pulse grows faster. You break into a cold sweat. You race toward the baby's crib and pick him up. Instantly, the piercing sound stops. The infant rests his head on your shoulder and nuzzles its small head in the crook of your neck. Tiny fingers graze your chest. Breathing in, you smell that indescribable baby scent. The baby's breath feels moist against your cheek, and you listen to his contented sounds. Relief and warmth envelop you. You are, after all, built to bond.

REFERENCES

Abramowitz, J. S., Schwartz, S. A., & Moore, K. M. (2003). Obsessional thoughts in postpartum females and their partners: Content, severity, and relationship with depression. *Journal of Clinical Psychology in Medical Settings, 10*(3), 157–164.

Abramowitz, J. S., Schwartz, S. A., Moore, K. M., & Luenzmann, K. R. (2003).

Obsessive-compulsive symptoms in pregnancy and the puerperium: A review of the literature. *Journal of Anxiety Disorders, 17*(4), 461–478.

Ainsworth, M. D. S., Blehar, M. C., Waters, E., & Wall, S. (1978). *Patterns of attachment: A psychological study of the Strange Situation.* Oxford, UK: Erlbaum.

Allen, R., Wasserman, G. A., & Seidman, S. (1990). Children with congenital anomalies: The preschool period. *Journal of Pediatric Psychology, 15*(3), 327–345.

Andrews, M. W., & Rosenblum, L. A. (1991). Attachment in monkey infants raised in variable-and-low-demand environments. *Child Development, 62*(4), 686–693.

Ashmead, D. H., Reilly, B. M., & Lipsitt, L. P. (1980). Neonates' heart rate, sucking rhythm, and sucking amplitude as a function of the sweet taste. *Journal of Experimental Child Psychology, 29*(2), 264–281.

Baillargeon, R. (2004). Infants' physical world. *Current Directions in Psychological Science, 13*(3), 89–94.

Bar-Haim, Y., Ziv, T., Lamy, D., & Hodes, R. M. (2006). Research article: Nature and nurture in own-race face processing. *Psychological Science, 17*(2), 159–163.

Barber, N. (1998). Sex differences in disposition towards kin, security of adult attachment, and sociosexuality as a function of parental divorce. *Evolution and Human Behavior, 19*(2), 125–132.

Barden, R. C., Ford, M. E., Jensen, A. G., Rogers-Salyer, M., & Salyer, K. E. (1989). Effects of craniofacial deformity in infancy on the quality of mother-infant interactions. *Child Development, 60*(4), 819–824.

Barr, R. G. (1990). The normal crying curve: What do we really know? *Developmental Medicine and Child Neurology, 32*(4), 356–362.

Beauchamp, G. K., & Mennella, J. A. (2011). Flavor perception in human infants: Development and functional significance. *Digestion, 83*(1), 1–6.

Bell, S. M., & Salter Ainsworth, M. D. (1972). Infant crying and maternal responsiveness. *Child Development, 43*(4), 1171–1190.

Belsky, J. (1993). Etiology of child maltreatment: A developmental ecological analysis. *Psychological Bulletin, 114*(3), 413–434.

Belsky, J., Steinberg, L., & Draper, P. (1991). Childhood experience, interpersonal development, and reproductive strategy: An evolutionary theory of socialization. *Child Development, 62*(4), 647–670.

Berman, C. M. (1982). The ontogeny of social relationships with group companions among free-ranging infant rhesus monkeys: I. Social networks and differentiation. *Animal Behaviour, 30*(1), 149–162.

Berman, P. W., Goodman, V., Sloan, V. L., & Fernander, L. (1978). Preference for infants among black and white children: Sex and age differences. *Child Development, 49*(3), 917–919.

Blass, E. M. (1990). Suckling: Determinants, changes, mechanisms, and lasting impressions. *Developmental Psychology, 26*(4), 520–533.

Bowlby, J. (1982). *Attachment and loss.* New York: Basic Books. (Original work published 1969)

Brazelton, T. B. (1985). Application of cry research to clinical perspectives. In B. Lester & C. F. Boukydis (Eds.), *Infant crying* (pp. 325–340). New York: Plenum Press.

Burnham, D., Kitamura, C., & Vollmer-Conna, U. (2002). What's new, pussycat? On talking to babies and animals. *Science, 296*(5572), 1435.

Bushnell, I. W. R. (2001). Mother's face recognition in newborn infants: Learning and memory. *Infant and Child Development, 10*(1–2), 67–74.

Bushnell, I. W. R., Sai, F., & Mullin, J. T. (1989). Neonatal recognition of the mother's face. *British Journal of Developmental Psychology, 7*(1), 3–15.

Carbajal, R., Veerapen, S., Couderc, S., Jugie, M., & Ville, Y. (2003). Analgesic effect of breast feeding in term neonates: Randomised controlled trial. *British Medical Journal, 326*(7379), 13–15.

Carter, C. S., & Altemus, M. (1997). *Integrative functions of lactational hormones in social behavior and stress management.* New York: New York Academy of Sciences.

Cernoch, J. M., & Porter, R. H. (1985). Recognition on maternal axillary odors by infants. *Child Development, 56*(6), 1593–1598.

Crockenberg, S. B. (1981). Infant irritability, mother responsiveness, and social support influences on the security of infant-mother attachment. *Child Development, 52*(3), 857–865.

DeCasper, A. J., & Fifer, W. P. (1980). Of human bonding: Newborns prefer their mothers' voices. *Science, 208*(4448), 1174–1176.

Delaunay-El Allam, M., Marlier, L., & Schaal, B. (2006). Learning at the breast: Preference formation for an artificial scent and its attraction against the odor of maternal milk. *Infant Behavior and Development, 29*(3), 308–321.

Delaunay-El Allam, M., Soussignan, R., Patris, B., Marlier, L., & Schaal, B. (2010). Long-lasting memory for an odor acquired at the mother's breast. *Developmental Science, 13*(6), 849–863.

Depue, R. A., & Morrone-Strupinsky, J. (2005). A neurobehavioral model of affiliative bonding: Implications for conceptualizing a human trait of affiliation. *Behavioral and Brain Sciences, 28*(3), 313–350.

Ellis, B. J., Bates, J. E., Dodge, K. A., Fergusson, D. M., Horwood, L. J., Pettit, G. S., et al. (2003). Does father absence place daughters at special risk for early sexual activity and teenage pregnancy? *Child Development, 74*(3), 801–821.

Ellis, B. J., Figueredo, A. J., Brumbach, B. H., & Schlomer, G. L. (2009). Fundamental dimensions of environmental risk: The impact of harsh versus unpredictable environments on the evolution and development of life history strategies. *Human Nature, 20*(2), 204–268.

Fernald, A. (1985). Four-month-old infants prefer to listen to motherese. *Infant Behavior and Development, 8*(2), 181–195.

Fernald, A. (2001). *Hearing, listening, and understanding: Auditory development in infancy.* In G. Bremner & A. Fogel (Eds.), *Blackwell handbook of infant development* (pp. 35–70). Malden, MA: Blackwell.

Fernald, A., & Kuhl, P. (1987). Acoustic determinants of infant preference for motherese speech. *Infant Behavior and Development, 10*(3), 279–293.

Field, T. M. (1998). Massage therapy effects. *American Psychologist, 53*(12), 1270–1281.

Field, T. M., Cohen, D., Garcia, R., & Greenberg, R. (1984). Mother–stranger face discrimination by the newborn. *Infant Behavior and Development, 7*, 19–25.

Field, T., Diego, M., & Hernandez-Reif, M. (2010). Preterm infant massage therapy research: A review. *Infant Behavior and Development, 33*(2), 115–124.

Field, T. M., & Vega-Lahr, N. (1984). Early interactions between infants with cranio-facial anomalies and their mothers. *Infant Behavior and Development, 7*(4), 527–530.

Fifer, W. P., & Moon, C. M. (1995). *The effects of fetal experience with sound.* In J. P. Lecanuet, W. P. Fifer, N. A. Krasnegor, & W. P. Smotherman (Eds.), *Fetal development: A psychobiological perspective* (pp. 351–366). Hillsdale, NJ: Erlbaum.

Fleming, A. S. (2005). Plasticity of innate behavior: Experiences throughout life affect maternal behavior and its neurobiology. In C. S. Carter, L. Ahnert, K. E. Grossmann, S. B. Hrdy, M. E. Lamb, S. W. Porges, et al. (Eds.), *Attachment and bonding: A new synthesis* (pp. 137–168). Cambridge, MA: MIT Press.

Fleming, A. S., Corter, C., Stallings, J., & Steiner, M. (2002). Testosterone and prolactin are associated with emotional responses to infant cries in new fathers. *Hormones and Behavior, 42*(4), 399–413.

Formby, D. (1967). Maternal recognition of infant's cry. *Developmental Medicine & Child Neurology, 9*(3), 293–298.

Fullard, W., & Reiling, A. M. (1976). An investigation of Lorenz's "babyness." *Child Development, 47*, 1191–1193.

Ganchrow, J. R., Steiner, J. E., & Daher, M. (1983). Neonatal facial expressions in response to different qualities and intensities of gustatory stimuli. *Infant Behavior and Development, 6*(2), 189–200.

Goren, C. C., Sarty, M., & Wu, P. Y. K. (1975). Visual following and pattern discrimination of face-like stimuli by the newborn infants. *Pediatrics, 56*, 544–549.

Green, W. H., Campbell, M., & David, R. (1984). Psychosocial dwarfism: A critical review of the evidence. *Journal of the American Academy of Child Psychiatry, 23*(1), 39–48.

Greenough, W. T., Black, J. E., & Wallace, C. S. (1987). Experience and brain development. *Child Development, 58*(3), 539–559.

Hahn-Holbrook, J., Holbrook, C., & Haselton, M. G. (2011). Parental precaution: Neurobiological means and adaptive ends. *Neuroscience and Biobehavioral Reviews, 35*(4), 1052–1066.

Hamlin, J., Wynn, K., & Bloom, P. (2010). Three-month-olds show a negativity bias in their social evaluations. *Developmental Science, 13*(6), 923–929.

Hancock, P. J. B., Bruce, V., & Burton, A. M. (2000). Recognition of unfamiliar faces. *Trends in Cognitive Sciences, 4*(9), 330–337.

Hofer, M. A. (1984). Relationships as regulators: A psychobiologic perspective on bereavement. *Psychosomatic Medicine, 46*(3), 183–197.

Hofer, M. A. (1994). Hidden regulators in attachment, separation and loss. *Monographs of the Society for Research in Child Development, 59*(2–3), 192–207, 250–283.

Hofer, M. A. (1995). Hidden regulators: Implications for a new understanding of attachment, separation, and loss. In S. Goldberg, R. Muir, & J. Kerr (Eds.), *Attachment theory: Social, developmental, and clinical perspectives* (pp. 203–230). Hillsdale, NJ: Analytic Press.

Hrdy, S. B. (2005). Evolutionary context of human development: The cooperative breeding model. In C. S. Carter, L. Ahnert, K. E. Grossmann, S. B. Hrdy, M. E. Lamb, S. W. Porges, et al. (Eds.), *Attachment and bonding: A new synthesis* (pp. 9–32). Cambridge, MA: MIT Press.

Hunziker, U. A., & Barr, R. G. (1986). Increased carrying reduces infant crying: A randomized controlled trial. *Pediatrics, 77*, 641–648.

Insel, T. R. (1997). A neurobiological basis of social attachment. *American Journal of Psychiatry, 154*(6), 726–735.

James, W. (1890). *The principles of psychology*. New York: Henry Holt.

Johnson, M. H., Dziurawiec, S., Ellis, H., & Morton, J. (1991). Newborns' preferential tracking of face-like stimuli and its subsequent decline. *Cognition, 40*(1–2), 1–19.

Kaitz, M., Good, A., Rokem, A. M., & Eidelman, A. I. (1987). Mothers' recognition of their newborns by olfactory cues. *Developmental Psychobiology, 20*(6), 587–591.

Kaitz, M., Good, A., Rokem, A. M., & Eidelman, A. I. (1988). Mothers' and fathers' recognition of their newborns photographs during the port-partum period. *Developmental and Behavioral Pediatrics, 9*(4), 223–226.

Kaitz, M., Lapidot, P., Bronner, R., & Eidelman, A. I. (1992). Parturient women can recognize their infants by touch. *Developmental Psychology, 28*(1), 35–39.

Kaitz, M., Shiri, S., Danziger, S., & Hershko, Z. (1994). Fathers can also recognize their newborns by touch. *Infant Behavior and Development, 17*(2), 205–207.

Kim, P., Leckman, J. F., Mayes, L. C., Feldman, R., Wang, X., & Swain, J. E. (2010). The plasticity of human maternal brain: Longitudinal changes in brain anatomy during the early postpartum period. *Behavioral Neuroscience, 124*(5), 695–700.

Kinsley, C. H., Madonia, L., Gifford, G. W., Tureski, K., Griffin, G. R., Lowry, C., et al. (1999). Motherhood improves learning and memory. *Nature, 402*(6758), 137–138.

Kitamura, C., Thanavishuth, C., Burnham, D., & Luksaneeyanawin, S. (2001). Universality and specificity in infant-directed speech: Pitch modifications as a function of infant age and sex in a tonal and non-tonal language. *Infant Behavior and Development, 24*(4), 372–392.

Konner, M. J. (1972). Aspects of the developmental ethology of a foraging people. In N. Blurton-Jones (Ed.), *Ethological studies of child behavior* (pp. 285–304). Cambridge, UK: Cambridge University Press.

Kozorovitskiy, Y., Hughes, M., Lee, K., & Gould, E. (2006). Fatherhood affects dendritic spines and vasopressin V1a receptors in the primate prefrontal cortex. *Nature Neuroscience, 9*(9), 1094–1095.

Kruger, A. C., & Konner, M. (2010). Who responds to crying? Maternal care and allocare among the !kung. *Human Nature, 21*(3), 309–329.

Langlois, J. H., Kalakanis, L., Rubenstein, A. J., Larson, A., Hallam, M., & Smoot, M. (2000). Maxims or myths of beauty? A meta-analytic and theoretical review. *Psychological Bulletin, 126*(3), 390–423.

Langlois, J. H., Ritter, J. M., Casey, R. J., & Sawin, D. B. (1995). Infant attractiveness predicts maternal behaviors and attitudes. *Developmental Psychology, 31*(3), 464–472.

Lecanuet, J., & Schaal, B. (2002). Sensory performances in the human foetus: A brief summary of research. *Intellectica, 34,* 29–56.

Leuner, B., Glasper, E. R., & Gould, E. (2010). Parenting and plasticity. *Trends in Neurosciences, 33*(10), 465–473.

Lorberbaum, J. P., Newman, J. D., Horwitz, A. R., Dubno, J. R., Lydiard, R. B., Hamner, M. B., et al. (2002). A potential role for thalamocingulate circuitry in human maternal behavior. *Biological Psychiatry, 51*(6), 431–445.

Lorenz, K. (1942). Die angeborenen formen möglicher erfahrung. [The inborn forms of possible experience]. *Zeitschrift Für Tierpsychologie, 5,* 235–409.

MacFarlane, A. J. (1975). Olfaction in the development of social preferences in the human neonate. *CIBA Foundation Symposium, 33,* 103–117.

Maestripieri, D., & Pelka, S. (2002). Sex differences in interest in infants across the lifespan. *Human Nature, 13*(3), 327–344.

Mahler, M. S. (1974). Symbiosis and individuation: The psychological birth of the human infant. *The Psychoanalytic Study of the Child, 29,* 89–106.

Marlier, L., & Schaal, B. (2005). Human newborns prefer human milk: Conspecific milk odor is attractive without postnatal exposure. *Child Development, 76*(1), 155–168.

Mason, C., & Elwood, R. (1995). Is there a physiological basis for the couvade and onset of paternal care? *International Journal of Nursing Studies, 32*(2), 137–148.

Mattson, B. J., Williams, S., Rosenblatt, J. S., & Morrell, J. I. (2001). Comparison of two positive reinforcing stimuli: Pups and cocaine throughout the postpartum period. *Behavioral Neuroscience, 115*(3), 683–694.

Maurer, D., & Lewis, T. L. (2001). Visual acuity: The role of visual input in inducing postnatal change. *Clinical Neuroscience Research, 1,* 239–247.

Meaney, M. J. (2001). Maternal care, gene expression, and the transmission of individual differences in stress reactivity across generations. *Annual Review of Neuroscience, 24,* 1161–1192.

Meaney, M. J. (2010). Epigenetics and the biological definition of gene × environment interactions. *Child Development, 81*(1), 41–79.

Mennella, J. A., & Beauchamp, G. K. (1998). Early flavor experiences: Research update. *Nutrition Reviews, 56*(7), 205–211.

Mennella, J. A., Jagnow, C. P., & Beauchamp, G. K. (2001). Prenatal and postnatal flavor learning by human infants. *Pediatrics, 107*(6), E88.

Mondloch, C. J., Lewis, T. L., Budreau, D. R., Maurer, D., Dannemiller, J. L., Stephens, B. R., et al. (1999). Face perception during early infancy. *Psychological Science, 10*(5), 419–422.

Moon, C., Cooper, R. P., & Fifer, W. P. (1993). Two-day-olds prefer their native language. *Infant Behavior and Development, 16*(4), 495–500.

Morton, J., & Johnson, M. H. (1991). CONSPEC and CONLERN: A two-process theory of infant face recognition. *Psychological Review, 98*(2), 164–181.

Muñoz-Hoyos, A., Molina-Carballo, A., Augustin-Morales, M., Contreras-Chova, F., Naranjo-Gómez, A., Justicia-Martínez, F., et al. (2011). Psychosocial dwarfism: Psychopathological aspects and putative neuroendocrine markers. *Psychiatry Research, 188*(1), 96–101.

Murray, L., & Trevarthen, C. (1986). The infant's role in mother-infant communications. *Journal of Child Language, 13*(1), 15–29.

Nadel, J., Carchon, I., Kervella, C., Marcelli, D., & Réserbat-Plantey, D. (1999). Expectancies for social contingency in 2-month-olds. *Developmental Science, 2*(2), 164–173.

Nagy, E. (2008). Innate intersubjectivity: Newborns' sensitivity to communication disturbance. *Developmental Psychology, 44*(6), 1779–1784.

Nelson, E. E., & Panksepp, J. (1998). Brain substrates of infant–mother attachment: Contributions of opioids, oxytocin, and norepinephrine. *Neuroscience and Biobehavioral Reviews, 22*(3), 437–452.

Newman, J. D. (1985). The infant cry of primates. In B. Lester & C. F. Boukydis (Eds.), *Infant crying* (pp. 307–323). New York: Plenum Press.

Newman, J. D. (2007). Neural circuits underlying crying and cry responding in mammals. *Behavioural Brain Research, 182*(2), 155–165.

Oatridge, A., Holdcroft, A., Saeed, N., Hajnal, J. V., Puri, B. K., Fusi, L., et al. (2002). Change in brain size during and after pregnancy: Study in healthy women and women with preeclampsia. *American Journal of Neuroradiology, 23*, 19–26.

Owings, D. H., & Zeifman, D. M. (2004). Human infant crying as an animal communication system: Insights from an assessment/management approach. In D. K. Oller & U. Griebel (Eds.), *Evolution of communication systems: A comparative approach* (pp. 151–170). Cambridge, MA: MIT Press.

Pagel, M. (1997). Desperately concealing father: A theory of parent–infant resemblance. *Animal Behaviour, 53*(5), 973–981.

Panksepp, J., Meeker, R., & Bean, N. J. (1980). The neurochemical control of crying. *Pharmocology, Biochemistry, and Behavior, 12*, 437–443.

Panksepp, J., Siviy, S. M., & Normansell, L. A. (1985). Brain opioids and social emotions. In M. Reite & T. Fields (Eds.), *The psychobiology of attachment and separation* (pp. 3–49). New York: Academic Press.

Pascalis, O., de Schonen, S., Morton, J., Deruelle, C., & Fabre-Grenet, M. (1995). Mother's face recognition by neonates: A replication and an extension. *Infant Behavior and Development, 18*(1), 79–85.

Pascalis, O., Scott, L. S., Kelly, D. J., Shannon, R. W., & Nicholson, E. (2005). Plasticity of face processing in infancy. *Proceedings of the National Academy of Sciences USA, 102*(14), 5297–5300.

Pawluski, J. L., Vanderbyl, B. L., Ragan, K., & Galea, L. A. M. (2006). First reproductive experience persistently affects spatial reference and working memory in the mother and these effects are not due to pregnancy or 'mothering' alone. *Behavioural Brain Research, 175*(1), 157–165.

Peláez-Nogueras, M., Gewirtz, J. L., Field, T., & Cigales, M. (1996). Infants' preference for touch stimulation in face-to-face interactions. *Journal of Applied Developmental Psychology, 17*(2), 199–213.

Pepper, G. V., & Roberts, S. C. (2006). Rates of nausea and vomiting in pregnancy and dietary characteristics across populations. *Proceedings of the Royal Society of London: B. Biological Sciences, 273*, 2675–2679.

Porter, R. H., Cernoch, J. M., & Balogh, R. D. (1984). Recognition of neonates by facial-visual characteristics. *Pediatrics, 74*, 501–504.

Porter, R. H., Cernoch, J. M., & McLaughlin, F. J. (1983). Maternal recognition of neonates through olfactory cues. *Physiology and Behavior, 30*(1), 151–154.

Quinn, P. C., Yahr, J., Kuhn, A., Slater, A. M., & Pascalis, O. (2002). Representation of the gender of human faces by infants: A preference for female. *Perception, 31*(9), 1109–1121.

Rosenstein, D., & Oster, H. (1988). Differential facial responses to four basic tastes in newborns. *Child Development, 59*(6), 1555–1568.

Russell, M. J. (1976). Human olfactory communication. *Nature, 260*(5551), 520–522.

Russell, M. J., Mendelson, T., & Peeke, H. V. (1983). Mothers' identification of their infant's odors. *Ethology and Sociobiology, 4*(1), 29–31.

Salapatek, P., Bechtold, A. G., & Bushnell, E. W. (1976). Infant visual acuity as a function of viewing distance. *Child Development, 47*(3), 860–863.

Scafidi, F. A., Field, T. M., Schanberg, S. M., Bauer, C. R., Tucci, K., Roberts, J., et al. (1990). Massage stimulates growth in preterm infants: A replication. *Infant Behavior and Development, 13*(2), 167–188.

Schanberg, S. M., & Field, T. M. (1987). Sensory deprivation stress and supplemental stimulation in the rat pup and preterm human neonate. *Child Development, 58*(6), 1431–1447.

Seifritz, E., Esposito, F., Neuhoff, J. G., Lüthi, A., Mustovic, H., Dammann, G., et al. (2003). Differential sex-independent amygdala response to infant crying and laughing in parents versus nonparents. *Biological Psychiatry, 54*(12), 1367–1375.

Sherrod, K. B., O'Connor, S., Vietze, P. M., & Altemeier, W. A. (1984). Child health and maltreatment. *Child Development, 55*(4), 1174–1183.

Shide, D. J., & Blass, E. M. (1989). Opioidlike effects of intraoral infusions of corn oil and polycose on stress reactions in 10-day-old rats. *Behavioral Neuroscience, 103*(6), 1168–1175.

Smith, B. A., Fillion, T. J., & Blass, E. M. (1990). Orally mediated sources of calming in 1- to 3-day-old human infants. *Developmental Psychology, 26*(5), 731–737.

Spangler, G., & Grossmann, K. E. (1993). Biobehavioral organization in securely and insecurely attached infants. *Child Development, 64*(5), 1439–1450.

Spelke, E. S., & Kinzler, K. D. (2007). Core knowledge. *Developmental Science, 10*(1), 89–96.

Stark, R. E., & Nathanson, S. N. (1973). Spontaneous crying in the newborn infant: Sounds and facial gestures. In J. F. Bosma (Ed.), *Fourth symposium oral sensation and perception: Development in the fetus and infant* (pp. 323–352). Bethesda, MD: U.S. Department of Health, Education, and Welfare.

Steinberg, L. D., Catalano, R., & Dooley, D. (1981). Economic antecedents of child abuse and neglect. *Child Development, 52*(3), 975–985.

Stern, D. N. (1977). *The first relationship: Infant and mother.* Cambridge, MA: Harvard University Press.

Storey, A. E., Walsh, C. J., Quinton, R. L., & Wynne-Edwards, K. (2000).

Hormonal correlates of paternal responsiveness in new and expectant fathers. *Evolution and Human Behavior, 21*(2), 79–95.

Strathearn, L., Li, J., Fonagy, P., & Montague, P. R. (2008). What's in a smile? Maternal brain responses to infant facial cues. *Pediatrics, 122*(1), 40–51.

Suomi, S. J. (1999). Attachment in rhesus monkeys. In J. Cassidy & P. Shaver (Eds.), *Handbook of attachment: Theory, research, and clinical applications* (pp. 181–197). New York: Guilford Press.

Swain, J. E., Lorberbaum, J. P., Kose, S., & Strathearn, L. (2007). Brain basis of early parent-infant interactions: Psychology, physiology, and in vivo functional neuroimaging studies. *Journal of Child Psychology and Psychiatry, 48*(3–4), 262–287.

Thoman, E. B., & Whitney, M. P. (1989). Sleep states of infants monitored in the home: Individual differences, developmental trends, and origins of diurnal cyclicity. *Infant Behavior and Development, 12*(1), 59–75.

Trevarthen, C. (2006). "Stepping away from the mirror: Pride and shame in adventures of companionship": Reflections on the nature and emotional needs of infant intersubjectivity. In C. S. Carter, L. Ahnert, K. E. Grossmann, S. B. Hrdy, M. E. Lamb, S. W. Porges, et al. (Eds.), *Attachment and bonding: A new synthesis* (pp. 55–84). Cambridge, MA: MIT Press.

Trevarthen, C., & Aitken, K. J. (2001). Infant intersubjectivity: Research, theory, and clinical applications. *Journal of Child Psychology and Psychiatry, 42*(1), 3–48.

Tronick, E., Als, H., Adamson, L., Wise, S., & Brazelton, T. (1978). The infant's response to entrapment between contradictory messages in face-to-face interaction. *Journal of the American Academy of Child Psychiatry, 17*, 1–13.

Tronick, E. Z., & Cohn, J. F. (1989). Infant-mother face-to-face interaction: Age and gender differences in coordination and the occurrence of miscoordination. *Child Development, 60*(1), 85–92.

Turati, C., Simion, F., Milani, I., & Umiltà, C. (2002). Newborns' preference for faces: What is crucial? *Developmental Psychology, 38*(6), 875–882.

Upadhyay, A., Aggarwal, R., Narayan, S., Joshi, M., Paul, V. K., & Deorari, A. K. (2004). Analgesic effects of expressed breast milk in procedural pain in term neonates: A randomized, placebo-controlled, double-blind trial. *Acta Paediatrics, 93*(4), 518–522.

Valenzà, E., Simion, F., Cassia, V. M., & Umiltà, C. (1996). Face preference at birth. *Journal of Experimental Psychology, 22*(4), 892–903.

van den Boom, D. (1994). The influence of temperament and mothering on attachment and exploration: An experimental manipulation of sensitive responsiveness among lower-class mothers with irritable infants. *Child Development, 65*(5), 1457–1477.

Walton, G. E., Bower, N. J., & Bower, T. G. (1992). Recognition of familiar faces by newborns. *Infant Behavior and Development, 15*(2), 265–269.

Webb, S. J., Monk, C. S., & Nelson, C. A. (2001). Mechanisms of postnatal neurobiological development: Implications for human development. *Developmental Neuropsychology, 19*(2), 147–171.

Weinberg, K. M., & Tronick, E. Z. (1996). Infant affective reactions to the resumption of maternal interaction after the still-face. *Child Development,* *67*(3), 905–914.

Werker, J. F. (1989). Becoming a native listener. *American Scientist, 77,* 54–59.

Werker, J. F., Pegg, J. E., & McLeod, P. J. (1994). A cross-language investigation of infant preference for infant-directed communication. *Infant Behavior and Development, 17*(3), 323–333.

Wiesenfeld, A. R., Malatesta, C. Z., & DeLoach, L. L. (1981). Differential parental response to familiar and unfamiliar infant distress signals. *Infant Behavior and Development, 4*(3), 281–295.

Wynn, K. (1992). Addition and subtraction by human infants. *Nature, 358*(6389), 749–750.

Zeifman, D. M. (2001). An ethological analysis of human infant crying: Answering Tinbergen's four questions. *Developmental Psychobiology, 39*(4), 265–285.

Zeifman, D. M. (2004). Colic and the early crying curve: A developmental account. *Behavioral and Brain Sciences, 27,* 476–477.

Zeifman, D., Delaney, S., & Blass, E. M. (1996). Sweet taste, looking, and calm in 2- and 4-week-old infants: The eyes have it. *Developmental Psychology, 32*(6), 1090–1099.

Chapter **3**

Developmental Trends and Bonding Milestones

From Parents to Partners

MARY I. CAMPA

*H*umans are social creatures. We spend much of our lives working or playing in the company of other people. Some of these people are central to, and permeate, our lives. The people who raise us, our best childhood friends, our first love, an inspirational teacher or coach—all of these people can shape our lives in profound ways. Relationships with parental figures are some of the most important and influential. As significant as they are, these relationships are but a fraction of the social connections we will make over the course of our lives. Starting in early childhood, we begin to branch out from parental relationships, and by the time we reach adolescence many of our connections are with people outside the family, particularly peers. Ultimately, our experiences and relationships during childhood and adolescence prepare us to make our own families. Thus, between infancy and early adulthood, we go from total dependence on caregivers to being able to care for ourselves and others.

The goal of the present chapter is to highlight some important trends and milestones that bridge the gap between early bonding experiences with parents and later bonding experiences with partners. The focus is largely on peer relationships because, as will be apparent, they occupy this developmental space. Specifically, the focus is on three broad areas of research: development of social competence in early childhood; normative changes in attachment behavior from middle childhood to adulthood; and biological, behavioral, and social-cognitive changes associated with puberty. At the end of the chapter, I also review the burgeoning body of literature on idiosyncratic preferences in romantic partner selection. Finally, gender becomes increasingly salient in this developmental period, and special attention is given to the topic throughout.

DEVELOPMENT OF SOCIAL COMPETENCE

Imagine two toddlers at play, and one has a toy the other wants. There are many ways a child might go about getting the desired toy: She could approach the other child with a different toy and try to trade, play alongside the other toddler until he's done with the toy, approach an adult to get sharing privileges, or just snatch the toy away. While all of these behaviors are likely to result in the toddler getting the toy (at least for a while), some strategies are more likely to result in positive social outcomes (e.g., getting the toy, not getting in trouble). Children who are socially competent engage a number of interrelated skills to produce positive outcomes. They are more likely to attend to and encode relevant information, understand how their actions affect others, regulate their emotions and behaviors, understand another's perspective, negotiate conflict, sustain positive interactions, and engage in cooperative behavior (Hay, Caplan, & Nash, 2009; Howes, 2009; Rose-Kransnor, 1997). Children who can flexibly engage a greater numbers of these skills across interactions with different social partners and in different social situations are considered socially competent (Rose-Kransnor, 1997; Thompson, 1994).

Play behavior is integral to children's social competence. When children play with other children, they simultaneously display their competence and practice the skills needed for successful social interaction (Coplan & Arbeau, 2009; Lindsey & Colwell, 2003). Children's play takes three basic forms: solitary play, mutually aware play, and socially interactive play. Although each form is present throughout the life course, the relative balance shifts during the preschool years (see Coplan & Arbeau, 2009, for a review). Notably, between 3 and 5 years of age, there are decreases in solitary play and increases in dyadic and group play. Parallel (or side-by-side) play continues to dominate in 4- to 5-year-old children, but during this time there is an increase in mutual awareness (e.g., more eye contact) and interactive play.

Just as there are developmental shifts in the type of play children engage in, there are also shifts in the adaptive value, or purpose, of play. For example, in early and middle childhood rough-and-tumble (RT) play provides an opportunity to practice reading the intentions of others to learn what is and is not perceived as playful. RT also helps children learn how to moderate their behavior to keep an interaction playful (Pellis & Pellis, 2007). In young adolescents, however, the purpose of RT play is more instrumental in delineating status boundaries in peer groups, particularly among males (Pellegrini, 2003). RT play in early and middle adolescence can also serve as an initial mechanism for youth to start interacting with the opposite sex.

Three important areas of research related to play and the development of social competence in young children are emotion regulation, perspective taking, and cooperative behavior. Although each of these areas reflects distinct abilities, they are nonetheless interrelated. For example, children's (and adult's) ability to attend to relevant and ignore irrelevant social information plays a role in affect regulation (Thompson, 1994) and accurate interpretation of the thoughts and feelings of others (Murphy, Laurie-Rose, Brinkman, & McNamara, 2007) and allows for cooperative interactions (Nagy & Molnar, 2004).

Emotion Regulation

Emotion regulation is broadly defined as the ability to monitor, evaluate, and modify one's emotional reactions, with optimal emotional regulation being situation and goal dependent (Thompson, 1994). Thus, an individual's ability to successfully regulate his or her emotions is likely to vary across settings and interaction partners. For example, children may find it more difficult to regulate their emotions in a maternal separation situation than in a peer-conflict situation. Although infant–caregiver relationships are the foundation of emotion regulation (see Dykas & Cassidy, Chapter 1, this volume), a sizable body of evidence shows that peer relationships also have important effects.

One form of play that appears to be especially important in facilitating social competence is pretend or sociodramatic play (Pearson, Russ, & Spannagel, 2008). Pretend play involves the use of symbolic behavior to mentally and physically generate different emotional and interpersonal situations. For example, in pretend play a child creates a situation where he or she can imagine how others think and feel (e.g., what it's like to be a mommy) or creates a potentially emotionally charged situation and modifies it (e.g., Mommy is leaving for vacation; what should the baby do?). Basic forms of pretend play develop early in the second year of life, increase steadily during the next several years, and then begin to decline in frequency.

Children can engage in pretend play alone or with others. Pretend play with others, particularly skilled others, is important in the development of self-regulatory abilities. For example, preschool children who played make-believe with peers showed greater control of their behavior during clean-up time (a social demand situation), whereas those who spent time pretending alone showed less behavioral control over time (Elias & Berk, 2002). Quality of play and self-regulatory behavior are also greater when interaction partners are more skilled (e.g., older, more knowledgeable, or verbal; DeKroon, Kyte, & Johnson, 2002; Werebe & Baudonnière, 1991). However, even interactions between 2-year olds can increase their self-control (Mathieson & Banerjee, 2010). As children approach school age, pretend play continues to be beneficial for girls but not for boys (Lindsey & Colwell, 2003). This may be related to a decrease in pretend play for boys as they age or to a different set of skills related to boys' regulatory behavior. Notably, Lindsey and Colwell (2003) found that RT play, more commonly observed among boys, was related to their emotional competence at this age, whereas pretend play was not. Overall, the more children work through emotional scenarios in their play, the more they are able to regulate their actual emotions in everyday life (Galyer & Evans, 2001).

Perspective Taking

Perspective taking is a broad term for the ability to understand another's emotions and cognitions and is a component of empathetic response (Dunn & Cutting, 1999; Selman, 1981). Children's ability to take another's perspective begins early in life with the development of joint attention (Charman et al., 2000). Some argue that true social understanding is not possible before children are able to differentiate themselves from others, a development that occurs in the second year of life (but see Nichols, Svetlova, & Brownell, 2010, for evidence of empathetic response in 12-month-olds). Also included in perspective taking is the ability to recognize and label emotional expressions, a skill that develops in early childhood and continues to improve through adolescence (Kolb, Wilson, & Taylor, 1992).

Like emotional regulation, perspective taking is related to children's pretend play. In particular, pretend play allows children to ascribe novel beliefs and emotions to make-believe people, thereby honing the skill of understanding others. For example, preschoolers who engage in more interactive play with peers are better able to identify facial expressions of emotion and are seen by parents and teachers as being more prosocial (Mathieson & Banerjee, 2010). Pretend play with a friend also increased children's ability to describe emotions relevant to specific situations (e.g., "This boy just got a new bike. How does he feel?"; Lindsey & Colwell, 2003). Unlike emotion regulation, perspective-taking abilities do not appear to be enhanced by pretend play with older versus younger playmates (Youngblade & Dunn, 1995). Rather, pretend-play partners who can help a child imagine a variety of different situations, even ones that are unlikely to occur in real life or are socially unacceptable, enhance emotional understanding. Finally, pretend play that requires object representation (e.g., imagining a block is a car) fosters the more cognitive aspects of perspective taking, including understanding others' beliefs (vs. emotions; Nielsen & Dissanayake, 2000).

Cooperative Behavior

Cooperative behavior involves both prosocial behaviors and the negotiation of conflict, but it begins with infants' first attempts to coordinate their own actions with others (Hay, Payne, & Chadwick, 2004). The basic ability to attend to and participate in a social interaction is present shortly after birth in the form of imitation (see Zeifman, Chapter 2, this volume, for more information about newborn skills). Although imitation may appear rudimentary when considering the intricacies of later social interaction, imitation requires orientation, attention, and motivation (Nagy & Molnar, 2004). Interestingly, observational data from neonates (3–36 hours after birth) indicate that they can produce gestures aimed to sustain an interaction, and heart rate data indicate that such gestures are different from mere imitation.

More complex cooperative behavior emerges in a predictable developmental sequence. Generally by the end of the first year children begin cooperative game play and by 2 years can engage in cooperative problem solving (Hay et al., 2009). Children will not play with just anyone, however. From very early on, children respond differently and reciprocally to each relationship partner, willingly engaging in play and sharing with some but not others (Ross & Lollis, 1989). The developmental time line of cooperative behaviors appears to be somewhat universal. For instance, research on children in Papua New Guinea indicates that although children play different types of games, increases in complexity over the first 3 years unfold similarly to Western samples (Eckerman & Whitehead, 1999). In addition, while themes and choice of play partners differ between American and Chinese families, children engage in the same forms of imaginative play behaviors across early childhood (Haight, Wang, Fung, Williams, & Mintz, 1999).

Parents typically direct social interactions with their children (see Zeifman, Chapter 2, this volume), whereas child-to-child interactions are the result of mutual engagement and cooperation. Children must choose to interact with a given peer and maintain that interaction in the face of potential adversity. However, conflict is common in peer interactions across the life course (e.g., Ross & Lollis, 1989), and conflict negotiation is itself an important component of children's play (Hay et al., 2009). As with other components of social competence, the turn-taking of pretend play may be especially useful in developing conflict resolution skills as children learn to negotiate shared creations.

Gender Differences in Social Competence

There are few differences in girls' and boys' social behaviors during infancy, but starting around age 3 children begin to self-segregate on the basis of gender (Fabes, Martin, & Hanish, 2004). By the time they reach preschool, children spend more than 50% of their time playing with children of the same sex and only 10% playing with those of the opposite sex. The gender-segregated nature of peer interactions intensifies through middle childhood and only begins to dissipate during early adolescence (Johnson, 2004; Maccoby & Jacklin, 1987). The most frequently cited explanation for gender segregation is that children prefer to play with others who are compatible in interaction style, and because boys and girls have different styles of interaction there is a de facto gender segregation (Fabes et al., 2004; Bohn-Gettler et al., 2010). Indeed, research has found gender differences in levels and responses to peer conflict (Sims, Hutchins, & Taylor, 1998), size and stability of peer groups (Johnson, 2004), and types of play (Zosuls et al., 2009).

Not all research supports the interaction style hypothesis, however. For example, Hoffmann and Powlishta (2001) found no evidence that girls' and boys' interaction styles differed in terms of aggressiveness, activity, or cooperation despite high levels of gender segregation in the sample. On the other hand, Bohn-Gettler et al. (2010) found gender differences in activity level, which were related to gender segregation. Specifically, highly active boys were least likely to play with girls, whereas highly active girls were most likely to play with boys. In addition, the highly active, gender-integrated girls were least well liked by their peers. The difference in results between the Hoffman and Powlishta and the Bohn-Gettler et al.

studies—gender differences in one and not the other—may be explained by more recent research on the role of gender schemas in children's gendered behavior.

Martin, Fabes, Hanish, Leonard, and Dinella (2011) proposed a two-part cognitive-behavioral similarity model to explain gender segregation in young children. Examining both type of play behavior (including activity, RT play, and aggression) and gendered cognitions (perceived self-similarity to boys and girls), the authors found that beliefs about one's similarity to one's gender was positively correlated with interactions within gender and negatively correlated with interactions outside one's gender. That is, girls who thought they were more girl-like were more likely to want to play with other girls; boys who thought they were more boy-like wanted to play with other boys. Importantly, this was true irrespective of interaction style. Furthermore, style of play, specifically RT play, was related only to boys'—and not to girls'—gender segregation. That is, boys who engaged in RT play were more likely to play with other boys, but girls who engaged in RT play were no more (or less) likely to play with other girls. This indicates that it is not just the type of play, or level of activity, that matters, but that children pick their play partners based on their ideas about who should be playing with whom and only then consider what they should be doing.

Research on gender differences in sharing behavior in children 2 to 4 years of age highlights the importance of gender norms in the onset of gender self-segregation (Hay, Castle, Davies, Demetriou, & Stimson, 1999). Sharing behavior with familiar peers tends to decline between the second and fourth years of life, particularly for boys. Girls' sharing behavior, however, is selective. Girls increase their sharing somewhat as they reach age 3 but only share with other girls, often rebuking boys' attempts to share. These findings support the idea that the early precursor of gender self-segregation may be adherence to gendered norms. That is, if Jill knows that sharing is only okay for girls, then she should not share with boys. In addition, like high-activity girls, boys who continue to share beyond the normal time frame are judged by parents and teachers to be problematic (Hay et al., 1999). Thus, evidence suggests that adults and peers alike exert considerable influence over gendered expectations through modeling, monitoring, and regulating gendered behavior (Glassman, 2000; Hibbard & Buhrmester, 1998).

Developmental Consequences of Social Competence

Consistent evidence indicates that children who are socially competent in preschool continue to be so across childhood (National Institute of Child

Health and Human Development, 2008) and adolescence (e.g., Masten, Morison, & Pellegrini, 1985). However, few studies have examined the effects of early childhood social competence on adult relationship functioning. A notable exception is the Minnesota Longitudinal Study of Risk and Adaptation, a 22-year longitudinal study of the effects of early emotion regulation (Simpson, Collins, & Salvatore, 2011). In particular, the authors found that children who were rated high in peer competence between 6 and 8 years of age reported more trust in their friends in adolescence and fewer expressions of negative emotion when resolving conflicts with romantic partners in young adulthood. These findings are particularly important as marital research implicates negative conflict styles as a main contributor to divorce (see Lee & Sbarra, Chapter 11, this volume).

NORMATIVE CHANGES IN ATTACHMENT BEHAVIOR

Who's the first person you turn to when you are upset about something? Who is the person you miss the most when you are away? Who is the person you know you can always count on no matter what? For most people, the answer to these questions changes over the course of development. Because humans are born in a state of extreme immaturity, infants are completely dependent on adult caregivers for food, shelter, physical safety, and emotional security. Humans (and other mammals; see Curtis, Chapter 6, this volume) are born with an attachment behavioral system that evolved to help ensure that these needs are met (Bowlby, 1969/1982; see Dykas & Cassidy, Chapter 1, this volume). Between childhood and adulthood, the list of people we rely on to meet our attachment needs expands from parental caregivers and family to include mentors, friends, and romantic partners. Generally, at some point in adulthood, a romantic partner becomes the primary the source for fulfilling attachment needs. In the following section, I review research on the changes in attachment behaviors and bonds that occur between middle childhood and young adulthood, focusing on the transition between parental and peer relationships.

Attachment Bonds and Behaviors

Attachment bonds are characterized by four behavioral features—proximity maintenance, secure base, safe haven, and separation distress—that together regulate affect by regulating *proximity* to an attachment figure (Hazan & Shaver, 2004). How much contact is needed depends on a variety of factors. Confidence that we can access our important people if needed is experienced as a sense of *secure base*, which in turn fosters exploration and active engagement in the world. Distress, whether a result of internal (e.g., physical illness) or external (e.g., threatening situations) factors, motivates us to seek out attachment figures as a *safe haven*. The prolonged or anticipated absence of an attachment figure causes *separation distress*. The attachment system is active across the life span. That is, at every age, we rely on others to meet our attachment needs. The amount and type of contact needed to feel secure change across development. An infant might need to be held to feel fully soothed, whereas a college student might be comforted by a phone call home.

Although these behavioral features work in concert, they are often experienced in isolation. For example, new couples might maintain constant proximity, spending every available minute together but still not see each other as bases of security. Bowlby (1969/1982) emphasized the importance of distinguishing between attachment behaviors and an attachment bond. Attachment bonds are enduring relationships characterized by all four behavioral features. Studies have shown that from middle childhood through old age, individuals have two or three attachment figures (i.e., relationships that include all four behavioral features) and an additional four or five people who meet some but not all attachment needs (Campa, Hazan, & Wolfe, 2009; Cicirelli, 2010; Seibert & Kerns, 2009). In some cases, the directing of one or more attachment behaviors to a nonattachment figure can be a precursor to the development of an attachment bond (Ainsworth, 1967; Hazan & Zeifman, 1994). For example, the repeated use of another as a haven of safety could ultimately lead to viewing this person as a base of security.

Developmental Trends in Attachment Behavior

As children begin spending more time with friends, they naturally begin to direct some attachment behaviors toward them. For example, when asked to choose the one person they would most like to spend time with, the majority of children aged 6–18 named a peer rather than a parent (Hazan & Zeifman, 1994; Nickerson & Nagle, 2005). The same studies found that starting about age 11, the majority of children began to seek out peers when feeling upset or down (i.e., the safe haven component of attachment). Before age 15 the most missed figure was a parent; after age 15 separation distress was displayed in reference to peers. However, not until early adulthood was there evidence for using peers as a secure base (Hazan & Zeifman, 1994; Markiewicz, Lawford, Doyle, & Haggart, 2006). The stepwise sequence of turning to peers for proximity maintenance, followed by safe haven, and finally separation distress and secure base has been replicated in a number of international samples (Friedlmeier & Granqvist, 2006; Zhang, Chan, & Teng, 2011). The type of peer that youth rely on changes across development; as they get older, they direct attachment behaviors less toward friends and more toward a romantic partner. Both theory and empirical evidence suggest that friendships are important developmental antecedents to positive romantic relationships and serve an intermediary role between parental and romantic relationships (e.g., Furman & Buhrmester, 1992; Sullivan, 1953).

Primary Attachment Figures

In theory, relationships that qualify as attachments are organized in a hierarchical fashion, with one person serving as the primary attachment figure (Bowlby, 1969/1982). This person is the one who is most preferred for meeting attachment needs. Although there is no definitive developmental time line of when a peer supplants a parent as the primary attachment figure, evidence suggests that it is rare until very late adolescence or early adulthood (Fraley & Davis, 1997; Markiewicz et al., 2006). Infant–caregiver attachments develop within the first year of life as a result of extensive interactions, including high levels of physical contact, with primary caregivers (Bowlby, 1969/1982; Ainsworth, 1967). There is some evidence that romantic attachments take an average of 2 years to develop and friendship attachments even longer (Fraley & Davis, 1997; Hazan & Zeifman, 1994). During adolescence, friendships and romantic relationships tend to be relatively short lived (Carver, Joyner, & Udry, 2003). It is thus unlikely that many peer bonds during this developmental period are of sufficient duration for attachment formation. These peer-to-peer relationships also tend to lack the intimacy and consistent proximity known to foster attachment bonds. The peer relationships that are most likely to become full-blown attachments are with romantic partners. In all studies examining attachment transfer during adolescences and young adulthood, it was individuals with romantic partners who were least likely to rely on a parent as their primary attachment figure (e.g., Fraley & Davis, 1997, Freeman & Brown, 2001; Friedlmeier & Granqvist, 2006; Hazan & Zeifman, 1994). Romantic relationships include features that support attachment formation, including physical intimacy (Hazan & Zeifman, 1994) and more consistent attachment need fulfillment (Campa et al., 2009).

Gender Differences in Attachment Behaviors

There are few gender differences in attachment behavior in infancy or early childhood, but some differences have been found in middle childhood and beyond (e.g., Schmitt et al., 2003). Consistent with the lack of gender effects on early attachment relationships, few studies have examined how girls and boys (or women and men) may differ in the way they use their attachment figures. Nonetheless, research on parent and peer social support suggests that differences may exist. For example, in a study of perceived support among 9- to 18-year-olds, Bokhorst, Sumter, and Westenberg (2010) found that girls reported more support from peers than did boys, but there was no gender difference in perceived support from parents (see also Helsen, Vollebergh, & Meeus, 2000). Nickerson and Nagle (2005) also reported gender differences in peer relationships, with girls reporting higher levels of attachment, trust, and communication. This may reflect general differences in boys' and girls' social networks. For example, although girls and boys have the same number of friends, boys interact with a larger number of people, suggesting that the proportion of superficial interactions is higher among boys (Johnson, 2004). The difference might also be due to the fact that the type of support boys provide, particularly to other boys, may not be conducive to the formation of attachment (Oransky & Marecek, 2009). However, in the two studies that reported gender differences in the transfer of attachment from parents to peers, the evidence was mixed; one study found girls more likely to direct attachment behavior toward peers than boys, and the other showed the opposite (Friedlmeier & Granqvist, 2006; Nickerson & Nagle, 2005). Clearly, more research is needed. The one gender difference that has been consistently reported is about parent, not peer relationships. Generally, youth of all ages report relying on their mothers, more than their fathers, to fulfill attachment needs, although boys turn to their fathers more than girls do, particularly when upset or sad (Freeman & Brown, 2001; Markiewicz et al., 2006).

Developmental Effects of Attachment Transfer

Individuals differ not just in *who* they use to meet their attachment needs but also in the *strategies* they use for fulfilling these needs. There are three primary strategies (also known as attachment "styles"), which vary along two dimensions of anxiety and avoidance (see Shaver & Mikulincer, Chapter 9, this volume). Individuals high in attachment anxiety report a lack of confidence in their ability to get their attachment needs met. Individuals high on avoidance are uncomfortable with interpersonal closeness and tend to distance themselves from others. The secure strategy is characterized by low scores on both the anxiety and avoidance dimensions. That is, secure individuals are comfortable seeking care from others and confident that care will be available if needed. Most youth use parents and peers for attachment needs (Bokhorst et al., 2010; Campa et al., 2009), but those with insecure attachment histories are more likely to transfer primary attachment functions to a peer, especially a romantic partner (Hazan & Zeifman, 1994; Markiewicz et al., 2006). A very supportive friend or romantic partner could, in theory, substitute for an unsupportive parent. However, friends of insecure youth are not more supportive on average than friends of secure youth (Freeman & Brown, 2001). Furthermore, even in late adolescence and early adulthood, relationships with parents and peers are not interchangeable. Early bonds with parents are unilateral and largely directed by the adult; it is not until early to mid-adulthood that attachment relationships transform into a more reciprocal bond. In contrast, peer attachments generally develop reciprocally, with each member of the pair receiving and providing support. Evidence suggests that exclusively relying on a peer for attachment needs during this period of development may be problematic. For example, Chinese young adults who named a peer as their base of security were lonelier and less positive than young adults whose base of security was a parent (Zhang et al., 2011). Importantly, this was true for secure as well as insecure youth, across all levels of perceived parent and peer support. This suggests that the negative feelings (i.e., loneliness, lack of positive emotion) reported by youth are not simply a function of having poor parental relationships. Rather, peer relationships at this age, which are generally less consistent and durable than parental ones, may not be capable of providing an effective secure base. Moreover, positive parental relationships can support youth so they can take interpersonal risks in peer relationships, increasing their emotional connections with, and eventual reliance on, peers for attachment needs (Helsen et al., 2000).

PUBERTAL DEVELOPMENT

The differences between boys and men, between girls and women, and between men and women are wide ranging and complex. Differences include their facial structure and body shape, voice quality, gait, and brain organization and function. Amazingly, all of these changes occur during a relatively short developmental window. Indeed, puberty is the second most rapid period of growth in the human lifespan, trailing only the growth rate from conception to age 3. Puberty is a process that begins with the reactivation of the hypothalamic–pituitary–gonadal (HPG) axis (last active during the fetal and neonatal periods) and ends in mid- to late adolescence, when hormones reach adult levels (Susman & Dorn, 2009). Although there is considerable individual variation in the onset and duration of puberty, the types of changes and the order in which they occur tend to be consistent across individuals (Cameron, 2004; Parent et al., 2003; Tanner & Whitehouse, 1976). I now review the biological, behavioral, and social-cognitive changes associated with puberty and their social implications.

Biological Changes

Pubertal biological changes can be categorized into three broad classes: changes in reproductive capacity, changes in sex-typical physical appearance, and changes in overall physical health. These changes are facilitated by the reactivation of HPG axis when pulsatile hypothalamic secretions of gonadotropin-releasing hormone begin stimulating a pituitary release of hormones (Susman & Dorn, 2009). Although the exact mechanism of initiation is not yet understood, it appears that a combination of genetic (Ge, Natsuaki, Neiderhiser, & Reiss, 2007) and environmental factors, including levels of leptin (or subcutaneous fat stores; Vizmanos & Marti-Henneberg, 2000) and family composition (Tither & Ellis, 2008), contribute to reactivation. Pituitary secretion of growth hormone is primarily responsible for the overall increase in body mass and the increase in heart and lung size, which provide greater circulatory and respiratory capacity (Parent et al., 2003). It is during the period of adolescence that individuals are at their peak physically. Males gain on average 52 pounds during puberty and show marked increases in lung capacity and cardiac output (Barnes, 1975; Nève, Girard, Flahault, & Boule, 2002). Females gain less weight overall, an average of 38 pounds, show a smaller increase in lung capacity, and produce fewer red blood cells. While girls gain between 2 and 10 inches in height over the course of roughly 2 years, boys gain between 4 and 12 inches in height over the course of roughly 4 years (Barnes, 1975). These changes in size and overall physicality are thought to have evolved to help females support the burden of childbearing (Sisk & Foster, 2004) and to help males increase their likelihood of successfully competing and providing for a mate (Miller, 1994; Puts, Gaulin & Verdolini, 2006).

In addition to growth hormone, the pituitary also releases follicle-stimulating hormone (FSH) and luteinizing hormone (LH; Cameron, 2004). FSH directly affects the production of ovarian follicles and sperm, enabling sexual reproduction. The primary role of LH is to stimulate the release of sex steroids from the gonads. In females, estrogen, progesterone, and androgens are produced by the ovaries, creating a cascade of effects in the brain as well as initiating (and later sustaining) the menstrual cycle. Estrogen and androgens are also responsible for female secondary sexual characteristics, including the development of breasts, fat redistribution, and pubic hair. In males, the testicles produce androgens, including testosterone, which is responsible for the deepening of the voice and the increasing of muscle mass and facial and body hair. With the processes of puberty, not only do individuals become reproductively capable but their bodies become prototypically male or female, and this difference figures in mate selection. For example, before puberty there is little difference between boys' and girls' bodies. After puberty, boys have a typical "V" male shape (high shoulder-to-waist ratio) and girls a typical "hourglass" female shape (low waist-to-hip ratio; Taylor, Grant, Williams, & Goulding, 2010). It has been shown repeatedly that males who conform to the "V" shape and females who conform to the "hourglass" shape are seen as more attractive (e.g., Braun & Bryan, 2006). The same hormonal increases that differentiate children from adults physically correspond with a shift in the appeal of baby features (Fullard & Reiling, 1976; Sprengelmeyer et al., 2009). Thus, at the same time boys and girls transform physically into sexually attractive men and women, they become capable of creating a child and are drawn to them.

Behavioral Changes

Biological changes associated with puberty also affect adolescent social behavior, especially sexual and romantic behavior. Youth often report sexual desire before the onset of puberty, as early as 10 years of age (Reynolds, Herbenick, & Bancroft, 2003). In a nationally representative sample of over 13,000 American adolescents ages 10–19, only 3.5% of youth reported no sexual interest (Udry & Chantala, 2005). Furthermore, there is a direct effect of hormones on adolescent sexuality, with higher levels of sex steroids (e.g., testosterone) associated with increased sexual desire and behavior (Udry, 1988). Adolescent sexual behavior is also influenced by social factors. For example, youth who had a sexually active best friend were more likely to be sexually active (Smith, Udry, & Morris, 1985). However, this was only true for girls who were physically developed. Those who were not developed (e.g., had little or no pubic hair) were not sexually active, regardless of what their friends were doing. Thus, it appears that boys' hormone levels (and social environments) have a direct and unmitigated effect on their sexual behavior, while girls' sexual behavior is influenced by an interaction between social and hormonal factors. These findings are consistent with theory and research on gender differences in adolescent sexuality, including same-sex sexuality (see Diamond, Chapter 8, this volume).

At about the time of puberty, youth begin to see themselves in the role of a romantic or sexual partner, although actual involvement in romantic relationships is heavily dependent on local culture, such as whether their peers are dating or not (Brown, 1999; Dornbusch et al., 1981). Between the ages of 12 and 18, adolescents generally spend more time with their romantic partners, invest more emotionally in their relationships, and engage in a greater number and type of sexual and romantic behaviors (Adams, Laursen, & Wilder, 2001; Carver et al., 2003). The majority of adolescents cite a romantic connection as the primary reason for initial intercourse, and adolescents in romantic relationships are more likely to have had intercourse (Michels, Kropp, Eyre, & Halpern-Felsher, 2005). With the average age of puberty in the United States being relatively early and the average age of marriage being relatively late, adolescents have a lengthy period during which to explore potential mates before selecting a long-term partner (Larson, Suzanne, Brown, Furstenberg, & Verma, 2002). Thus, although romantic relationships in adolescence tend to be short in duration, they provide adolescents with valuable experiences and skills, including companionship, reciprocity, cooperation, support provision and acceptance, love, and bonding (Furman & Wehner, 1994). Furthermore, the quality and experiences of romantic relationships during adolescence influence mental and sexual health and relationship functioning into young adulthood (Adam et al., 2011; Simpson et al., 2011).

Social-Cognitive Changes

A new line of research suggests that pubertal hormones also affect adolescent social-cognitive processing via brain changes. Adolescence represents a time of considerable brain reorganization characterized by patterned increases in gray matter, significant synaptic pruning, and increased myelination that continues into young adulthood (Giedd et al., 1999). All of these changes serve to make the adolescent brain function with increased specificity. The brain developments do not occur uniformly; rather, the brain matures from the back to the front so the regions implicated in executive planning, organization and judgment, impulse control, and reasoning are the last to mature (Lenroot & Giedd, 2006). In comparison, the limbic system, responsible for reward sensitivity and instinctive emotional reactions, is hyperactive during adolescence, creating an imbalance in emotional and cognitive functioning that influences adolescent social interactions (Steinberg, 2004). For example, compared with adults, adolescents focus more on rewards and less on potential risks, particularly in social situations. Thus, adolescents are more likely to engage in risky but socially rewarding behaviors (e.g., girls sneaking boys into their slumber party against their parents' wishes). Interestingly, brain reorganization associated with puberty results in temporary decreases in an adolescent's ability to engage in some basic social processing. Although the ability to label facial expressions of emotion peaks in early childhood, young adolescents suffer a temporary deficit in this skill (McGivern, Andersen, Byrd, Mutter, & Reilly, 2002). Neurological studies have also found that adolescents are distracted by emotional information when attempting to focus their attention (Monk et al., 2003). Overall, changes in the adolescent brain create a social redirection of behavior and cognitions such that adolescents are increasingly focused on peers, including romantic and sexual relationships (Forbes & Dahl, 2010).

Gender Differences and Developmental Consequences Associated with Puberty

Puberty unfolds similarly in many respects for boys and girls, although there are notable differences. On average, girls begin puberty at about 10 or 11 years of age, and the time frame from onset of puberty to completion is about 6 years. Boys, on the other hand, begin puberty closer to 12 years of age but proceed somewhat faster, completing the process about the same time as girls. Therefore, during adolescence there are more girls than boys, in a given age category, undergoing pubertal changes. This difference is especially relevant for girls who mature early, because they are early not just compared with other girls but compared with other adolescents. With the importance of social relationships during adolescence, off-time pubertal development can lead early-maturing girls to seek out peers who appear more similar to them, generally older peers who are engaging in more mature behaviors. Often this includes sexual and romantic involvement with older boys, which predisposes them to risky sexual and romantic behaviors in young adulthood (Susman & Dorn, 2009). Early-maturing girls are also at a social disadvantage because the physical changes associated with puberty make them more sexually attractive to males but less similar to the cultural ideal of physical attractiveness, which can be both confusing and damaging to their sense of self (e.g., Frisén & Holmqvist, 2010). All of this makes the experience of puberty more stressful for girls, particularly those who mature early. For boys, the physical transition is often easier (but see Cheung, Ng, & McBride-Chang, 2007). However, the change in relationship expectations as boys and girls start to comingle can be more challenging for boys (Leaper & Anderson, 1997).

Although some have argued that with puberty comes a widening of the gap between males and females—a so-called gender intensification (Hill & Lynch, 1983)—there is little evidence that girls become more girl-like or boys become more boy-like, at least in terms of gender-role identity (Galambos, Almeida, & Petersen, 1990). There are, however, some differences between girls and boys that are heightened around puberty that influence the nature of heterosexual interactions into adulthood. One notable example is the differences in girls' and boys' emotional expression. Compared with girls, teenage boys report less intimacy, affection, and companionship in their same-sex friendships; moreover, boys say that they disclose less about themselves in their friendships than do girls (Johnson, 2004). There is some evidence that this difference becomes more prominent during adolescence, with older boys feeling less emotionally expressive (i.e., disclosing their feelings less often and feeling less like others could "read" their feelings; Polce-Lynch, Myers, Kliewer, & Kilmartin, 2001). It may be that as they begin engaging in more mixed-sex relationships, boys turn to girls to fulfill their needs for emotional intimacy (e.g., Furman & Burhmester, 1992), but this may also indicate that boys find intimacy through alternative means than the emotional expression and disclosure that is so important for girls (Camarena, Sarigiani, & Peterson, 1990). This early-appearing difference in boys' emotionally intimate interactions is evident in their adult relationships as well and influences their romantic partners' perceptions of responsive care, a key factor in relationship satisfaction (Laurenceau, Barrett, & Rovine, 2005).

CHILDHOOD AND ADOLESCENT INFLUENCES ON ROMANTIC PARTNER PREFERENCES

Common lore has it that we choose partners who resemble our parents in some way. Several studies provide evidence that this may occur in humans in the form of sexual imprinting. Sexual imprinting can be positive or negative and refers to early experiences with models, often parents or siblings, that affect future behavior toward sexual or romantic partners. Positive sexual imprinting occurs when partners similar to the model are preferred; negative sexual imprinting occurs when partners similar to the model are avoided (Westermarck, 1891). A classic example of negative imprinting draws on data from Israeli kibbutzim (Shepher, 1971). From birth to age, children raised in this kind of communal setting spend most of their time in gender-integrated, single-age peer groups. According to principles of negative imprinting, this type of close contact during the early years of development should create a romantic and sexual aversion. In support of this hypothesis, an examination of over 2,700 marriages in kibbutz children found that there were only five cases of marriage between youth who lived in the same peer group before the age of 6 and none for youth who lived together for more than 2 years during this time (Shepher, 1971). Furthermore, adolescents in the same peer group did not engage in any sexual contact, a choice that appeared to be voluntary because there was no pressure to refrain from normative sexual exploration or any negative consequences for doing so; indeed, sexual explorations were relatively common in youth from different peer groups.

The primary mechanism of the type of sexual imprinting in the kibbutz studies is likely incest avoidance (Westermarck, 1891). Individuals who live in close proximity during the early years of life are generally blood related, and it benefits mates in terms of offspring number and health to avoid mating with close blood relatives (Keller & Waller, 2002). For example, studies of Chinese and Taiwanese *shim-pua* ("little daughter-in-law") arranged marriages found early exposure to a future spouse to be particularly important in influencing mating behavior (Wolf, 1985, as cited in Rantala & Marcinkowska, 2011). It was common practice in *shim-pua* marriages for girls to be sold to their husbands' families early in life and raised alongside the betrothed as siblings. As the children reached marrying age, they experienced great discomfort at the thought of engaging in sexual behavior with their spouse/sibling and had fewer offspring than spouses not reared together. Furthermore, the younger the older spouse was at the time the couple met, the greater the discomfort and the fewer offspring, suggesting an important role for continued exposure during early development in particular (Lieberman, 2009).

Although imprinting in the form of incest avoidance has a clear evolutionary advantage, there is some debate over the mechanisms and evolutionary benefits of positive imprinting. Generally, mating with moderately similar (e.g., like close family but not close family) others may increase genetic compatibility. For example, couples who show moderate similarity in the major histocompatibilty complex (MHC) have more immunocompetent offspring relative to other couples (Tregenza & Wedell, 2000). However, assortive MHC mating is unlikely to be an imprinting process since the transmission is at the genetic level (offspring inherit codominant MHC alleles from each parent; Alberts & Ober, 1993). Positive sexual imprinting in humans may be more akin to a preferential learning process where individuals develop a template for acceptable mates based on people frequently encountered (Bereczkei, Gyuris, Koves, & Bernath, 2002). Although the exact mechanisms remain to be explained, there is evidence of parental influence on the sexual preference and mate choice of a partner's eye color (Little, Penton-Voak, Burt, & Perrett, 2003), smoking behavior (Aronsson, Lind, Ghirlanda, & Enquist, 2011), personality

(Gyuris, Járai, & Bereczkei, 2010), and facial features (Wiszewska, Paw-lowski, & Boothroyd, 2007).

An interesting feature of human sexual imprinting is that it is opposite-sex parents who serve as the models. For example, in a study of eye color preference, the eye color of women's (heterosexual) partners was similar to their fathers but not their mothers, and the eye color of men's (heterosexual) partners was similar to their mothers but not their fathers (Little et al., 2003). Although these findings are consistent with an imprinting process, it may also be the case that children inherit partner preferences from their same-sex parents (e.g., a mother passes to her daughter a preference for brown-eyed men). While the genetic explanation is intriguing, two studies support the imprinting mechanism. Specifically, Aronsson et al. (2011) found that heterosexual males had a sexual preference for a smoking partner if their mothers smoked during their childhood, whereas homosexual males desired a smoking partner if either their mothers or fathers smoked. Furthermore, smoking is a relatively new invention, and smoking preference is unlikely to be a trait that is genetically coded (or one that confers any evolutionary mating advantage). The best evidence that parent–partner characteristics are based on some type of imprinting mechanism comes from Bereczkei, Gyuris, and Weisfeld (2004), who found a link between the facial features of adopted women's husbands and their adoptive fathers.

An important component to the imprinting (or imprinting-like) argument is the timing of the modeling. True imprinting requires a critical period of modeling, which is generally unmodifiable thereafter. Thus far, no evidence of positive sexual imprinting-like behavior in humans meets these strict criteria (Rantala & Marcinkowska, 2011). Several studies have demonstrated, however, a differential influence of parental characteristics based on the quality of early relationships. For example, women who frequently had positive interactions with their fathers during the first 7 years of life tended to show a strong preference for a partner with facial features similar to the father, whereas women who had less positive relationships with their fathers during this time period did not (Bereczkei et al., 2004; Wiszewska et al., 2007). Thus, the evidence suggests that the experiences that we have with our parents during childhood and adolescents and their idiosyncratic characteristics shape our adult mate choices.

CONCLUSION

The goal of this chapter was to describe the developmental trends and milestones that occur between infant attachments to caregivers and adult attachments to romantic partners. Successful mating and reproducing is the ultimate goal of the social human and requires an ability to find an appropriate partner and produce offspring. It also requires a transition from being completely dependent on a caregiver to being the person capable of providing care, both to offspring and partners. The research reviewed here suggests that these transitions occur across the period from early childhood to early adulthood, and that relationships during this phase of life, including those with peers, have lasting and profound developmental consequences for future relationships.

ACKNOWLEDGMENT

Preparation of this chapter was facilitated by a grant from Skidmore College.

REFERENCES

Adam, E. K., Chyu, L., Hoyt, L. T., Doane, L. D., Boisjoly, J., Duncan, G. J., et al. (2011). Adverse adolescent relationship histories and young adult health: Cumulative effects of loneliness, low parental support, relationship instability, intimate partner violence, and loss. *Journal of Adolescent Health, 49*(3), 278–286.

Adams, R. E., Laursen, B., & Wilder, D. (2001). Characteristics of closeness in adolescent romantic relationships. *Journal of Adolescence, 24*(3), 353–363.

Ainsworth, M. D. S. (1967). *Infancy in Uganda: Infant care and the growth of love.* Baltimore: Johns Hopkins University Press.

Alberts, S., & Ober, C. (1993). Genetic variability in the major histocompatibility complex: A review of non-pathogen-mediated. *Yearbook of Physical Anthropology, 36*, 71–89.

Aronsson, H. H., Lind, J. J., Ghirlanda, S. S., & Enquist, M. M. (2011). Parental influences on sexual preferences: The case of attraction to smoking. *Journal of Evolutionary Psychology, 9*(1), 21–41.

Barnes, H. (1975). Physical growth and development during puberty. *Medical Clinics of North America, 59*(6), 1305–1317.

Bereczkei, T. T., Gyuris, P. P., Koves, P. P., & Bernath, L. L. (2002). Homogamy, genetic similarity and imprinting: Parental influence on mate choice preferences. *Personality and Individual Differences, 33*(5), 677–690.

Bereczkei, T., Gyuris, P., & Weisfeld, G. (2004). Sexual imprinting in human mate choice. *Proceedings of the Royal Society of London: B. Biological Sciences, 271*(1544), 1129–1134.

Bohn-Gettler, C. M., Pellegrini, A. D., Dupuis, D., Hickey, M., Hou, Y., Roseth, C., et al. (2010). A longitudinal study of preschool children's (homo sapiens) sex segregation. *Journal of Comparative Psychology, 124*(2), 219–228.

Bokhorst, C. L., Sumter, S. R., & Westenberg, P. (2010). Social support from parents, friends, classmates, and teachers in children and adolescents aged 9 to 18 years: Who is perceived as most supportive? *Social Development, 19*(2), 417–426.

Bowlby, J. (1982). *Attachment and loss* (2nd ed.). New York: Basic Books. (Original work published 1969)

Braun, M. F., & Bryan, A. (2006). Female waist-to-hip and male waist-to-shoulder ratios as determinants of romantic partner desirability. *Journal of Social and Personal Relationships, 23*, 805–819.

Brown, B. (1999). "You're going out with who?": Peer group influences on adolescent romantic relationships. In W. Furman, B. Brown, & C. Feiring (Eds.), *The development of romantic relationships in adolescence* (pp. 291–329). Cambridge, UK: Cambridge University Press.

Camarena, P. M., Sarigiani, P. A., & Petersen, A. C. (1990). Gender-specific pathways to intimacy in early adolescence. *Journal of Youth and Adolescence, 19*, 19–32.

Cameron, J. L. (2004). Interrelationships between hormones, behavior, and affect during adolescence: Understanding hormonal, physical, and brain changes occurring in association with pubertal activation of the reproductive axis: Introduction to part III. In R. E. Dahl & L. Spear (Eds.), *Adolescent brain development: Vulnerabilities and opportunities* (pp. 110–123). New York: New York Academy of Sciences.

Campa, M. I., Hazan, C., & Wolfe, J. E. (2009). The form and function of attachment behavior in the daily lives of young adults. *Social Development, 18*(2), 288–304.

Carver, K., Joyner, K., & Udry, J. (2003). National estimates of adolescent romantic relationships. In P. Florsheim (Ed.), *Adolescent romantic relations and sexual behavior: Theory, research, and practical implications* (pp. 23–56). Mahwah, NJ: Erlbaum.

Charman, T., Baron-Cohen, S., Swettenham, J., Baird, G., Cox, A., & Drew, A. (2000). Testing joint attention, imitation, and play as infancy precursors to language and theory of mind. *Cognitive Development, 15*(4), 481–498.

Cheung, C. S., Ng, V. N., & McBride-Chang, C. (2007). Perceived pubertal timing, life satisfaction, and depression among early Hong Kong adolescents: Boys at risk? *Journal of Psychology in Chinese Societies, 8*(2), 179–198.

Cicirelli, V. G. (2010). Attachment relationships in old age. *Journal of Social and Personal Relationships, 27*(2), 191–199.

Coplan, R. J., & Arbeau, K. A. (2009). Peer interactions and play in early childhood. In K. H. Rubin, W. M. Bukowski, & B. Laursen (Eds.), *Handbook of peer interactions, relationships, and groups* (pp. 143–161). New York: Guilford Press.

DeKroon, D. A., Kyte, C. S., & Johnson, C. J. (2002). Partner influences on the social pretend play of children with language impairments. *Language, Speech, and Hearing Services in Schools, 33*(4), 253–267.

Dornbusch, S., Carlsmith, J. M., Gross, R., Martin, J., Jennings, D., Rosenberg, et al. (1981). Sexual development, age and dating: A comparison of biological and social influence upon one set of behaviors. *Child Development, 52*, 179–185.

Dunn, J., & Cutting, A. L. (1999). Understanding others, and individual differences in friendship interactions in young children. *Social Development, 8*(2), 201–219.

Eckerman, C. O., & Whitehead, H. (1999). How toddler peers generate coordinated action: A cross cultural exploration. *Early Education and Development, 10*(3), 241–226.

Elias, C. L., & Berk, L. E. (2002). Self-regulation in young children: Is there a role for sociodramatic play? *Early Childhood Research Quarterly, 17*(2), 216–238.

Fabes, R. A., Martin, C., & Hanish, L. D. (2004). The next 50 years: Considering gender as a context for understanding young children's peer relationships. *Merrill-Palmer Quarterly: Journal of Developmental Psychology, 50*(3), 260–273.

Forbes, E. E., & Dahl, R. E. (2010). Pubertal development and behavior: Hormonal activation of social and motivational tendencies. *Brain and Cognition, 72*(1), 66–72.

Fraley, R., & Davis, K. E. (1997). Attachment formation and transfer in young adults' close friendships and romantic relationships. *Personal Relationships, 4*(2), 131–144.

Freeman, H., & Brown, B. (2001). Primary attachment to parents and peers during adolescence: Differences by attachment style. *Journal of Youth and Adolescence, 30*(6), 653–674.

Friedlmeier, W., & Granqvist, P. (2006). Attachment transfer among Swedish and German adolescents: A prospective longitudinal study. *Personal Relationships, 13*(3), 261–279.

Frisén, A., & Holmqvist, K. (2010). Physical, sociocultural, and behavioral factors associated with body-esteem in 16-year-old Swedish boys and girls. *Sex Roles, 63*(5/6), 373–385.

Fullard, W., & Reiling, A. M. (1976). An investigation of Lorenz's "babyness." *Child Development, 47,* 1191–1193.

Furman, W., & Buhrmester, D. D. (1992). Age and sex differences in perceptions of networks of personal relationships. *Child Development, 63*(1), 103.

Furman, W., & Wehner, E. A. (1994). Romantic views: Toward a theory of adolescent romantic relationships. In R. Montemayor, G. R. Adams, & T. P. Gullotta (Eds.), *Personal relationships during adolescence* (pp. 168–195). Thousand Oaks, CA: Sage.

Galambos, N. L., Almeida, D. M., & Petersen, A. C. (1990). Masculinity, femininity, and sex role attitudes in early adolescence: Exploring gender intensification. *Child Development, 61*(6), 1905–1914.

Galyer, K. T., & Evans, I. M. (2001). Pretend play and the development of emotion regulation in preschool children. *Early Child Development and Care, 166,* 93–108.

Ge, X., Natsuaki, M. N., Neiderhiser, J. M., & Reiss, D. (2007). Genetic and environmental influences on pubertal timing: Results from two national sibling studies. *Journal of Research on Adolescence, 17*(4), 767–788.

Giedd, J. N., Blumenthal, J., Jeffries, N. O., Castellanos, F. X., Liu, H., Zijdenbos, A., et al. (1999). Brain development during childhood and adolescence: A longitudinal MRI study. *Nature Neuroscience, 2*(10), 861–863.

Glassman, M. (2000). Adult and peer social interactions during preschool activity: A combination for gender segregation? *Early Child Development and Care, 165*, 1–16.

Gyuris, P., Járai, R., & Bereczkei, T. (2010). The effect of childhood experiences on mate choice in personality traits: Homogamy and sexual imprinting. *Personality and Individual Differences, 49*(5), 467–472.

Haight, W. L., Wang, X., Fung, H., Williams, K., & Mintz, J. (1999). Universal, developmental, and variable aspects of young children's play: A cross-cultural comparison of pretending at home. *Child Development, 70*(6), 1477–1488.

Hay, D. F. (1985). Learning to form relationships in infancy: Parallel attainments with parents and peers. *Developmental Review, 5*(2), 122–161.

Hay, D. F., Caplan, M., & Nash, A. (2009). The beginnings of peer relations. In K. H. Rubin, W. M. Bukowski, & B. Laursen (Eds.), *Handbook of peer interactions, relationships, and groups* (pp. 121–142). New York: Guilford Press.

Hay, D. F., Castle, J., Davies, L., Demetriou, H., & Stimson, C. A. (1999). Prosocial action in very early childhood. *Journal of Child Psychology and Psychiatry, 40*(6), 905–916.

Hay, D. F., Payne, A., & Chadwick, A. (2004). Peer relations in childhood. *Journal of Child Psychology and Psychiatry, 45*(1), 84–108.

Hazan, C., & Shaver, P. R. (2004). Attachment as an organizational framework for research on close relationships. In H. T. Reis & C. E. Rusbult (Eds.), *Close relationships: Key readings* (pp. 153–174). Philadelphia: Taylor & Francis.

Hazan, C., & Zeifman, D. (1994). Sex and the psychological tether. *Advances in Personal Relationships, 5*, 151–178.

Helsen, M., Vollebergh, W., & Meeus, W. (2000). Social support from parents and friends and emotional problems in adolescence. *Journal of Youth and Adolescence, 29*(3), 319–335.

Hibbard, D. R., & Buhrmester, D. (1998). The role of peers in the socialization of gender-related social interaction styles. *Sex Roles, 39*(3–4), 185–202.

Hill, J. P., & Lynch, M. E. (1983). The intensification of gender-related role expectations during early adolescence. In J. Brooks-Gunn & A. C. Petersen (Eds.), *Girls at puberty: Biological and psychosocial perspectives* (pp. 201–228). New York: Plenum.

Hoffmann, M. L., & Powlishta, K. K. (2001). Gender segregation in childhood: A test of the interaction style theory. *Journal of Genetic Psychology, 162*(3), 298–313.

Howes, C. (2009). Friendship in early childhood. In K. H. Rubin, W. M. Bukowski, & B. Laursen (Eds.), *Handbook of peer interactions, relationships, and groups* (pp. 180–194). New York: Guilford Press.

Johnson, H. (2004). Gender, grade, and relationship differences in emotional closeness within adolescent friendships. *Adolescence, 39*(154), 243–255.

Keller, L. F., & Waller, D. M. (2002). Inbreeding effects in wild populations. *Trends in Ecology and Evolution, 17*, 230–241.

Kolb, B., Wilson, B., & Taylor, L. (1992). Developmental changes in the recognition and comprehension of facial expression: Implications for frontal lobe function. *Brain and Cognition, 20*(1), 74–84.

Larson, R. W., Suzanne, W., Brown, B., Furstenberg, F. R., & Verma, S. (2002).

Changes in adolescents' interpersonal experiences: Are they being prepared for adult relationships in the twenty-first century? *Journal of Research on Adolescence, 12*(1), 31–68.

Laurenceau, J., Barrett, L., & Rovine, M. J. (2005). The interpersonal process model of intimacy in marriage: A daily-diary and multilevel modeling approach. *Journal of Family Psychology, 19*(2), 314–323.

Leaper, C., & Anderson, K. J. (1997). Gender development and heterosexual romantic relationships during adolescence. In S. Shulman & W. Collins (Eds.), *Romantic relationships in adolescence: Developmental perspectives* (pp. 85–103). San Francisco: Jossey-Bass.

Lenroot, R. K., & Giedd, J. N. (2006). Brain development in children and adolescents: Insights from anatomical magnetic resonance imaging. *Neuroscience and Biobehavioral Reviews, 30*(6), 718–729.

Lieberman, D. (2009). Rethinking the Taiwanese minor marriage data: Evidence the mind uses multiple kinship cues to regulate inbreeding avoidance. *Evolution and Human Behavior, 30*, 153–160.

Lindsey, E. W., & Colwell, M. J. (2003). Preschoolers' emotional competence: Links to pretend and physical play. *Child Study Journal, 33*(1), 39–52.

Little, A. C., Penton-Voak, I. S., Burt, D. M., & Perrett, D. I. (2003). Investigating an imprinting-like phenomenon in humans: Partners and opposite-sex parents have similar hair and eye colour. *Evolution and Human Behavior, 24*(1), 43–51.

Maccoby, E. E., & Jacklin, C. (1987). Gender segregation in childhood. In H. W. Reese (Ed.), *Advances in child development and behavior* (Vol. 20, pp. 239–287). San Diego, CA: Academic Press.

Markiewicz, D., Lawford, H., Doyle, A., & Haggart, N. (2006). Developmental differences in adolescents' and young adults' use of mothers, fathers, best friends, and romantic partners to fulfill attachment needs. *Journal of Youth and Adolescence, 35*(1), 127–140.

Martin, C., Fabes, R. A., Hanish, L., Leonard, S., & Dinella, L. M. (2011). Experienced and expected similarity to same-gender peers: Moving toward a comprehensive model of gender segregation. *Sex Roles, 65*(5–6), 421–434.

Masten, A. S., Morison, P., & Pellegrini, D. S. (1985). A revised class play method of peer assessment. *Developmental Psychology, 21*(3), 523–533.

Mathieson, K., & Banerjee, R. (2010). Pre-school peer play: The beginnings of social competence. *Educational and Child Psychology, 27*(1), 9–20.

McGivern, R. F., Andersen, J., Byrd, D., Mutter, K. L., & Reilly, J. (2002). Cognitive efficiency on a match to sample task decreases at the onset of puberty in children. *Brain and Cognition, 50*(1), 73–89.

Michels, T. M., Kropp, R. Y., Eyre, S. L., & Halpern-Felsher, B. L. (2005). Initiating sexual experiences: How do young adolescents make decisions regarding early sexual activity? *Journal of Research on Adolescence, 15*(4), 583–607.

Miller, E. M. (1994). Paternal provisioning versus mate seeking in human populations. *Personality and Individual Differences, 17*(2), 227–255.

Monk, C. S., Grillon, C., Baas, J. P., McClure, E. B., Nelson, E. E., Zarahn, E., et al. (2003). A neuroimaging method for the study of threat in adolescents. *Developmental Psychobiology, 43*(4), 359–366.

Murphy, L., Laurie-Rose, C., Brinkman, T. M., & McNamara, K. A. (2007). Sustained attention and social competence in typically developing preschool-aged children. *Early Child Development and Care, 177*(2), 133–149.

Nagy, E., & Molnar, P. (2004). Homo imitans or homo provocans? Human imprinting model of neonatal imitation. *Infant Behavior and Development, 27*(1), 54–63.

National Institute of Child Health and Human Development (2008). Social competence with peers in third grade: Associations with earlier peer experiences in child care. *Social Development, 17*, 419–453.

Nève, V., Girard, F., Flahault, A., & Boule, M. (2002). Lung and thorax development during adolescence. Relationship with pubertal status. *European Respiratory Journal, 20*, 1292–1298.

Nichols, S. R., Svetlova, M., & Brownell, C. A. (2010). Toddlers' understanding of peers' emotions. *Journal of Genetic Psychology: Research and Theory on Human Development, 171*(1), 35–53.

Nickerson, A. B., & Nagle, R. J. (2005). Parent and peer attachment in late childhood and early adolescence. *Journal of Early Adolescence, 25*(2), 223–249.

Nielsen, M., & Dissanayake, C. (2000). An investigation of pretend play, mental state terms and false belief understanding: In search of a metarepresentational link. *British Journal of Developmental Psychology, 18*(4), 609–624.

Oransky, M., & Marecek, J. (2009). "I'm not going to be a girl": Masculinity and emotions in boys' friendships and peer groups. *Journal of Adolescent Research, 24*(2), 218–241.

Parent, A., Teilmann, G., Juul, A., Skakkebaek, N., Toppari, J., & Bourguignon, J. (2003). The timing of normal puberty and the age limits of sexual precocity: Variations around the world, secular trends, and changes after migration. *Endocrine Reviews, 24*(5), 668–693.

Pearson, B. L., Russ, S. W., & Spannagel, S. (2008). Pretend play and positive psychology: Natural companions. *Journal of Positive Psychology, 3*(2), 110–119.

Pellegrini, A. D. (2003). Perceptions and functions of play and real fighting in early adolescence. *Child Development, 74*(5), 1522–1533.

Pellis, S. M., & Pellis, V. C. (2007). Rough-and-tumble play and the development of the social brain. *Current Directions in Psychological Science, 16*(2), 95–98.

Polce-Lynch, M., Myers, B. J., Kliewer, W., & Kilmartin, C. (2001). Adolescent self-esteem and gender: Exploring relations to sexual harassment, body image, media influence, and emotional expression. *Journal of Youth and Adolescence, 30*(2), 225.

Puts, D., Gaulin, S. C., & Verdolini, K. (2006). Dominance and the evolution of sexual dimorphism in human voice pitch. *Evolution and Human Behavior, 27*(4), 283–296.

Rantala, M. J., & Marcinkowska, U. M. (2011). The role of sexual imprinting and the Westermarck effect in mate choice in humans. *Behavioral Ecology and Sociobiology, 65*(5), 859–873.

Reynolds, M. A., Herbenick, D. L., & Bancroft, J. (2003). The nature of childhood sexual experiences: Two studies 50 years apart. In J. Bancroft (Ed.), *Sexual development in childhood* (pp. 134–155). Bloomington: Indiana University Press.

Rose-Krasnor, L. (1997). The nature of social competence: A theoretical review. *Social Development, 6*(1), 111–135.

Ross, H. S., & Lollis, S. P. (1989). A social relations analysis of toddler peer relationships. *Child Development, 60*(5), 1082.

Schmitt, D. P., Alcalay, L., Allensworth, M., Allik, J., Ault, L., Austers, I., et al. (2003). Are men universally more dismissing than women? Gender differences in romantic attachment across 62 cultural regions. *Personal Relationships, 10*(3), 307–331.

Seibert, A. C., & Kerns, K. A. (2009). Attachment figures in middle childhood. *International Journal of Behavioral Development, 33*(4), 347–355.

Selman, R. L. (1981). The development of interpersonal competence: The role of understanding in conduct. *Developmental Review, 1*(4), 401–422.

Shepher, J. (1971). Mate selection among second generation kibbutz adolescents and adults: Incest avoidance and negative imprinting. *Archives of Sexual Behavior, 1,* 293–307.

Simpson, J. A., Collins, W. A., & Salvatore, J. E. (2011). The impact of early interpersonal experience on adult romantic relationship functioning: Recent findings from the Minnesota longitudinal study of risk and adaptation. *Current Directions in Psychological Science, 20,* 355–359.

Sims, M., Hutchins, T., & Taylor, M. (1998). Gender segregation in young children's conflict behavior in child care settings. *Child Study Journal, 28*(1), 1–16.

Sisk, C. L., & Foster, D. L. (2004). The neural basis of puberty and adolescence. *Nature Neuroscience, 7*(10), 1040–1042.

Smith, E. A., Udry, J., & Morris, N. M. (1985). Pubertal development and friends: A biosocial explanation of adolescent sexual behavior. *Journal of Health and Social Behavior, 26*(3), 183–192.

Sprengelmeyer, R. R., Perrett, D. I., Fagan, E. C., Cornwell, R. E., Lobmaier, J. S., Sprengelmeyer, A. A., et al. (2009). The cutest little baby face: A hormonal link to sensitivity to cuteness in infant faces. *Psychological Science, 20*(2), 149–154.

Steinberg, L. (2004). Risk taking in adolescence: What changes, and why? In R. E. Dahl & L. Spear (Eds.), *Adolescent brain development: Vulnerabilities and opportunities* (pp. 51–58). New York: New York Academy of Sciences.

Sullivan, H. (1953). *The interpersonal theory of psychiatry.* New York: Norton.

Susman, E. J., & Dorn, L. D. (2009). Puberty: Its role in development. In R. M. Lerner & L. Steinberg (Eds.), *Handbook of adolescent psychology: Vol. 1. Individual bases of adolescent development* (3rd ed., pp. 116–151). Hoboken, NJ: Wiley.

Tanner, J. M., & Whitehouse, R. H. (1976). Clinical longitudinal standards for height, weight, height velocity, weight velocity, and stages of puberty. *Archives of Disease in Childhood, 51*(3), 170–179.

Taylor, R., Grant, A., Williams, S., & Goulding, A. (2010). Sex differences in regional body fat distribution from pre- to postpuberty. *Obesity, 18*(7), 1410–1416.

Thompson, R. A. (1994). Emotion regulation: A theme in search of definition. *Monographs of the Society for Research in Child Development, 59,* 25–52.

Tither, J. M., & Ellis, B. J. (2008). Impact of fathers on daughters' age at menarche: A genetically and environmentally controlled sibling study. *Developmental Psychology, 44*(5), 1409–1420.

Tregenza, T., & Wedell, N. (2000). Genetic compatibility, mate choice and patterns of parentage: Invited review. *Molecular Ecology, 9*, 1013–1027.

Udry, J. (1988). Biological predispositions and social control in adolescent sexual behavior. *American Sociological Review, 53*(5), 709–722.

Udry, J. R., & Chantala, K. (2005). Risk factors differ according to same-sex or opposite-sex interest. *Journal of Biosocial Science, 37*, 481–497.

Vizmanos, B. B., & Marti-Henneberg, C. C. (2000). Puberty begins with a characteristic subcutaneous body fat mass in each sex. *European Journal of Clinical Nutrition, 54*(3), 203–208.

Werebe, M. G., & Baudonnière, P. (1991). Social pretend play among friends and familiar preschoolers. *International Journal of Behavioral Development, 14*(4), 411–428.

Westermarck, E. (1891). *The history of human marriage.* London: Macmillan.

Wiszewska, A., Pawlowski, B., & Boothroyd, L. G. (2007). Father-daughter relationship as a moderator of sexual imprinting: A facial metric study. *Evolution and Human Behavior, 28*(4), 248–252.

Youngblade, L. M., & Dunn, J. (1995). Individual differences in young children's pretend play with mother and sibling: Links to relationships and understanding of other people's feelings and beliefs. *Child Development, 66*(5), 1472–1492.

Zhang, H., Chan, D. S., & Teng, F. (2011). Transfer of attachment functions and adjustment among young adults in China. *Journal of Social Psychology, 151*(3), 257–273.

Zosuls, K. M., Ruble, D. N., Tamis-LeMonda, C. S., Shrout, P. E., Bornstein, M. H., & Greulich, F. K. (2009). The acquisition of gender labels in infancy: Implications for gender-typed play. *Developmental Psychology, 45*(3), 688–701.

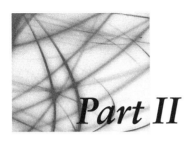

Part II

CONTEMPORARY APPROACHES TO MATING

Chapter **4**

Finding the One

A Process Model of Human Mate Selection

GÜL GÜNAYDIN
EMRE SELCUK
CINDY HAZAN

> Of all the gin joints, in all the towns, in all the world,
> she walks into mine.
> > —RICK BLAINE (portrayed by Humphrey Bogart)
> > in the 1942 film *Casablanca*

*T*he selection of a mate may well be the most important personal decision of a lifetime. Not only one's happiness, overall well-being, and productivity (e.g., Ryff & Singer, 2001) but even the very length of one's life can be significantly and profoundly affected by this singular choice (e.g., Selcuk & Ong, 2013). The reality that the world's population is currently more than 7 billion and rising (World Bank, 2012) means that at any given time there are literally millions of individuals of a suitable age and preferred sex from which to choose a mate. Of course, not all potential mates have equal probability of being selected. Still, among the many, how do people go about finding "the one?" How systematic or conscious is the choice? How much are mating "decisions" the result of hard-wired tendencies or random circumstantial factors? Researchers from a wide variety of fields—psychology, sociology, communication, anthropology, ethology, biology, economics—have sought to answer these questions. The work has been guided by an equally broad array of theoretical perspectives, including cognitive consistency theories (e.g., Heider, 1958), social exchange and interdependence theories (e.g., Kelley et al., 2003), ethological attachment theory (e.g., Hazan & Diamond, 2000), evolutionary theory (e.g., Buss, 1989), and self-perception models (e.g., Buston & Emlen, 2003) to name just a few. Detailed discussions of these theoretical approaches can be found elsewhere (e.g., Sprecher, Wenzel, & Harvey, 2008). The central aim of the present chapter is to survey the range of empirical findings that have been generated by these various theoretical perspectives with a view to providing an integrated process model of human mate selection. In organizing the factors that have been shown to influence mate selection, we start with the least constraining and end with the most constraining. More specifically, we move from the broadest level of "Who is accessible?" to the narrower category of "Who is appealing?" to the even smaller group of "Who is interested and attainable?" to, finally, "Who is the one?"

Before starting, it is worth noting that the majority of research on mate selection focuses on heterosexual couples. Although more research is definitely needed to systematically examine mate selection in lesbians and gay men, extant literature on mate selection in same-sex couples suggests that the factors that influence mate selection in heterosexual couples generally apply to same-sex couples as well (e.g., Felmlee, Orzechowicz, & Fortes, 2010; Peplau & Fingerhut, 2007; Peplau, Padesky, & Hamilton, 1982).

STEP 1: WHO IS ACCESSIBLE AS A POTENTIAL MATE?

It is a truism that mating requires meeting. One's ideal mate might reside across town or across the globe, but either way there will be no mating in the absence of an actual encounter. Propinquity, or distance in space, is one of the most influential factors in narrowing the pool of potential mates. Although we have good intuitions about the importance of propinquity, its role in mate selection is typically underappreciated. Let's say your partner has a crush on a celebrity. You might be mildly annoyed but probably not deeply concerned. Imagine, however, that by some unexpected turn of events you find yourselves living next door to this celebrity. In all likelihood, your concern would be elevated precisely because you understand intuitively that close physical proximity provides opportunities for interaction that can foster interpersonal attraction. Yet if you were to be asked on what basis you chose your current partner, it is doubtful you would cite propinquity as a factor.

Physical Propinquity

The importance of propinquity in relationship initiation was first documented in a seminal study by Festinger, Schachter, and Back (1950), who observed that the specific apartment in a university student housing complex to which people were randomly assigned had a profound influence on their subsequent social networks. For instance, individuals were almost 10 times as likely to become friends with someone living in the same building compared with someone living in a different building and about twice as likely to become friends with someone living on the same floor within the same building compared with someone living on a different floor. Festinger and colleagues' findings have been well replicated in studies of relationship initiation (e.g., Marmaros & Sacerdote, 2006; Mayer & Puller, 2008).

Thanks to the rapid increase in the use of online social networking, researchers now have access to invaluable archival data on social relationships. Analyses of such data provide converging evidence that people predominantly interact with others who are geographically close. For example, an analysis of the social networks of more than 500,000 LiveJournal bloggers revealed that geographical proximity significantly increased the probability of friendship formation. In this community, two-thirds of an average user's friends were geographically close (Liben-Nowell, Novak, Kumar, Raghavan, & Tomkins, 2005). The finding is notable precisely because online networks are not restricted by geographical location. Similarly, analyses of data from popular social networking websites such as Facebook and MySpace found that the people listed as best friends in online profiles tend to reside geographically close (e.g., DeScioli, Kurzban, Koch, & Liben-Nowell, 2011). Moreover, the frequency and duration of online communication increase as the geographical distance between individuals decreases (Leskovec & Horvitz, 2007). Collectively, these studies provide strong and consistent evidence that geographical propinquity plays a leading role in relationship development.

Kossinets and Watts's (2006) longitudinal study offers further evidence that physical propinquity bolsters initial attraction. This study analyzed e-mail exchanges of 43,553 students, faculty, and staff over the course of an academic year. For students who did not share a single acquaintance, simply taking a class together increased the likelihood of interacting by a staggering 140 times. Even students who did share an acquaintance were three times more likely to interact if they took a class together. Moreover, manipulating small and seemingly arbitrary differences in physical proximity in classroom settings, such as where students were assigned to sit in an auditorium, influenced later friendships (Back, Schmukle, & Egloff, 2008).

Cyber Propinquity

The development of Internet technology enables individuals to achieve virtual proximity through common Internet media—online dating websites, forums, and chat rooms—even if they are not geographically close. For example, being in the same "chat room" with another person is similar to being in the same room in the sense that both situations decrease interpersonal distance. Hence, one may extend the definition of propinquity to include not only closeness in physical space but also closeness in cyberspace. According to a recent survey of a nationally representative sample of U.S. adults (Rosenfeld & Thomas, 2012), "online" ranks only second to "through friends" as the most common way heterosexual couples meet, whereas it is by far the most common way same-sex couples meet.

Individuals may get acquainted online unintentionally, for example, while seeking information in a news discussion group (e.g., McKenna, Green, & Gleason, 2002; Ridings & Gefen, 2004). In a survey of users of such groups, Parks and Floyd (1996) found that 61% reported forming a close online relationship with someone they met on a newsgroup, 33% reported meeting their "cyber friends" face to face, and 8% of online relationships evolved to be romantic. A more recent survey of newsgroup users suggested a dramatic 62% increase in online relationships moving to the face-to-face realm (McKenna et al., 2002).

Individuals may also join online communities to search actively for potential mates; online dating websites are the best example. Although the extent to which online dating websites improve romantic outcomes remains highly questionable (Finkel, Eastwick, Karney, Reis, & Sprecher, 2012), these websites provide unprecedented access to potential mates who may otherwise have been unknown or inaccessible through other means.

Social Propinquity

Propinquity can also be considered in terms of closeness in social space or ties in a social network. One can meet a potential mate through mutual contacts—acquaintances, friends, family members (Rosenfeld & Thomas,

2012). Individuals may ask their friends and family to introduce them to potential mates; friends and family might take the initiative to engineer meetings; or potential mates might be encountered incidentally at social gatherings hosted by friends and family. Indeed, simply sharing an acquaintance dramatically increases the probability of getting acquainted with someone new. Hammer (1980) longitudinally followed individuals in three small networks: a church, a doughnut shop, and a factory. In all three networks, two people who shared an acquaintance at a given time were more likely to become acquainted at a later time. This finding was conceptually replicated in a more recent study by Kossinets and Watts (2006), who showed that two individuals sharing an acquaintance were 30 times more likely to exchange e-mails than those who did not. In both studies, the likelihood of initiating contact steadily increased as the number of mutual acquaintances increased.

In summary, there is ample empirical evidence that propinquity—whether physical, cyber, or social—plays a central role in mate selection. Evidence further suggests that geographical closeness and face-to-face interactions, whether they come early or later in the process, are crucially important. Our online and offline social networks and our daily activities determine to a large extent who we will cross paths with. These are the factors that reduce the millions of potential mates to the smaller pool of those who are accessible and thus have an increased probability of being selected.

STEP 2: WHO IS APPEALING AS A POTENTIAL MATE?

Of this smaller group of individuals who are accessible as potential mates, some will be more appealing than others and, therefore, more likely to be chosen. Two of these appeal factors—similarity and familiarity—are inherently related to propinquity. We tend to affiliate and socialize with others who are similar to us in important ways, a phenomenon known as *social homogamy* (e.g., Kalmijn, 1998). In addition, it is a fundamental aspect of human nature to be drawn to familiar things and persons. To complicate matters even further, repeated contact increases familiarity, and people who are similar seem familiar whether in actuality they are or not (Moreland & Zajonc, 1982). Thus, similarity and familiarity are inextricably linked to propinquity. Other factors that influence the appeal of potential mates include characteristics such as physical appearance, social status and resources, and personality of the potential mate, along with one's affective state.

Similarity

Romantic partners tend to be similar to each other in numerous ways (e.g., Kalmijn, 1998). One reason partners are so alike is that individuals are more attracted to others whom they perceive as similar to themselves (Chapdelaine, Kenny, & LaFontana, 1994)—the "likes-attract" phenomenon (Buston & Emlen, 2003). Accordingly, researchers have investigated similarity in such domains as demographics (e.g., Kurzban & Weeden, 2005), attitudes (e.g., Newcomb, 1956), personality (e.g., Byrne, Griffitt, & Stefaniak, 1967), and physical attractiveness (e.g., Buston & Emlen, 2003).

Demographic Similarity

Similarity in ethnicity is a major factor shaping interpersonal attraction and mate selection. This is not surprising given that individuals tend to display an implicit preference toward people of their own ethnicity (e.g., Greenwald, McGhee, & Schwartz, 1998). In line with this preference, Verbrugge (1977) found that friends, particularly close friends, were likely to be of the same ethnicity. Similarly, Marmaros and Sacerdote (2006) found that race was one of the most important predictors of e-mail exchanges between college students: An e-mail exchange between two Caucasian students was three times more likely than between a Caucasian and an African American student.

Results of speed-dating experiments also show that individuals, particularly women and White conservatives, tend to prefer to date others of their own ethnicity (Eastwick, Richeson, Son, & Finkel, 2009; Fisman, Iyengar, Kamenica, & Simonson, 2006, 2008; Kurzban & Weeden, 2005). In addition, a recent study investigating partner preferences in an online dating website showed that both men and women preferred to contact individuals of their own ethnicity after browsing through online profiles of potential mates (Hitsch, Hortaçsu, & Ariely, 2010).

Ethnicity is not the only demographic characteristic on which mates tend to be similar. Research has shown that both heterosexual and gay/lesbian individuals prefer to befriend, date, and marry those who are similar to themselves on other demographic characteristics, including age, education, financial resources, and religion (e.g., Buston & Emlen, 2003; Hitsch et al., 2010; Leskovec & Horvitz, 2007; Mayer & Puller, 2008; Peplau et al., 1982; Verbrugge, 1977).

The fact that people tend to affiliate with others who are like them naturally limits contact with others who are unlike them. Whether mates are similar on any specific characteristic may result from an active seeking of similarity or may be a more passive consequence of social homogamy (Sakai & Johnson, 1997).

Attitudinal Similarity

Attitudinal similarity has also been found to facilitate interpersonal attraction. In a classic study on this topic, students randomly assigned to rooms in a dorm were found to like fellow students with similar attitudes more than those with dissimilar attitudes (Newcomb, 1956). In a series of subsequent experiments, Byrne and colleagues (e.g., Byrne & Nelson, 1965) manipulated attitude similarity by varying the degree of overlap between participants' self-reported attitudes and attitude ratings ostensibly provided by another participant. Self–other similarity in attitudes was found to be positively related to participants' initial attraction scores. Supporting these early findings, more recent studies showed that individuals are more likely to become friends and romantically involved with those who share similar political views (e.g., Mayer & Puller, 2008; Watson et al., 2004).

Similarity in Personality

Studies investigating whether similarity in personality characteristics increases attraction have produced mixed findings. Some studies found that personality similarity increased attraction (Byrne et al., 1967; Klohnen & Luo, 2003). Yet other studies found weak or no evidence of personality similarity facilitating attraction (e.g., Back, Schmukle, & Egloff, 2011; Luo & Zhang, 2009).

These mixed findings suggest potential factors moderating the association between personality similarity and interpersonal attraction. For instance, individuals show a greater liking of people whose personality matches their ideal personality but not those whose personality matches their own actual personality (e.g., Herbst, Gaertner, & Insko, 2003). Other studies provided evidence that perceived but not actual similarity in personality (e.g., Selfhout, Denissen, Branje, & Meeus, 2009) and likability of the target person (Taylor & Mettee, 1971) appear to moderate the relationship between similarity and attraction. Finally, for certain traits, such as dominance, complementarity rather than similarity may lead to greater attraction (Dryer & Horowitz, 1997).

Similarity in Physical Attractiveness

Individuals prefer to date a person who is similar to themselves in physical attractiveness (Buston & Emlen, 2003; Todd, Penke, Fasolo, & Lenton, 2007; but see Kurzban & Weeden, 2005). Moreover, attractive individuals expect to date more attractive people, whereas unattractive individuals expect to date less attractive people (Montoya, 2008). Similarly, a study analyzing data from HotOrNot.com, a website where users rate the "hotness" of photographs submitted by other users, revealed that attractive individuals were more likely to accept dating requests of individuals who were also high on attractiveness (Lee, Loewenstein, Ariely, Hong, & Young, 2008). Studies on established relationships also demonstrate that partners are similar in terms of observer ratings of attractiveness (e.g., Stevens, Owens, & Schaefer, 1990). Thus, although everyone might desire a highly attractive partner, in actuality most end up with someone who is similar to themselves in attractiveness.

In summary, individuals tend to be attracted to others who are similar to themselves in attitudes, physical attractiveness, and a variety of demographic characteristics. Although some studies provided evidence that similarity in personality also enhances attraction, others demonstrated that this association depends on which personality traits are investigated, whether similarity to the actual-self or the ideal self is assessed, and whether perceived or actual measures of similarity are used. Exceptions notwithstanding, the evidence overwhelmingly shows that it is likes, and not opposites, that attract.

Familiarity

Feelings of familiarity created by repeated exposure to a person can also increase liking. Indeed, in the groundbreaking Festinger et al. (1950) study described previously, propinquity facilitated liking precisely because it afforded opportunities for interaction that resulted in increased familiarity. The effect of familiarity is so robust that repeated exposure increases liking for faces presented for such a short time as to not be consciously detected (Bornstein, Leone, & Galley, 1987). The effect extends to more naturalistic settings such as face-to-face interactions and online conversations (e.g., Reis, Maniaci, Caprariello, Eastwick, & Finkel, 2011). A powerful demonstration of the influence of familiarity on attraction in everyday life was provided by Moreland and Beach (1992), who manipulated mere exposure by having four female confederates attend different numbers of sessions in a course without interacting with students. The greater number of sessions the women attended, the greater the attraction reported by students. Although such studies provide strong evidence that familiarity increases attraction, the effect appears to hold only when initial impressions are either neutral or mildly positive. For disliked others, repeated exposure, in fact, decreases liking (e.g., Ebbesen, Kjos, & Konecni, 1976).

Affective State

In a famous study on interpersonal attraction, Dutton and Aron (1974) had an attractive female experimenter approach male participants as they were crossing either "a fear-arousing suspension bridge or a non-fear-arousing bridge." Participants crossing the fear-arousing bridge (vs. the non-fear-arousing bridge) afterward used more sexual imagery in the stories they were asked to write and were also more likely to telephone the female experimenter. These findings have been conceptually replicated in subsequent studies using diverse methods for inducing arousal (for a review, see Foster, Witcher, Campbell, & Green, 1998), including physical exercise (e.g., White, Fishbein, & Rutstein, 1981), threat of electric shock (Dutton & Aron, 1974), and exposure to sexual material (e.g., Griffitt, May, & Veitch, 1974).

Why does arousal lead to attraction? One explanation is that when individuals encounter a potential mate in an arousing context, they misattribute the source of arousal to the other person (Dutton & Aron, 1974). According to an alternative view, arousal enhances a specific dominant response in a given situation (Allen, Kenrick, Linder, & McCall, 1989). The dominant response toward an attractive potential mate in an arousing context is romantic attraction, whereas the dominant response toward an unattractive potential mate is aversion. Indeed, arousal only increases attraction to physically attractive targets and, in fact, has the opposite effect for unattractive targets (e.g., Foster et al., 1998; White et al., 1981).

Whether individuals are in a good or a bad mood can also influence attraction. Individuals in a positive mood—induced by watching a happy film (Gouaux, 1971), getting favorable performance feedback (Forgas & Bower, 1987), or experiencing a pleasant temperature (Griffitt, 1970)—showed greater interpersonal attraction than individuals in a negative mood. Those feeling good (vs. bad) also engaged in more mimicry (van Baaren, Fockenberg, Holland, Janssen, & van Knippenberg, 2006) and self-disclosure (Forgas, 2011), both of which are conducive to attraction and liking.

Physical Appearance

Perhaps the most studied factor in mate selection is physical appearance. Physically attractive individuals are rated as more desirable potential mates than are less attractive individuals by both heterosexual and gay/lesbian individuals (e.g., Ha, van den Berg, Engels, & Lichtwarck-Aschoff, 2012). In a meta-analysis of more than 900 studies, Langlois and colleagues (2000) found that across cultures physically attractive individuals are judged and treated more favorably than unattractive individuals. Strikingly, attractiveness judgments can be made as rapidly as within 20 milliseconds of exposure to a target (Olson & Marshuetz, 2005), suggesting that they are highly automatic.

Normative Cues of Attractiveness

Facial, bodily, vocal, and more recently olfactory cues have all been linked with attractiveness. One such cue is the extent to which a face looks typical. Averageness of a face is positively associated with judgments of attractiveness. In fact, composite faces created by averaging multiple faces are rated more attractive than the individual faces (e.g., Langlois & Roggman, 1990). One effect of averaging faces is increased symmetry. Most faces have some degree of asymmetry, but when faces are averaged the asymmetries tend to cancel each other out. Symmetrical faces are rated as more attractive than asymmetrical faces (e.g., Perrett et al., 1999). Similarly, individuals with symmetrical bodies are judged as more attractive (Gangestad, Thornhill, & Yeo, 1994) and are more desirable as mates than those with asymmetrical bodies (Thornhill & Gangestad, 1994). One explanation for these findings is that symmetry signals mate quality or "good genes." Indeed, in both human and nonhuman animals, fluctuating asymmetries (i.e., random deviations from perfect symmetry in bilaterally paired traits) are associated with developmental instability (e.g., Gangestad et al., 1994). In a range of species, males with low fluctuating asymmetry attract more mates than their less symmetrical counterparts (Watson & Thornhill, 1994).

Sexual maturity of facial, bodily, and vocal features is also associated with attractiveness. Male and female faces are virtually indistinguishable prior to puberty. However, the hormonal changes associated with pubertal onset alter faces dramatically and in sex-typical ways (e.g., Thornhill & Møller, 1997). Surges in testosterone cause disproportionate growth in the chin and jaw region and also brow thickening, making a face appear more masculine. A smaller chin and jaw and less prominent brow, along with such estrogen-driven changes as lip plumping, make a face appear more feminine. Men tend to judge female faces with feminine features as more attractive than those with masculine features (e.g., Cunningham, Roberts, Barbee, Druen, & Wu, 1995). Interestingly, women find slightly feminized versions of male faces more attractive than those that are modified to look even more masculine, theoretically because femininity signals trustworthiness (e.g., Perrett et al., 1998). However, women's preferences vary as a function of their menstrual cycle: Women prefer more masculine male faces when they are in the fertile phase of their menstrual cycle than during the infertile phase (e.g., Penton-Voak, Perrett, Castles, Kobayashi, Burt, Murray et al., 1999).

Pubertal onset is also associated with bodily changes, including the differentiation of male and female body shapes (e.g., Thornhill & Møller, 1997). Increases in testosterone trigger growth in the upper body and shoulders while suppressing growth in the gluteofemoral region (hips and thighs). In contrast, estrogen causes disproportionate growth in the hips and thighs. Body shapes that signal sex-typical maturation—a high shoulder-to-hip ratio in men and a low waist-to-hip ratio in women—are judged as more attractive (e.g., Dijkstra & Buunk, 2001; Singh, 1993).

The same hormones responsible for changes in facial and bodily features also produce sex-differentiated changes in voice (Abitol, Abitol, & Abitol, 1999). Men find women with higher pitched voices more attractive (e.g., Collins & Missing, 2003), whereas women, particularly those in the fertile phase of their menstrual cycle, find men with lower pitched voices more attractive (e.g., Feinberg et al., 2006).

Menstrual cycle phase is also a factor in men's judgments of female attractiveness, with men judging women in the fertile phase of their menstrual cycle as more attractive than those in the infertile phase (Roberts et al., 2004). In an interesting demonstration of this effect, Miller, Tybur, and Jordan (2007) showed that lap dancers earned more tips while in the fertile (vs. infertile) phase of their menstrual cycle. Parallel to these findings, men found the body scent of women more attractive (Havlíček, Dvořákova, Bartoš, & Flegr, 2006; Singh & Bronstad, 2001) and had elevated testosterone in response to these scents (Miller & Maner, 2010) when women were in the fertile (vs. infertile) phase of their menstrual cycle.

Heterosexual women are similarly sensitive to olfactory cues when it comes to odors signaling men's disease resistance. Having a mate with a dissimilar major histocompatibility complex (MHC)—a gene family involved in the immune system—is thought to increase the likelihood of reproducing offspring with good immunocompetence (Thornhill et al., 2003), and this information is transmitted by body scent. Women prefer the body scent of men whose MHC is dissimilar from their own as compared to the scent of men with a similar MHC (e.g., Wedekind, Seebeck, Bettens, & Paepke, 1995). Women in the fertile phase of their menstrual cycle were also found to prefer the body scent of men with high (vs. low) facial symmetry, another cue that signals disease resistance (e.g., Rikowski & Grammer, 1999).

The attraction factors discussed thus far are by and large difficult to alter, whereas others are more changeable. One example is emotional reaction. Raised eyebrows and dilated pupils increase attractiveness ratings of female faces (Cunningham, 1986), presumably because both indicate a positive mood state and favorable emotional reaction. A big smile has also been found to boost the attractiveness ratings of female as well as male faces (Cunningham, 1986; Cunningham, Barbee, & Pike, 1990). For women, even the color of one's clothing can make a difference. In a series of studies, men found women more attractive if they were wearing red compared with blue, consistent with the common association of the color red with female sexual arousal (Elliot & Niesta, 2008).

Idiosyncratic Cues to Attractiveness

The existence of features that are consistently associated with judgments of attractiveness seems to support the contention that standards of beauty are widely shared. Consistent with this view, past work has repeatedly reported considerable agreement across individuals about who is attractive and who is not, thus further strengthening the view that attractiveness is objective and not subjective (e.g., Langlois et al., 2000). Hönekopp (2006) challenged this notion on the charge that current methods of calculating interjudge agreement (e.g., Cronbach's alpha) actually overestimate the role of shared versus idiosyncratic taste in judgments of attractiveness. That is, when the number of judges (i.e., participants rating the attractiveness of faces) is large, as in a typical behavioral experiment, interjudge agreement might seem very high even if the intercorrelations between judges are small. To estimate the relative roles of idiosyncratic and shared taste on judgments of attractiveness, Hönekopp (2006) asked participants to repeatedly rate the same set of faces. Results showed that idiosyncratic taste and shared taste accounted for roughly equal variance in judgments of attractiveness. In other words, idiosyncratic taste was just as important as shared preferences in who participants found attractive.

One possible source of idiosyncratic preferences is one's experiences in past relationships. Extensive research shows that individuals may apply aspects of their past relationships to new relationships, a phenomenon referred to as *transference* (e.g., Andersen & Chen, 2002). One study found that individuals judged faces that resembled their romantic partner more attractive than faces that did not (Günaydin, Zayas, Selcuk, & Hazan, 2012). Another factor likely to shape idiosyncratic preferences is physical similarity of a potential mate to oneself. For instance, studies have consistently shown that individuals rate pairs of faces that represent actual couples as more similar to one another compared with random pairs of faces (e.g., Bereczkei, Gyuris, & Weisfeld, 2004).

Situational Factors Affecting Judgments of Attractiveness

A number of situational factors have been found to influence judgments of attractiveness. For example, in a classic study, Pennebaker et al. (1979) showed that individuals in a bar found opposite-sex targets more attractive as closing time approached and hence potential mates became more scarce. In addition to perceived scarcity of potential mates, scarcity of resources was found to alter standards of beauty. Nelson and Morrison (2005) showed that when men were lacking in resources—hungry (vs. sated) or dissatisfied (vs. satisfied) with their finances—they lowered their standards when evaluating women as potential mates.

Alcohol consumption, which is known to impair judgments of all sorts, also has been shown to influence judgments of attractiveness. For example, heterosexual individuals who consumed alcohol found opposite-sex targets more attractive than those who did not consume alcohol (e.g., Parker, Penton-Voak, Attwood, & Munafò, 2008). Finally, even mere exposure to highly attractive others can shift perceivers' standards of beauty by creating a contrast effect. For example, men exposed to unusually attractive women in a TV show (i.e., *Charlie's Angels*) or in a magazine ad subsequently rated a woman of average attractiveness less attractive than men who were not exposed to women of above-average attractiveness (Kenrick & Gutierres, 1980).

Social Status/Resources

High social status and good earning prospects are desirable in a mate potentially because they both help secure resources necessary to promote child care. Indeed, both male and female conceptions of an ideal partner include characteristics signaling high social status and good financial prospects, such as having a good job and a nice home and being successful and financially secure (Fletcher, Simpson, Thomas, & Giles, 1999). A recent study that asked participants to indicate their interest in dating individuals based on their profile descriptions found similar results (Ha et al., 2012). Specifically, both heterosexual and gay/lesbian individuals were interested in dating potential mates with higher (vs. lower) social status and financial resources.

Personality

Another important consideration in mate selection is personality. Studies across many different cultures consistently find that both heterosexual and gay/lesbian individuals prefer partners who are kind, warm, and trustworthy (e.g., Buss, 1989; Felmlee et al., 2010; Fletcher et al., 1999). A review of the evolution of morality also identified warmth, trustworthiness, and kindness as well as other morally relevant traits, such as heroism, fidelity, and empathy, as virtues that individuals typically look for in potential mates (Miller, 2007).

These personality judgments can be made by looking at a person's face for a fraction of a second (e.g., Willis & Todorov, 2006). Such snap judgments are based on a number of cues. For one, perceivers are more likely to ascribe trustworthiness and kindness to physically attractive targets than to unattractive ones (e.g., Berry & Zebrowitz-McArthur, 1985; Dion, Berscheid, & Walster, 1972). Other cues associated with these judgments are babyfacedness and facial width-to-height ratio. An objective measure of babyfacedness derived from facial features (e.g., large eyes, bulging forehead, receding chin) as well as subjective judgments based on photographs were found to be positively correlated with judgments of honesty and kindness, even after controlling for facial attractiveness (e.g., Berry & Zebrowitz-McArthur, 1985). Facial width-to-height ratio—a cue related to aggression in men (e.g., Carre & McCormick, 2008)—also influences judgments of male trustworthiness, with wider faces being perceived as less trustworthy (Stirrat & Perrett, 2010). Moreover, men with wider (vs. narrower) faces were more likely to betray the trust of others, deceive others during negotiation, and cheat to enhance financial gain (Haselhuhn & Wong, 2012; Stirrat & Perrett, 2010), showing that there is some grain of truth in perceivers' initial impressions of trustworthiness.

Why do humans across virtually all cultures value traits like trustworthiness, kindness, warmth, and empathy in mates? One reason is that these traits are indicators of good mental health and hence reproductive fitness (Miller, 2007). For instance, capacity for empathic response advertises genetic quality since it is easily disrupted by several mental health problems (e.g., autism spectrum conditions; Baron-Cohen, 2009). These traits are associated with reproductive fitness also by way of the ability and willingness to commit in the relationship (e.g., Schmitt, 2004) and care for the offspring (e.g., Prinzie, Stams, Dekovic, Reijntjes, & Belsky, 2009).

Sex Differences in the Importance of Attractiveness, Resources, and Personality in Mate Selection

Do women and men value similar or different characteristics in a potential mate? According to sexual strategies theory (Buss, 1989; Buss & Schmitt, 1993), attractiveness and resources are differentially important for men and women because women's investment in offspring care is much higher than that of men. As a result, for women, the adaptive mate selection strategy that increases chances of offspring survival is to look for cues in potential mates signaling ability to care for the offspring (financial resources and traits such as ambitiousness), whereas the adaptive mating strategy for men is to look for cues signaling reproductive ability (physical attractiveness).

The best known study testing this theory is Buss's (1989) survey of 10,047 respondents in 37 cultures. Respondents were asked to rank order their preferences for a potential mate. This study showed that physical attractiveness ranked higher on men's lists compared with women's lists, whereas good earning potential ranked higher on women's lists compared with men's lists, supporting the predictions of sexual strategies theory. More important, between-sex similarities in partner preferences outweighed between-sex differences in this study. Neither men nor women found either attractiveness or social status as the most important characteristic of a mate. The most preferred four traits in a potential mate were identical for both sexes, with "kind and understanding" topping the list.

Of course, individuals often encounter various trade-offs in their relationship experiences. After all, a potential partner may be a really nice person but not so physically attractive, another may be of high social status but cold, and so on. Hence, another way to study the relative importance of attractiveness, social status/resources, and personality in mate preference is to systematically manipulate these trade-offs. This is exactly what Fletcher, Tither, O'Loughlin, Friesen, and Overall (2004) did. Results of this study showed that when warmth/trustworthiness was pitted against attractiveness or status/resources in a long-term mate, both men and women preferred warmth/trustworthiness. When attractiveness was pitted against status/resources in a long-term mate, men preferred attractiveness over status/resources, whereas women were equally likely to choose either characteristic. Again, this study suggests that between-sex similarities in partner preferences are as prominent as between-sex differences.

The majority of studies investigating sex differences, including those just reviewed, relied on self-reported preferences. Yet from an evolutionary perspective actual mate choice is more relevant for offspring survival than stated preferences (e.g., Todd et al., 2007). Studies focusing on actual mate choice generally lend no support or mixed support for sex differences in mate preferences (e.g., Conley, Moors, Matsick, Ziegler, & Valentine, 2011; Eastwick & Finkel, 2008; Kurzban & Weeden, 2005; but see Schmitt et al., 2012). In summary, sex differences in mate choice are much smaller than is popularly assumed.

STEP 3: WHO IS INTERESTED AND ATTAINABLE AS A POTENTIAL MATE?

All things being equal, people tend to like those who like them back. Reciprocity of romantic interest is a strong signal that the other person is interested and attainable as a potential mate. Signs of reciprocity help avoid social rejection, which humans find highly aversive and painful (Williams & Nida, 2011). In a seminal study demonstrating the effect of reciprocity on attraction, Backman and Secord (1959) asked participants to engage in a group discussion with unknown others. Prior to the discussion, participants were given the names of three other participants who, on the basis of a personality analysis, would most probably like them. After the group discussion, participants were asked to name three individuals they wanted to be partnered with in an upcoming interaction. Participants were significantly more likely to select individuals whom they thought would like them compared with other members of the group.

Backman and Secord's (1959) findings were subsequently replicated in getting-acquainted interactions (e.g., Chapdelaine et al., 1994; Kenny, Bond, Mohr, & Horn, 1996) and dating contexts. In two speed-dating studies, participants flirted more with, showed more romantic desire for, and eventually wanted to date those who reciprocated their interest (Back et al., 2011; Eastwick, Finkel, Mochon, & Ariely, 2007).

Converging evidence for reciprocal liking comes from studies of online social networks. For example, an analysis of the friend rankings of 11 million users in the MySpace network revealed that an individual's best friend choices reflected how others had ranked that individual in their own online profile (DeScioli et al., 2011). Specifically, 69% percent of users chose as their best friend someone who had given them a high ranking. A study of the LiveJournal community also found that 80% of online friendships were reciprocal (Liben-Nowell et al., 2005).

Although reciprocity is the norm, people also take selectivity into account when deciding whether to reciprocate interest on the part of a potential mate. As reviewed previously, individuals are motivated to seek characteristics such as attractiveness, resources, and good personality in a potential mate. Extensive research shows that individuals who possess these qualities are selective when signaling romantic interest (e.g., Lee et al., 2008). Thus, seeking a potential mate who selectively reciprocates one's interest ensures that the other person is attainable yet desirable as a mate. To manipulate selectivity, Walster, Walster, Piliavin, and Schmidt (1973) had male participants read profiles of women who were ostensibly potential dates. One of the women was described as selective in her mate choice; she was willing to date the participant but not anyone else. Another woman was described as not wanting to date anybody. A third was reportedly willing to date everyone. The profile for the fourth woman provided no information about her dating preferences. Participants liked the woman who was selective in her dating choice more than the other three women, and most selected her for a date.

Similarly, in speed-dating studies, individuals, particularly men, who indiscriminately showed romantic desire and dating interest were judged unselective and, in turn, less appealing as dates (Back et al., 2011, Eastwick et al., 2007; Kurzban & Weeden, 2005; Luo & Zhang, 2009).

STEP 4: WHO IS "THE ONE"?

How do these multiple and diverse factors—from chance encounters to split-second judgments of attractiveness to one's affective state at the time of meeting—come together to influence mate selection? We propose that mate selection can be characterized as a series of steps in a process of narrowing the pool of eligible mates from the many to "the one" (see Figure 4.1). Arguably the most influential factor in narrowing the pool of "eligibles" is propinquity—be it physical, cyber, or social—because this is what determines the probability of actually meeting a potential mate. Also, as argued previously, similarity and familiarity are inextricably linked to propinquity. Our social networks tend to be composed of people who are similar to us on a wide range of dimensions; the similarity makes them seem familiar, and the increased exposure afforded by propinquity makes them actually more familiar. Within this smaller pool of eligible mates, some individuals will appeal more than others. This includes considerations of physical appearance, social standing and resources, and personality as well as our affective state when we encounter these individuals.

There are two very important and interesting questions about this narrowing-down process. First, to what degree is the process driven by consciously held criteria? That is, do we know what we are looking for in a mate, and do our mate choices match our conscious selection criteria? Research findings indicate that what individuals say they are looking for in a mate does not in general coincide with their actual mate choices (e.g., Eastwick & Finkel, 2008). Rather, mate "selection" is more likely the result of "adventitious" or chance factors like propinquity (Lykken & Tellegen, 1993) and unconscious processes such as transference (e.g., Günaydin et al., 2012).

The second important and interesting question is this: If mate selection involves the narrowing down of a pool of "eligibles" to a smaller number of individuals who are equally accessible, appealing, and attainable, what

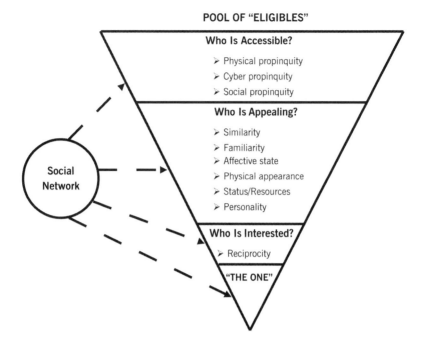

FIGURE 4.1. A process model of mate selection.

accounts for the selection of one to the exclusion of the others? This is where the fourth and final step in our process model comes into play. A sign of reciprocated interest on the part of a potential mate who is accessible, appealing, and attainable may suffice to trigger romantic infatuation. On the basis of interviews with hundreds of individuals, Tennov (1979) identified the common characteristics of infatuation, which later became the subject of much empirical research. Studies have shown that physiological arousal and anxiety (Marazziti & Canale, 2004), mental preoccupation with (Marazziti, Akiskal, Rossi, & Cassano, 1999) and idealization of (Niehuis, Lee, Reifman, Swenson, & Hunsaker, 2011) the target of attraction, as well as an intense longing for contact with this person (Aron et al., 2005) indeed characterize feelings of infatuation, as Tennov originally proposed. Such feelings narrow one's focus even further by focusing attention on one potential mate to the exclusion of all others.

Intense infatuation toward a potential mate can be triggered by any one or a combination of factors covered in this chapter. Regardless, when infatuation kicks in, it tends to "lock the emotional gates against further intrusion" from attractive others (Tennov, 1979, p. 254). In laboratory as well as online dating contexts, simply thinking that one's romantic interest is reciprocated has the effect of directing attention away from attractive alternatives (Koranyi & Rothermund, 2012).

THE INFLUENCE OF SOCIAL NETWORKS AT EVERY STEP IN THE PROCESS

An individual's social network can play a major role in mate selection. In a previous section, we have reviewed evidence that having mutual social ties decreases social distance, thereby increasing the likelihood of interaction and interpersonal attraction. However, reducing social distance is not the only means by which social networks influence mate choice. Network members can exert influence by approving or disapproving of a potential mate, by playing matchmaker, and by doing the actual choosing, as in arranged marriage.

Network Members Approve or Disapprove

Friends and family may not always agree with one's mate choices (Buunk, Park, & Dubbs, 2008), and their approval or lack thereof has consequences for a budding relationship. Network members exert an influence in all stages of relationship development (Sprecher, 2011), although this influence is strongest when the couple is transitioning from casual dating to serious involvement (Knobloch & Donovan-Kicken, 2006). Indeed, increased network approval is associated with increased commitment, love, and satisfaction and lower likelihood of breakup over time (e.g., Etcheverry & Agnew, 2004; Sprecher & Felmlee, 1992). In contrast, when network members disapprove, they engage in behaviors intended to undermine the relationship (e.g., preventing the couple from spending time together) and avoid behaving in a manner that encourages the relationship (e.g., saying anything positive about the partner; Sprecher, 2011). Of course, such attempts can also backfire by fueling attraction, a phenomenon referred to as the "Romeo and Juliet effect" (Driscoll, Davis, & Lipetz, 1972). However, more often evidence supports the view that social network disapproval leads to lesser rather than greater attraction (Sprecher, 2011; Sprecher & Felmlee, 1992).

   Not surprisingly, the impact of social network approval or disapproval depends on how much people care about what their network members have to say about their relationships. When individuals are motivated to comply with the opinions of their network members, approval leads to greater commitment, which in turn prospectively predicts relationship stability (Etcheverry & Agnew, 2004).

Network Members Play Matchmaker

It is not uncommon for friends or family to introduce members of their social networks to each other in the hopes of making a good match. To play matchmaker, one has to make an assessment of whether two people are compatible in ways that matter (Chapdelaine et al., 1994). For example, if Kate believes Jessie will like Jamie, she might assume that Jamie will reciprocate Jessie's liking. Alternatively, because Kate herself likes Jamie, she assumes Jessie will agree on Jamie's likability. Kate could also assume Jessie and Jamie will like each other because they are similar in a variety of ways. In a reanalysis of five studies of initial attraction, Kenny et al. (1996) showed that individuals are indeed quite accurate—albeit not perfect—at assessing whether two of their acquaintances, particularly those whom they know well, might like one another. So people might actually be quite good at playing matchmaker for members of their social networks. To our knowledge, however, relationship outcomes of network-initiated matches have yet to be empirically investigated. Whether matches set up by friends and family are happier or more enduring than those resulting from chance encounters is a matter for future research.

Network Members Arrange Marriages

The most direct form of social influence on mate selection is the arranged marriage. Arranged marriages are common in many parts of the world (Goodwin, 1999), such as Japan, China, India (e.g., Sprecher & Chandak, 1992), and Turkey (e.g., Hortaçsu, 2007). As opposed to individual "choice marriages" prevalent in Western cultures, spouses in arranged marriages are selected by the couple's parents, sometimes with the help of other kin and typically with little or no input from the couple. Interestingly, spouses in arranged marriages and so-called choice marriages were found to be equally similar in terms of age, education, and family background (e.g., Fox, 1975). It appears that whether mates are chosen by individuals or arranged by their families, the pool of eligibles is roughly the same—that is, a social network defined by propinquity.

CONCLUDING REMARKS

Research guided by numerous theoretical perspectives has identified myriad factors that influence human mate selection. However, the richness of the insights brought about by these diverse perspectives and empirical advances has not been fully utilized in the sense of organizing them into a unified framework. The process model of mate selection we presented in this chapter is one plausible way of integrating the vast literature on human mate selection. Future investigations that take multiple factors into account simultaneously (see Eastwick & Finkel, 2008; Hitsch et al., 2010; Kurzban & Weeden, 2005; Liben-Nowell et al., 2005, for examples of such an approach) rather than a single factor in isolation have the potential to advance theory and research greatly. Whether our process model holds up under empirical testing or not, we hope it will encourage others to join us in the search for an integrated process model of human mate selection.

REFERENCES

Abitbol, J., Abitbol, P., & Abitbol, B. (1999). Sex hormones and the female voice. *Journal of Voice, 13*, 424–446.

Allen, J. B., Kenrick, D. T., Linder, D. E., & McCall, M. A. (1989). Arousal and attraction: A response-facilitation alternative to misattribution and negative-reinforcement models. *Journal of Personality and Social Psychology, 57*, 261–270.

Andersen, S. M., & Chen, S. (2002). The relational self: An interpersonal social–cognitive theory. *Psychological Review, 109*, 619–645.

Aron, A., Fisher, H., Mashek, D. J., Strong, G., Li, H., & Brown, L. L. (2005). Reward, motivation, and emotion systems associated with early-stage intense romantic love. *Journal of Neurophysiology, 94*, 327–337.

Back, M. D., Penke, L., Schmukle, S. C., Sachse, K., Borkenau, P., & Asendorpf, J. B. (2011). Why mate choices are not as reciprocal as we assume: The role of personality, flirting and physical attractiveness. *European Journal of Personality, 25*, 120–132.

Back, M. D., Schmukle, S. C., & Egloff, B. (2008). Becoming friends by chance. *Psychological Science, 19*, 439–440.

Back, M. D., Schmukle, S. C., & Egloff, B. (2011). A closer look at first sight: Social relations lens model analyses of personality and interpersonal attraction at zero acquaintance. *European Journal of Personality, 25*, 225–238.

Backman, C. W., & Secord, P. F. (1959). The effect of perceived liking on interpersonal attraction. *Human Relations, 12*, 379–384.

Baron-Cohen, S. (2009). Autism: The empathizing–systemizing (E-S) theory. *Annals of New York Academy of Sciences, 1156*, 68–80.

Bereczkei, T., Gyuris, P., & Weisfeld, G. E. (2004). Sexual imprinting in human mate choice. *Proceedings of the Royal Society of London: B. Biological Sciences, 271*, 1129–1134.

Berry, D. S., & Zebrowitz-McArthur, L. (1985). Some components and consequences of a babyface. *Journal of Personality and Social Psychology, 48*, 312–323.

Bornstein, R. F., Leone, D. R., & Galley, D. J. (1987). The generalizability of subliminal mere exposure effects: Influence of stimuli perceived without awareness on social behavior. *Journal of Personality and Social Psychology, 53,* 1070–1079.

Buss, D. M. (1989). Sex differences in human mate preferences: Evolutionary hypotheses tested in 37 cultures. *Behavioral and Brain Sciences, 12,* 1–49.

Buss, D. M., & Schmitt, D. P. (1993). Sexual strategies theory: An evolutionary perspective on human mating. *Psychological Review, 100,* 204–232.

Buston, P. M., & Emlen, S. T. (2003). Cognitive processes underlying human mate choice: The relationship between self-perception and mate preference in Western society. *Proceedings of the National Academy of Sciences USA, 100,* 8805–8810.

Buunk, A. P., Park, J. H., & Dubbs, S. L. (2008). Parent–offspring conflict in mate preferences. *Review of General Psychology, 12,* 47–62.

Byrne, D., Griffitt, W., & Stefaniak, D. (1967). Attraction and similarity of personality characteristics. *Journal of Personality and Social Psychology, 5,* 82–90.

Byrne, D., & Nelson, D. (1965). Attraction as a linear function of proportion of positive reinforcements. *Journal of Personality and Social Psychology, 1,* 659–663.

Carre, J. M., & McCormick, C. M. (2008). In your face: Facial metrics predict aggressive behaviour in the laboratory and in varsity and professional hockey players. *Proceedings of the Royal Society of London: B. Biological Sciences, 275,* 2651–2656.

Chapdelaine, A., Kenny, D. A., & LaFontana, K. M. (1994). Matchmaker, matchmaker, can you make me a match? Predicting liking between two unacquainted persons. *Journal of Personality and Social Psychology, 67,* 83–91.

Collins, S. A., & Missing, C. (2003). Vocal and visual attractiveness are related in women. *Animal Behaviour, 65,* 997–1004.

Conley, T. D., Moors, A. C., Matsick, J. L., Ziegler, A., & Valentine, B. A. (2011). Women, men, and the bedroom: Methodological and conceptual insights that narrow, reframe, and eliminate gender differences in sexuality. *Current Directions in Psychological Science, 20,* 296–300.

Cunningham, M. R. (1986). Measuring the physical in physical attractiveness: Quasi-experiments on the sociobiology of female facial beauty. *Journal of Personality and Social Psychology, 50,* 925–935.

Cunningham, M. R., Barbee, A. P., & Pike, C. L. (1990). What do women want? Facialmetric assessment of multiple motives in the perception of male facial physical attractiveness. *Journal of Personality and Social Psychology, 59,* 61–72.

Cunningham, M. R., Roberts, A. R., Barbee, A. P., Druen, P. B., & Wu, C. H. (1995). Their ideas of beauty are, on the whole, the same as ours: Consistency and variability in the cross-cultural perception of female physical attractiveness. *Journal of Personality and Social Psychology, 68,* 261–279.

DeScioli, P., Kurzban, R., Koch, E. N., & Liben-Nowell, D. (2011). Best friends: Alliances, friend ranking, and the MySpace social network. *Perspectives on Psychological Science, 6,* 6–8.

Dijkstra, P., & Buunk, A. P. (2001). Sex differences in the jealousy-evoking nature of a rival's body build. *Evolution and Human Behavior, 22,* 335–341.

Dion, K., Berscheid, E., & Walster, E. (1972). What is beautiful is good. *Journal of Personality and Social Psychology, 24*, 285–290.

Driscoll, R., Davis, K. E., & Lipetz, M. E. (1972). Parental interference and romantic love: The Romeo and Juliet effect. *Journal of Personality and Social Psychology, 24*, 1–10.

Dryer, D. C., & Horowitz, L. M. (1997). When do opposites attract? Interpersonal complementarity versus similarity. *Journal of Personality and Social Psychology, 72*, 592–603.

Dutton, D., & Aron, A. P. (1974). Some evidence for heightened sexual attraction under conditions of high anxiety. *Journal of Personality and Social Psychology, 23*, 510–517.

Eastwick, P. W., & Finkel, E. J. (2008). Sex differences in mate preferences revisited: Do people know what they initially desire in a romantic partner? *Journal of Personality and Social Psychology, 94*, 245–264.

Eastwick, P. W., Finkel, E. J., Mochon, D., & Ariely, D. (2007). Selective versus unselective romantic desire: Not all reciprocity is created equal. *Psychological Science, 18*, 317–319.

Eastwick, P. W., Richeson, J. A., Son, D., & Finkel, E. J. (2009). Is love colorblind? Political orientation moderates interracial romantic desire. *Personality and Social Psychology Bulletin, 35*, 1258–1268.

Ebbesen, E. B., Kjos, G. L., & Konecni, V. J. (1976). Spatial ecology: Its effects on the choice of friends and enemies. *Journal of Experimental Social Psychology, 12*, 505–518.

Elliot, A. J., & Niesta, D. (2008). Romantic red: Red enhances men's attraction to women. *Journal of Personality and Social Psychology, 95*, 1150–1164.

Etcheverry, P. E., & Agnew, C. R. (2004). Subjective norms and the prediction of romantic relationship state and fate. *Personal Relationships, 11*, 409–428.

Feinberg, D. R., Jones, B. C., Law Smith, M. J., Moore, F. R., DeBruine, L. M., Cornwell, R. E., et al. (2006). Menstrual cycle, trait estrogen level and masculinity preferences in the human voice. *Hormones and Behavior, 49*, 215–222.

Felmlee, D., Orzechowicz, D., & Fortes, C. (2010). Fairy tales: Attraction and stereotypes in same-gender relationships. *Sex Roles, 62*, 226–240.

Festinger, L., Schachter, S., & Back, K. (1950). *Social processes in informal groups.* Stanford, CA: Stanford University Press.

Finkel, E. J., Eastwick, P. W., Karney, B. R., Reis, H. T., & Sprecher, S. (2012). Online dating: A critical analysis from the perspective of psychological science. *Psychological Science in the Public Interest, 13*, 3–66.

Fisman, R., Iyengar, S., Kamenica, E., & Simonson, I. (2006). Gender differences in mate selection: Evidence from a speed dating experiment. *Quarterly Journal of Economics, 121*, 673–697.

Fisman, R., Iyengar, S.S., Kamenica, E., & Simonson, I. (2008). Racial preferences in dating. *Review of Economic Studies, 75*, 117–132.

Fletcher, G. J. O., Simpson, J. A., Thomas, G., & Giles, L. (1999). Ideals in intimate relationships. *Journal of Personality and Social Psychology, 76*, 72–89.

Fletcher, G. J. O., Tither, J. M., O'Loughlin, C., Friesen, M., & Overall, N. (2004). Warm and homely or cold and beautiful? Sex differences in trading off traits in mate selection. *Personality and Social Psychology Bulletin, 30*, 659–672.

Forgas, J. P. (2011). Affective influences on self-disclosure: Mood effects on the intimacy and reciprocity of disclosing personal information. *Journal of Personality and Social Psychology, 100*, 449–461.

Forgas, J. P., & Bower, G. H. (1987). Mood effects on person perception judgments. *Journal of Personality and Social Psychology, 53*, 53–60.

Foster, C. A., Witcher, B. S., Campbell, W. K., & Green, J. D. (1998). Arousal and attraction: Evidence for automatic and controlled processes. *Journal of Personality and Social Psychology, 74*, 86–101.

Fox, G. L. (1975). Love match and arranged marriage in a modernizing nation: Mate selection in Ankara, Turkey. *Journal of Marriage and Family, 37*, 180–193.

Gangestad, S., Thornhill, R., & Yeo, R. (1994). Facial attractiveness, developmental stability and fluctuating asymmetry. *Ethology and Sociobiology, 15*, 73–85.

Goodwin, R. (1999). *Personal relationships across cultures.* London: Routledge.

Gouaux, C. (1971). Induced affective states and interpersonal attraction. *Journal of Personality and Social Psychology, 20*, 37–43.

Greenwald, A. G., McGhee, D. E., & Schwartz, J. L. K. (1998). Measuring individual differences in implicit cognition: The Implicit Association Test. *Journal of Personality and Social Psychology, 74*, 1464–1480.

Griffitt, W. (1970). Environmental effects on interpersonal affective behavior: Ambient effective temperature and attraction. *Journal of Personality and Social Psychology, 15*, 240–244.

Griffitt, W., May, J., & Veitch, R. (1974). Sexual stimulation and interpersonal behavior: Heterosexual evaluative responses, visual behavior, and physical proximity. *Journal of Personality and Social Psychology, 30*, 367–377.

Günaydin, G., Zayas, V., Selcuk, E., & Hazan, C. (2012). I like you but I don't know why: Objective facial resemblance to significant others influences snap judgments. *Journal of Experimental Social Psychology, 48*, 350–353.

Ha, T., van den Berg, J., Engels, R., & Lichtwarck-Aschoff, A. (2012). Effects of attractiveness and status in dating desire in homosexual and heterosexual men and women. *Archives of Sexual Behavior, 41*, 673–682.

Hammer, M. (1980). Predictability of social connections over time. *Social Networks, 2*, 165–180.

Haselhuhn, M. P., & Wong, E. M. (2012). Bad to the bone: Facial structure predicts unethical behaviour. *Proceedings of the Royal Society of London: B. Biological Sciences, 279*, 571–576.

Havlíček, J., Dvořákova, R., Bartoš, L., & Flegr, J. (2006). Non-advertized does not mean concealed: Body odour changes across the human menstrual cycle. *Ethology, 112*, 81–90.

Hazan, C., & Diamond, L. M. (2000). The place of attachment in human mating. *Review of General Psychology, 4*, 186–204.

Heider, F. (1958). *The psychology of interpersonal relations.* New York: Wiley.

Herbst, K. C., Gaertner, L., & Insko, C. A. (2003). My head says yes but my heart says no: Cognitive and affective attraction as a function of similarity to the ideal self. *Journal of Personality and Social Psychology, 84*, 1206–1219.

Hitsch, G. J., Hortaçsu, A., & Ariely, D. (2010). Matching and sorting in online dating. *American Economic Review, 100*, 130–163.

Hönekopp, J. (2006). Once more: Is beauty in the eye of the beholder? Relative contributions of private and shared taste to judgments of facial attractiveness. *Journal of Experimental Psychology: Human Perception and Performance, 32*, 199–209.

Hortaçsu, N. (2007). Family-versus couple-initiated marriages in Turkey: Similarities and differences over the family life cycle. *Asian Journal of Social Psychology, 10*, 103–116.

Kalmijn, M. (1998). Intermarriage and homogamy: Causes, patterns and trends. *Annual Review of Sociology, 24*, 395–421.

Kelley, H. H., Holmes, J. G., Kerr, N. L., Reis, H. T., Rusbult, C. E., & Van Lange, P. A. M. (2003). *An atlas of interpersonal situations.* Cambridge, UK: Cambridge University Press.

Kenny, D. A., Bond, C. F., Jr., Mohr, C. D., & Horn, E. M. (1996). Do we know how much people like one another? *Journal of Personality and Social Psychology, 71*, 928–936.

Kenrick, D. T., & Gutierres, S. E. (1980). Contrast effects and judgments of physical attractiveness: When beauty becomes a social problem. *Journal of Personality and Social Psychology, 38*, 131–140.

Klohnen, E. C., & Luo, S. (2003). Interpersonal attraction and personality: What is attractive—self similarity, ideal similarity, complementarity, or attachment security? *Journal of Personality and Social Psychology, 85*, 709–722.

Knobloch, L. K., & Donovan-Kicken, E. (2006). Perceived involvement of network members in courtships: A test of the relational turbulence model. *Personal Relationships, 13*, 281–301.

Koranyi, N., & Rothermund, K. (2012). When the grass on the other side of the fence doesn't matter: Reciprocal romantic interest neutralizes attentional bias towards attractive alternatives. *Journal of Experimental Social Psychology, 48*, 186–191.

Kossinets, G., & Watts, D. J. (2006). Empirical analysis of an evolving social network. *Science, 311*, 88–90.

Kurzban, R., & Weeden, J. (2005). HurryDate: Mate preferences in action. *Evolution and Human Behavior, 26*, 227–244.

Langlois, J. H., Kalakanis, L., Rubenstein, A. J., Larson, A., Hallam, M., & Smoot, M. (2000). Maxims or myths of beauty? A meta-analytic and theoretical review. *Psychological Bulletin, 126*, 390–423.

Langlois, J. H., & Roggman, L. A. (1990). Attractive faces are only average. *Psychological Science, 1*, 115–121.

Lee, L., Loewenstein, G., Ariely, D., Hong, J., & Young, J. (2008). If I'm not hot, are you hot or not: Physical attractiveness evaluation and dating preferences as a function of one's own attractiveness. *Psychological Science, 19*, 669–677.

Leskovec, J., & Horvitz, E. (2007). *Worldwide buzz: Planetary-scale views on an instant-messaging network* (Microsoft Research Technical Report MSR-TR-2006-186). Retrieved September 29, 2011, from *http://research.microsoft.com/en-us/um/people/horvitz/msn-paper.pdf.*

Liben-Nowell, D., Novak, J., Kumar, R., Raghavan, P., & Tomkins, A. (2005).

Geographic routing in social networks. *Proceedings of the National Academy of Sciences USA, 102*, 623–628.

Luo, S., & Zhang, G. (2009). What leads to romantic attraction: Similarity, reciprocity, security, or beauty? Evidence from a speed-dating study. *Journal of Personality, 77*, 933–964.

Lykken, D. T., & Tellegen, A. (1993). Is human mating adventitious or the result of lawful choice? A twin study of mate selection. *Journal of Personality and Social Psychology, 65*, 56–68.

Marazziti, A., Akiskal, H. S., Rossi, A., & Cassano, G. B. (1999). Alteration of the platelet serotonin transporter in romantic love. *Psychological Medicine, 29*, 741–745.

Marazziti, D., & Canale, D. (2004). Hormonal changes when falling in love. *Psychoneuroendocrinology, 29*, 931–936.

Marmaros, D., & Sacerdote, B. (2006). How do friendships form? *Quarterly Journal of Economics, 121*, 79–119.

Mayer, A., & Puller, S. (2008). The old boy (and girl) network: Social network formation on university campuses. *Journal of Public Economics, 92*, 329–347.

McKenna, K. Y. A., Green, A., & Gleason, M. (2002). Relationship formation on the Internet: What's the big attraction? *Journal of Social Issues, 58*, 9–31.

Miller, G. F., Tybur, J. M., & Jordan, B. D. (2007). Ovulatory cycle effects on tip earnings by lap dancers: Economic evidence for human estrus? *Evolution and Human Behavior, 28*, 375–381.

Miller, G. F. (2007). Sexual selection for moral virtues. *Quarterly Review of Biology, 82*, 97–125.

Miller, S. L., & Maner, J. K. (2010). Scent of a woman: Men's testosterone responses to olfactory ovulation cues. *Psychological Science, 21*, 276–283.

Montoya, R. M. (2008). I'm hot, so I'd say you're not: The influence of objective physical attractiveness on mate selection. *Personality and Social Psychology Bulletin, 34*, 1315–1331.

Moreland, R. L., & Beach, S. R. (1992). Exposure effects in the classroom: The development of affinity among students. *Journal of Experimental Social Psychology, 28*, 255–276.

Moreland, R. L., & Zajonc, R. B. (1982). Exposure effects in person perception: Familiarity, similarity, and attraction. *Journal of Experimental Social Psychology, 18*, 395–415.

Nelson, L. D., & Morrison, E. L. (2005). The symptoms of resource scarcity: Judgments of food and finances influence preferences for potential partners. *Psychological Science, 16*, 167–173.

Newcomb, T. M. (1956). The prediction of interpersonal attraction. *American Psychologist, 11*, 575–586.

Niehuis, S., Lee, K., Reifman, A., Swenson, A., & Hunsaker, S. (2011). Idealization and disillusionment in intimate relationships: A review of theory, method, and research. *Journal of Family Theory and Review, 3*, 273–302.

Olson, I. R., & Marshuetz, C. (2005). Facial attractiveness is appraised in a glance. *Emotion, 5*, 498–502.

Parker, L. L. C., Penton-Voak, I. S., Attwood, A. S., & Munafò, M. R. (2008). Effects of acute alcohol consumption on ratings of attractiveness of facial stimuli: Evidence of long-term encoding. *Alcohol and Alcoholism, 43,* 636–640.

Parks, M. R., & Floyd, K. (1996). Making friends in cyberspace. *Journal of Communication, 46,* 80–97.

Pennebaker, J. W., Dyer, M. A., Caulkins, R. S., Litowitz, D. L., Ackreman, P. L., Anderson, D. B., et al. (1979). Don't the girls get prettier at closing time: A country and western application to psychology. *Personality and Social Psychology Bulletin, 5,* 122–125.

Penton-Voak, I. S., Perrett, D. I., Castles, D. L., Kobayashi, T., Burt, D. M., Murray, L. K., et al. (1999). Menstrual cycle alters face preference. *Nature, 399,* 741–742.

Peplau, L. A., & Fingerhut, A. W. (2007). The close relationships of lesbians and gay men. *Annual Review of Psychology, 58,* 405–424.

Peplau, L. A., Padesky, C., & Hamilton, M. (1982). Satisfaction in lesbian relationships. *Journal of Homosexuality, 8,* 23–35.

Perrett, D. I., Burt, D. M., Penton-Voak, I. S., Lee, K. J., Rowland, D. A., & Edwards, R. (1999). Symmetry and human facial attractiveness. *Evolution and Human Behavior, 20,* 295–307.

Perrett, D. I., Lee, K. J., Penton-Voak, I., Rowland, D., Yoshikawa, S., Burt, D. M., et al. (1998). Effects of sexual dimorphism on facial attractiveness. *Nature, 394,* 884–887.

Prinzie, P., Stams, G. J. J. M., Dekovic, M., Reijntjes, A. H. A., & Belsky, J. (2009). The relations between parents' Big Five personality factors and parenting: A meta-analytic review. *Journal of Personality and Social Psychology, 97,* 351–362.

Reis, H. T., Maniaci, M. R., Caprariello, P. A., Eastwick, P. W., & Finkel, E. J. (2011). Familiarity does indeed promote attraction in live interaction. *Journal of Personality and Social Psychology, 101,* 557–570.

Ridings, C., & Gefen, D. (2004). Virtual community attraction: Why people hang out online. *Journal of Computer-Mediated Communication, 10.*

Rikowski, A., & Grammer, K. (1999). Human body odour, symmetry and attractiveness. *Proceedings of the Royal Society of London: B. Biological Sciences, 266,* 869–874.

Roberts, S. C., Havlíćek, J., Flegr, J., Hruskova, M., Little, A. C., Jones, B. C., et al. (2004). Female facial attractiveness increases during the fertile phase of the menstrual cycle. *Proceedings of the Royal Society of London Series: B. Biological Sciences, 271,* S270-S272.

Rosenfeld, M. J., & Thomas, R. J. (2012). Searching for a mate: The rise of the Internet as a social intermediary. *American Sociological Review, 77,* 523–547.

Ryff, C. D., & Singer, B. H. (2001). *Emotions, social relationships, and health.* New York: Oxford University Press.

Sakai, D. K., & Johnson, R. C. (1997). Active phenotypic assortment in mate selection: Self descriptions and sought-for attributes of mates in dating advertisements. *Biodemography and Social Biology, 44,* 258–264.

Schmitt, D. P. (2004). The Big Five related to risky sexual behaviour across 10 world regions: Differential personality associations of sexual promiscuity and relationship infidelity. *European Journal of Personality, 18,* 301–319.

Schmitt, D. P., Jonason, P. K., Byerley, G. J., Flores, S. D., Illbeck, B. E., O'Leary, K. N., et al. (2012). A reexamination of sex differences in sexuality: New studies reveal old truths. *Current Directions in Psychological Science, 21*, 135–139.

Selcuk, E., & Ong, A. D. (2013). Perceived partner responsiveness moderates the association between received emotional support and all-cause mortality. *Health Psychology, 32*, 231–235.

Selfhout, M., Denissen, J., Branje, S., & Meeus, W. (2009). In the eye of the beholder: Perceived, actual, and peer-rated similarity in personality, communication, and friendship intensity during the acquaintanceship process. *Journal of Personality and Social Psychology, 96*, 1152–1165.

Singh, D. (1993). Adaptive significance of female physical attractiveness: Role of the waist-to-hip ratio. *Journal of Personality and Social Psychology, 65*, 293–307.

Singh, D., & Bronstad, P. M. (2001). Female body odour is a potential cue to ovulation. *Proceedings of the Royal Society of London: B. Biological Sciences, 268*, 797–801.

Sprecher, S. (2011). The influence of social networks on romantic relationships: Through the lens of the social network. *Personal Relationships, 18*, 630–644.

Sprecher, S., & Chandak, R. (1992). Attitudes about arranged marriages and dating among men and women from India. *Free Inquiry in Creative Sociology, 20*, 59–69.

Sprecher, S., & Felmlee, D. (1992). The influence of parents and friends on the quality and stability of romantic relationships: A three-wave longitudinal investigation. *Journal of Marriage and the Family, 54*, 888–900.

Sprecher, S., Wenzel, A., & Harvey, J. (Eds.). (2008). *Handbook of relationship initiation.* New York: Psychology Press.

Stevens, G., Owens, D., & Schaefer, E. C. (1990). Education and attractiveness in marriage choices. *Social Psychology Quarterly, 53*, 62–70.

Stirrat, M., & Perrett, D. I. (2010). Valid facial cues to cooperation and trust: Male facial width and trustworthiness. *Psychological Science, 21*, 349–354.

Taylor, S. E., & Mettee, D. R. (1971). When similarity breeds contempt. *Journal of Personality and Social Psychology, 20*, 75–81.

Tennov, D. (1979). *Love and limerence. The experience of being in love.* New York: Stein and Day.

Thornhill, R., & Gangestad, S. W. (1994). Human fluctuating asymmetry and sexual behavior. *Psychological Science, 5*, 297–302.

Thornhill, R., Gangestad, S. W., Miller, R., Scheyd, G., McCollough, J., & Franklin, M. (2003). MHC, symmetry and body scent attractiveness in men and women (*Homo sapiens*). *Behavioral Ecology, 14*, 668–678.

Thornhill, R., & Møller, A. P. (1997). Developmental stability, disease and medicine. *Biological Reviews, 72*, 497–548.

Todd, P. M., Penke, L., Fasolo, B., & Lenton, A. P. (2007). Different cognitive processes underlie human mate choices and mate preferences. *Proceedings of the National Academy of Sciences USA, 104*, 15011–15016.

van Baaren, R. B., Fockenberg, D. A., Holland, R. W., Janssen, L., & van Knippenberg, A. (2006). The moody chameleon: The effect of mood on non-conscious mimicry. *Social Cognition, 24*, 426–437.

Verbrugge, L. M. (1977). The structure of adult friendship choices. *Social Forces, 56*, 576–597.

Walster, E., Walster, G. W., Piliavin, J., & Schmidt, L. (1973). "Playing hard to get": Understanding an elusive phenomenon. *Journal of Personality and Social Psychology, 26*, 113–121.

Watson, D., Klohnen, E. C., Casillas, A., Simms, E. N., Haig, J., & Berry, D. S. (2004). Match makers and deal breakers: Analyses of assortative mating in newlywed couples. *Journal of Personality, 72*, 1029–1068.

Watson, P. J., & Thornhill, R. (1994). Fluctuating asymmetry and sexual selection. *Trends in Ecology and Evolution, 9*, 21–25.

Wedekind, C., Seebeck, T., Bettens, F., & Paepke, A. J. (1995). MHC dependent mate preference in humans. *Proceedings of the Royal Society of London: B. Biological Sciences, 260*, 245–249.

White, G. L., Fishbein, S., & Rutstein, J. (1981). Passionate love and the misattribution of arousal. *Journal of Personality and Social Psychology, 41*, 56–62.

Williams, K. D., & Nida, S. A. (2011). Ostracism: Consequences and coping. *Current Directions in Psychological Science, 20*, 71–75.

Willis, J., & Todorov, A. (2006). First impressions: Making up your mind after a 100-ms exposure to a face. *Psychological Science, 17*, 592–598.

World Bank. (2012). *World development indicators 2012.* Retrieved July 18, 2012, from *http://data.worldbank.org/data-catalog/world-development-indicators/wdi-2012.*

Chapter 5

To Pair Bond or Not

The Evolutionary Psychological Approach to Human Mating

PAUL W. EASTWICK
NATASHA D. TIDWELL

*A*s detailed in several other chapters in this volume, pair bonds are an enormously important component of humans' evolutionary heritage (Günaydin, Selcuk, & Hazan, Chapter 4, and Zeifman, Chapter 2, this volume). As members of the genus *Homo* were adapting to life on the African savannah between 1.5 and 2 million years ago, pair bonds between adult mating partners emerged as a mating strategy that conferred vast reproductive benefits (Eastwick, 2009). The offspring of these early hominids were exceptionally immature at birth and required considerable parental care in order to satisfy the energy requirements of their large brains (Smith & Tompkins, 1995). Pair bonds would have encouraged early *Homo*, especially males, to invest in the offspring produced by this primary partnership (Hazan & Diamond, 2000; L. C. Miller & Fishkin, 1997; Zeifman & Hazan, 2008), thus increasing the likelihood that those offspring would ultimately survive to reproduce themselves (Geary, 2000). This evolved legacy of pair bonding remains evident in the mating behavior of modern human beings, as detailed by an enormous literature on attachment that stretches across anthropology (Gray & Anderson, 2010), psychology (Cassidy & Shaver, 2008), and neurobiology (Curtis, Chapter 6, this volume; cf. Barash & Lipton, 2001).

Nevertheless, pair bonding is not the only strategy in the human mating repertoire. Some situations and some romantic partners are not conducive to pair bonding, and humans can use sex to fulfill a wide variety of motives that are unrelated to pair bonding, including the motive to feel good about oneself and the motive to impress others (Cooper, Shapiro, & Powers, 1998). Thus, mating researchers must explain not only the inner workings of the romantic pair bond but also how and why humans mate when attachment concerns are irrelevant and under what circumstances pair bonds become a likely or unlikely mating option.

The present chapter reviews these non-pair-bonding elements of the human mating psychology, with a particular emphasis on an influential branch of psychological science called *evolutionary psychology*. Evolutionary psychologists apply the principles of evolutionary biology to the study of the mind. Research in this tradition addresses questions about the adaptive function of particular mental features; that is, how was the human psyche designed by natural selection to solve particular problems in our evolutionary past? Using this functional approach, evolutionary psychology has achieved new insights across a wide variety of psychological domains, such as social exchange (Cosmides & Tooby, 2005), emotion (Oaten, Stevenson, & Case, 2009), and attention (Maner et al., 2005). However, evolutionary psychology has examined the mating domain more than any other (Buss & Reeve, 2003), and no review of the mating research landscape can be complete without considering this work.

This chapter begins with a brief historical overview of the intellectual roots of evolutionary psychology. We then describe the explosion of evolutionary research on mating topics that began in the late 1980s and continued throughout the 1990s, a literature with a strong focus on between-sex differences in mating behavior. Next, we describe several newer evolutionary psychological programs of research that address within-sex differences and strive to explain how people negotiate the trade-off between long-term and short-term mating strategies. Finally, we review nascent evolutionary perspectives that promise a conceptual integration of research in the evolutionary psychological and relationship science traditions, the latter of which includes the voluminous literature on adult romantic attachment and pair bonds (Hazan & Diamond, 2000).

THE ORIGINS OF EVOLUTIONARY PSYCHOLOGY

Evolutionary psychology owes much to Charles Darwin and the theory of natural selection (Darwin, 1859). Many features of organisms are at least partially heritable, which means that organisms will pass these features on to their offspring. Although Mendel's research on genetics was not widely appreciated during Darwin's time, by the early 20th century, scientists recognized that genetic transmission was the primary means by which organisms passed features to subsequent generations. Depending on the current environment, some genes have more beneficial effects on an organism's fitness than other genes; that is, some genes make it more likely that an organism will survive and reproduce. By affecting reproductive success in this way, an environment exerts natural selection on a population of organisms by changing the likelihood that some genes will increase in prevalence and some will decrease in prevalence. Given consistent environmental forces and a sufficient amount of time, natural selection can cause a particular gene or set of genes to proceed to fixation, which means that all members of the population possess the beneficial genes.

Through this process of natural selection, adaptations are born. *Adaptations* are inherited features of organisms that arose in the past through natural selection because they directly or indirectly contributed to reproductive success (Buss, Haselton, Shackelford, Bleske, & Wakefield, 1998). Thus, the function of an adaptation is to solve a reproductive problem—to help an organism avoid predators, find food, mate successfully, or perform any behavior that promotes the transmission of genes to subsequent generations. Many morphological features of organisms are straightforward examples of adaptations: Eyes are adaptations that serve the function of sensing light, and forelimbs are adaptations that serve the function of grasping, scratching, running, or flying. Just as natural selection operates on these features of organisms, it also operates on brains, thus natural selection can produce mental adaptations that function to increase reproductive success. For example, fear is an adaptation that serves the function of avoiding life-threatening dangers, and showy behaviors (e.g., a peacock's tail display) are adaptations that serve the function of attracting mates.

The concept of the adaptation was not widely applied to humans until E. O. Wilson's advanced the idea in *Sociobiology* (1975). Wilson argued that evolutionary principles could explain and predict human behavior, as these behaviors should also have been shaped by natural selection to promote reproductive fitness. That is, the same adaptive logic that explains the function of an animal's wing or mating display could also explain why humans engage in certain behaviors, including mating behaviors.

This emerging perspective intersected with Trivers's (1972) influential theory of differential parental investment. Trivers's insight was that the sex that invested most heavily in offspring would be the sex that is more discriminating in the mating domain. In most mammals, females invest more heavily in offspring than males in terms of pregnancy, lactation, and nurturing, and because these activities are costly, the consequences of a poor mating decision (i.e., mating with a low-quality male) are considerably higher for females. The theory of differential parental investment proposes that some mental adaptations should facilitate different strategies for males and females: For example, females should have evolved behavioral strategies to be cautious and choosy in selecting mates, whereas males should have evolved strategies that help them to acquire a large number of sexual opportunities. The synthesis of Wilson's and Trivers's perspectives suggested that the application of evolutionary concepts to humans could explain and predict a number of differences between men and women in the mating domain.

One other critical foundational concept grew out of research on social exchange by Cosmides and Tooby (Cosmides, 1989; Tooby & Cosmides, 1992). These studies focused on reasoning behavior, as revealed by the Wason selection task (Wason, 1966), which tests how well people reason about *If P, then Q* rules. When these rules are abstract (e.g., If a person has a "D" rating, then his documents must be marked code "3"), participants do a poor job of detecting violations of a rule. However, when researchers frame these same rules as a social contract (e.g., If a person is drinking beer, then he must be over 20 years old), participants' ability to detect violations increases substantially. Cosmides and Tooby suggest that this content effect reveals that humans have specialized psychological mechanisms devoted to the detection of cheaters that are not activated when people perform abstract exercises in logic. Furthermore, this cheater-detection mechanism was honed by natural selection for its adaptive benefits in humans' evolutionary past.

The Cosmides and Tooby perspective had two important implications for the mating research that followed. First, their research deemphasized the adaptive function of specific behaviors, which was the standard approach in the animal behavior literature, and emphasized instead the adaptive function of underlying psychological mechanisms (Driscoll, 2004). By suggesting that certain psychological mechanisms could have evolved for their adaptive benefits, Cosmides and Tooby connected the sociobiological theories of Wilson with the vernacular of empirical psychologists (who strive to understand mental mechanisms); thus, the field of evolutionary psychology was born. The second implication of this perspective was Tooby and

Cosmides's (1992) postulate that the human psyche must be composed largely of distinct psychological mechanisms, sometimes called *domain-specific* mechanisms, each designed to solve a specific adaptive problem. That is, a human brain should contain few domain-general mechanisms (e.g., all-purpose learning mechanisms) because such content-free designs would not be as successful as domain-specific mechanisms, like the cheater-detection mechanism identified in their experiments. Thus, the evolutionary psychological approach to mating initially involved the search for domain-specific mechanisms that were honed by natural selection to increase men's and women's reproductive success. Furthermore, because this approach drew heavily from parental investment theory (Trivers, 1972), researchers hypothesized that many of these mechanisms would be different for men and women.

THE CLASSIC EVOLUTIONARY PSYCHOLOGICAL PERSPECTIVE ON MATING

David Buss pioneered the evolutionary psychological approach to mating in the late 1980s and early 1990s. His work on mate preferences (Buss, 1989), jealousy (Buss, Larsen, Westen, & Semmelroth, 1992), and short-term versus long-term sexual strategies (Buss & Schmitt, 1993) are the *Rubber Soul*, *Revolver*, and *Sgt. Pepper*, respectively, of evolutionary mating research. We review each of these programs of research next.

Mate Preferences

For many decades, sociologists and psychologists have been interested in the qualities that people desire in a romantic partner (e.g., Hill, 1945). For example, people tend to prefer mates who are kind and who have an exciting personality (Buss & Barnes, 1986). Having a mate with these sorts of positive traits can have beneficial consequences for oneself: A kind mate may be skilled in providing support, whereas an exciting partner may offer thrills and adventure.

Both sexes desire kindness and an exciting personality in an ideal romantic partner to a similar extent, but men and women may differ in the importance they place on other traits. Buss (1989) proposed that some sex differences in mate preferences reflected psychological adaptations honed by natural selection to increase men's and women's reproductive success. As predicted by parental investment theory (Trivers, 1972), human females invest in offspring more than males. However, human males can monopolize and defend resources, and they frequently choose to invest these resources in offspring. Therefore, Buss argues, ancestral females would have faced the adaptive problem of identifying which males were able to make such an investment, and women should reveal evidence of evolved mechanisms that direct them to mate with men who have accrued or have the strong potential to accrue resources. Alternatively, men's reproductive success is limited by the availability of partners who have a high reproductive capacity (i.e., fertile partners). Reproductive capacity is associated with youth in women, and youth can be inferred by the presence of clear skin, lustrous hair, and other markers of physical attractiveness (Buss, 1992). Men's reproductive capacity, however, is not associated as strongly with age; thus, a male's physical attractiveness is not a strong indicator of his fertility. Therefore, to solve the problem of identifying fertile partners, Buss predicted that men would have evolved a stronger preference for young, attractive partners than women.

In a survey of 10,047 participants from 37 different cultures, Buss (1989) found strong evidence for these predicted sex differences when men and women rated the importance they placed on various qualities in a mate. Specifically, women (more than men) rated the items "good financial prospect" and "ambition and industriousness" as important in a mate, and men (more than women) rated the item "good looks" as important in a mate. Also, women in every sampled culture desired a mate who was older than they were, and men in every culture desired a mate who was younger. Other scholars have replicated these sex differences in representative samples within the United States (Sprecher, Sullivan, & Hatfield, 1994), in participants' evaluations of descriptions or photographs of opposite-sex individuals (e.g., Townsend & Wasserman, 1998), and in meta-analyses of the existing mate preferences literature (Feingold, 1990, 1992). These sex differences are consistent with the parental investment logic: Men desire youth and physical attractiveness in a mate because these traits provide strong cues to a women's fertility, whereas women desire age and ambition in a mate because older, ambitious men are likely to have or eventually acquire resources that will contribute to the health and survival of offspring.

Jealousy

In humans' ancestral past, men would have faced an adaptive problem that women did not, namely the problem of paternity certainty. Given that mammals exhibit internal female fertilization and gestation, men can never be 100% sure that the offspring of their mate is actually their own. If a woman engaged in sexual contact with multiple male partners, her mate could potentially invest time and resources in raising another man's off-spring, thus decreasing his own reproductive success. For this reason, Buss and others (e.g., M. I. Wilson & Daly, 1992) proposed that a naturally selected mental mechanism that caused men to be hypervigilant for and guard against signs of a mate's sexual infidelity would have solved this ancestral problem. Women, on the other hand, would have faced a different adaptive problem: If a woman's mate became emotionally attached to another female partner, he might choose to divert his resources to this alternative relationship, and his original partner would experience reduced reproductive success. Therefore, women might exhibit evidence of a naturally selected mental mechanism that caused them to be hypervigilant for and guard against signs of a mate's emotional infidelity, which would have been a strong cue to her impending loss of his resources.

Buss and colleagues (1992) explored these two hypotheses simultaneously in a study of jealousy. Presumably, people who are jealous of a potential romantic rival would be motivated to take steps to counter this threat to their current relationship (e.g., by restricting their partner's access to the rival). Yet the reproductive fitness costs of sexual versus emotional threats could have differed for men and women in humans' ancestral past, as noted previously, and thus the situations or events that trigger jealousy could have evolved to be sex differentiated. Specifically, Buss and colleagues predicted that men would be more upset than women by the prospect of their mate committing sexual infidelity, whereas women would be more upset than men by the prospect of their mate committing emotional infidelity. In one study, Buss et al. (1992) asked participants to select which of the following two scenarios would distress or upset them more: (1) imagining their partner enjoying passionate sexual intercourse with another person or (2) imagining their partner forming a deep emotional attachment to another person. The results revealed that 60% of men selected the sexual option as more distressing, whereas only 17% of women selected the sexual option. In other words, men tended to select the sexual option as worse than the emotional option (60% sexual vs. 40% emotional), whereas women overwhelmingly selected the emotional option (83% emotional vs. 17% sexual). A subsequent study also found that men exhibited greater autonomic arousal (a physiological measure of distress) in response to the sexual than the emotional infidelity scenario, whereas women again exhibited the opposite pattern. In short, the situations that inspire jealousy may differ for men and women, and this sex difference is consistent with the evolutionary psychological perspective that the sexes have evolved different solutions to sex-specific adaptive problems.

Short-Term versus Long-Term Sexual Strategies

As noted at the beginning of this chapter, humans mate outside of long-term pair bonds; some mating relationships can last for very short periods of time and involve little or no emotional and material investment. This distinction between short-term and long-term mating is a key component of sexual strategies theory (Buss & Schmitt, 1993). Sexual strategies theory also draws from the parental investment logic (Trivers, 1972) to arrive at the prediction that men and women should differentially emphasize the amount of time and effort that they devote to short-term strategies. The investment required by women in gestating, nursing, and raising offspring is considerably higher than that required for men, and thus the upper ceiling on a man's reproductive success is conceivably limited only by the number of sexual partners he can attract. After all, it is possible, in principle, for a man to sire an offspring after just one act of copulation, and men who desired and successfully pursued large numbers of short-term sexual relationships would achieve greater reproductive success than a woman who pursued a similar strategy. Therefore, men should desire large numbers of short-term sexual relationships to a greater extent than women do, as ancestral women could not have appreciably increased their own reproductive success by using a short-term strategy.

Buss and Schmitt (1993) reported results from several studies that were consistent with this prediction. For example, although the sexes did not differ in the extent to which they claim they are currently seeking a long-term partner, men were more likely than women to report that they were seeking a short-term partner. Also, men reported on average that they desired a larger number of sexual partners than women did: Over a lifetime, men desired approximately 18 partners on average, whereas women desired 4–5 partners. Another indication of men's desire to acquire a large number of sexual partners is reflected in their relaxed standards for a short-term mate. Indeed, men were more likely than women to report that they would be willing to have a sexual relationship with a partner they had known for only a short period of time (e.g., 1 week). All three of these sex differences also emerged in a subsequent 52-nation study that sampled more than 16,000 participants (Schmitt et al., 2003).

One fascinating study, by Clark and Hatfield (1989), examined men's and women's willingness to have a sexual encounter with a previously unknown individual after a genuine face-to-face request. In this study, research assistants initiated contact with attractive individuals on a college campus by saying, "I have been noticing you around campus. I find you to be very attractive." They then followed up this contact with one of three questions: "Would you go out with me tonight?", "Would you come over to my apartment tonight?", or "Would you go to bed with me tonight?" Approximately 50% of both sexes were likely to say "yes" to the simple "go out" request. However, men were much more likely than women to say "yes" to the "apartment" request (69% vs. 3%) and "bed" request (72% vs. 0%). Although few people commonly encounter such bold solicitations, the participants believed the requests to be genuine, and the data clearly demonstrated that men were more interested than women in having a sexual encounter with someone they did not really know.

Some of the most comprehensive data on sex differences in the emphasis on short-term relationships is found in the literature on *sociosexuality*, an individual difference that refers to people's tendency or willingness to have short-term, uncommitted sexual relationships. Common measures of sociosexuality (e.g., Simpson & Gangestad, 1991) ask respondents to indicate how many partners they foresee themselves having sex with during the next 5 years and the extent to which they agree with statements such as "Sex without love is OK." In the same 52-nation data set investigated by Schmitt and colleagues (2005), men reported a more unrestricted sociosexual orientation (i.e., a greater willingness to have short-term uncommitted sex) than women across all the cultures sampled. The weight of the evidence indicates that men are more interested in short-term sexual relationships than women, and this sex difference could reflect sex-differentiated mental adaptations that evolved in response to parental investment considerations (Trivers, 1972).

Other Classic Evolutionary Psychological Topics

Above and beyond the "big three" (i.e., mate preferences, jealousy, and short-term sexual strategies), evolutionary psychologists made other novel empirical contributions to the study of mating throughout the 1990s. Many of these studies documented sex differences that were similarly consistent with the parental investment logic: men emphasize their resources and women emphasize their physical attractiveness when trying to attract new mates (Buss, 1988) and retain their current mates (Buss & Shackelford, 1997). Similarly, when people attempt to attract a mate who is already in a relationship with someone else (i.e., mate "poaching"), resource-demonstration tactics are judged more effective for men and appearance-enhancement tactics more effective for women (Schmitt & Buss, 2001). Other programs of research blended the short-term versus long-term distinction with the study of mate preferences, finding that sex differences in the qualities people desire in romantic partners are especially prominent in short-term contexts (Kenrick, Groth, Trost, & Sadalla, 1993). Finally, even though the ideal attractiveness standard for women's weight has varied over time (Barber, 1998) and across cultures (J. L. Anderson, Crawford, Nadeau, & Lindberg, 1992), an influential program of research suggested that a waist-to-hip ratio of approximately 0.7 in women may be a consistent predictor of attractiveness across time and cultures (Singh, 1993; Singh & Luis, 1995).

Limitations of Classic Evolutionary Psychological Findings

The programs of research reviewed previously were extremely influential in elevating the evolutionary perspective to the forefront of modern empirical psychology. Currently, most psychologists are comfortable with the idea that human behavior can be elucidated by the evolutionary program known as adaptationism—the general research strategy that seeks to identify adaptations that were produced by natural selection (Andrews, Gangestad, & Matthews, 2002)—and psychologists routinely rely on such functional reasoning to make predictions and explain data. Furthermore, evolutionary psychology successfully generated a host of novel predictions throughout its first decade of prominence (Buss & Reeve, 2003).

Nevertheless, elements of the evolutionary psychological program of research have sparked healthy and vigorous academic debate. For one, some evolutionary psychological findings are subject to alternative explanations that do not rely on domain-specific naturally selected mechanisms. Social role theory is one leading alternative framework (Eagly & Wood, 1999; Wood & Eagly, 2002). Social role theory suggests that the behaviors of men and women differ because each sex acquires through development and socialization the traits and preferences that best equip them for their anticipated roles. As women are more likely than men to fulfill homemaker/caretaker roles and men are more likely than women to fulfill provider roles in most industrialized societies, social role theory predicts that men and women will differentially adopt the traits and preferences that facilitate their performance of these roles (e.g., nurturance for women, ambition for men). Furthermore, these sex differences eventually become enshrined in broader gender roles, and these gender roles in turn shape people's expectations about how the sexes do and should behave in general (Prentice & Carranza, 2002). Consistent with this perspective, Eagly and Wood (1999) reanalyzed Buss's 37-cultures data (1989) and found that sex differences in the preference for good financial prospects and youth in a mate were smaller in countries that had greater gender equality. In other words, when the roles performed by men and women in a society were more similar, their romantic partner preferences were similar as well (see also Kasser &

Sharma, 1999). Subsequent research has demonstrated that many evolutionary psychological effects vary across cultures, such as the sociosexuality (Schmitt et al., 2005) and waist-to-hip ratio (Yu & Shepard, 1998) findings noted previously, and this cross-cultural variability can be explained by appealing to both evolutionary and social role perspectives (Eastwick, 2013; Gangestad, Haselton, & Buss, 2006).

Other findings have challenged whether the evolutionary sex differences have the functional implications assumed by the adaptationist perspective. Many of these challenges originated as methodological concerns: The sex differences research, for example, relied heavily on self-reported preferences and decontextualized, hypothetical scenarios (Clark & Hatfield, 1989, is a prominent exception). This literature ultimately intersected little with a decades-long, methodologically strong tradition of relationship science that examines how people initiate and maintain romantic relationships in their actual everyday lives (Berscheid, 1999; Reis, 2007). Initially, some evolutionary psychologists were openly hostile to the relationships approach, considering it "simplistic" and suggesting that relationships theories had "failed miserably" (Buss & Reeve, 2003, p. 849). However, without demonstrations that the evolutionary sex differences also describe people's actual mating relationships, assumptions about their function and adaptive relevance remain speculative.

In fact, recent research from the relationships tradition paints a different picture than the evolutionary psychological approach for some topics. For example, if men desire physical attractiveness in a romantic partner more than women and women desire earning prospects in a romantic partner more than men, the functional rationale predicts that these traits should differentially inspire men's and women's romantic interest in real-life romantic partners. That is, the physical attractiveness of a potential partner should be a stronger predictor of men's than women's romantic interest in that partner (e.g., men should strongly prefer attractive to unattractive partners, whereas women should only slightly prefer attractive to unattractive partners); the opposite pattern should exist for earning prospects. However, recent research has failed to find evidence for these sex differences (Eastwick & Finkel, 2008): Physical attractiveness predicts romantic interest equally for men and women (r's = ~.40), and earning prospects predicts romantic interest equally for men and women (r's = ~.20). Thus, people's mate preference ratings for specific traits may not be guiding their actual romantic choices (see also Eastwick, Eagly, Finkel, & Johnson, 2011; Eastwick, Finkel, & Eagly, 2011).

The jealousy research has encountered similar predictive difficulties. For one, the jealousy sex differences tend not to emerge when people report on actual past infidelity experiences; in these cases, both men and women focus on the emotional aspects of the infidelity more than the sexual aspects (Harris, 2002). Furthermore, findings in the relationships research tradition suggest (perhaps counterintuitively) that people's relationships are actually better off when they *neglect* a potential relationship threat, not when they notice the threat and take action against it (Simpson, Ickes, & Blackstone, 1995; Simpson, Ickes, & Grich, 1999). In fact, people experience decreases in closeness and are more likely to break up to the extent that they accurately attend to threats (Simpson et al., 1999; Simpson, Orina, & Ickes, 2003). This corpus of research is inconsistent with an (unproven) assumption of the functional evolutionary perspective: the hypothesis that jealousy causes people to successfully guard their relationships against threats like sexual and emotional infidelity.

Another consequence of the lack of overlap between evolutionary psychology and relationship science is that adult attachment research (e.g., Hazan & Shaver, 1994) and evolutionary psychology proceeded in largely separate streams during the 1990s. Thus, evolutionary psychology did not extensively consider the attachment bond in its portrayal of human mating processes. Of course, evolutionary psychology did examine long-term mating; long-term mating is a vital component of sexual strategies theory (Buss & Schmitt, 1993), for example. However, in the classic evolutionary psychological studies, long-term mating was largely about men's ability to provide resources and defend against possible rivals to achieve paternity certainty. Thus, evolutionary psychologists acknowledged long-term relationships without examining the adaptive benefits of the attachment bond, such as emotional coregulation and social support processes (Zeifman, Chapter 2, this volume). Hazan and Diamond (2000) suggested that pair bonds are more likely to be the "species-typical" form of long-term mating than the pairing of young women with wealthy men, and they challenged scholars to incorporate both evolutionary and attachment considerations into their models of human mating. This challenge inspired a new generation of researchers, and in the decade that followed, the evolutionary and attachment perspectives started to converge (Eastwick, 2009; see Phylogeny and Evolutionary Psychology, p. 151).

EVOLUTIONARY PSYCHOLOGY, THE NEXT GENERATION: STRATEGIC TRADE-OFFS

The long-term versus short-term mating distinction highlighted by Buss and Schmitt (1993) suggests a trade-off in how humans spend their mating-related energies. That is, people can expend effort pursuing short-term casual sex, or they can pursue long-term relationships that would also have entailed some degree of parental caregiving. This postulate was also central to parental investment theory (Trivers, 1972): An investment of time and resources in a current offspring (i.e., parenting effort) comes at the cost of investing time and resources in the creation of additional offspring (i.e., mating effort). As mating effort can lead to greater reproductive success for men than for women, men express more interest in short-term relationships than women do, as discussed previously.

Strategic Pluralism Theory

Gangestad and Simpson's (2000) strategic pluralism theory offered an important extension of the trade-off logic: specifically, that trade-offs between mating and parenting effort apply not only between sex (e.g., men vs. women) but also within sex. Some ancestral men, given their natural gifts and proclivities, might have been able to achieve reproductive success through short-term casual sex, and so these men practiced a short-term strategy. Yet other men might not have been able to pursue a short-term strategy successfully, and instead they, like most women, favored a long-term approach to mating relationships. This insight offers an important caveat to the Buss and Schmitt (1993) sex difference in the pursuit of short-term mating: Men's greater desire of short-term relationships does not mean that the pursuit of short-term relationships would have been an adaptive strategy for all men. In fact, most men might have experienced the greatest benefit from a long-term strategy.

The first major issue for strategic pluralism theory to address was the a priori identification of men who were likely to pursue and achieve success using a short-term mating strategy. Gangestad and Simpson (2000) turned to good-genes sexual selection for guidance. According to models of good-genes sexual selection in nonhumans (Andersson, 1986; Kirkpatrick, 1996), some genes increase an organism's fitness because they help the organism to fight pathogens and resist disease, and organisms might signal to potential mates that they possess such beneficial genes through observable indicators. One such indicator is fluctuating asymmetry (FA), or the degree to which an organism's bilateral features (e.g., ears, feet, hands) are discrepant in size (e.g., the left ear is longer than the right). Greater FA is associated with deviations from the optimal developmental trajectory, perhaps reflecting the organism's inability to resist pathogens or affliction with a large number of deleterious mutations (Møller & Swaddle, 1997). Given that FA is partially heritable (Møller & Thornhill, 1997), female humans might have evolved a preference for low FA (i.e., more symmetry) in mates because their offspring could benefit from the "good genes" that men with low FA possess. Therefore, FA should be negatively associated with the use of short-term, casual-sex strategies in men, as low-FA symmetrical men are the ones who are likely to be desirable to women for their genetic endowment alone.

Several studies have documented evidence in support of this hypothesis. For example, men who are low in FA (i.e., more symmetrical) report greater sociosexuality, have more sex partners, and are more likely to have sex at a younger age than men who are high in FA (Gangestad & Simpson, 2000; Thornhill & Gangestad, 1994). Low FA in men is also associated with the tendency to be selected by women as extra-pair sex partners (Gangestad & Thornhill, 1997). In addition, FA is associated with traits that might facilitate successful competition with other men for mates, such as physicality and social dominance (Gangestad & Simpson, 2000). Indeed, one study found that men with lower FA were more likely to use dominant tactics (e.g., derogating a rival male) than men high in FA when competing for a date (Simpson, Gangestad, Christensen, & Leck, 1999). In summary, symmetry (i.e., low FA) may be an indicator of the extent to which human males possess genes that help them to resist pathogens, compete with other males, and ultimately implement a short-term sexual strategy.

Evolutionary scholars have documented other physical indicators beyond FA that predict men's preferences for certain types of relationships. For example, the ratio of index finger length to ring finger length (2D:4D) is a rough indicator of the amount of estrogen relative to testosterone to which an individual was exposed prenatally. Specifically, a shorter index finger relative to the ring finger (i.e., a smaller 2D:4D ratio) indicates that prenatal testosterone had a large influence on an individual's brain during fetal development (Malas, Dogan, Hilal Evcil, & Desdicioglu, 2006; Manning, 2002). Schwarz, Mustafíc, Hassebrauck, and Jörg (2011) found that male participants' 2D:4D finger-length ratio predicted their orientation toward short-term relationships: Men were more willing to have multiple casual-sex partners to the extent that they had a smaller 2D:4D. Female participants did not show this same pattern. As prenatal testosterone is also associated with traits like masculinity and dominance, which facilitate successful competition with other men (Neave, Laing, Fink, & Manning, 2003), 2D:4D may be another morphological indicator of men's likelihood of implementing a short-term mating strategy.

However, women are not simply the passive recipients of men's sexual strategies. On the contrary, strategic pluralism theory suggests that women should adaptively negotiate trade-offs between short-term and long-term mating as well. If women can extract genetic benefits from certain men by engaging in short-term mating with them, such a strategy might have been adaptive under certain circumstances, even if it meant that the woman would receive little long-term investment from such a mate. For example, women who receive insufficient parental care during childhood might later come to believe that they will be unable to find a mate who can invest in their offspring (Belsky, Steinberg, & Draper, 1991); thus, a mate with good genes might be an optimal choice under such circumstances. One recent line of research has pursued female choice in considerable detail, examining how shifts in women's ovulatory cycles are related to the short-term versus long-term trade-off. We now turn to this burgeoning literature.

Ovulatory Shifts

The female in many primate species gives a clear visual indication that she is ovulating (e.g., sex skin swellings among baboons), but human females do not (Burley, 1979). Yet the timing of ovulation may be relevant to *Homo sapiens'* mating behavior, and evolutionary scholars have explored whether the behaviors and preferences of naturally cycling women (i.e., women who do not use hormonal forms of contraception) vary depending on ovulatory cycle phase (Gangestad, Thornhill, & Garver-Apgar, 2005). As women are most likely to conceive when they have intercourse just prior to ovulation (approximately midcycle; Wilcox, Duncan, Weinberg, Trussell, & Baird, 2001), they might have evolved a tendency to pursue good genes for their offspring at this point in their menstrual cycle.

Several scent preference studies have produced data consistent with this hypothesis. In one compelling demonstration (Gangestad & Thornhill, 1998), men wore t-shirts for two nights without using scented products and subsequently returned the t-shirts to the experimenters. At a separate session, women then rated the attractiveness of the smell of the t-shirts. Women who were close to ovulation revealed a preference for the scent of the men who were low in FA—the symmetrical men—over the men who were high in FA (see also Thornhill & Gangestad, 1999). According to models of good-genes sexual selection, low-FA men have genes that promote robust, healthy development. Therefore, women's ovulatory shift in preference for the smell of these men is consistent with the strategic pluralism theory postulate that women may have evolved to seek out the genes of symmetrical men for their offspring specifically when they are likely to conceive. Other scent-preference studies have revealed that fertile women, especially those who are single, prefer the scent of men who rate themselves as dominant (Havlíček, Roberts, & Flegr, 2005).

Researchers have also documented ovulatory shifts in women's preferences for other attributes in men. For example, women viewed videos of men competing for a date and found certain personality traits to be more or less attractive depending on ovulatory cycle phase (Gangestad, Garver-Apgar, Simpson, & Cousins, 2007). Specifically, women rated traits such as physical attractiveness, muscularity, and social respectability as particularly attractive in a short-term mating partner (but not a long-term partner) when they were most fertile. Highly fertile women also judged men to be especially desirable for a short-term relationship when the men behaved in a dominant manner toward other men (Gangestad, Simpson, Cousins, Garver-Apgar, & Christensen, 2004) and when the men's voices had a low pitch (Puts, 2005). Similarly, women rated masculine male faces as desirable for short-term (but not long-term) relationships when they were close to ovulation (Jones et al., 2008).

These studies collectively suggest that women, during the fertile phase of their cycle, might seek particular men as short-term partners who have genes that promote health and successful intrasexual competition. But do ovulatory shifts emerge if women already have a relationship partner? A number of studies have examined possible trade-offs between the benefits women receive from a current partner and a possible extra-pair partner. For example, women who were dating unattractive men reported in a daily diary study that they were more attracted to and flirtatious with other potential partners when they were fertile than when they were not fertile (Haselton & Gangestad, 2006). Women who were dating attractive men did not reveal the same ovulatory shift in their attraction to extra-pair partners. Similarly, researchers have also explored ovulatory shifts in women's desire for similarity in major histocompatibility complex (MHC) genes. Organisms that have diverse MHC genes tend to have healthier immune systems; thus, a woman's relationship partner who happened to share her MHC genes might present more of a genetic liability for her offspring than a partner who did not. Indeed, one study found that women were more attracted to and more likely to engage in extra-pair sex with alternative partners when they shared MHC genes with their current partner than when their partner's MHC genes were dissimilar (Garver-Apgar, Gangestad, Thornhill, Miller, & Olp, 2006). These results suggest that ovulatory shifts might have been designed by natural selection to encourage women to pursue desirable genes, especially if her current partner does not offer the same genetic benefits.

Women demonstrate other behavioral differences across the menstrual cycle as well. In one study, researchers asked women to draw pictures of the clothing that they would want to wear to a social event that evening.

They found that when the women were close to ovulation, they drew more revealing clothing than when they were in the nonfertile phase of their cycle (Durante, Li, & Haselton, 2008). In another study, independent judges examined photographs of women taken during the fertile and nonfertile phases their cycles, and guessed 60% of the time that the women were trying to look attractive in the photograph taken at high fertility (Haselton, Mortenzaie, Pillsworth, Bleske-Rechek, & Frederick, 2007). Furthermore, an eye-tracking study found that women close to ovulation looked at attractive men longer than did women who were not in the fertile phase of their cycle (U. S. Anderson et al., 2010). These studies suggest that women may use subtle cues such as clothing and eye contact to communicate sexual interest when fertile.

Finally, several studies have suggested that men's judgments about women differ depending on the woman's ovulatory cycle phase. For example, men rate women's voices as increasingly attractive as women approach ovulation (Pipitone & Gallup, 2008). Also, men find the scent of fertile women to be particularly appealing, and men's testosterone, a hormone that facilitates mating effort, increases after smelling t-shirts worn by ovulating women (S. L. Miller & Maner, 2010b; Thornhill et al., 2003). Men also demonstrate behavioral changes in mating contexts depending on women's fertility status. In one study, researchers found that female lap dancers received more money in tips the closer they were to ovulation (G. Miller, Tybur, & Jordan, 2007). Another study found that men made riskier decisions in a game of blackjack when in the presence of an ovulating versus a nonovulating female confederate (S. L. Miller & Maner, 2011). Furthermore, these men were also more likely to engage in the affiliative behavior of mimicry when interacting with the ovulating capered with the nonovulating woman. These results suggest that men may be more motivated to try to impress and win the affections of women to the extent that the women are close to ovulation.

In summary, strategic pluralism theory has inspired a productive line of research on women's ovulatory cycles and generated considerable interest in within-sex variation in mating strategies. This research program has employed an impressive variety of methods: For example, the studies reviewed in this section successfully incorporated physiological and hormonal assessments to explain mating phenomena, and like the Clark and Hatfield (1989) study, much of this work has examined participants' evaluations of real-life potential partners. Furthermore, the findings have generally converged on theoretically sensible conclusions. This new generation of evolutionary psychological research, however, has yet to dovetail substantially with relationship science and attachment theory. Thus, pair bonds and other attachment-related processes have not yet been integrated with strategic pluralism theory. Nevertheless, new work that preserves the methodological strengths of this new evolutionary literature has recently started to highlight the possible synthesis of relationship science and evolutionary psychology.

BUILDING CONNECTIONS WITH THE SOCIAL PSYCHOLOGY OF ROMANTIC RELATIONSHIPS

Several evolutionary scholars have started to incorporate theories and methods from relationship science, which is a subdiscipline of social psychology (Berscheid & Reis, 1998). We first review several studies using social-cognitive approaches that have focused on early-stage visual perception in mating situations, and then present some work that attempts to integrate evolutionary and attachment topics into a common theoretical framework.

Social-Cognitive Approaches

An extensive program of research by Maner and colleagues has examined how adaptive psychological mechanisms might be evident in the early stages of human social perception. In one study, participants looked at an array of attractive and unattractive faces while wearing an eye-tracking device that determined the precise location of their gaze. Participants on average tended to visually fixate on attractive members of the opposite sex; this attentional bias toward attractive faces was especially pronounced for individuals who were high in sociosexuality (Maner et al., 2003). In another study, this effect was exacerbated when participants were primed with sexual thoughts. That is, participants high in sociosexuality were more likely to direct their attention to attractive opposite-sex faces when sexually aroused relative to a control condition (Maner, Gailliot, Rouby, & Miller, 2007). On the other hand, participants were more likely to direct their attention to attractive *same*-sex faces when they were primed with jealous thoughts, but only to the extent that they described themselves as high in "intrasexual vigilance"—that is, they tended to worry chronically about potential rivals. These studies provide insight into the adaptive functioning of social attention: People tend to focus their attention, albeit unintentionally, on social targets who are relevant to their temporarily active (i.e., mate searching, mate guarding) and chronically active (i.e., sociosexuality, intrasexual vigilance) goals.

Maner's work on visual attention has intersected with relationship scholars' research on how people in committed relationships defend against possible temptations. In general, the act of paying attention to attractive alternative partners is not a promising indicator of the health and longevity of one's committed relationship (Rusbult, Martz, & Agnew, 1998). For example, R. S. Miller (1997) found that participants in relationships who chose to look at pictures of attractive members of the opposite sex for longer (vs. shorter) periods of time reported lower levels of relationship satisfaction and were more likely to end their relationships. Maner, Gailliot, and Miller (2009) examined this phenomenon in the early stages of visual perception by using a visual cueing task that required participants to direct their attention away from photos of faces. Among participants who were single, those who were subtly primed with mating words like *kiss* and *lust* were more likely to attend to attractive opposite-sex faces than participants exposed to nonmating control words like *talk* and *floor*. In contrast, participants who were involved in a relationship revealed the opposite pattern: They were less likely to attend to attractive opposite-sex faces when primed with mating words than control words. Participants involved in a romantic relationship were also less likely to attend to attractive opposite-sex faces after writing about a memory of experiencing love for their romantic partner than after writing a control essay about a time they felt happy (Maner, Rouby, & Gonzaga, 2008). A related study found that people in relationships were more likely to quickly label attractive members of the opposite sex as threats in a "shoot/don't shoot" scenario, suggesting that these committed individuals perceive attractive alternative partners as threatening even at an unconscious level (Plant, Kunstman, & Maner, 2010). Finally, a similar effect emerged in the study of men's evaluations of the ovulating or nonovulating female confederate described previously: Men in committed relationships actually rated the attractiveness of the woman as *less* appealing when she was ovulating than when she was not ovulating, suggesting that partnered men automatically engage in relationship-protective behaviors in response to olfactory cues (S. L. Miller & Maner, 2010a).

Taken together, these studies suggest that people exhibit evidence of functional mental adaptations even during the initial, unconscious stages of social perception. In some cases, people exhibit adaptive attentional strategies that help them to locate new potential partners, and in other cases, these adaptive strategies enable them to protect their relationships against possible threats. These new applications of social-cognitive methods and relationships theories to the study of human mating illustrate how evolutionary perspectives can make important contributions to relationship science and vice versa.

Phylogeny and Evolutionary Psychology

The major evolutionary perspectives reviewed in this chapter have focused on the adaptive design of psychological mechanisms in humans. However, this functional perspective does not typically incorporate systematic comparisons between related species or the actual time course of evolutionary events, an approach in evolutionary biology known as *phylogeny*. Scholars have argued that evolutionary hypotheses could be informed by a more detailed consideration of these timing issues (Gosling & Graybeal, 2007). For example, one study that examined phylogenetic relationships among mammals found that pair bonding tended to evolve in species in which paternal care for offspring was prevalent (Fraley, Brumbaugh, & Marks, 2005), lending weight to the hypothesis that pair bonding is an evolved adaptation that encourages paternal contributions to offspring. The phylogenetic perspective has also been applied to the evolution of the self (Leary & Buttermore, 2003) and spatial cognition (Wynn, 2002) in humans and can help scholars to make more informed adaptive hypotheses.

Eastwick (2009) argued that information about the time course of human evolution could generate new predictions about how different components of the mating psychology intersect. Specifically, Eastwick (2009) proposed that adaptations for adult attachment bonds could have evolved to counteract some older features of the human mating psyche. As mentioned earlier, natural selection generated adult pair bonds as an adaptive solution to encourage paternal investment in offspring about 1.5 to 2 million years ago around the emergence of the genus *Homo*. However, other mating-relevant adaptations already existed in the minds of early members of *Homo*, and natural selection would be unlikely to or unable to eliminate some of these adaptations, even if they worked at cross-purposes with the pair bond. Therefore, adult pair bonds might function as an "adaptive workaround" that serves as an evolutionary corrective to older adaptations. Specifically, attachment bonds might function to mute or refocus the effects of older adaptations—even adaptations that typically facilitated intra- or intersexual competition—toward the new adaptive purpose of protecting and strengthening the attachment bond.

Some recent evidence is consistent with this adaptive workaround logic. For example, the hormone testosterone promotes mating effort in primates and predated the evolution of the pair bond in the *Homo* lineage. However, testosterone could have produced maladaptive effects by directing mating activities away from an existing pair bond. Consistent with the hypothesis that attachment bonds can function as an adaptive workaround, several studies have demonstrated that men's testosterone levels decrease when they are involved in a relationship and increase when they become single again (Gray et al., 2004; Mazur & Michalek, 1998). Relationship status (single vs. partnered) is a weak indicator of attachment bond activation, however, as people can be in committed relationships without experiencing strong attachment to their partner. Intriguingly, one study found that men's testosterone levels were lower to the extent that they invested in and spent time with their spouse, a better indicator of the presence of an attachment bond (Gray, Kahlenberg, Barrett, Lipson, & Ellison, 2002). These findings are consistent with the hypothesis that attachment bonds, when activated, will mute the influence of prior adaptations that have the potential to work at cross-purposes with the attachment bond.

Other recent data suggest that attachment bonds might refocus the effects of earlier adaptations toward the entirely new adaptive purpose of maintaining or strengthening the bond. One set of studies examined whether adaptations associated with ovulatory shifts, which also predate the evolution of pair bonds in hominids, might serve a different function when attachment bonds are activated (Eastwick & Finkel, 2012). Women reported the strength of their attachment bonds to their current partner by agreeing or disagreeing with items like "When I am away from my partner, I feel down" and "My partner is the first person that I would turn to if I had a problem." They also reported the extent to which they wanted to have romantic physical intimacy (e.g., intimate or emotionally fulfilling sex) with their current partner, a behavior that can strengthen an attachment bond (Hazan & Diamond, 2000). To the extent that a woman's attachment bond to her current partner was strong, she was actually more likely to desire romantic physical intimacy with her partner when she was fertile than when she was not fertile. In other words, even though ovulatory adaptations can increase women's desire for "good genes" under many circumstances as reviewed previously, they can also be co-opted by a strong attachment bond, sending women in search not of good genes but of attachment-building sex with her current partner. These findings lend weight to the phylogenetic concept of the "adaptive workaround" and hint at how attachment processes might intersect with mating features typically associated with evolutionary psychology.

CONCLUSION

The evolutionary psychological perspective has been both productive and influential: Many scholars discovered new findings under the guidance of the adaptive framework of evolutionary psychology, and functional reasoning is now commonplace throughout psychological science. The early evolutionary psychological focus on sex differences has been supplemented over the past decade by additional considerations of within-sex differences in mating strategies. Furthermore, this recent work has laudable methodological strengths in that it examines hormones and physiology in addition to self-reports. New directions in evolutionary psychological research promise a stronger integration of evolutionary psychology with relationship science, a subdiscipline of social psychology that examines how people form and maintain the pair bond. Scholars from these two traditions are frequently interested in similar questions about human mating, and their efforts to explain these mysteries should become more synergistic in the years to come.

REFERENCES

Anderson, J. L., Crawford, C. B., Nadeau, J., & Lindberg, T. (1992). Was the Duchess of Windsor right? A cross-cultural review of the socioecology of ideals of female body shape. *Ethology and Sociobiology, 13*, 197–227.

Anderson, U. S., Perea, E. F., Becker, D. V., Ackerman, J. M., Shapiro, J. R., Neuberg, S. L., et al. (2010). I only have eyes for you: Ovulation redirects attention (but not memory) to attractive men. *Journal of Experimental Social Psychology, 46*, 804–808.

Andersson, M. (1986). Evolution of condition-dependent sex ornaments and mating preferences: Sexual selection based on viability differences. *Evolution, 40*, 804–816.

Andrews, P. W., Gangestad, S. W., & Matthews, D. (2002). Adaptationism: How to carry out an exaptationist program. *Behavioral and Brain Sciences, 25*, 489–553.

Barash, D. P., & Lipton, J. E. (2001). *Myth of monogamy: Fidelity and infidelity in animals and people.* New York: Freeman.

Barber, N. (1998). Secular changes in standards of bodily attractiveness in women: Tests of a reproductive model. *International Journal of Eating Disorders, 23*, 449–454.

Belsky, J., Steinberg, L., & Draper, P. (1991). Childhood experience, interpersonal development, and reproductive strategy: An evolutionary theory of socialization. *Child Development, 62*, 647–670.

Berscheid, E. (1999). The greening of relationship science. *American Psychologist, 54*, 260–266.

Berscheid, E., & Reis, H. T. (1998). Attraction and close relationships. In D. T. Gilbert, S. T. Fiske, & G. Lindzey (Eds.), *The handbook of social psychology* (4th ed., Vol. 2, pp. 193–281). New York: McGraw-Hill.

Burley, N. (1979). The evolution of concealed ovulation. *American Naturalist, 114*, 835–858.

Buss, D. M. (1988). The evolution of human intrasexual competition: Tactics of mate attraction. *Journal of Personality and Social Psychology, 54*, 616–628.

Buss, D. M. (1989). Sex differences in human mate preferences: Evolutionary hypotheses tested in 37 cultures. *Behavioral and Brain Sciences, 12*, 1–49.

Buss, D. M. (1992). Mate preference mechanisms: Consequences for partner choice and intrasexual competition. In J. H. Barkow, L. Cosmides, & J. Tooby (Eds.), *The adapted mind: Evolutionary psychology and the generation of culture* (pp. 249–266). New York: Oxford University Press.

Buss, D. M., & Barnes, M. (1986). Preferences in human mate selection. *Journal of Personality and Social Psychology, 50*, 559–570.

Buss, D. M., Haselton, M. G., Shackelford, T. K., Bleske, A. L., & Wakefield, J. C. (1998). Adaptations, exaptations, and spandrels. *American Psychologist, 53*, 533–548.

Buss, D. M., Larsen, R. J., Westen, D., & Semmelroth, J. (1992). Sex differences in jealousy: Evolution, physiology, and psychology. *Psychological Science, 3*, 251–255.

Buss, D. M., & Reeve, H. K. (2003). Evolutionary psychology and developmental dynamics: Comment on Lickliter and Honeycutt (2003). *Psychological Bulletin, 129*, 848–853.

Buss, D. M., & Schmitt, D. P. (1993). Sexual strategies theory: An evolutionary perspective on human mating. *Psychological Review, 100*, 204–232.

Buss, D. M., & Shackelford, T. K. (1997). From vigilance to violence: Mate retention tactics in married couples. *Journal of Personality and Social Psychology, 72*, 346–361.

Cassidy, J. E., & Shaver, P. R. (2008). *Handbook of attachment: Theory, research, and clinical applications* (2nd ed.). New York: Guilford Press.

Clark, R. D., & Hatfield, E. (1989). Gender differences in receptivity to sexual offers. *Journal of Psychology and Human Sexuality, 2*, 39–55.

Cooper, M. L., Shapiro, C. M., & Powers, A. M. (1998). Motivations for sex and risky sexual behavior among adolescents and young adults: A functional perspective. *Journal of Personality and Social Psychology, 75*, 1528–1558.

Cosmides, L. (1989). The logic of social exchange: Has natural selection shaped how humans reason? Studies with the Wason selection task. *Cognition, 31*, 187–276.

Cosmides, L., & Tooby, J. (2005). Neurocognitive adaptations designed for social exchange. In D. M. Buss (Ed.), *The handbook of evolutionary psychology* (pp. 584–627). Hoboken, NJ: Wiley.

Darwin, C. (1859). *On the origin of species by means of natural selection*. London: Murray.

Driscoll, C. (2004). Can behaviors be adaptations? *Philosophy of Science, 71*, 16–35.

Durante, K. M., Li, N. P., & Haselton, M. G. (2008). Changes in women's choice of dress across the ovulatory cycle: Naturalistic and laboratory task-based evidence. *Personality and Social Psychology Bulletin, 34*, 1451–1460.

Eagly, A. H., & Wood, W. (1999). The origins of sex differences in human behavior: Evolved dispositions versus social roles. *American Psychologist, 54*, 408–423.

Eastwick, P. W. (2009). Beyond the Pleistocene: Using phylogeny and constraint to inform the evolutionary psychology of human mating. *Psychological Bulletin, 135*, 794–821.

Eastwick, P. W. (2013). Cultural influences on attraction. In J. A. Simpson & L. Campbell (Eds.), *Oxford handbook of close relationships* (pp. 161–182). New York: Oxford University Press.

Eastwick, P. W., Eagly, A. H., Finkel, E. J., & Johnson, S. E. (2011). Implicit and explicit preferences for physical attractiveness in a romantic partner: A double dissociation in predictive validity. *Journal of Personality and Social Psychology, 101*, 993–1011.

Eastwick, P. W., & Finkel, E. J. (2008). Sex differences in mate preferences revisited: Do people know what they initially desire in a romantic partner? *Journal of Personality and Social Psychology, 94*, 245–264.

Eastwick, P. W., & Finkel, E. J. (2012). The evolutionary armistice: Attachment bonds moderate the function of ovulatory cycle effects. *Personality and Social Psychology Bulletin, 38*, 174–184.

Eastwick, P. W., Finkel, E. J., & Eagly, A. H. (2011). When and why do ideal partner preferences affect the process of initiating and maintaining romantic relationships? *Journal of Personality and Social Psychology, 101*, 1012–1032.

Feingold, A. (1990). Gender differences in effects of physical attractiveness on romantic attraction: A comparison across five research paradigms. *Journal of Personality and Social Psychology, 59*, 981–993.

Feingold, A. (1992). Gender differences in mate selection preferences: A test of the parental investment model. *Psychological Bulletin, 112*, 125–139.

Fraley, R. C., Brumbaugh, C. C., & Marks, M. J. (2005). The evolution and function of adult attachment: A comparative and phylogenetic analysis. *Journal of Personality and Social Psychology, 89*, 731–746.

Gangestad, S. W., Garver-Apgar, C. E., Simpson, J. A., & Cousins, A. J. (2007). Changes in women's mate preferences across the ovulatory cycle. *Journal of Personality and Social Psychology, 92*, 151–163.

Gangestad, S. W., Haselton, M. G., & Buss, D. M. (2006). Evolutionary foundations of cultural variation: Evoked culture and mate preferences. *Psychological Inquiry, 17*, 75–95.

Gangestad, S. W., & Simpson, J. A. (2000). The evolution of human mating: Trade-offs and strategic pluralism. *Behavioral and Brain Sciences, 23*, 573–644.

Gangestad, S. W., Simpson, J. A., Cousins, A. J., Garver-Apgar, C. E., & Christensen, P. (2004). Women's preferences for male behavioral displays change across the menstrual cycle. *Psychological Science, 15*, 203–206.

Gangestad, S. W., & Thornhill, R. (1997). The evolutionary psychology of extra-pair sex: The role of fluctuating asymmetry. *Evolution and Human Behavior, 18*, 69–88.

Gangestad, S. W., & Thornhill, R. (1998). Menstrual cycle variation in women's preference for the scent of symmetrical men. *Proceedings of the Royal Society of London: B. Biological Sciences, 265*, 927–933.

Gangestad, S. W., Thornhill, R., & Garver-Apgar, C. E. (2005). Adaptations to ovulation: Implications for sexual and social behavior. *Current Directions in Psychological Science, 14,* 312–316.

Garver-Apgar, C. E., Gangestad, S. W., Thornhill, R., Miller, R. D., & Olp, J. J. (2006). Major histocompatibility complex alleles, sexual responsivity, and unfaithfulness in romantic couples. *Psychological Science, 17,* 830–835.

Geary, D. C. (2000). Evolution and proximate expression of human paternal investment. *Psychological Bulletin, 126,* 55–77.

Gosling, S. D., & Graybeal, A. (2007). Tree thinking: A new paradigm for integrating comparative data in psychology. *Journal of General Psychology, 134,* 259–277.

Gray, P. B., & Anderson, K. G. (2010). *Fatherhood: Evolution and human paternal behavior.* Cambridge, MA: Harvard University Press.

Gray, P. B., Chapman, J. F., Burnham, T. C., McIntyre, M. H., Lipson, S. F., & Ellison, P. T. (2004). Human male pair bonding and testosterone. *Human Nature, 15,* 119–131.

Gray, P. B., Kahlenberg, S. M., Barrett, E. S., Lipson, S. F., & Ellison, P. T. (2002). Marriage and fatherhood are associated with lower testosterone in males. *Evolution and Human Behavior, 23,* 193–201.

Harris, C. R. (2002). Sexual and romantic jealousy in heterosexual and homosexual adults. *Psychological Science, 13,* 7–12.

Haselton, M. G., & Gangestad, S. W. (2006). Conditional expression of women's desires and men's mate guarding across the ovulatory cycle. *Hormones and Behavior, 49,* 509–518.

Haselton, M. G., Mortezaie, M., Pillsworth, E. G., Bleske-Rechek, A., & Frederick, D. A. (2007). Ovulatory shifts in human female ornamentation: Near ovulation, women dress to impress. *Hormones and Behavior, 51,* 40–45.

Havlíček, J., Roberts, S. C., & Flegr, J. (2005). Women's preference for dominant male odour: Effects of menstrual cycle and relationship status. *Biology Letters, 1,* 256–259.

Hazan, C., & Diamond, L. M. (2000). The place of attachment in human mating. *Review of General Psychology, 4,* 186–204.

Hazan, C., & Shaver, P. R. (1994). Attachment as an organizational framework for research on close relationships. *Psychological Inquiry, 5,* 1–22.

Hill, R. (1945). Campus values in mate-selection. *Journal of Home Economics, 37,* 554–558.

Jones, B. C., DeBruine, L. M., Perrett, D. I., Little, A. C., Feinberg, D. R., & Law Smith, M. J. (2008). Effects of menstrual cycle phase on face preferences. *Archives of Sexual Behavior, 37,* 78–84.

Kasser, T., & Sharma, Y. S. (1999). Reproductive freedom, educational equality, and females' preference for resource-acquisition characteristics in mates. *Psychological Science, 10,* 374–377.

Kenrick, D. T., Groth, G. E., Trost, M. R., & Sadalla, E. K. (1993). Integrating evolutionary and social exchange perspectives on relationships: Effects of gender, self-appraisal, and involvement level on mate selection criteria. *Journal of Personality and Social Psychology, 64,* 951–969.

Kirkpatrick, M. (1996). Good genes and direct selection in the evolution of mating preferences. *Evolution, 50*, 2125–2140.

Leary, M. R., & Buttermore, N. R. (2003). The evolution of the human self: Tracing the natural history of self-awareness. *Journal for the Theory of Social Behaviour, 33*, 365–404.

Malas, M. A., Dogan, S., Hilal Evcil, E., & Desdicioglu, K. (2006). Fetal development of the hand, digits and digit ratio (2d:4d). *Early Human Development, 82*, 469–475.

Maner, J. K., Gailliot, M. T., & Miller, S. L. (2009). The implicit cognition of relationship maintenance: Inattention to attractive alternatives. *Journal of Experimental Social Psychology, 45*, 174–179.

Maner, J. K., Gailliot, M. T., Rouby, D. A., & Miller, S. L. (2007). Can't take my eyes off you: Attentional adhesion to mates and rivals. *Journal of Personality and Social Psychology, 93*, 389–401.

Maner, J. K., Kenrick, D. T., Becker, D., Delton, A. W., Hofer, B., Wilbur, C. J., et al. (2003). Sexually selective cognition: Beauty captures the mind of the beholder. *Journal of Personality and Social Psychology, 85*, 1107–1120.

Maner, J. K., Kenrick, D. T., Becker, D. V., Robertson, T. E., Hofer, B., Neuberg, S. L., et al. (2005). Functional projection: How fundamental social motives can bias interpersonal perception. *Journal of Personality and Social Psychology, 88*, 63–78.

Maner, J. K., Rouby, D. A., & Gonzaga, G. C. (2008). Automatic inattention to attractive alternatives: The evolved psychology of relationship maintenance. *Evolution and Human Behavior, 29*, 343–349.

Manning, J. (2002). *Digit ratio: A pointer to fertility, behavior, and health.* New Brunswick, NJ: Rutgers University Press.

Mazur, A., & Michalek, J. (1998). Marriage, divorce, and male testosterone. *Social Forces, 77*, 315–330.

Miller, G., Tybur, J. M., & Jordan, B. D. (2007). Ovulatory cycle effects on tip earnings by lap dancers: Economic evidence for human estrus? *Evolution and Human Behavior, 28*, 375–381.

Miller, L. C., & Fishkin, S. A. (1997). On the dynamics of human bonding and reproductive success: Seeking windows on the adapted-for human-environmental interface. In J. A. Simpson & D. T. Kenrick (Eds.), *Evolutionary social psychology* (pp. 197–236). Mahwah, NJ: Erlbaum.

Miller, R. S. (1997). Inattentive and contented: Relationship commitment and attention to alternatives. *Journal of Personality and Social Psychology, 73*, 758–766.

Miller, S. L., & Maner, J. K. (2010a). Evolution and relationship maintenance: Fertility cues lead committed men to devalue relationship alternatives. *Journal of Experimental Social Psychology, 46*, 1081–1084.

Miller, S. L., & Maner, J. K. (2010b). Scent of a woman: Men's testosterone responses to olfactory ovulation cues. *Psychological Science, 21*, 276–283.

Miller, S. L., & Maner, J. K. (2011). Ovulation as a male mating prime: Subtle signs of women's fertility influence men's mating cognition and behavior. *Journal of Personality and Social Psychology, 100*, 295–308.

Møller, A. P., & Swaddle, J. P. (1997). *Asymmetry, developmental stability, and evolution*. Oxford, UK: Oxford University Press.

Møller, A. P., & Thornhill, R. (1997). A meta analysis of the heritability of developmental stability. *Journal of Evolutionary Biology, 10*, 1–16.

Neave, N., Laing, S., Fink, B., & Manning, J. T. (2003). Second to fourth digit ratio, testosterone and perceived male dominance. *Proceedings of the Royal Society of London. Series: B. Biological Sciences, 270*, 2167–2172.

Oaten, M., Stevenson, R. J., & Case, T. I. (2009). Disgust as a disease-avoidance mechanism. *Psychological Bulletin, 135*, 303–321.

Pipitone, R. N., & Gallup, G. G. (2008). Women's voice attractiveness varies across the menstrual cycle. *Evolution and Human Behavior, 29*, 268–274.

Plant, E. A., Kunstman, J. W., & Maner, J. K. (2010). You do not only hurt the one you love: Self-protective responses to attractive relationship alternatives. *Journal of Experimental Social Psychology, 46*, 474–477.

Prentice, D. A., & Carranza, E. (2002). What women and men should be, shouldn't be, are allowed to be, and don't have to be: The contents of prescriptive gender stereotypes. *Psychology of Women Quarterly, 26*, 269–281.

Puts, D. A. (2005). Mating context and menstrual phase affect women's preferences for male voice pitch. *Evolution and Human Behavior, 26*, 388–397.

Reis, H. T. (2007). Steps toward the ripening of relationship science. *Personal Relationships, 14*, 1–23.

Rusbult, C. E., Martz, J. M., & Agnew, C. R. (1998). The investment model scale: Measuring commitment level, satisfaction level, quality of alternatives, and investment size. *Personal Relationships, 5*, 357–387.

Schmitt, D. P., Alcalay, L., Allensworth, M., Allik, J., Ault, L., Austers, I., et al. (2003). Universal sex differences in the desire for sexual variety: Tests from 52 nations, 6 continents, and 13 islands. *Journal of Personality and Social Psychology, 85*, 85–104.

Schmitt, D. P., Alcalay, L., Allensworth, M., Allik, J., Ault, L., Austers, I., et al. (2005). Sociosexuality from Argentina to Zimbabwe: A 48-nation study of sex, culture, and the strategies of human mating. *Behavioral and Brain Sciences, 28*, 247–311.

Schmitt, D. P., & Buss, D. M. (2001). Human mate poaching: Tactics and temptations for infiltrating existing mateships. *Journal of Personality and Social Psychology, 80*, 894–917.

Schwarz, S., Mustafíc, M., Hassebrauck, M., & Jörg, J. (2011). Short-and long-term relationship orientation and 2d:4d finger-length ratio. *Archives of Sexual Behavior, 40*, 1–10.

Simpson, J. A., & Gangestad, S. W. (1991). Individual differences in sociosexuality: Evidence for convergent and discriminant validity. *Journal of Personality and Social Psychology, 60*, 870–883.

Simpson, J. A., Gangestad, S. W., Christensen, P. N., & Leck, K. (1999). Fluctuating asymmetry, sociosexuality, and intrasexual competitive tactics. *Journal of Personality and Social Psychology, 76*, 159–172.

Simpson, J. A., Ickes, W., & Blackstone, T. (1995). When the head protects the heart: Empathic accuracy in dating relationships. *Journal of Personality and Social Psychology, 69*, 629–641.

Simpson, J. A., Ickes, W., & Grich, J. (1999). When accuracy hurts: Reactions of anxious-ambivalent dating partners to a relationship-threatening situation. *Journal of Personality and Social Psychology, 76*, 754–769.

Simpson, J. A., Orina, M. M., & Ickes, W. (2003). When accuracy hurts, and when it helps: A test of the empathic accuracy model in marital interactions. *Journal of Personality and Social Psychology, 85*, 881–893.

Singh, D. (1993). Adaptive significance of female physical attractiveness: Role of waist-to-hip ratio. *Journal of Personality and Social Psychology, 65*, 293–307.

Singh, D., & Luis, S. (1995). Ethnic and gender consensus for the effect of waist-to-hip ratio on judgment of women's attractiveness. *Human Nature, 6*, 51–65.

Smith, B. H., & Tompkins, R. L. (1995). Toward a life history of the Hominidae. *Annual Review of Anthropology, 24*, 257–279.

Sprecher, S., Sullivan, Q., & Hatfield, E. (1994). Mate selection preferences: Gender differences examined in a national sample. *Journal of Personality and Social Psychology, 66*, 1074–1080.

Thornhill, R., & Gangestad, S. W. (1994). Human fluctuating asymmetry and sexual behavior. *Psychological Science, 5*, 297–302.

Thornhill, R., & Gangestad, S. W. (1999). The scent of symmetry: A human sex pheromone that signals fitness? *Evolution and Human Behavior, 20*, 175–201.

Thornhill, R., Gangestad, S. W., Miller, R., Scheyd, G., McCollough, J. K., & Franklin, M. (2003). Major histocompatibility complex genes, symmetry, and body scent attractiveness in men and women. *Behavioral Ecology, 14*, 668–678.

Tooby, J., & Cosmides, L. (1992). The psychological foundations of culture. In J. H. Barkow, L. Cosmides, & J. Tooby (Eds.), *The adapted mind: Evolutionary psychology and the generation of culture* (pp. 19–136). New York: Oxford University Press.

Townsend, J. M., & Wasserman, T. (1998). Sexual attractiveness: Sex differences in assessment and criteria. *Evolution and Human Behavior, 19*, 171–191.

Trivers, R. L. (1972). Parental investment and sexual selection. In B. G. Campbell (Ed.), *Sexual selection and the descent of man, 1871–1971* (pp. 136–179). Chicago: Aldine.

Wason, P. C. (1966). Reasoning. In B. M. Foss (Ed.), *New horizons in psychology* (pp. 135–151). Harmondsworth, UK: Penguin.

Wilcox, A. J., Duncan, D. B., Weinberg, C. R., Trussell, J., & Baird, D. D. (2001). Likelihood of conception with a single act of intercourse: Providing benchmark rates for assessment of post-coital contraceptives. *Contraception, 63*, 211–215.

Wilson, E. O. (1975). *Sociobiology: The new synthesis.* Cambridge, MA: Harvard University Press.

Wilson, M. I., & Daly, M. (1992). The man who mistook his wife for a chattel. In J. H. Barkow, L. Cosmides, & J. Tooby (Eds.), *The adapted mind: Evolutionary psychology and the generation of culture* (pp. 289–322). New York: Oxford University Press.

Wood, W., & Eagly, A. H. (2002). A cross-cultural analysis of the behavior of women and men: Implications for the origins of sex differences. *Psychological Bulletin, 128*, 699–727.

Wynn, T. (2002). Archaeology and cognitive evolution. *Behavioral and Brain Sciences, 25*, 389–438.

Yu, D. W., & Shepard, G. H. (1998). Is beauty in the eye of the beholder? *Nature, 396*, 321–322.

Zeifman, D., & Hazan, C. (2008). Pair bonds as attachments: Reevaluating the evidence. In J. Cassidy & P. R. Shaver (Eds.), *The handbook of attachment* (2nd ed., pp. 436–455). New York: Guilford Press.

Chapter **6**

Insights from Animal Models of Social Bonding

J. THOMAS CURTIS

Affiliative behavior is a fundamental aspect of the natural histories of many animal species, including humans, and has been shown to confer survival advantages. For example, group formations such as schooling by fish and flocking by birds may help to reduce the risk of predation (Hass & Valenzuela, 2002; Seghers, 1974). At the individual level, young baboons are more likely to survive if the mother has established strong social ties with other adults (Silk, Alberts, & Altmann, 2003). As an extreme example, intimate contact between human mothers and their infants can alter the rate at which the autonomic nervous system develops (Feldman & Eidelman, 2003).

Despite the ubiquity of affiliative behavior within a social group, the formation of bonds between individuals is less common and typically involves mother–infant bonds. Rarer still are bonds between two unrelated adults. Nonetheless, bonds between individuals appear to share common traits, such as approach and avoidance responses, social recognition, the formation of conditioned preferences, and motivation (Depue & Collins, 1999; Insel & Fernald, 2004; Young, 2002; Young, Lim, Gingrich, & Insel,

2001). Thus, mother–infant bonds and social bonds between adults (including human romantic bonds and friendships) likely derive from the same basic mechanism (Bartels & Zeki, 2004; Depue & Morrone-Strupinsky, 2005; Fraley & Shaver, 2000; Insel, 1997; Pedersen, 2004).

Among nonhuman species, bonds between adults typically are tightly associated with reproduction. Most animal species display promiscuous mating systems, with males and females remaining in contact only long enough for mating to occur. Promiscuous mating strategies are quite varied. At one extreme is broadcast spawning (e.g., Levitan et al., 2004), wherein multiple individuals of both sexes contribute to a communal mating effort (common in aquatic environments). At the other extreme is harem formation (perhaps best exemplified by some pinniped species; e.g., Cassini, 1999), wherein one individual (typically a male) attempts to monopolize the reproductive efforts of many opposite-sex individuals. Occasionally, however, selection pressures favor a monogamous mating system manifested by strong reciprocal bonds between the members of a breeding pair.

CHARACTERISTICS OF MONOGAMOUS PAIR BONDING

Monogamous social organization is usually characterized by selective affiliation with a familiar partner, parental care provided by males as well as by females, and intense aggression toward unfamiliar conspecifics of either sex (Clutton-Brock, 1991; Dewsbury, 1987; Lukas & Clutton-Brock, 2012). Further, pairs may synchronize activities such as foraging and parental care (Hofmann, Getz, & Gavish, 1984; Kellam, 2003; Kleiman, 1981), and in some cases remain together and defend a common territory throughout the year (Black, 2001; Herr & Rosell, 2004; Ralls, Cypher, & Spiegel, 2007). Often, monogamous pairings are maintained until the death of one individual (Black, 2001; Ralls et al., 2007). In extreme cases, some individuals will not form a second bond after the loss of their original partner (Pizzuto & Getz, 1998), although they may still mate. Physically, many monogamous species display little sexual dimorphism, with both sexes being of similar size and coloration (Herr & Rosell, 2004; Ophir, Phelps, Sorin, & Wolff, 2007) and, in many cases, sharing a common suite of behaviors that may serve to reinforce the pair bond (Nuechterlein & Storer, 1982; Rodgers, 1980). Moreover, males tend to have smaller testes relative to those of similar sized congeners, possibly reflecting a reduction in the role that intermale competition plays in mate acquisition in monogamous species (Cartar, 1985). In general, monogamous species tend to fall more toward the "k-selected" end of the evolutionary spectrum, focusing resources on producing fewer but better provisioned young. Thus, monogamous species tend toward small litters, some evidence suggests that the young tend to be precocial (especially in birds), and development often is delayed compared with closely related but promiscuous relatives (Kleiman, 1977, 1981).

ADVANTAGES OF MONOGAMOUS PAIR BONDING

Remaining with the same partner can enhance lifetime reproductive success (Ribble, 1992), often as a result of the male's involvement in parental care (Wright & Brown, 2002). Having both parents involved in the care of offspring may increase offspring survival, allowing the female to reduce the number of offspring produced, which in turn decreases the reproductive strain associated with each litter. Further, monogamous mating reduces the risks of sexually transmitted diseases (Kokko, Ranta, Ruxton, & Lundberg, 2002). From the male's perspective, monogamous mating allows him to be confident of the paternity of offspring in which he is investing. Further, monogamy may allow males to reduce investment in characteristics associated with intermale competition (e.g., reduced testis size relative to polygamous species). As a result of reduced investment in components of sexual conflict, energetic expenses are reduced, potentially allowing monogamous species to occupy or expand into niches in which single-parent offspring care would be insufficient for successful reproduction. In short, both sexes may benefit from monogamous pairing.

PHYLOGENETICS OF MONOGAMOUS PAIR BONDING

Although monogamous pair bonding is relatively uncommon in any given phylogenetic family, this social structure is displayed by species throughout the animal kingdom, including some crustaceans, possibly some insects, and most of the vertebrate classes. Traditionally, birds have been considered to be among the exemplars for monogamous bonding, and although it has been suggested that as many as 90% of bird species are monogamous, persistent pairings between individuals probably are far less common. Black (1996) identified "persistent bonding" as occurring in about one-fifth of bird families, with some species displaying not just behaviors associated with bond formation but also complex ritual behaviors that serve to reinforce or maintain the bond (Kellam, 2003). Among mammals, monogamy is represented in the marsupials, insectivora (shrews), chiroptera (bats), primates, rodents, at least one whale species, carnivora, some seals, and a few antelope species (Kleiman, 1981), and thus appears to have evolved independently several times (Komers & Brotherton, 1997). Nonetheless, monogamy is rare among mammals (Kleiman, 1977); only about 3% of mammal species display such bonds, and even fewer exhibit obligate monogamy (Kleiman, 1977). Humans are among the few mammal species considered to be monogamous. Worldwide, the vast majority of men and women marry, and, even in cultures where multiple partners are permitted (or may even be the preferred marriage pattern), monogamous pairing is the modal arrangement (Fisher, 1989). This does not mean, however, that monogamous pairings are permanent. Rather, although an individual may be bonded to a single partner at any given time, monogamous pair bonds may be expressed with different partners over a lifetime (i.e., serial monogamy; Fisher, 1989).

STUDYING SOCIAL BONDING IN ANIMALS

The processes underlying the formation and maintenance of pair bonds between individuals occur not in the heart but in the mind. Although it is possible to gain insight into the mechanisms that underlie pair bonds in humans via instruments such as questionnaires, retrospective studies, and noninvasive analytical techniques such as functional magnetic resonance imaging (Fisher, Aron, & Brown, 2005), a firm understanding of most complex processes requires the ability to manipulate the system of interest. Clearly, it would be unethical to manipulate pair-bond formation in humans; thus, we must rely on animal models for the testing of hypotheses regarding the neurochemical and neuroanatomical bases of social bonding.

Social contact in humans elicits a suite of physiological responses that are highly conserved evolutionarily and may serve to reinforce the motivation to engage in such contact (Depue & Collins, 1999). In other words, these responses appear to be "rewarding" (as defined by Ikemoto & Panksepp, 1999) in that they "elicit approach responses." Importantly, activation of the central pathways associated with reward processing can occur in humans despite a lack of conscious perception (Berns, Cohen, & Mintun, 1997) (i.e., no intellectual processing or volition is necessary). Thus, it is possible to employ animal models to examine certain aspects of the central processes underlying the formation and maintenance of pair bonds.

Numerous theories have been advanced regarding the evolution of social bonding, especially monogamous bonding (Kleiman, 1977; Orians, 1969; Wittenberger & Tilson, 1980). Unfortunately, it is unlikely that any single theory accounts for all monogamous bonding since monogamy is not a unitary process, but rather can have species-specific manifestations (Dewsbury, 1987). Given their long-established reputation as being monogamous (Lack, 1940), birds have been the source of the largest body of literature regarding monogamous pair bonding. Thus, it is not surprising that much of the theoretical work on, and study of the ecological and evolutionary bases for, pair-bond formation, maintenance, and dissolution has focused on avian species (Dubois, Wajnberg, & Cezilly, 2004; Linden, 1991; Otter & Ratcliffe, 1996; Cezilly & Nager, 1995; Cezilly, Preault, Dubois, Faivre, & Patris, 2000; Choudhury, 1995; McNamara & Forslund, 1996). There are, however, some important limitations to studies of social bonding, particularly monogamous bonding, in birds, especially when the goal is to extrapolate the results to human bonding. First, most bird species are unsuited to laboratory studies. Although individuals of many bird species do form socially and/or sexually monogamous bonds during the breeding season, those same individual birds may be solitary or part of large foraging flocks outside of the breeding season (Emery, Seed, von Bayern, & Clayton, 2007). In fact, some seabird pairs may be in close proximity to each other for only a short period each year, even during the breeding period (Creelman & Storey, 1991). Further, in many cases, the sexes often are segregated during the nonbreeding periods (Stinson, Crawford, & Lauthner, 1981). As such, it is possible that the neurochemistry, or even neuroanatomy, associated with social bonding may not be constant throughout the year. Such seasonal changes have been noted for central processes associated with other avian behaviors (Emery et al., 2007). Although evidence from migratory species suggests that spatial memories may be retained for at least 1 year (Mettke-Hofmann & Gwinner, 2003), it is unclear whether social memories are similarly retained. This issue is exemplified by the question of whether individuals are bonded to each other or to a specific nest site to which both individuals return independently each year (Bried & Jouventin, 1999; Gunnarsson, Gill, Sigurbjornsson, & Sutherland, 2004). The latter would be consistent with long-term spatial memory but provides little insight into social memory. Finally, in some cases, avian monogamy may be driven by factors that produce de facto monogamy by reducing nonmonogamous opportunities. Mock (1985) notes that the relatively short female investment in producing the primary reproductive unit, the egg, forces the male to attend closely, at least until all available ova are fertilized. Given the relatively tight timing of breeding in many bird species, in some cases, by the time all available ova from a particular female are fertilized there may be no other female in breeding condition. Given these limitations, we focus our discussion on mammalian pair bonding.

SOCIAL BONDING IN MAMMALS

Over the past three decades, an extensive literature has been built around research on social bonding focusing on two mammalian genera: *Microtus* and *Peromyscus*. Species within these genera often display very similar nonsocial behaviors such as activity and feeding patterns (Madison, 1985) but differ significantly in their mating systems and thus in the ways that individuals interact socially (Bester-Meredith, Young, & Marler, 1999; Dewsbury, 1987). In fact, species within *Peromyscus* and *Microtus* provide a microcosm of mammalian social structures. Most species display a promiscuous mating system, displaying little evidence of social ties, typically defending individual territories; females usually are the sole caretakers of pups. A few species, however, display the shared parental care, shared nests throughout the year, and selective aggression toward strangers but not toward the partner that characterize monogamous pair bonding. These animals form strong pair bonds with their mate, which are manifested by a preference for social contact with the partner even when other conspecifics are present.

Prairie vole social behavior, especially, has been well characterized. Field studies show that prairie voles are highly social: Pairs share a nest and parental duties; in fact, both members often are found in the same trap (Getz, Carter, & Gavish, 1981). In the laboratory, voles appear to avoid isolation by seeking out conspecifics and, in fact, suffer significant stress when isolated (DeVries, 2002; DeVries, DeVries, Taymans, & Carter, 1996; DeVries, Glasper, & Detillion, 2003; DeVries, Taymans, & Carter, 1997; Klein, Hairston, DeVries, & Nelson, 1997). In contrast to more traditional laboratory animals, prairie vole social behaviors actually are remarkably similar to those of humans: long-term pair bonding, care of offspring by both parents, and sharing of a nest year-round (Carter & Getz, 1993). Further, autonomic responses in voles are more like those of humans than of other rodent species (Grippo, Lamb, Carter, & Porges, 2007). These parallels have led to the extensive use of voles to study quantitatively the behavioral, neural, and physiological bases of social attachment (Aragona, Liu, Curtis, Stephan, & Wang, 2003; Carter & Getz, 1993; Curtis, Liu, & Wang, 2001; Curtis, Stowe, & Wang, 2003; Cushing, Martin, Young, & Carter, 2001; DeVries et al., 1996; Gingrich, Liu, Cascio, Wang, & Insel, 2000; Insel, 2003; Insel, Preston, & Winslow, 1995; Liu, Curtis, & Wang, 2001; Liu & Wang, 2003; Wang, Yu, Cascio, Liu, Gingrich, & Insel, 1999; Williams, Catania, & Carter, 1992; Winslow, Hastings, Carter, Harbaugh, & Insel, 1993). Studies using voles have examined reciprocal interactions between social bonding and neurochemistry (especially dopamine, oxytocin, and vasopressin); neuroanatomy (both receptor and fiber distributions); autonomic, endocrine, and immune functions; gene expression; substance abuse; adult neurogenesis; aggression; maternal and paternal behavior; social recognition; and reproductive suppression (Aragona et al., 2006; Cho, DeVries, Williams, & Carter, 1999; Curtis & Wang, 2005a; DeVries & Carter, 1999; Fowler, Liu, Ouimet, & Wang, 2002; Gobrogge, Liu, Jia, & Wang, 2007; Grippo, Wu, Hassan, & Carter, 2008; Hammock & Young, 2004; Insel, Wang, & Ferris, 1994; Klein et al., 1997; Wang, Ferris, & De Vries, 1994; Williams, Insel, Harbaugh, & Carter, 1994). As a result of this diversity of studies, both the behavioral repertoire and the physiology of voles are well documented, so there is a strong literature base upon which future studies can rest.

Developmental Factors

Species differences associated with social behavior arise early in development, even among closely related species. In general, pups of promiscuous species such as montane (*M. montanus*) and meadow (*M. pennsylvanicus*) voles and white-footed mice (*P. leucopus*) develop more rapidly than do pups from monogamous pine (M. *pinetorum*) and prairie (*M. ochrogaster*) voles or California mice (*P. californicus*) (McGuire & Novak, 1984; McGuire & Novak, 1986; Nadeau, 1985; Prohazka, Novak, & Meyer, 1986) (reviewed by Layne, 1968). Indeed, several studies have shown that brain development may be delayed in monogamous species. Vole species with differing mating systems display different allometric relationships between brain mass and body mass during development. Promiscuous vole species switch from an immature allometric growth pattern to an adult pattern earlier in development than do the monogamous voles (Gutierrez, Meyer, & Novak, 1989), suggesting that brain development is delayed in monogamous voles. These species differences in brain growth may be attributable to the proliferation of new cells. Indices of cell proliferation suggest that the brains of monogamous pine vole are still undergoing considerable mitotic activity at 5 days postnatally. At the same age, however, mitotic activity is significantly reduced in meadow voles and in other non-pair-bonding species such as rats and mice (Gutierrez et al., 1989). In the same study, monogamous vole species were also found to display a greater increase in cell proliferation in the cerebellum between 2 and 5 days of age compared with promiscuous voles, again suggesting that brain development is delayed in monogamous species. This difference may account for the more advanced neuromuscular development displayed by promiscuous vole pups (Prohazka et al., 1986).

In addition to differences in brain growth, the development of neuro-chemical systems differs between species with differing social systems. For example, brain-derived neurotrophic factor (BDNF) is important for the proliferation, survival, and growth of neurons. In some brain areas, the promiscuous meadow vole displays adult patterns of BDNF expression at about 2 weeks of age, while the monogamous prairie vole does not show adult patterns until at least 3 weeks of age (Liu, Fowler, & Wang, 2001). Monogamous prairie voles and promiscuous montane voles also differ in temporal and regional expression of the genes for receptors that bind the neurochemicals vasopressin or oxytocin (Wang & Young, 1997; Wang, Young, Liu, & Insel, 1997), which are critical for social memory and/or for the formation of adult social attachments in monogamous species (Dantzer, Koob, Bluthe, & Le Moal, 1988; Wang, Young, De Vries, & Insel, 1998; Williams et al., 1994).

The differences in central developmental are manifested in behavioral differences in monogamous and promiscuous pups. Promiscuous vole pups become independent at a younger age: These pups begin eating solid food as early as 8 days of age and wean at 13–14 days while pups of monogamous vole species are not weaned until about 1 week later (McGuire & Novak, 1984). It is interesting to note that the timing of weaning and independence in each species parallels the timing of the switch to adult patterns of BDNF expression. A similar pattern is seen in promiscuous and monogamous mice. Among *Peromyscus*, pups from promiscuous species open their eyes earlier and wean earlier than do pups of monogamous mice (Layne, 1968).

Juvenile Behaviors

Behavioral differences reflecting the various social structures also are reflected to some extent in the interactions among juvenile rodents (Pellis, Pellis, & Dewsbury, 1989). In fact, juvenile play behavior may prepare relevant brain circuitry responsible for adult social behavior (Cooke, Chowanadisai, & Breedlove, 2000). For example, rats that lack opportunities to engage in play as pups may display abnormal social behavior as adults (van den Berg et al., 1999). Young prairie voles display a propensity for intimate contact and mutual grooming, while these behaviors are much less common in meadow voles (Wilson, 1982). These differences parallel the species-specific adult social behaviors: Adult prairie voles are much more social than adult meadow voles. The play behaviors of juveniles also reflect species differences in adult social behavior. The play behaviors of juveniles of highly social vole species are more complex (Pellis & Iwaniuk, 1999), and the types of play differ between the species (Pellis et al., 1989; Pierce, Pellis, Dewsbury, & Pellis, 1991). During play fighting, social species are more likely to display "passive" defense postures, while nonsocial species display more "aggressive" defense postures (Pellis et al., 1989). Interestingly, the species differences in play appear to reflect species differences in adult precopulatory behavioral patterns (Pellis et al., 1989; Pierce et al., 1991).

Nature or Nurture?

Collectively, these observations demonstrate clear species differences in the ontogeny of the brain that may contribute to species-specific social structures. However, it is not clear whether "nature" or "nurture" drive such differences. Such questions typically are addressed by cross-fostering pups between parents of the different species. Monogamous California mice (*P. californicus*) raised by promiscuous white-footed foster parents (*P. leucopus*) display some behavior patterns typical of their foster parents as adults, and the behavioral differences are correlated with changes within the brain (Bester-Meredith & Marler, 2001, 2003). In studies in which pups of a promiscuous vole species were raised by monogamous foster parents or cross-fostered to unrelated promiscuous parents, the fostered pups showed a slight preference for the species by which they were reared (McGuire & Novak, 1987) and displayed parental behaviors at a level closer to that of their fostering parents (McGuire, 1988). These results suggest that, at minimum, environmental factors can interact with genetics to influence the social behavior of rodents.

Neurochemistry of Bonding

The neurochemistry of social bonding involves a complex interplay between a number of neurotransmitter/neuromodulator systems and multiple brain regions. Following are summaries of the most well-studied neurochemical systems. It should be noted that none are comprehensive, as each would require its own chapter to provide an exhaustive survey of the information known about the roles of these neurotransmitters in social bonding. For more in-depth analyses, the reader is referred to reviews by Young and colleagues (Lim & Young, 2006; Young, Liu, & Wang, 2008), Insel (1997), Carter (1998; Carter, Williams, & Witt, 1990), Curtis (Curtis, Liu, Aragona, & Wang, 2006), and Wang (Wang et al., 1998).

Oxytocin

Examination of oxytocin involvement in social bonding originally was rooted in observations that oxytocin facilitated the formation of bonds between mothers and their offspring. A role for oxytocin in adult pair-bond formation was confirmed when it was found that administration of oxytocin into the lateral ventricle in female prairie voles could induce pair bonding (Williams et al., 1994; Witt, Carter, & Walton, 1990). Similar treatments were ineffective in promiscuous vole species (Insel, 2000). Such findings were strengthened by observations that blockade of oxytocin receptors using selective oxytocin receptor antagonists inhibited the formation of the natural mating-induced pair bonds (Insel & Hulihan, 1995).

Comparative studies of the distribution of oxytocinergic cells and fibers have found subtle differences between monogamous and promiscuous vole species (Wang, Zhou, Hulihan, & Insel, 1996), but no consistent pattern differentiating the two groups has emerged. The story is different, however, when the distribution patterns for oxytocin receptors are examined. Vole species that share similar social structures display the most similar receptor distribution patterns (Insel & Shapiro, 1992). Importantly, the species-specific patterns are apparent throughout development and are not the result of different receptor subtypes, since all voles express the same oxytocin receptor. The species-specific receptor distribution patterns may, however, be related to subtle differences in the promoter regions for the oxytocin receptor genes. Support for this possibility came when researchers were able to direct the expression of a reporter gene to socially relevant brain regions in mice by linking the reporter gene to the oxytocin promoter region from social voles (Young, Waymire, et al., 1997).

Interestingly, after the birth of young, oxytocin receptor distribution in the nonsocial montane vole female grows to resemble that of social voles (Insel & Shapiro, 1992). This to some extent brings the story full circle, since the original experiments examining a potential role for oxytocin in pair bonding were based on oxytocin's role in maternal bonding. The maternal "circuit" includes most of the neural components implicated in pair bonding. Thus, one possibility for the origin of pair bonding is that pair-bonding species have co-opted the mechanism(s) by which maternal bonds are formed. This possibility is further supported by observations that even sexually naïve male prairie voles display maternal-type behaviors when exposed to pups (Lonstein & De Vries, 1999), and that, among females, prairie vole mothers display considerably more maternal care than do meadow vole mothers (McGuire & Novak, 1984).

Vasopressin

Vasopressin (AVP) is probably most widely known for its peripheral effects as a potent vasoconstrictor and its role in body fluid regulation via effects at the level of the kidney. However, in addition to its peripheral effects, AVP can also act in the brain. Within the central nervous system, the majority of AVP innervation is found in the amygdala–bed nucleus of the stria terminalis (BNST)–lateral septum circuit (De Vries & Miller, 1998). This extrahypothalamic AVP system is sexually dimorphic in rodents. Castration of neonatal male rats produces an AVP innervation pattern similar to that in females (De Vries & Miller, 1998), suggesting that this dimorphism is regulated by perinatal exposure to gonadal hormones (Axelson, Smith, & Duarte, 1999; De Vries & Miller, 1998; Wang, Bullock, & De Vries, 1993).

As with oxytocin, central administration of AVP also can affect social behavior. This neurochemical can induce paternal behavior (Wang et al., 1994), selective aggression (Winslow et al., 1993), and the formation of partner preferences in monogamous voles (Cho et al., 1999; Winslow et al., 1993). In some cases, the effects of central AVP are species specific. For example, in monogamous prairie voles, central administration of AVP induces aggression (Young, Winslow, Nilsen, & Insel, 1997) while the same treatment in promiscuous montane voles does not alter aggression (Young et al., 1997). Consistent with these observations, there appears to be a relationship between the numbers of vasopressin receptors and/or the density of AVP innervation and species-specific social structures. The distributions of AVP fibers in the brain differ between monogamous and promiscuous species within both *Microtus* and *Peromyscus*. However, between genera, they differ in opposite directions. Males of a monogamous *Peromyscus* species, the California mouse, display a higher density of AVP immunoreactive staining in the BNST than the promiscuous white-footed mouse (Bester-Meredith & Marler, 2001; Bester-Meredith et al., 1999). In *Microtus*, the opposite pattern is found: Monogamous species display less AVP innervation in BNST than promiscuous species (Wang, 1995).

Vasopressin receptor densities also differ between species with differing social structures. Again, however, although there are species differences within each genus, a consistent correlation between vasopressin receptors and social structure is not found. For example, monogamous *Peromyscus* species have a higher density of vasopressin receptors in the lateral septum than promiscuous species (Bester-Meredith et al., 1999; Insel, Gelhard, & Shapiro, 1991), exactly opposite the patterns seen for vasopressin receptors in the lateral septum in monogamous and promiscuous *Microtus* species (Insel et al., 1994). There is a consistent correlation between vasopressin receptor densities and mating system in only one brain region—the ventral pallidum (Bester-Meredith et al., 1999)—and this region has recently become the focus of several studies (cf. Pitkow et al., 2001).

Dopamine

Biogenic amine involvement in the central processes important for pair bonding appears to be phylogenetically very old (Nestler, 2002) and may originally have mediated the formation of associations between behavior and positive outcome. For example, forming an association between a particularly nutritious food source and the cues that facilitate locating that food source would likely have adaptive value. In mammals, such associations appear to be mediated via activation of central dopamine pathways (reviewed by Ikemoto & Panksepp, 1999). This type of process would be ideally suited for co-opting as a mechanism to ensure the appropriate motivations and behaviors as mating strategies shifted from broadcast spawning to an orientation toward particular individuals (Parker, 1984). Once tied to reproduction, it is a short step to involvement in processes such as parental bonding that may enhance the survival of offspring.

It is well known that central dopamine release accompanies sexual activity in some species, including rats, voles, and hamsters (Becker, Rudick, & Jenkins, 2001; Gingrich et al., 2000; Kohlert & Meisel, 1999; Pfaus et al., 1990). Those observations, plus the fact that mating facilitates pair-bond formation in monogamous prairie voles (Williams et al., 1992), led to the hypothesis that dopamine might play a role in social attachment. This hypothesis was supported when it was shown that mating-induced pair bonding in prairie voles was impaired by blocking the activity of dopamine, while dopamine receptor activation could induce pair bonds in the absence of mating (Aragona et al., 2003; Wang et al., 1999). Interestingly, doses of dopamine agonist that induced partner preferences in female voles (Wang et al., 1999) were ineffective in males (Aragona et al., 2003), suggesting sex differences in sensitivity to dopamine manipulations. The fact that administration of dopaminergic drugs directly into the brain produced similar results as peripheral treatment established central dopamine systems as critical for pair bonding (Wang et al., 1999).

There are three major dopaminergic pathways in the brain (Melis & Argiolas, 1995): the nigrostriatal pathway (Swanson, 1982), the incertohypothalamic pathway (Cheung, Ballew, Moore, & Lookingland, 1998), and the mesocorticolimbic pathway (Swanson, 1982). Although it is possible that all of these pathways may play at least indirect roles in social bonding, the mesolimbic pathway, consisting of reciprocal innervation between the ventral tegmental area (VTA) and the medial prefrontal cortex, and projections from each to the nucleus accumbens (Carr & Sesack, 2000; McFarland & Kalivas, 2001; Swanson, 1982), has been most strongly implicated in mediating the motivated behaviors and in reward processing that likely are central to social bonding. In fact, mesolimbic areas are activated in humans when subjects view images of their respective love interests (Bartels & Zeki, 2000, 2004; Fisher et al., 2005). Thus, considerable effort has been expended studying the role of the mesolimbic dopamine system in social attachment, particularly in the formation and maintenance of pair bonds between male and female mates. (Aragona et al., 2003, 2006; Curtis et al., 2001, 2003; Curtis & Wang, 2003, 2005a, 2005b; Gingrich et al., 2000; Keer & Stern, 1999; Lorrain, Riolo, Matuszewich, & Hull, 1999; Mermelstein & Becker, 1995; Mitchell & Gratton, 1992; Tidey & Miczek, 1996).

Just as direct administration of dopamine drugs into the brain established a role for central dopamine in social bonding, so too did direct administration of dopamine drugs establish the importance of specific brain regions. Using this approach, the mesolimbic dopamine pathway was shown to be of critical importance in the formation and maintenance of pair bonds in both sexes (Aragona et al., 2003, 2006; Gingrich et al., 2000). Site-specific manipulations of dopamine processing, especially of the activity of the D_2-type dopamine receptors, in the nucleus accumbens can fundamentally alter pair-bonding behavior. Further, even within the nucleus accumbens, there appears to be functional segregation along an anterior–posterior gradient within the core and shell subregions of the nucleus accumbens (Zahm, 2000; Reynolds & Berridge, 2002). Administration of a D_2 dopamine receptor agonist into the rostral shell effectively induced pair bonds in the absence of mating, while administration into the rostral core or into the caudal shell was ineffective (Aragona et al., 2006).

Social functioning in humans also involves dopamine receptor activation (Lawford et al., 2003). For example, people expressing a genotype associated with reduced postsynaptic D_2 activity have negative parenting perceptions (Lucht et al., 2006). Similarly, compared with healthy subjects, patients with social phobias have lower D_2 binding (Schneier et al., 2000). Finally, other members of the D_2 family of receptors also can impact human social bonding. For example, disorganized mother–infant attachment is associated with a polymorphism of the gene for the D_4 dopamine receptor (Gervai et al., 2005).

Corticosterone

Sex differences in the effects of oxytocin, AVP, and dopamine have commonly been reported; however, these differences primarily have been in terms of sensitivity rather than direction of effects. Such is not the case when the effects of the stress hormone corticosterone are examined. In contrast to the effects of the other neurochemicals, the effects of elevated corticosterone on pair bonding are sexually dimorphic in monogamous voles. In males, the effects of stress, presumably including increased circulating corticosterone, enhance the formation of pair bonds (DeVries et al., 1996). Conversely, adrenalectomy, which reduces circulating corticosterone, inhibits pair bonding (DeVries et al., 1996). In females, the opposite pattern is found: Adrenalectomy enhances pair bonding, whereas stress reduces pair-bond formation (DeVries, DeVries, Taymans, & Carter, 1995; DeVries et al., 1996).

Other Neurochemicals

The neurochemicals listed previously have received the majority of the attention in studies of the neurochemistry of social bonding. However, the list of neurochemicals that are involved in social bonding also includes some less well-studied compounds. The excitatory neurotransmitter glutamate and the inhibitory neurotransmitter gamma-aminobutyric acid (GABA) have each been indirectly implicated in social bonding via their role in regulating dopamine neurotransmission in the mesolimbic dopamine pathway. The dopaminergic innervation of the NAcc originates primarily from within the VTA in the ventral midbrain (Hasue & Shammah-Lagnado, 2002; Swanson, 1982). Modulation of dopaminergic output from the VTA appears to involve a complex interplay between excitatory and inhibitory inputs as well as inhibitory interneurons within the VTA itself. Interestingly, blockade of either the excitatory glutamate activity or inhibitory GABA activity within the VTA can induce pair-bond formation in monogamous voles (Curtis & Wang, 2005b).

Neurochemical Interactions

Although the neurochemicals/hormones just presented all have been implicated in pair bonding, it is unknown whether they act in concert or independently to regulate behavior. In addition, the nature of any interactions and the brain circuits in which such interactions occur remain to be fully determined. Nonetheless, there is some evidence that concurrent activation or cross-talk between neurotransmitter systems also may be involved in pair-bond formation. Recently, researchers have begun to address these questions. Early studies suggested sex-specific roles for oxytocin and AVP: Oxytocin was the "pair-bond hormone" in females, while AVP was responsible for pair-bond formation in males (Carter & Getz, 1993). Subsequent studies, however, have shown that the idea of a simple sexual dichotomy in the roles of AVP and oxytocin in the regulation of pair bonding was an oversimplification. Central administration of either oxytocin or AVP at relatively high doses can induce partner preferences in both sexes. Further, pair bonding in both sexes can be impaired by blocking either type of receptor (Cho et al., 1999). Further, when injected into the lateral septum in male prairie voles, oxytocin, like AVP, can induce pair bonding (Liu, Curtis, et al., 2001). These data indicate that both AVP and oxytocin are involved in pair bonding in both sexes of prairie voles. Despite these findings, it should not be concluded that there are no sex differences in oxytocin and AVP effects. Important sex differences in responses to various doses of the peptides suggest that the sexes may differ in their relative sensitivities to each peptide. Further, where sex differences are found, they tend to reinforce the notion that AVP is more effective in males while oxytocin is more effective in females. Finally, sex differences may also exist in other systems that interact with AVP and oxytocin in the regulation of pair bonding. In male prairie voles, AVP administration in lateral septum induces pair bonding. This effect is blocked by coadministration of either vasopressin or oxytocin receptor antagonists, suggesting that access to both receptors is essential for AVP induction of pair bonding (Liu, Curtis, et al., 2001). In NAcc, which contains both oxytocin and D_2 dopamine receptors, administration of either oxytocin or D_2 agonists induces pair bonding in female prairie voles (Liu & Wang, 2003). Interestingly, the abilities of both oxytocin and D_2 agonists to induce pair bonds can be blocked by antagonists to either type of receptor (Liu & Wang, 2003). These results suggest that oxytocin and dopamine may act synergistically in NAcc to regulate pair bonding.

As noted, the effects of corticosterone on adult pair bonding are sexually dimorphic. Exactly how this sexually dimorphic response is mediated is unknown, but it is likely that the responses arise via corticosterone interactions with other neurochemical systems. For example, removal of the adrenal glands, which reduces corticosterone, also reduces the density of vasopressin receptors in the lateral septum and BNST, both of which have been implicated in social bonding, and this effect can be reversed by hormone replacement (Watters, Wilkinson, & Dorsa, 1996). Interestingly, hormone replacement targeting the "Type I" glucocorticoid receptors reversed adrenalectomy effects on vasopressin receptor density only in the BNST, whereas targeting "Type II" glucocorticoid receptors restored receptor densities in both the lateral septum and the BNST (Watters et al., 1996). These results show that changes in circulating corticosterone levels may alter AVP-induced responses. Given the sexual dimorphism in the extrahypothalamic AVP system, it is possible that the sex-specific effects of corticosterone are secondary to its effects on AVP activity.

Corticosterone also can interact with central dopamine (Curtis & Wang, 2005a). Stress can alter excitatory glutamate receptors on dopaminergic cells in the VTA, and glucocorticoid receptors are found on those same cells (Saal, Dong, Bonci, & Malenka, 2003). Importantly, the stress-induced changes in the VTA were blocked by glucocorticoid receptor antagonists (Saal et al., 2003). Since the VTA is the primary source of dopamine input to the nucleus accumbens (Swanson, 1982), these results suggest that glucocorticoid receptor activation in the VTA could impact dopamine release in the nucleus accumbens. Direct effects of glucocorticoid receptor activation within the nucleus accumbens also are possible. For example, dopamine transporter (DAT) activity in the nucleus accumbens is directly correlated with corticosterone levels (Sarnyai, McKittrick, McEwen, & Kreek, 1998). Since corticosterone levels are lower in voles that are paired (DeVries et al., 1995, 1997), it is possible that DAT activity also is decreased, reducing clearance of dopamine from the synapse and thus potentiating the effects of released dopamine.

Adult Social Interactions

We have examined evolutionary, natural history, and developmental aspects of adult social bonding, and have outlined the central processes that underlie the formation of adult social bonds. We now turn to the adult social interactions that are directly linked with the formation, maintenance, and, in some cases, dissolution of adult social bonds. Although relationships such as friendships are important aspects of human behavior, we focus on the bonds between the individuals that make up a mating pair. Note again that although we focus on pair bonds associated with mating, the mechanisms involved likely also are involved in other types of social bonds.

Courtship

Courtship rituals play an important role in the initial selection of a mate and the formation of the pair bond. It has been suggested that the often elaborate courtship rituals may serve to coordinate a pair's reproductive physiology (Lehrman, 1959). It is likely that the vomeronasal organ (VNO) serves as a primary component of reproductive activation in female rodents and thus may play an important role in the coordination of reproductive behaviors such as pair bonding. Evidence for such a possibility includes that from studies that examine the role of the olfactory system(s) in pair bonding. The VNO system or accessory olfactory pathway is a chemosensory system, which is anatomically and functionally distinct from the main olfactory pathway (Døving & Trotier, 1998; Halpern, 1987). The VNO is located in the anteroventral part of the nasal cavity and projects exclusively to the accessory olfactory bulb. Information from the VNO is transmitted to a variety of brain regions, including the vomeronasal amygdala. Importantly, nearly all of the central structures that receive input from the VNO are involved in reproductive physiology and behavior. The significance of these observations is apparent in the fact that pair bonding can alter the activity of many of these regions (Curtis & Wang, 2003; Cushing, Mogekwu, Le, Hoffman, & Carter, 2002; Wang, Hulihan, & Insel, 1997; Schwab, Solomon, Isaacson, & Callahan, 2004). Further, lesions of the amygdala diminish social attachment (Kirkpatrick, Carter, Newman, & Insel, 1994).

The VNO system has been implicated in a wide variety of chemo-signal-induced and reproductively associated behaviors and neuroendocrine responses (Døving & Trotier, 1998; Keverne, 2002). For example, the VNO appears to contribute to social recognition. Olfactory investigation of conspecific juveniles (juvenile recognition) often is used to examine mechanisms underlying social recognition. Removal of the VNO has been found to impair juvenile recognition significantly and to prevent animals from responding to the vasopressin receptor antagonist (Bluthe & Dantzer, 1993), suggesting the importance of the VNO in regulation of individual recognition, a process presumably involved in pair-bond formation in voles. A role for the VNO in pair bonding was verified when it was shown that pair-bond formation was impaired in prairie voles from which the VNO had been surgically removed (Curtis et al., 2001).

One critical question in the present context is whether there is a role for a VNO in social bonding in humans as occurs in rodents. In fact, the very existence of a functional VNO in adult humans is controversial (see Meredith, 2001, for a detailed treatment of the issue). Nonetheless, a potential role for accessory olfactory input in human bonding is supported by studies showing possible pheromonal effects on human mate choice, human reproductive physiology, and sex- and sexual orientation-specific responses to putative pheromonal signals (Cowley & Brooksbank, 1991; Savic, Berglund, & Lindstrom, 2005; Stern & McClintock, 1998; Wysocki & Preti, 2004).

Maintenance of Social Bonds

Brotherton and Komers (2003) concluded that monogamy derives from a mate-guarding strategy, which often involves an aggression component. In line with the premise that many social behaviors derive from the mating system, in some species mating can produce fundamental changes in social behaviors, including aggression. Pair-bonded male prairie voles and non-bonded males are very different animals (Gammie & Nelson, 2000; Insel et al., 1995; Winslow et al., 1993). Sexually naïve male prairie voles display little aggression when exposed to a novel male (Winslow et al., 1993). However, after 24 hours of mating, these males develop a strong preference for contact with the familiar partner, and at the same time they also become less fearful and more aggressive toward strangers (Insel et al., 1995). Even the pattern of agonistic behavior changes: Attack bites are added to the premating repertoire of defensive and threat-type behaviors (Insel et al., 1995). The transition from defense to attack appears to be mediated, at least in part, by AVP since blockade of vasopressin receptors prior to mating eliminates mating-induced aggression (Winslow et al., 1993). Within species, differential AVP innervation has been associated with individual differences in aggressiveness (Compaan, Buijs, Pool, De Ruiter, & Koolhaas, 1993; Everts, De Ruiter, & Koolhaas, 1997). In the rat, there is a negative correlation between individual aggression and AVP fiber density in the lateral septum (Everts et al., 1997), and aggressive mice have a lower density of AVP fibers in the BNST than nonaggressive mice (Compaan et al., 1993). Consistent with a negative correlation between AVP innervation and aggression, pair-bonded male prairie voles have lower AVP fiber density in the lateral septum relative to virgin males (Bamshad, Novak, & De Vries, 1993). Interestingly, no change in AVP fiber density is seen in promiscuous meadow vole males after the birth of pups (Bamshad et al., 1993). This difference may reflect the fact that, after mating, monogamous prairie vole males display extensive parental and nest- and mate-guarding behaviors that are not seen in male meadow voles. These observations suggest that AVP may play a role in the aggressive responses to strangers that are manifested as mate guarding, which may serve in pair-bond maintenance. Changes in aggression after mating are not limited to males. Sexually experienced breeder female prairie voles display more aggression and less affiliative behavior than do sexually naïve females (Bowler, Cushing, & Carter, 2002), and postpartum female common voles (*M. arvalis*) become more aggressive toward males as pups develop (Heise & Lippke, 1997). Whether the increases in aggression in females are attributable to mating or to gestational or postpartum changes is unknown, but changes in AVP gene expression after the birth of pups are known to occur (Wang, Liu, Young, & Insel, 2000).

The importance of AVP in mediating at least some aspects of aggressive behavior suggests involvement of the amygdala–BNST–lateral septum circuit. This notion is supported by studies in a variety of species. For example, agonistic behavior activates this circuit in male hamsters (Kollack-Walker & Newman, 1995) and female mice (Gammie & Nelson, 2001). Similarly, in a resident/intruder test, previously mated male prairie voles displayed increased neuronal activity in all three brain regions (Wang, Hulihan, et al., 1997), suggesting that these areas are activated during aggression in voles as well. These results establish a consistent pattern of involvement of this circuit associated with aggression regardless of species or gender. Interestingly, in monogamous voles, activation of this system occurred only in response to a stranger, not after reexposure to the familiar partner, suggesting that aggression can be modified by familiarity (Wang, Hulihan, et al., 1997).

Although aggression per se may be mediated by AVP, the differential responses to strangers versus to the partner may require central dopamine activity, in particular, the increase in extracellular dopamine that accompanies exposure to novelty (Hooks & Kalivas, 1995). In addition to D_2 dopamine receptors, the nucleus accumbens contains the D_1 dopamine receptor subtype. D_1 receptors originally were thought to play no role in pair bonding (Wang et al., 1999). This is probably true in terms of pair-bond *formation*, but increasing evidence suggests that D_1 dopamine receptors may be critical for pair-bond *maintenance*. More recent work has shown that activation of D_1 dopamine receptors impairs the formation of pair bonds (Aragona et al., 2003). Interestingly, pair-bonded male prairie voles display D_1 dopamine receptor densities that are substantially greater than those seen in non-pair-bonded voles (Aragona et al., 2003), and the higher densities of D_1 receptors, in conjunction with novelty-induced increases in dopamine release in response to a unfamiliar vole, appear to underlie the aversive responses to strangers by pair-bonded voles. Such responses likely prevent the formation of a second pair bond, which in turn may serve to maintain a monogamous life strategy. Importantly, because of familiarity with the partner, there is no novelty-induced dopamine release, and thus no aversive response is directed toward to the partner upon reuniting after separation. It would be interesting to examine whether a similar reorganization of central dopamine activity occurs in species that display serial monogamy, or whether there are sex differences in species such as Mongolian gerbil (*Meriones unguicalatus*) that appear to display sex-specific types of social bonds (Starkey & Hendrie, 1998). Finally, it also would be of interest to learn whether there are individual differences in the regulation of D_1 receptor expression in pair-bonded voles. Although considered to be a monogamous species, a small percentage of prairie voles can form a second pair bond (Pizzuto & Getz, 1998). Differences in the ability to increase D_1

receptors may account for the small percentage of monogamous voles that form new pair bonds after losing a mate.

Divorce

As noted earlier, individuals can accrue significant fitness advantages as a result of forming monogamous pair bonds. However, such pairings are not without costs. In fact, monogamous animals face an important challenge: if and when to abandon a partner with whom they may not be reproductively compatible. Although not universally accepted, a number of studies in humans suggest that childless couples are more likely to divorce (Andersson, 1997; Day, 1964; Fisher, 1989; White, 1990; Wineberg, 1988). Cohen (1971) noted that for the Kanuri people "not all long marriages are fertile, but almost all fertile marriages tend to be longer." Lest one think a higher incidence of divorce among childless couples is a modern phenomenon, Willcox (1897) found that childless couples in the United States in the 1800s were three to four times more likely to separate than couples with children. Similarly, in the first half of the 1900s, about 60% of divorced couples had no children (Jacobson, 1950). Thus, it is clear that any relationship between childlessness and marital dissolution is not a recent development. What is unclear, however, is whether this relationship is solely a cultural derivative or an evolutionary "holdover" that reflects previously adaptive behavior (Choudhury, 1995). To test this latter possibility, pair bonding in prairie voles was assessed as a function of reproductive success (Curtis, 2010). It was found that male prairie voles whose mates became pregnant within a short period after pairing displayed the typical strong preference for affiliation with his mate. In contrast, males whose partners did not become pregnant did not show the typical partner preference, nor did those males whose partners' pregnancies were delayed. Rather, these males alternated between spending time with the mate and spending time with a stranger. Importantly, the differences in male behavior were not secondary to the timing of copulation, since males that mated within the normal time period—but with females that were ovariectomized and thus incapable of pregnancy—also displayed the switching behavior (Curtis, 2010). These results suggest that, among monogamous mammals, successful reproduction may be important in consolidating pair bonds. Fisher (2000) proposed interrelationships among three discrete emotion systems—lust, attraction, and attachment—that parallel mating, reproduction, and parenting. One might speculate that, in primitive humans, the transition from attraction to attachment coincided with the birth of a child. Here again, our biological heritage can affect modern behavior. For some, the transition from attraction to attachment may not be made in the absence of successful reproduction. Thus, as suggested by Rasmussen (1981), from an evolutionary perspective, poor reproductive success should lead to a weakening of the bonds between mates. For some humans, as for voles, pair-bond formation may be a two-step process, with childbirth contributing to consolidation of the bond. In other words, we may be "wired" to fall out of love in the absence of evidence for reproductive compatibility.

BROADER IMPLICATIONS

Interpersonal interactions such as parent–child, spousal, friendship, and work relationships all rely to some extent on the ability to form and maintain social ties. In fact, such ties can be beneficial to human health and well-being. For example, a network of strong social attachments may reduce a person's chances of developing substance abuse problems, and for those already afflicted, strong social ties can facilitate recovery and reduce the likelihood of relapse. In contrast, deficits in the ability to form meaningful social bonds are associated with a variety of human psychological impairments: Autism, traumatic brain injury, and disorders such as schizophrenia and depression all may have a strong social withdrawal component. In fact, the loss of a significant relationship can exacerbate depression. Thus, gaining an understanding of the neural processes that underlie social attachment may provide insights into not only aspects of human "natural history" but also into the causes of some psychological disorders.

REFERENCES

Andersson, G. (1997). The impact of children on divorce risks of Swedish women. *European Journal of Population, 13*(2), 109–145.

Aragona, B. J., Liu, Y., Curtis, J. T., Stephan, F. K., & Wang, Z. (2003). A critical role for nucleus accumbens dopamine in partner-preference formation in male prairie voles. *Journal of Neuroscience, 23*(8), 3483–3490.

Aragona, B. J., Liu, Y., Yu, Y. J., Curtis, J. T., Detwiler, J. M., Insel, T. R., et al. (2006). Nucleus accumbens dopamine differentially mediates the formation and maintenance of monogamous pair bonds. *Nature Neuroscience, 9*(1), 133–139.

Axelson, J. F., Smith, M., & Duarte, M. (1999). Prenatal flutamide treatment eliminates the adult male rat's dependency upon vasopressin when forming social-olfactory memories. *Hormones and Behavior, 36*(2), 109–118.

Bamshad, M., Novak, M. A., & De Vries, G. J. (1993). Sex and species differences in the vasopressin innervation of sexually naive and parental prairie voles,

Microtus ochrogaster and meadow voles, *Microtus pennsylvanicus. Journal of Neuroendocrinology, 5*, 247–255.

Bartels, A., & Zeki, S. (2000). The neural basis of romantic love. *NeuroReport, 11*(17), 3829–3834.

Bartels, A., & Zeki, S. (2004). The neural correlates of maternal and romantic love. *NeuroImage, 21*(3), 1155–1166.

Becker, J. B., Rudick, C. N., & Jenkins, W. J. (2001). The role of dopamine in the nucleus accumbens and striatum during sexual behavior in the female rat. *Journal of Neuroscience, 21*(9), 3236–3241.

Berns, G. S., Cohen, J. D., & Mintun, M. A. (1997). Brain regions responsive to novelty in the absence of awareness. *Science, 276*(5316), 1272–1275.

Bester-Meredith, J. K., & Marler, C. A. (2001). Vasopressin and aggression in cross-fostered California mice (*Peromyscus californicus*) and white-footed mice (*Peromyscus leucopus*). *Hormones and Behavior, 40*(1), 51–64.

Bester-Meredith, J. K., & Marler, C. A. (2003). Vasopressin and the transmission of paternal behavior across generations in mated, cross-fostered *Peromyscus* mice. *Behavioral Neuroscience, 117*(3), 455–463.

Bester-Meredith, J. K., Young, L. J., & Marler, C. A. (1999). Species differences in paternal behavior and aggression in *Peromyscus* and their associations with vasopressin immunoreactivity and receptors. *Hormones and Behavior, 36*(1), 25–38.

Black, J. M. (1996). Introduction: Pair bonds and partnerships. In J. M. Black (Ed.), *Partnerships in birds: The study of monogamy* (pp. 3–20). Oxford, UK: Oxford University Press.

Black, J. M. (2001). Fitness consequences of long-term pair bonds in barnacle geese: Monogamy in the extreme. *Behavioral Ecology, 12*(5), 640–645.

Bluthe, R. M., & Dantzer, R. (1993). Role of the vomeronasal system in vasopressinergic modulation of social recognition in rats. *Brain Research, 604*(1–2), 205–210.

Bowler, C. M., Cushing, B. S., & Carter, C. S. (2002). Social factors regulate female-female aggression and affiliation in prairie voles. *Physiology and Behavior, 76*, 559–566.

Bried, J., & Jouventin, P. (1999). Influence of breeding success on fidelity in long-lived birds: An experimental study. *Journal of Avian Biology, 30*(4), 392–398.

Brotherton, P. N. M., & Komers, P. E. (2003). Mate guarding and the evolution of social monogamy in mammals. In U. H. Reichard & C. Boesch (Eds.), *Monogamy: Mating strategies and partnerships in birds, humans and other mammals* (pp. 42–58). Cambridge, UK: Cambridge University Press.

Carr, D. B., & Sesack, S. R. (2000). Projections from the rat prefrontal cortex to the ventral tegmental area: Target specificity in the synaptic associations with mesoaccumbens and mesocortical neurons. *Journal of Neuroscience, 20*(10), 3864–3873.

Cartar, R. V. (1985). Testis size in sandpipers: The fertilization frequency hypothesis. *Naturwissenschaften, 72*(3), 157–158.

Carter, C. S. (1998). Neuroendocrine perspectives on social attachment and love. *Psychoneuroendocrinology, 23*(8), 779–818.

Carter, C. S., & Getz, L. L. (1993). Monogamy and the prairie vole. *Scientific American, 268*, 100–106.

Carter, C. S., Williams, J. R., & Witt, D. M. (1990). The biology of social bonding in a monogamous male. *Comparative Physiology, 9*, 154–164.

Cassini, M. H. (1999). The evolution of reproductive systems in pinnipeds. *Behavioral Ecology, 10*(5), 612–616.

Cezilly, F., & Nager, R. G. (1995). Comparative evidence for a positive association between divorce and extra-pair paternity in birds. *Proceedings of the Royal Society of London: B. Biological Sciences, 262*(1363), 7–12.

Cezilly, F., Preault, M., Dubois, F., Faivre, B., & Patris, B. (2000). Pair-bonding in birds and the active role of females: A critical review of the empirical evidence. *Behavioural Processes, 51*(1–3), 83–92.

Cheung, S., Ballew, J. R., Moore, K. E., & Lookingland, K. J. (1998). Contribution of dopamine neurons in the medial zona incerta to the innervation of the central nucleus of the amygdala, horizontal diagonal band of Broca and hypothalamic paraventricular nucleus. *Brain Research, 808*(2), 174–181.

Cho, M. M., DeVries, A. C., Williams, J. R., & Carter, C. S. (1999). The effects of oxytocin and vasopressin on partner preferences in male and female prairie voles (*Microtus ochrogaster*). *Behavioral Neuroscience, 113*(5), 1071–1079.

Choudhury, S. (1995). Divorce in birds: A review of the hypotheses. *Animal Behaviour, 50*, 413–429.

Clutton-Brock, T. (1991). *The evolution of parental care*. Princeton, NJ: Princeton University Press.

Cohen, R. (1971). *Dominance and defiance: A study of marital stability in an Islamic African society*. Washington DC: American Anthropological Association.

Compaan, J. C., Buijs, R. M., Pool, C. W., De Ruiter, A. J., & Koolhaas, J. M. (1993). Differential lateral septal vasopressin innervation in aggressive and nonaggressive male mice. *Brain Research Bulletin, 30*(1–2), 1–6.

Cooke, B. M., Chowanadisai, W., & Breedlove, S. M. (2000). Post-weaning social isolation of male rats reduces the volume of the medial amygdala and leads to deficits in adult sexual behavior. *Behavioral Brain Research, 117*(1–2), 107–113.

Cowley, J. J., & Brooksbank, B. W. L. (1991). Human exposure to putative pheromones and changes in aspects of social behavior. *Journal of Steroid Biochemistry and Molecular Biology, 39*(4B), 647–659.

Creelman, E., & Storey, A. E. (1991). Sex-differences in reproductive-behavior of Atlantic puffins. *Condor, 93*(2), 390–398.

Curtis, J. T. (2010). Does fertility trump monogamy? *Animal Behaviour, 80*, 319–328.

Curtis, J. T., Liu, Y., Aragona, B. J., & Wang, Z. X. (2006). Dopamine and monogamy. *Brain Research, 1126*, 6–90.

Curtis, J. T., Liu, Y., & Wang, Z. (2001). Lesions of the vomeronasal organ disrupt mating-induced pair bonding in female prairie voles (*Microtus ochrogaster*). *Brain Research, 901*(1–2), 167–174.

Curtis, J. T., Stowe, J. R., & Wang, Z. (2003). Differential effects of intraspecific interactions on the striatal dopamine system in social and non-social voles. *Neuroscience, 118*(4), 1165–1173.

Curtis, J. T., & Wang, Z. (2003). Forebrain c-fos expression under conditions conducive to pair bonding in female prairie voles (*Microtus ochrogaster*). *Physiology and Behavior, 80*(1), 95–101.

Curtis, J. T., & Wang, Z. (2005a). Glucocorticoid receptor involvement in pair bonding in female prairie voles: The effects of acute blockade and interactions with central dopamine reward systems. *Neuroscience, 134*(2), 369–376.

Curtis, J. T., & Wang, Z. (2005b). Ventral tegmental area involvement in pair bonding in male prairie voles. *Physiology and Behavior, 86*, 338–346.

Cushing, B. S., Martin, J. O., Young, L. J., & Carter, C. S. (2001). The effects of peptides on partner preference formation are predicted by habitat in prairie voles. *Hormones and Behavior, 39*(1), 48–58.

Cushing, B. S., Mogekwu, N., Le, W. W., Hoffman, G. E., & Carter, C. S. (2002). Cohabitation induced Fos immunoreactivity in the monogamous prairie vole. *Brain Research, 965*(1–2), 203–211.

Dantzer, R., Koob, G. F., Bluthe, R. M., & Le Moal, M. (1988). Septal vasopressin modulates social memory in male rats. *Brain Research, 457*(1), 143–147.

Day, L. H. (1964). Patterns of divorce in Australia and the United States. *American Sociological Review, 29*(4), 509–522.

Depue, R. A., & Collins, P. F. (1999). Neurobiology of the structure of personality: Dopamine, facilitation of incentive motivation, and extraversion. *Behavioral and Brain Sciences, 22*(3), 491–529.

Depue, R. A., & Morrone-Strupinsky, J. V. (2005). A neurobehavioral model of affiliative bonding: Implications for conceptualizing a human trait of affiliation. *Behavioral and Brain Sciences, 28*(3), 313–395.

DeVries, A. C. (2002). Interaction among social environment, the hypothalamic-pituitary-adrenal axis, and behavior. *Hormones and Behavior, 41*(4), 405–413.

DeVries, A. C., & Carter, C. S. (1999). Sex differences in temporal parameters of partner preference in prairie voles (*Microtus ochrogaster*). *Canadian Journal of Zoology, 77*(6), 885–889.

DeVries, A. C., DeVries, M. B., Taymans, S., & Carter, C. S. (1995). Modulation of pair bonding in female prairie voles (*Microtus ochrogaster*) by corticosterone. *Proceedings of the National Academy of Sciences USA, 92*(17), 7744–7748.

DeVries, A. C., DeVries, M. B., Taymans, S. E., & Carter, C. S. (1996). The effects of stress on social preferences are sexually dimorphic in prairie voles. *Proceedings of the National Academy of Sciences USA, 93*(21), 11980–11984.

DeVries, A. C., Glasper, E. R., & Detillion, C. E. (2003). Social modulation of stress responses. *Physiology and Behavior, 79*(3), 399–407.

DeVries, A. C., Taymans, S. E., & Carter, C. S. (1997). Social modulation of corticosteroid responses in male prairie voles. *Annals of the New York Academy of Sciences, 807*, 494–497.

De Vries, G. J., & Miller, M. A. (1998). Anatomy and function of extrahypothalamic vasopressin systems in the brain. *Progress in Brain Research, 119*, 3–20.

Dewsbury, D. A. (1987). The comparative psychology of monogamy. *Nebraska Symposium on Motivation, 35*, 1–50.

Døving, K. B., & Trotier, D. (1998). Structure and function of the vomeronasal organ. *Journal of Experimental Biology, 201*(21), 2913–2925.

Dubois, F., Wajnberg, E., & Cezilly, F. (2004). Optimal divorce and re-mating strategies for monogamous female birds: A simulation model. *Behavioral Ecology and Sociobiology, 56*(3), 228–236.

Emery, N. J., Seed, A. M., von Bayern, A. M. P., & Clayton, N. S. (2007). Cognitive adaptations of social bonding in birds. *Philosophical Transactions of the Royal Society: B. Biological Sciences, 362*(1480), 489–505.

Everts, H. G., De Ruiter, A. J., & Koolhaas, J. M. (1997). Differential lateral septal vasopressin in wild-type rats: Correlation with aggression. *Hormones and Behavior, 31*(2), 136–144.

Feldman, R., & Eidelman, A. I. (2003). Skin-to-skin contact (kangaroo care) accelerates autonomic and neurobehavioural maturation in preterm infants. *Developmental Medicine and Child Neurology, 45*(4), 274–281.

Fisher, H., Aron, A., & Brown, L. L. (2005). Romantic love: An fMRI study of a neural mechanism for mate choice. *Journal of Comparative Neurology, 493*(1), 58–62.

Fisher, H. E. (1989). Evolution of human serial pairbonding. *American Journal of Physical Anthropology, 78*, 331–354.

Fisher, H. E. (2000). Lust, attraction, attachment: Biology and evolution of the three primary emotion systems for mating, reproduction, and parenting. *Journal of Sex Education and Therepy, 25*(1), 96–104.

Fowler, C. D., Liu, Y., Ouimet, C., & Wang, Z. (2002). The effects of social environment on adult neurogenesis in the female prairie vole. *Journal of Neurobiology, 51*(2), 115–128.

Fraley, R. C., & Shaver, P. R. (2000). Adult attachment theory: Theoretical developments, emerging controversies, and unanswered questions. *Review of General Psychology, 4*(2), 132–154.

Gammie, S. C., & Nelson, R. J. (2000). Maternal and mating-induced aggression is associated with elevated citrulline immunoreactivity in the paraventricular nucleus in prairie voles. *Journal of Comparative Neurology, 418*(2), 182–192.

Gammie, S. C., & Nelson, R. J. (2001). cFOS and pCREB activation and maternal aggression in mice. *Brain Research, 898*(2), 232–241.

Gervai, J., Nemoda, Z., Lakatos, K., Ronai, Z., Toth, I., Ney, K., et al. (2005). Transmission disequilibrium tests confirm the link between DRD4 gene polymorphism and infant attachment. *American Journal of Medical Genetics: Part B. Neuropsychiatric Genetics, 132B*(1), 126–130.

Getz, L. L., Carter, C. S., & Gavish, L. (1981). The mating system of the prairie vole, *Microtus ochrogaster*: Field and laboratory evidence for pair-bonding. *Behavioral Ecology and Sociobiology, 8*, 189–194.

Gingrich, B., Liu, Y., Cascio, C., Wang, Z., & Insel, T. R. (2000). Dopamine D_2 receptors in the nucleus accumbens are important for social attachment in female prairie voles (*Microtus ochrogaster*). *Behavioral Neuroscience, 114*(1), 173–183.

Gobrogge, K. L., Liu, Y., Jia, X. X., & Wang, Z. X. (2007). Anterior hypothalamic neural activation and neurochemical associations with aggression in pair-bonded male prairie voles. *Journal of Comparative Neurology, 502*(6), 1109–1122.

Grippo, A. J., Lamb, D. G., Carter, C. S., & Porges, S. W. (2007). Cardiac regulation in the socially monogamous prairie vole. *Physiology and Behavior, 90*(2–3), 386–393.

Grippo, A. J., Wu, K. D., Hassan, B. S., & Carter, C. S. (2008). Social isolation in prairie voles induces behaviors relevant to negative affect: Toward the development of a rodent model focused on co-occuring depression and anxiety. *Depression and Anxiety, 25*(6), E17–26.

Gunnarsson, T. G., Gill, J. A., Sigurbjornsson, T., & Sutherland, W. J. (2004). Pair bonds: Arrival synchrony in migratory birds. *Nature, 431*(7009), 646.

Gutierrez, P. J., Meyer, J. S., & Novak, M. (1989). Comparison of postnatal brain development in meadow voles (*Microtus pennsylvanicus*) and pine voles (*M. pinatorum*). *Journal of Mammalogy, 70*(2), 292–299.

Halpern, M. (1987). The organization and function of the vomeronasal system. *Annual Reviews Neuroscience, 10*, 325–362.

Hammock, E. A. D., & Young, L. J. (2004). Functional microsatellite polymorphism associated with divergent social structure in vole species. *Molecular Biology and Evolution, 21*(6), 1057–1063.

Hass, C. C., & Valenzuela, D. (2002). Anti-predator benefits of group living in white-nosed coatis (*Nasua narica*). *Behavioral Ecology and Sociobiology, 51*(6), 570–578.

Hasue, R. H., & Shammah-Lagnado, S. J. (2002). Origin of the dopaminergic innervation of the central extended amygdala and accumbens shell: A combined retrograde tracing and immunohistochemical study in the rat. *Journal of Comparative Neurology, 454*(1), 15–33.

Heise, S., & Lippke, J. (1997). Role of female aggression in prevention of infanticidal behavior in male common voles, *Microtus arvalis* (Pallas, 1779). *Aggressive Behavior, 23*, 293–298.

Herr, J., & Rosell, F. (2004). Use of space and movement patterns in monogamous adult Eurasian beavers (*Castor fiber*). *Journal of Zoology, 262*, 257–264.

Hofmann, J. E., Getz, L. L., & Gavish, L. (1984). Home range overlap and nest cohabitation of male and female prairie voles. *American Midland Naturalist, 112*(2), 314–319.

Hooks, M. S., & Kalivas, P. W. (1995). The role of the mesoaccumbens-pallidal circuitry in novelty-induced activation. *Neuroscience, 64*(3), 587–597.

Ikemoto, S., & Panksepp, J. (1999). The role of nucleus accumbens dopamine in motivated behavior: A unifying interpretation with special reference to reward-seeking. *Brain Research Reviews, 31*(1), 6–41.

Insel, T. R. (1997). A neurobiological basis of social attachment. *American Journal of Psychiatry, 154*(6), 726–735.

Insel, T. R. (2000). Toward a neurobiology of attachment. *Review of General Psychology, 4*(2), 176–185.

Insel, T. R. (2003). Is social attachment an addictive disorder? *Physiology and Behavior, 79*(3), 351–357.

Insel, T. R., & Fernald, R. D. (2004). How the brain processes social information: Searching for the social brain. *Annual Review of Neuroscience, 27*, 697–722.

Insel, T. R., Gelhard, R., & Shapiro, L. E. (1991). The comparative distribution of forebrain receptors for neurohypophyseal peptides in monogamous and polygamous mice. *Neuroscience, 43*(2–3), 623–630.

Insel, T. R., & Hulihan, T. J. (1995). A gender-specific mechanism for pair bonding: Oxytocin and partner preference formation in monogamous voles. *Behavioral Neuroscience, 109*(4), 782–789.

Insel, T. R., Preston, S., & Winslow, J. T. (1995). Mating in the monogamous male: Behavioral consequences. *Physiology and Behavior, 57*(4), 615–627.

Insel, T. R., & Shapiro, L. E. (1992). Oxytocin receptor distribution reflects social organization in monogamous and polygamous voles. *Proceedings of the National Academy of Sciences USA, 89*(13), 5981–5985.

Insel, T. R., Wang, Z.-X., & Ferris, C. F. (1994). Patterns of brain vasopressin receptor distribution associated with social organization in microtine rodents. *Journal of Neuroscience, 14*(9), 5381–5392.

Jacobson, P. H. (1950). Differentials in divorce by duration of marriage and size of family. *American Sociological Review, 15*(2), 235–244.

Keer, S. E., & Stern, J. M. (1999). Dopamine receptor blockade in the nucleus accumbens inhibits maternal retrieval and licking, but enhances nursing behavior in lactating rats. *Physiology and Behavior, 67*(5), 659–669.

Kellam, J. S. (2003). Pair bond maintenance in pileated woodpeckers at roost sites during autumn. *Wilson Bulletin, 115*(2), 186–192.

Keverne, E. B. (2002). Mammalian pheromones: From genes to behaviour. *Current Biology, 12*(23), R807–809.

Kirkpatrick, B., Carter, C. S., Newman, S. W., & Insel, T. R. (1994). Axon-sparing lesions of the medial nucleus of the amygdala decrease affiliative behaviors in the prairie vole (*Microtus ochrogaster*): Behavioral and anatomical specificity. *Behavioral Neuroscience, 108*(3), 501–513.

Kleiman, D. G. (1977). Monogamy in mammals. *Quarterly Review of Biology, 52*(1), 39–69.

Kleiman, D. G. (1981). Correlations among life history characteristics of mammalian species exhibiting two extreme forms of monogamy. In R. D. Alexander & D. W. Tinkle (Eds.), *Natural selection and social behavior: Recent research and new theory* (pp. 332–344). New York: Chiron Press.

Klein, S. L., Hairston, J. E., DeVries, A. C., & Nelson, R. J. (1997). Social environment and steroid hormones affect species and sex differences in immune function among voles. *Hormones and Behavior, 32*(1), 30–39.

Kohlert, J. G., & Meisel, R. L. (1999). Sexual experience sensitizes mating-related nucleus accumbens dopamine responses of female Syrian hamsters. *Behavioral Brain Research, 99*(1), 45–52.

Kokko, H., Ranta, E., Ruxton, G., & Lundberg, P. (2002). Sexually transmitted disease and the evolution of mating systems. *Evolution, 56*(6), 1091–1100.

Kollack-Walker, S., & Newman, S. W. (1995). Mating and agonistic behavior produce different patterns of Fos immunolabeling in the male Syrian hamster brain. *Neuroscience, 66*(3), 721–736.

Komers, P. E., & Brotherton, P. N. M. (1997). Female space use is the best predictor of monogamy in mammals. *Proceedings of the Royal Society of London: B. Biological Sciences, 264*(1386), 1261–1270.

Lack, D. (1940). Pair-formation in birds. *Condor, 42*(6), 269–286.

Lawford, B. R., Young, R. M., Noble, E. P., Kann, B., Arnold, L., Rowell, J., et al. (2003). D2 dopamine receptor gene polymorphism: Paroxetine and social functioning in posttraumatic stress disorder. *European Neuropsychopharmacology, 13*(5), 313–320.

Layne, J. N. (1968). Ontogeny. In J. A. King (Ed.), *Biology of Peromyscus (Rodentia)* (Special Publication No. 2) (pp. 148–253). Shippensburg, PA: American Society of Mammalogists.

Lehrman, D. S. (1959). Hormonal responses to external stimuli in birds. *Ibis, 101*, 478–496.

Levitan, D. R., Fukami, H., Jara, J., Kline, D., McGovern, T. M., McGhee, K. E., et al. (2004). Mechanisms of reproductive isolation among sympatric broadcast-spawning corals of the *Montastraea annularis* species complex. *Evolution, 58*(2), 308–323.

Lim, M. M., & Young, L. J. (2006). Neuropeptidergic regulation of affiliative behavior and social bonding in animals. *Hormones and Behavior, 50*(4), 506–517.

Linden, M. (1991). Divorce in great tits—chance or choice? An experimental approach. *American Naturalist, 138*(4), 1039–1048.

Liu, Y., Curtis, J. T., & Wang, Z. (2001). Vasopressin in the lateral septum regulates pair bond formation in male prairie voles (*Microtus ochrogaster*). *Behavioral Neuroscience, 115*(4), 910–919.

Liu, Y., Fowler, C. D., & Wang, Z. (2001). Ontogeny of brain-derived neurotrophic factor gene expression in the forebrain of prairie and montane voles. *Developmental Brain Research, 127*(1), 51–61.

Liu, Y., & Wang, Z. X. (2003). Nucleus accumbens oxytocin and dopamine interact to regulate pair bond formation in female prairie voles. *Neuroscience, 121*(3), 537–544.

Lonstein, J. S., & De Vries, G. J. (1999). Sex differences in the parental behaviour of adult virgin prairie voles: Independence from gonadal hormones and vasopressin. *Journal of Neuroendocrinology, 11*(6), 441–449.

Lorrain, D. S., Riolo, J. V., Matuszewich, L., & Hull, E. M. (1999). Lateral hypothalamic serotonin inhibits nucleus accumbens dopamine: Implications for sexual satiety. *Journal of Neuroscience, 19*(17), 7648–7652.

Lucht, M., Barnow, S., Schroeder, W., Grabe, H. J., Finckh, U., John, U., et al. (2006). Negative perceived paternal parenting is associated with dopamine D-2 receptor exon 8 and GABA(A) alpha 6 receptor variants: An explorative study. *American Journal of Medical Genetics: Part B. Neuropsychiatric Genetics, 141B*(2), 167–172.

Lukas, D., & Clutton-Brock, T. (2012). Cooperative breeding and monogamy in mammalian species. *Proceedings of the Royal Society of London: B. Biological Sciences, 279*, 2151–2156.

Madison, D. M. (1985). Activity rhythms and spacing. In R. H. Tamarin (Ed.), *Biology of New World Microtus* (Special Publication No. 2) (pp. 373–419). Shippensburg, PA: American Society of Mammalogists.

McFarland, K., & Kalivas, P. W. (2001). The circuitry mediating cocaine-induced reinstatement of drug-seeking behavior. *Journal of Neuroscience, 21*(21), 8655–8663.

McGuire, B. (1988). Effects of cross-fostering on parental behavior of meadow voles (*Microtus pennsylvanicus*). *Journal of Mammalogy, 69*(2), 332–341.

McGuire, B., & Novak, M. (1984). A comparison of maternal behaviour in the meadow vole (*Microtus pennsylvanicus*), prairie vole (*M. ochrogaster*) and pine vole (*M. pinatorum*). *Animal Behavior, 32*, 1132–1141.

McGuire, B., & Novak, M. (1986). Parental care and its relationship to social organization in the montane vole (*Microtus montanus*). *Journal of Mammalogy, 67*, 305–311.

McGuire, B., & Novak, M. (1987). The effects of cross-fostering on the development of social preferences in meadow voles (*Microtus pennsylvanicus*). *Behavioral and Neural Biology, 47*(2), 167–172.

McNamara, J. M., & Forslund, P. (1996). Divorce rates in birds: Predictions from an optimization model. *American Naturalist, 147*(4), 609–640.

Melis, M. R., & Argiolas, A. (1995). Dopamine and sexual behavior. *Neuroscience and Biobehavioral Reviews, 19*(1), 19–38.

Meredith, M. (2001). Human vomeronasal organ function: A critical review of best and worst cases. *Chemical Senses, 26*(4), 433–445.

Mermelstein, P. G., & Becker, J. B. (1995). Increased extracellular dopamine in the nucleus accumbens and striatum of the female rat during paced copulatory behavior. *Behavioral Neuroscience, 109*(2), 354–365.

Mettke-Hofmann, C., & Gwinner, E. (2003). Long-term memory for a life on the move. *Proceedings of the National Academy of Sciences USA, 100*(10), 5863–5866.

Mitchell, J. B., & Gratton, A. (1992). Mesolimbic dopamine release elicited by activation of the accessory olfactory system: A high speed chronoamperometric study. *Neuroscience Letters, 140*(1), 81–84.

Mock, D. W. (1985). An introduction to the neglected mating system. In P. A. Gowaty & D. W. Mock (Eds.), *Avian monogamy: Ornithological Monographs No. 37* (pp. 1–10). Washington, DC: American Ornithologists Union.

Nadeau, J. H. (1985). Ontogeny. In R. H. Tamarin (Ed.), Biology of New World Microtus (Special Publication No. 2) (pp. 254–285). Shippensburg, PA: American Society of Mammalogists.

Nestler, E. J. (2002). From neurobiology to treatment: Progress against addiction. *Nature Neuroscience, 5*, 1076–1079.

Nuechterlein, G. L., & Storer, R. W. (1982). The pair-formation displays of the Western Grebe. *Condor, 84*(4), 350–369.

Ophir, A. G., Phelps, S. M., Sorin, A. B., & Wolff, J. O. (2007). Morphological, genetic and behavioral comparisons of two prairie vole populations in the field and laboratory. *Journal of Mammalogy, 88*(4), 989–999.

Orians, G. H. (1969). On the evolution of mating systems in birds and mammals. *American Naturalist, 103*(934), 589–603.

Otter, K., & Ratcliffe, L. (1996). Female initiated divorce in a monogamous songbird: Abandoning mates for males of higher quality. *Proceedings of the Royal Society of London: B. Biological Sciences, 263*(1368), 351–355.

Parker, G. A. (1984). Sperm competition and the evolution of animal mating strategies. In R. L. Smith (Ed.), *Sperm competition and the evolution of animal mating systems* (pp. 1–60). New York: Academic Press.

Pedersen, C. A. (2004). Biological aspects of social bonding and the roots of human violence. *Annals of the New York Academy of Science, 1036*, 106–127.

Pellis, S. M., & Iwaniuk, A. N. (1999). The roles of phylogeny and sociality in the evolution of social play in muroid rodents. *Animal Behaviour, 58*(2), 361–373.

Pellis, S. M., Pellis, V. C., & Dewsbury, D. A. (1989). Different levels of complexity in the play-fighting by muroid rodents appear to result from different levels of intensity of attack and defense. *Aggressive Behavior, 15*(4), 297–310.

Pfaus, J. G., Damsma, G., Nomikos, G. G., Wenkstern, D. G., Blaha, C. D., Phillips, A. G., et al. (1990). Sexual behavior enhances central dopamine transmission in the male rat. *Brain Research, 530*(2), 345–348.

Pierce, J. D., Jr., Pellis, V. C., Dewsbury, D. A., & Pellis, S. M. (1991). Targets and tactics of agonistic and precopulatory behavior in montane and prairie voles: Their relationship to juvenile play-fighting. *Aggressive Behavior, 17*(6), 337–349.

Pitkow, L. J., Sharer, C. A., Ren, X., Insel, T. R., Terwilliger, E. F., & Young, L. J. (2001). Facilitation of affiliation and pair-bond formation by vasopressin receptor gene transfer into the ventral forebrain of a monogamous vole. *Journal of Neuroscience, 21*(18), 7392–7396.

Pizzuto, T., & Getz, L. L. (1998). Female prairie voles (*Microtus ochrogaster*) fail to form a new pair after loss of mate. *Behavioural Processes, 43*, 79–86.

Prohazka, D., Novak, M. A., & Meyer, J. S. (1986). Divergent effects of early hydrocortisone treatment on behavioral and brain development in meadow and pine voles. *Developmental Psychobiology, 19*(6), 521–535.

Ralls, K., Cypher, B., & Spiegel, L. K. (2007). Social monogamy in kit foxes: Formation, association, duration, and dissolution of mated pairs. *Journal of Mammalogy, 88*(6), 1439–1446.

Rasmussen, D. R. (1981). Pair-bond strength and stability and reproductive success. *Psychological Review, 88*(3), 274–290.

Reynolds, S. M., & Berridge, K. C. (2002). Positive and negative motivation in nucleus accumbens shell: Bivalent rostrocaudal gradients for GABA-elicited eating, taste "liking"/"disliking" reactions, place preference/avoidance, and fear. *Journal of Neuroscience, 22*(16), 7308–7320.

Ribble, D. O. (1992). Lifetime reproductive success and its correlates in the monogamous rodent, *Peromyscus californicus. Journal of Animal Ecology, 61*(2), 457–468.

Rodgers, J. A. (1980). Little Blue Heron breeding behavior. *Auk, 97*(2), 371–384.

Saal, D., Dong, Y., Bonci, A., & Malenka, R. C. (2003). Drugs of abuse and stress trigger a common synaptic adaptation in dopamine neurons. *Neuron, 37*(4), 577–582.

Sarnyai, Z., McKittrick, C. R., McEwen, B. S., & Kreek, M. J. (1998). Selective regulation of dopamine transporter binding in the shell of the nucleus accumbens by adrenalectomy and corticosterone-replacement. *Synapse, 30*(3), 334–337.

Savic, I., Berglund, H., & Lindstrom, P. (2005). Brain response to putative pheromones in homosexual men. *Proceedings of the National Academy of Sciences USA, 102*(20), 7356–7361.

Schneier, F. R., Liebowitz, M. R., Abi-Dargham, A., Zea-Ponce, Y., Lin, S. H., & Laruelle, M. (2000). Low dopamine D-2 receptor binding potential in social phobia. *American Journal of Psychiatry, 157*(3), 457–459.

Schwab, J. M., Solomon, N. G., Isaacson, L. G., Callahan, P. (2004). Reproductive activation of pine voles (*Microtus pinetorum*): Examination of physiological markers. *Brain Research, 1021,* 256–263.

Seghers, B. H. (1974). Schooling behavior in guppy (*Poecilia reticulata*): An evolutionary response to predation. *Evolution, 28*(3), 486–489.

Silk, J. B., Alberts, S. C., & Altmann, J. (2003). Social bonds of female baboons enhance infant survival. *Science, 302*(5648), 1231–1234.

Starkey, N. J., & Hendrie, C. A. (1998). Disruption of pairs produces pair-bond disruption in male but not female Mongolian gerbils. *Physiology and Behavior, 65*(3), 497–503.

Stern, K., & McClintock, M. K. (1998). Regulation of ovulation by human pheromones. *Nature, 392*(6672), 177–179.

Stinson, C. H., Crawford, D. L., & Lauthner, J. (1981). Sex-differences in winter habitat of American kestrels in Georgia. *Journal of Field Ornithology, 52*(1), 29–35.

Swanson, L. W. (1982). The projections of the ventral tegmental area and adjacent regions: A combined fluorescent retrograde tracer and immunofluorescence study in the rat. *Brain Research Bulletin, 9*(1–6), 321–353.

Tidey, J. W., & Miczek, K. A. (1996). Social defeat stress selectively alters mesocorticolimbic dopamine release: An *in vivo* microdialysis study. *Brain Research, 721*(1–2), 140–149.

van den Berg, C. L., Hol, T., Van Ree, J. M., Spruijt, B. M., Everts, H., & Koolhaas, J. M. (1999). Play is indispensable for an adequate development of coping with social challenges in the rat. *Developmental Psychobiology, 34*(2), 129–138.

Wang, Z. (1995). Species differences in the vasopressin-immunoreactive pathways in the bed nucleus of the stria terminalis and medial amygdaloid nucleus in prairie voles (*Microtus ochrogaster*) and meadow voles (*Microtus pennsylvanicus*). *Behavioral Neuroscience, 109*(2), 305–311.

Wang, Z., Bullock, N. A., & De Vries, G. J. (1993). Sexual differentiation of vasopressin projections of the bed nucleus of the stria terminals and medial amygdaloid nucleus in rats. *Endocrinology, 132*(6), 2299–2306.

Wang, Z., Ferris, C. F., & De Vries, G. J. (1994). Role of septal vasopressin innervation in paternal behavior in prairie voles (*Microtus ochrogaster*). *Proceedings of the National Academy of Sciences USA, 91*(1), 400–404.

Wang, Z., Hulihan, T. J., & Insel, T. R. (1997). Sexual and social experience is associated with different patterns of behavior and neural activation in male prairie voles. *Brain Research, 767*(2), 321–332.

Wang, Z., & Young, L. J. (1997). Ontogeny of oxytocin and vasopressin receptor binding in the lateral septum in prairie and montane voles. *Developmental Brain Research, 104*(1–2), 191–195.

Wang, Z., Young, L. J., De Vries, G. J., & Insel, T. R. (1998). Voles and vasopressin:

A review of molecular, cellular, and behavioral studies of pair bonding and paternal behaviors. *Progress in Brain Research, 119*, 483–499.

Wang, Z., Young, L. J., Liu, Y., & Insel, T. R. (1997). Species differences in vasopressin receptor binding are evident early in development: Comparative anatomic studies in prairie and montane voles. *Journal of Comparative Neurology, 378*(4), 535–546.

Wang, Z., Yu, G., Cascio, C., Liu, Y., Gingrich, B., & Insel, T. R. (1999). Dopamine D_2 receptor-mediated regulation of partner preferences in female prairie voles (*Microtus ochrogaster*): A mechanism for pair bonding? *Behavioral Neuroscience, 113*(3), 602–611.

Wang, Z., Zhou, L., Hulihan, T. J., & Insel, T. R. (1996). Immunoreactivity of central vasopressin and oxytocin pathways in microtine rodents: A quantitative comparative study. *Journal of Comparative Neurology, 366*, 726–737.

Wang, Z. X., Liu, Y., Young, L. J., & Insel, T. R. (2000). Hypothalamic vasopressin gene expression increases in both males and females postpartum in a biparental rodent. *Journal of Neuroendocrinology, 12*(2), 111–120.

Watters, J. J., Wilkinson, C. W., & Dorsa, D. M. (1996). Glucocorticoid regulation of vasopressin V1a receptors in rat forebrain. *Molecular Brain Research, 38*(2), 276–284.

White, L. K. (1990). Determinants of divorce—A review of research in the 80s. *Journal of Marriage and the Family, 52*(4), 904–912.

Willcox, W. F. (1897). *The divorce problem: A study in statistics* (2nd ed., pp. 1–75). New York: Columbia University.

Williams, J. R., Catania, K. C., & Carter, C. S. (1992). Development of partner preferences in female prairie voles (*Microtus ochrogaster*): The role of social and sexual experience. *Hormones and Behavior, 26*(3), 339–349.

Williams, J. R., Insel, T. R., Harbaugh, C. R., & Carter, C. S. (1994). Oxytocin administered centrally facilitates formation of a partner preference in female prairie voles (*Microtus ochrogaster*). *Journal of Neuroendocrinology, 6*, 247–250.

Wilson, S. C. (1982). The development of social behaviour between siblings and non-siblings of the voles *Microtus ochrogaster* and *Microtus pennsylvanicus*. *Animal Behaviour, 30*(2), 426–437.

Wineberg, H. (1988). Duration between marriage and first birth and marital instability. *Social Biology, 35*(1–2), 91–102.

Winslow, J. T., Hastings, N., Carter, C. S., Harbaugh, C. R., & Insel, T. R. (1993). A role for central vasopressin in pair bonding in monogamous prairie voles. *Nature, 365*(6446), 545–548.

Witt, D. M., Carter, C. S., & Walton, D. M. (1990). Central and peripheral effects of oxytocin administration in prairie voles (*Microtus ochrogaster*). *Pharmacology, Biochemistry and Behavior, 37*(1), 63–69.

Wittenberger, J. F., & Tilson, R. L. (1980). The evolution of monogamy: Hypotheses and evidence. *Annual Review of Ecology and Systematics, 11*, 197–232.

Wright, S. L., & Brown, R. E. (2002). The importance of paternal care on pup survival and pup growth in *Peromyscus californicus* when required to work for food. *Behavioural Processes, 60*(1), 41–52.

Wysocki, C. J., & Preti, G. (2004). Facts, fallacies, fears, and frustrations with human pheromones. *Anatomical Record: Part A. Discoveries in Molecular Cellular and Evolutionary Biology, 281A*(1), 1201–1211.

Young, K. A., Liu, Y., & Wang, Z. X. (2008). The neurobiology of social attachment: A comparative approach to behavioral, neuroanatomical, and neurochemical studies. *Comparative Biochemistry and Physiology: C. Toxicology and Pharmacology, 148*(4), 401–410.

Young, L. J. (2002). The neurobiology of social recognition, approach, and avoidance. *Biological Psychiatry, 51*(1), 18–26.

Young, L. J., Lim, M. M., Gingrich, B., & Insel, T. R. (2001). Cellular mechanisms of social attachment. *Hormones and Behavior, 40*(2), 133–138.

Young, L. J., Waymire, K. G., Nilsen, R., MacGregor, G. R., Wang, Z., & Insel, T. R. (1997). The 5' flanking region of the monogamous prairie vole oxytocin receptor gene directs tissue-specific expression in transgenic mice. *Annals of the New York Academy of Sciences, 807*, 515–517.

Young, L. J., Winslow, J. T., Nilsen, R., & Insel, T. R. (1997). Species differences in V_{1a} receptor gene expression in monogamous and nonmonogamous voles: Behavioral consequences. *Behavioral Neuroscience, 111*(3), 599–605.

Zahm, D. S. (2000). An integrative neuroanatomical perspective on some subcortical substrates of adaptive responding with emphasis on the nucleus accumbens. *Neuroscience and Biobehavioral Reviews, 24*(1), 85–105.

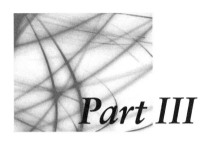

Part III

NEW TOPICS, IDEAS, AND DEVELOPMENTS

Chapter 7

Logging On, Hooking Up

The Changing Nature of Romantic
Relationship Initiation and Romantic Relating

SUSAN SPRECHER
SANDRA METTS

*I*magine two friends catching up on recent events in their lives. One says to the other, "I hear you are dating again. How did you two meet?" Which of the following responses would you most likely expect?

1. "I am sure we were destined to meet. We grew up in the same community, and although we didn't go to the same schools, our families attended the same church, and we occasionally interacted there. I think my family always hoped we would end up together."
2. "Oh, just luck of the draw—we happened to be assigned to the same lab section in our biology class. We began studying together and then eventually started dating."
3. "Well, kind of weird. We were at a party hanging out. I got what I thought was a wink from across the room; we hooked up that very

night, and just kind of kept going. I just changed my Facebook status so I hope this works out."

4. "We met online. The dating site said we would make a compatible match because of our answers to a set of questions. We communicated for weeks over the computer and then set up our first meeting. I was nervous about meeting but it was a great first date and we both just sort of stopped looking."

If you find all responses plausible, but had to select the most typical response for young adults and selected the second one, you would likely be correct. However, what if the scenario involved two middle-aged coworkers, and the inquiry began with "I hear you are dating again after your divorce"? Both Options 1 and 4 would seem realistic. What if this question was posed to someone of your grandparents' generation? Option 1 would be most plausible, Options 2 and 3 highly unlikely, and Option 4, although possible, nevertheless atypical. Our point here is simply that finding a potential partner is not an easy, direct path common to all cohort groups or at all times. In this chapter, we focus on the changing nature of romantic relationship initiation.

Romantic relationship initiation, partner selection, and dating are not static processes in Western society but are subject to change over time (e.g., Cate & Lloyd, 1992). Some of the changes occur because of the emergence of new social norms. For example, it has become normative to delay marriage beyond the early 20s. As a result, romantic initiation and dating in adolescence and young adulthood have become more focused on filling needs for companionship, sexual intimacy, and fun rather than a step toward a long-term commitment or marriage (Giordano, Manning, & Longmore, 2009). An aspect of casual dating in adolescence that has evolved with this normative transition is "group dating" or "hanging out," in which mixed-sex groups of adolescents meet at a specific location (e.g., mall, movie) for fun and socializing (Bredow, Cate, & Huston, 2008; Glenn & Marquardt, 2001). In addition, increasing divorce rates and changing norms about dating and courtship for middle-aged and older adults have resulted in more dating and partner seeking in midlife and later (Sassler, 2010). Two changes of particular relevance within the domain of romantic relationship initiation include the availability of technology as a virtual location for meeting potential partners and the reformulation of sexual norms within the traditional phases of relationship development.

The availability of personal computers and the Internet, linking people at great distances, has changed how people initiate relationships (Wellman, 2001). People of diverse ages are finding and interacting with partners through Internet dating sites, social network sites (e.g., Facebook), and other online venues (e.g., McKenna, 2008; Sprecher, 2009). Furthermore, hookups, which are casual, often unplanned, sexual encounters that occur outside of a dating or romantic context, have become more common and acceptable among college students and adolescents (Paul, Wenzel, & Harvey, 2008). Although hookups are characterized by spontaneous physical intimacy that occurs without the intent to develop a relationship, one potential outcome of the hookup experience is the development of a romantic relationship (e.g., Bogle, 2008).

Internet connections and sexual hookups, as two new ways of meeting potential romantic partners, deviate from the typical pathway to intimacy common in traditional dating, discussed further later in this chapter. They exist, however, side by side with traditional ways of meeting partners. People still meet partners through their social networks (e.g., friends introduce friends), fall in love with the person in the cubicle next to them at the office, and go to singles bars and neighborhood pubs to meet others and socialize. Our discussion here of the new ways of forming romantic relationships includes a comparison with the more traditional ways of meeting partners.

Although the Internet and hooking up serve as ways that relationships are initiated, these contexts are also used to engage in casual interactions with no expectations or desire for a relationship to develop. Internet dating and hooking up are of scientific interest to relationship scholars not only because relationships can be formed from the experiences but also because they represent new ways that people can meet their sexual, social, and other needs even in the absence of the development of a relationship— that is, they provide new ways of human bonding.

THE TRADITIONAL SCRIPT FOR ROMANTIC RELATIONSHIP INITIATION

In the "traditional" Western script for romantic relationship initiation, people met, and still meet, partners in various face-to-face contexts, including the workplace, school, bars, and just "hanging out" with friends. If a romantic spark occurs between two people in an initial face-to-face encounter, one or both people (but usually the male in heterosexual connections) initiate further contact through a first date. Traditionally defined, dates are formally planned and often include an activity (e.g., dinner, movie). The first date is a time of initial self-disclosure and some physical affection but rarely full sexual intimacy (Mongeau & Johnson, 1995; Rose & Frieze, 1993). First dates for heterosexuals have been described as strongly influenced by gender-role cultural scripts, in which men initiate, plan, and pay and women engage in more subordinate roles (e.g., Eaton & Rose, 2011; Laner & Ventrone, 2000). If there is attraction after the first date, the traditional courtship process continues and results in subsequent dates (Mongeau, Morr Serewicz, & Therrien, 2004). During this early phase, the traditional gender-role script casts men as the initiators of sexual behaviors and women as the responders or restrictors (Bartoli & Clark, 2006). If the couple progresses through subsequent dates, sexual intimacy increases (Cohen & Shotland, 1996), as does the degree of information and knowledge the partners gain about each other through reciprocal self-disclosure (Derlega, Winstead, & Greene, 2008).

DATA ON HOW COUPLES MEET

Perhaps the best data available on how people met partners in the pre-Internet era, before sexual mores changed to include casual hookup experiences, come from the 1992 National Health and Social Life Survey conducted with a representative sample of 3,432 Americans (Laumann, Gagnon, Michael, & Michaels, 1994). The survey revealed that most people met their partner in one of four venues: school, work, private party, and bar. Approximately 33% of the relationships began through an introduction by a friend, another 33% through an introduction by another network member (e.g., a family member, coworker, neighbor), and the final 33% through self-introductions; 1% or less of respondents met their partner through personal want ads in print magazines and newspapers.

Since the early 1990s, however, the Internet has become a prominent place to meet partners. The first national study that demonstrated the growing influence of the Internet in romantic initiation and relating was conducted in 2005 by the Pew Internet & American Life Project, a nonprofit research center that monitors the social effects of the Internet on Americans. The Pew survey involved telephone interviews with a national representative sample of 3,215 adults, ranging in age from 18 to over 65 (Madden & Lenhart, 2006). Of the single adults in the sample who were Internet users and currently seeking a romantic partner, 37% reported that they had gone to a dating website or other online venue to meet potential partners. In addition, 15% of the participants knew of someone who was in a marriage or long-term relationship with someone they had met online, and 31% knew of someone who had experimented with Internet dating. However, of those in the sample who were married or in a committed relationship, most reported meeting their partner in real-world settings, such as work or school (38%), through family or friends (34%), or at a nightclub, bar, café, or other social venues (13%). Only 3% reported meeting their partner through the Internet.

In interpreting the relatively low percentage of respondents who met their partner online, it should be noted that a majority of the sample was involved in relationships that had originated years earlier, before the era of the Internet. Evidence suggests that of relationships formed more recently, the percentage originating online has been increasing exponentially. A 2009 study with a nationally representative sample of 4,002 participants (Rosenfeld & Thomas, 2012) found that of the participants who had met their partner in the 2 years (2007–2009) prior to the administration of the survey, approximately 22% of the heterosexual couples met on the Internet; 17% of heterosexual respondents met their partner within a 10-year period prior to the survey. Data collected in other countries, beyond the United States, also show an increasing incidence of relationship formation via the Internet (e.g., Dutton et al., 2009; Hogan, Li, & Dutton, 2011; Shtatfeld & Barak, 2009).

It is more difficult to document how many people meet partners through sexual hookups. Questions about hookup experiences have not been included in the national representative studies referred to previously. Studies conducted with convenience samples of college students, however, suggest that a large proportion of college students, especially by the time they reach their senior year, have had a hookup experience (McClintock, 2010; Paul, McManus, & Hayes, 2000). Only a small percentage (10–12%) of the total number of hookups, however, have actually resulted in a dating relationship (Bisson & Levine, 2009; Paul et al., 2000).

In the next section, we discuss in more detail how the Internet has been used as a way to initiate romantic relationships and as a format for other romantic relating. Following this, we discuss hookups as a form of romantic relationship initiation and romantic/sexual relating.

USE OF THE INTERNET FOR ROMANTIC RELATIONSHIP INITIATION AND RELATING

Online dating is an omnibus term used to refer to meeting a partner online, but it can be misleading for several reasons. First, dating in the traditional sense rarely occurs online. Instead, people meet a partner online, typically have their initial communication through computer-mediated communication (CMC), but then move the relationship offline relatively quickly. Second, the term does not capture the diverse ways that people can initiate a relationship online. With these caveats in mind, we begin this section by distinguishing among various types of online relationship initiation. We then discuss the implications for relationship development when initial communication and information obtained about the other occurs via the Internet versus face-to-face interaction, with a focus on the differences in pathways to romantic intimacy.

Diversity of Online Initiation

McKenna (2007, 2008) and others (e.g., Sprecher, 2009; Whitty, 2007) have distinguished among types of Internet venues for meeting others. These online venues can vary on several dimensions, including the users' motivations for visiting a particular venue, whether the communication is synchronous or asynchronous, the degree of anonymity, the amount of information that is potentially available about the other prior to a potential face-to-face meeting, and the length of time two people interact with each other in CMC before meeting.

Naturally Forming Relationships

Relationships can develop as a by-product of interaction in online venues that have a primary purpose other than relationship formation. For example, people may go to particular Internet sites to play interactive games, participate in a newsgroup or blog, or to be part of a social group. Studies have shown that relationships commonly begin through such online venues. For example, Parks and Floyd (1996) sampled people who posted messages to Internet newsgroups to investigate trends regarding the development of new acquaintances, friendships, or other personal relationships stemming from their participation. They found that 61% of respondents formed a relationship with someone they met for the first time through the Internet newsgroup. Most of the relationships were described as friendships and some as romantic. In Parks and Roberts's (1998) follow-up study of individuals engaging in Internet multiuser games and discussions, 94% of respondents reported that they had formed a personal relationship with someone they met through this online venue; 26% of these relationships were described as romantic. In another study based on surveys sent to hundreds of Internet newsgroup members who participated in online group discussions, McKenna, Green, and Gleason (2002) found that most users had formed friendships with other group members, and approximately 20% had entered a romantic relationship with someone they met through these online interactions. A 2-year follow-up study of this sample indicated that the relationships remained relatively stable over time. Utz (2000) found that 77% of a sample who were involved in interactive role-playing online games reported forming an online relationship, 25% of which were romantic. Recent research continues to show that naturally forming relationships, particularly friendships, frequently develop from interactions that occur in online venues focused on specific activities (e.g., Wellman, Salaff, Dimitrova, Yuan, & Gay, 2006).

Online interactions in such venues can facilitate relationship development because of the experience of pleasant interactions in the context of engaging in common activities, the perception of similarity, and the opportunity to express one's true self through CMC (Bargh, McKenna, & Fitzsimons, 2002; McKenna et al., 2002). In addition, CMC can lead to high levels of self-disclosure (e.g., Joinson, 2001), discussed later. The newest form of an online venue in which naturally forming relationships can develop are virtual worlds such as SIMS and Second Life, which allow interactions with others through avatars (e.g., Vasalou & Joinson, 2009). The social interactions that occur online in such virtual venues, even if they do not evolve into face-to-face relationships, can nonetheless help people meet their need for belonging and for connecting with others. For example, some people spend several hours each week playing multiuser games, sometimes with people from around the world (Yee, 2006).

Social Network Relationships

People also interact and form relationships through online social network sites. Facebook, the most widely used social network site at the time of this writing,[1] began in 2004 as a tool for college students and then expanded to include high school and junior high students and adults (Boyd & Ellison, 2007; Madden & Zickuhr, 2011). Facebook members use it primarily to keep in touch with family and with old and new friends (Ellison, Steinfield, & Lampe, 2007; Joinson, 2008; Smith, 2011). Facebook and other social network sites can also contribute to the development of relationships and in a variety of ways.

Through Facebook, people can engage in "social browsing" (Lampe, Ellison, & Steinfield, 2006) to learn information about people they do not know but who may be connected to their friends. Awareness of another, afforded by browsing, is considered to be the first stage of relationship development (Levinger, 1974). The information obtained about another through Facebook can then lead to a request through Facebook to make

---

[1]Friendster and Myspace were other early social network sites. LinkedIn, another social network site, allows people to connect for both professional and social purposes.

the other a "friend." Facebook further facilitates the process of acquiring new friends by recommending friends based on having friends in common. In addition, Facebook provides an opportunity for romantic relationship initiation by facilitating reconnections and announcing relationship status changes of network members. For example, through Facebook postings, people can learn that old flames and peripheral members of their network have changed their relationship status and are now "available," which can motivate reconnections (Bryant, Marmo, & Ramirez, 2011). Facebook also facilitates relationship initiation by providing the opportunity for users to join virtual groups based on common interests and to organize social gatherings (Ellison et al., 2007).

Regardless of whether the target of one's romantic interest was previously known offline or known only through Facebook, access to information provided in Facebook about the target individual, in the form of profile information, photos, and posts, allows people to learn about the other's background, religious and political views, hobbies, friendships, and activities. Considerable research in social psychology has shown that knowledge leads to familiarity and attraction (for a review, see Berscheid & Reis, 1998).

The first academic research on Facebook and other network sites (e.g., Myspace) focused on topics such as identity presentation and the association of use of the network sites with well-being (e.g., Ellison et al., 2007; Valkenburg, Peter, & Schouten, 2006). More recent research has examined the association between the use of Facebook and young adults' social opportunities, including the development of relationships and offline social capital (i.e., resources becoming available through social connections). In one frequently cited study on the social implications of Facebook use, Ellison et al. (2007) surveyed college students about Facebook usage, including the degree to which Facebook was used to meet new people. They found that the respondents were more likely to use Facebook as a way to stay in touch with those with whom they already had an offline connection than to meet new people. Raacke and Bonds-Raacke (2008), however, found that more than half of a sample of Facebook and Myspace members reported using a social network site to make new friends (see also Bonds-Raacke & Raacke, 2010; Lenhart & Madden, 2007). People who are shy or socially anxious may be especially likely to use social network sites to form new relationships (e.g., Baker & Oswald, 2010).

Facebook and other Internet venues also provide assistance in the development of relationships that originated offline. That is, people can meet in real-world settings but then use Facebook or another Internet site to assist in the relationship initiation process (Sprecher, 2009). For example, it is very common for young adults, particularly in college settings, to search a person's social network profile after they meet for the first time in a class or party (Ellison et al., 2007). As noted, considerable information can be available about others on Facebook, including friendship networks, study major or type of employment, interests, and hometown. In addition, post-college adults meet others in social settings and professional settings and then use Internet search engines ("googling") to acquire information about the other and sometimes to verify the information the other reveals about his or her background (e.g., occupation, education). According to the 2005 Pew Internet & American Life Project survey, 17% of the Internet users who were single and looking for a partner reported that they searched for information on the Internet about someone they were dating or about to date (Madden & Lenhart, 2006), although no doubt that rate is much higher today, several years later. In addition, it is not uncommon for two people to meet for the first time in a face-to-face setting, exchange e-mail addresses in addition to phone numbers, and then become acquainted through CMC before meeting again (Rabby & Walther, 2003). Potential dating partners may also use CMC to make plans to get together. According to the Pew survey results (Madden & Lenhart, 2006), 26% of single Internet users said they had asked someone out on a date through the Internet.

Targeted Relationships

Of the relationships that originate through the Internet, those that begin at a dating or matching site have received the greatest attention in the media. McKenna (2008) referred to these as "targeted relationships." Compared with relationships that begin through online communities or social network sites, relationships that develop through Internet dating sites often occur more rapidly and are more likely to be defined as romantic (rather than as friendship) from the start. This more rapid progression to romantic intimacy likely occurs because single adults visit the dating sites for the specific and explicit purpose of finding a partner, and assume (most often accurately) that others enrolled at the site are also single and interested in finding a partner.

The first mainstream Internet matching site, Match (launched in 1995), is still one of the most frequently used self-selection sites in the United States. At this and other similar sites, members post profile information, including demographics, personality descriptions, interests, and photographs. Members view others' profile and use the site's search engine to narrow the pool of potential partners who meet their particular criteria, for example, to those in a particular geographical location, age group, or with specific interests. It is estimated that currently there are hundreds of such Internet dating sites, which offer users the opportunity to advertise themselves in a way similar to the printed want ads of prior decades but without limitations on space (see Cocks, 2009). Some sites charge users a fee, but many (e.g., PlentyOfFish, OkCupid) are free, generating revenue through advertising. Match and other such self-selection sites are for the general population of singles, whereas other sites target special niches: for example, particular age groups (e.g., seniorpeoplemeet.com), religious groups (e.g., jdate.com, christianmingle.com), and sexual orientations (e.g., GaySinglesOnline.com).

A smaller number of dating websites offer a scientific approach to matching, and claim to be able to find "compatible" matches based on algorithms applied to users' answers to scientific-based surveys that assess their personality characteristics, interests, attitudes, and desires in a part-ner. Among these sites are eHarmony, the first science-based matching service, launched in 2000; PerfectMatch, launched in 2002; and Chemis-try, launched in 2005 (for a journalistic description of the scientific sites, see Gottlieb, 2006). The dating sites claim that their matching systems are based on "science," including the social scientific literature on close relationships. For example, Galen Buckwalter, the primary creator of the matching survey at eHarmony, stated that he initially reviewed the psychol-ogy literature "to identify the areas that might be relevant in predicting success in long-term relationships" (Gottlieb, 2006, p. 60). The Duet Total Compatibility System at PerfectMatch and the personality test at Chemis-try are also described as based on scientific literature (for further discus-sion, see Sprecher, 2011).

In addition, many of the sites now include in their algorithms data based on members' actual use behaviors, including how often they log in and who they contact (Humphries, 2010). The scientific sites have not published their matching formulas or subjected them to peer review, but information on their websites and press releases suggests that the focus is primarily on creating compatible matches based on principles of similarity. PerfectMatch and Chemistry also cite *complementarity* (being opposite on certain characteristics) as a factor in their compatibility science (for a dis-cussion, see Finkel, Eastwick, Karney, Reis, & Sprecher, 2012; Sprecher, 2011).

Most of the Internet dating sites, regardless of the matching system used, typically provide a multiple-stage procedure for initial communica-tion to help potential matches learn about each other in a nonthreatening way. The communication features include preprogrammed icebreaker mes-sages; a procedure for sharing "must haves," "can't stands," and responses to multiple-choice items; voice and video greetings; and anonymous instant messaging and e-mails.

Factors such as physical attractiveness (a subjective evaluation based on photographs), occupation and other signs of resources, and similarity in traits, leisure interests, and other characteristics influence whether members choose to initiate or respond to communication with potential partners (e.g., Fiore & Donath, 2004; Hitsch, Hortaçsu, & Ariely, 2010a, 2010b). Once communication is initiated, other factors influence the continuation of communication, including speed of response and writing ability (Baker, 1998). If there is online attraction and rapport, based on the information gleaned through the profile information and the initial online communication, the two may move their relationship offline, a progression that usually begins with phone calls followed by face-to-face meeting in a safe, public place (Long, 2010). Many people may have an online attraction to another, only to be disappointed when meeting in person. Many people who seek a partner through an Internet service may meet several potential matches before becoming involved with one of them, an attraction process that is described later.

Implications for Relationship Development of Meeting Online

An interesting question is whether relationships that begin online differ from those that begin in traditional contexts in how they develop. In this section, we consider various implications of having initial communication and information seeking about potential dates via the Internet, and discuss how the pathway to intimacy online may differ from that in a traditional face-to-face context.

Effects of Computer-Mediated Communication

An almost certainty of meeting someone online is that communication begins through CMC, in the form of e-mails, instant messages, Facebook communication, or private messages through an Internet dating site.

Early research on the effects of CMC, conducted primarily with work groups comparing computer network communication with face-to-face (FtF) communication, found that people were more likely to be rude and say negative comments when using an electronic medium versus FtF interactions (Walther & Parks, 2002) and also to relate in a more impersonal, task-oriented way (for a review, see Walther, 1996; Siegel, Dubrovsky, Kiesler, & McGuire, 1986). This early research, then, suggested that meeting someone online would not be conducive to forming an intimate bond.

The early theoretical perspective that argued that CMC would hinder communication was referred to as "cues-filtered-out" (Culnan & Markus, 1987). This perspective argued that CMC would be less personal (than FtF) because of reduced nonverbal communication, such as facial expressions and tone of voice.

Evidence then emerged, however, to show that personal communication was possible through computer communication despite reduced nonverbal cues. To account for the new findings, Walther (1995) proposed the social information processing theory, which states that relationship development is possible via CMC but may just take longer than with FtF. This perspective argues that people will substitute other cues, such as self-disclosure, to compensate for limited nonverbal cues.

More recently, Walther (2007) argued that online communication can be even more personal than FtF communication. Hyperpersonal communication can emerge over CMC because self-disclosure can occur more easily. Furthermore, the intensity of self-disclosure can lead to the development of affinity and closeness. Closeness in CMC contexts can also be enhanced by the ability to present oneself carefully by editing messages, referred to as selective self-presentation (Walther, 2007). Another CMC factor that contributes to closeness is the tendency to assume idealistic attributes of the other (Jiang, Bazarova, & Hancock, 2011).

A growing number of experimental studies have examined the degree or intimacy of self-disclosure among previously unacquainted pairs as a function of whether their communication occurs online or in FtF settings. A recent meta-analysis (Kim & Dindia, 2011) of 11 such studies concluded that there was little evidence for the hyperpersonal perspective; only two studies found online self-disclosure to be greater than FtF self-disclosure (i.e., Joinson, 2001; Schouten, Valkenburg, & Peter, 2009). In three studies (e.g., Parks & Roberts, 1998) reviewed by Kim and Dindia (2011), no differences were found between FtF and online self-disclosure levels, suggesting evidence for the social information processing perspective. In six studies analyzed by Kim and Dindia (2011), however, self-disclosure was higher in FtF than in CMC (e.g., Cho, 2007). In their meta-analyses, Kim and Dindia (2011) found that the overall effect size was not significantly different from zero, suggesting no overall effect across the studies for the medium of communication on degree or intimacy of self-disclosure.

There is also a small amount of literature on the effects of modality switching (e.g., engaging in CMC initially and then switching to FtF interaction); this research has focused more on impressions and attraction as the dependent variables rather than the level of self-disclosure. For example,

McKenna et al. (2002) found that participants who had an initial CMC interaction followed by a FtF interaction (in the same session) had more positive impressions of the interaction partner than those who interacted FtF in both conditions of the study. Other research, however, that has included varying lengths of time of CMC prior to FtF interaction suggests that if CMC is too prolonged (e.g., via e-mail for several weeks), there may not be benefits of the CMC once FtF interaction occurs (e.g., Ramirez & Wang, 2008; Ramirez & Zhang, 2007).

Implications of Having Extensive Information about the Other

When people meet potential partners online, particularly at the dating sites, they often acquire extensive information about others before they ever begin communicating, and certainly before they meet. The information may be in the form of open-ended information provided in a profile (e.g., "I like long walks") and trait information provided by answers to predetermined questions (e.g., regarding occupation, religion, religious beliefs, interests, attitudes). Although in FtF settings people may also acquire information about others prior to meeting them, such as through friends, most often they would have less information compared with the breadth and depth of information that can be obtained online (Toma & Hancock, 2011). Information obtained online has also been distinguished in other ways from that obtained in FtF settings. For example, online information has been described as primarily in the form of "searchable traits"—objective attributes (e.g., income, religion) that can be provided in a profile or in response to predetermined questions (Frost, Chance, Norton, & Ariely, 2008). Searchable traits are compared with "experiential attributes," which require some personal interaction to judge (e.g., sense of humor) (Frost et al., 2008).

One possible positive implication of having extensive information about others is that it can be possible, in theory, to search for a partner with certain desired characteristics. This may be especially important for those who are looking for a partner with certain characteristics that might be difficult to find in traditional avenues for mate seeking (Rosenfeld & Thomas, 2012).

However, there are also potential negative implications of having extensive information about potential partners available online. Significant among them is that the "marketplace" phenomenon of dating and mating becomes particularly salient. The search and selection process that occurs online prior to the formation of relationships has been described as a crass transaction, with each person possessing a market value and being reduced to a commodity. According to Ahuvia, Adelman, and Izberk-Bilgin (2009), a major criticism of Internet matching and other commercial means for finding a partner is that they represent a "McDonaldizing" of romance that is "systematizing, rationalizing, and rendering into a calculative mate quest what is supposed to be a magical process" (p. 239). People interviewed about the online selection process have likened it to shopping in a supermarket, catalog, or candy store (Heino, Ellison, & Gibbs, 2010; Lawson & Leck, 2006). Every seeker who is exploring, selecting, and rejecting the "candy," however, is also keenly aware that they likewise are being rejected by others because they do not meet others' standards. This salience of the exchange of economic and interpersonal assets may explain why online dating is viewed as less fun than offline dating, which involves a social activity like going to a movie (e.g., Frost et al., 2008, Study 1).

Another potentially negative aspect of the availability of extensive trait information is that that too much weight can be given to characteristics that do not actually lead to attraction once in FtF interaction. Members of dating sites often process extensive information about multiple others and use search engines to narrow the pool of potential partners based on "searchable attributes" (Frost et al., 2008). Users relying on search engines may assume they can find compatible partners based on their beliefs about what traits will appeal to them or will result in compatible relationships. However, in premeeting contexts, people do not always have good insight into what they would actually like in a partner once in a FtF situation (Eastwick & Finkel, 2008; Sprecher, 1989). In addition, research suggests that when people have too many options from which to choose, they can experience *choice overload*, which can lead to misremembering information and thus poorly informed decisions (Lenton & Stewart, 2008; Lenton, Fasolo, & Todd, 2008; Wu & Chiou, 2009; see a discussion in Finkel et al., 2012).

Pathway to Intimacy in Online versus Offline Relationship Development

Factors that can influence attraction and falling in love include similarity in attitudes and values, physical proximity, physical attractiveness of the partner, rewards of self-disclosure, and support for the relationship from family and friends (Berscheid & Reis, 1998). Each of these factors may affect attraction and falling in love both over the Internet and in the real world, but likely play out in different ways or at different points in time, in the different ways of meeting.

According to Merkle and Richardson (2000), the process of attraction in FtF romantic relationships is likely to involve first the influence of spatial factors and physical attractiveness and then the discovery of similarity and the role of self-disclosure. They argued that, in contrast, Internet-initiated romantic relationships involve "an inverted developmental sequence"; initially a high level of mutual and sometimes intense self-disclosure (although see Kim & Dindia, 2011) and a minimal role for physical attractiveness and proximity. Physical attractiveness will likely still play a role once two people meet in person, but, as noted by Cooper and Sportolari (1997), its impact may be less because it follows learning other information about each other. Cooper and Sportolari speculated that by the time two people meet, "the felt intensity and meaning of any unappealing physical traits are then more likely to be mitigated by the overall attraction that exists" (p. 9). On a related note, Ben-Ze'ev (2004, p. 161) discussed how the "attractiveness halo" found in FtF interactions (whereby a person who is viewed to be physically attractive is assumed to have a number of other desirable traits) is replaced by a "personality halo," whereby a person who "is perceived as having a specific, positive personality trait is assumed to have other good characteristics—sometimes even those connected to external appearance" (p. 161). Therefore, people can be attracted online to others because of personality characteristics that would not be salient in get-acquainted interactions in FtF settings, where physical appearance and other salient characteristics can serve as gating features (McKenna, 2008).

Once two people meet through a dating site and continue to be attracted to each other in FtF interaction, they must deal with two issues that often are the factors that bring people together in the first place in traditional settings. First, they must, in some cases, overcome geographical distance. People who meet online are generally at a greater distance than people who meet in FtF settings, and considerable research has shown the importance of proximity (see Parks, 2007). Second, people who meet partners over the Internet must integrate their new partner into their larger social network. Research indicates the important role of the social network for both relationship formation and relationship maintenance (for reviews, see Parks, 2007; Sprecher, Felmlee, Orbuch, & Willetts, 2002).

We turn now to an alternative, and even more complicated, route to relationship formation: sexual hookups and other forms of casual sex. Unlike online venues, where meeting a potential mate is the explicit goal, partners involved in casual sexual episodes seldom acknowledge this goal, even when it is present; if a romantic relationship does develop, it is emergent and serendipitous.

SEXUAL HOOKUPS AS RELATIONSHIP INITIATION AND BONDING

Whereas Internet dating is more common among working adults and retirees (Rosenfeld & Thomas, 2012; Stephure, Boon, MacKinnon, & Deveau, 2009), hooking up is more common among young adults, particularly on college campuses (e.g., Glenn & Marquardt, 2001; Paul et al., 2008). Hookups are generally defined as casual sex that occurs outside a relational context and without the explicit expectation of forming a relationship (e.g., Glenn & Marquardt, 2001). Although the use of the term *hookup* is relatively new, casual sex is not. *Casual sex* is an umbrella term referring to sex that occurs outside of traditional dating or romantic relationships; it became more common beginning with the sexual revolution of the 1960s (Perlman & Sprecher, 2012). We first discuss distinctions among types of hookup experiences, followed by the implications for relationship development when sexual involvement is the defining feature of an initial interaction and/or the fundamental element that motivates continued interactions over time.

Variation in Hookups and Casual Sex

One-Night Stands or Hookups

The one-night stand is typically defined as sexual behavior, ranging from intimate kissing to intercourse, between strangers or brief acquaintances who have no expectation of developing a romantic relationship or arranging future interactions (Paul et al., 2000). Although specific circumstances may differ, the hookup script typically includes a party or bar, drinking alcohol, and dancing (Epstein, Calzo, Smiler, & Ward, 2009). In general, hookups are considered a convenient and uncomplicated means of achieving sexual gratification without the constraints of interdependence and commitment to exclusivity. In actual practice, however, hookups bring the risk of losing a friendship or dealing with a sexual partner who expected a more enduring relationship (Bradshaw, Kahn, & Seville, 2010). They can also be a source of confusion and ambivalence if one's own expectations or goals are not fully understood (Paul & Hayes, 2002), particularly compared with the benefits and stability associated with sex in a dating relationship (Bradshaw et al., 2010). Indeed, college students, particularly men, reported feeling moderately positive reactions following a hookup, but the source of the positive reactions was attributed to the possibility of a romantic relationship developing or the hookup relationship being clarified (Owen & Fincham, 2011b).

Booty Calls

The "booty call" is an interesting sexual phenomenon that shares the same presumption of the hookup—that no romantic relationship will develop—but also shares the pattern of repeated sexual episodes characteristic of friends with benefits (discussed next). As defined by Jonason, Li, and Cason (2009), "A booty call involves the solicitation of a non-long-term partner for explicit or implicit intent of engaging in sexual activity" (p. 460). Although an unconventional relational formulation, booty call relationships seem to serve the relationship goals of men for sexual gratification with few costs and the goal of women for a relatively stable relationship marked by compatibility.

Unlike the hookup, a booty call relationship has some degree of investment and may include signs of affection such as kissing (Grello, Welsh, & Harper, 2006). More specifically, in a comparison of intimacy behaviors reported by college students in hookups, booty calls, and dating relationships, Jonason, Li, and Richardson (2010) found that talking and holding hands were more common in dating relationships than booty calls, and that leaving after sex (for both men and women) was more common in booty call relationships than serious relationships or hookups. Jonason et al. (2010) speculated that avoiding displays of emotional intimacy and parting after sex are strategic (though perhaps unconscious) ways for partners to prevent booty call relationships from becoming romantic.

Friends with Benefits

Although sometimes considered to be synonymous with the booty call relationship, the friends-with-benefits relationship is unique in its merger of sexual and relational intimacy (e.g., Hughes, Morrison, & Asada, 2005). Other than the sexual component, this relationship is comparable to any other close friendship. In fact, the inclusion of sexual intimacy increases the perceived quality of the friendship but does not redefine it as a dating or romantic relationship (Afifi & Faulkner, 2000), and the relationship is associated with more positive (e.g., happy, pleased) than negative (e.g., disappointed, awkward, used) emotions, especially for men (Owen & Fincham, 2011b). The exception to this pattern stems from the influence of psychological distress and feeling constrained by the relationship, which reduces the positive response (Owen & Fincham, 2011a). Consistent with gender-role patterns noted previously, however, women seem to be more emotionally involved in the relationship, whereas men are more sexually involved (e.g., desiring sex more often) (McGinty, Knox, & Zusman, 2007).

In summary, there is variation in the sexual experiences that are referred to as hookups. In addition to the various types discussed previously, hookup experiences can vary by the degree of sexual activity (ranging from kissing to sexual intercourse), by the motivations of the partners, and by whether the relationship is concurrent with committed relationships (Paul et al., 2008). However, the diverse experiences, ranging from a one-night stand to friends with benefits, share the quality that they occur outside the context of a dating, committed relationship.

Implications for Relationship Development of Sex Occurring before Affection

In the standard script for romantic relationship development, affection comes first in a relationship and then sex (Perlman & Sprecher, 2012). Indeed, the occurrence of first sexual involvement is identified by dating couples as a significant "turning point" in the development of the relationship (Baxter & Pittman, 2001). Moreover, when the explicit expression of affection (i.e., "I love you") precedes the first sexual episode, couples report greater relationship satisfaction and stability following the episode (Metts, 2004).

The lack of a dating relationship within which to frame sexual experiences, however, does not necessarily mean that individuals engaging in casual sexual encounters are completely free of expectations associated with normative dating scripts and the sex roles embedded within them. For example, five broad categories of goals characterize traditional first dates: have fun, reduce uncertainty, investigate romantic potential, initiate a friendship, and engage in sexual activity (Mongeau et al., 2004). Clearly, in the case of casual sexual encounters, the goal of sexual activity is the primary motivation.

However, the goal of investigating romantic potential is also present in college students' accounts of their casual sex experiences, particularly for women. For example, consistent with evolutionary theory, Townsend and Wasserman (2011) found that women are more likely than men to gauge their own and a partner's investment potential when involved in hookup relationships. In a study by Grello et al. (2006), approximately 20% of the women who participated in hookups believed that the most recent hookup experience was the beginning of a relationship, compared with only 3% of the men. Even in a context where a platonic relationship exists prior to sexual involvement, as with friends with benefits, women are more likely than men to hope that the friendship will evolve into a romantic relationship (Owen & Fincham, 2011b). In a study of individuals currently in a friends-with-benefits relationship, both men and women were committed to the friendship and reported a desire to feel close as a motive for entering in a sexual relationship with a friend; however, men were more motivated to enter the friends-with-benefits relationship because of the sexual component and women were more motivated by the emotional aspect (Lehmiller, VanderDrift, & Kelly, 2011). Similarly, women tend to place more importance on the value of the friendship and to experience greater emotional involvement than men, whereas men tend to emphasize the benefits of sexual gratification (McGinty et al., 2007). Similar gender patterns are evident in booty call relationships as well. On the basis of results of two studies using college student samples, Jonason et al. (2009) concluded that booty call relationships offer a type of compromise in mating strategies for both men and women, providing men with an easily available sexual partner and women with the opportunity to assess the quality of a potential mate.

The likelihood that relationships that begin with and focus on sexual activity will develop into committed romantic relationships depends on a number of circumstantial and individual factors. A one-night stand that occurs when one or both individuals are already in a romantic relationship is unlikely to progress any further. However, as Paul et al. (2008) noted, factors that enhance the likelihood that hookups will become longer term romantic relationships include voluntarily having sex (rather than being forced), engaging in discussion about the meaning of the sexual encounter, a positive emotional experience (and lack of regret), and network support for the relationship.

More broadly, given the ambiguity inherent in the various formulations of casual sex relationships, definitional uncertainty is high. In a review of theoretical approaches to the uncertainty construct, Bradac (2001) noted that although uncertainty may be an uncomfortable state in some circumstances, it may also be welcome in others (e.g., medical evaluations/prognosis). The key is to establish and maintain "optimality" in levels of uncertainty (p. 471). We can speculate that in nontraditional sexual relationships, uncertainty management involves reducing uncertainty about expected behavioral sequences (e.g., when, where, how, and to what extent sex will occur), but allowing relatively high levels of uncertainty regarding the possibility of an emergent romantic dating relationship. Assuming that a romantic relationship does emerge, previous norms for maintaining a sexually focused relationship must be reevaluated and negotiated. This process may be a unique challenge for friends-with-benefits relationships that are embedded within social networks (Hughes et al., 2005) and/or do not manifest open communication about the nature of the relationship (Bisson & Levine, 2009).

CONCLUSION

Our goal in this chapter was to provide a summary profile of two alternative approaches to the traditional social practices of courtship: Internet dating and sexual hookups. Given the increasing availability of online resources and the loosening of sexual norms in the current population of college-age adults, both initiation options are becoming more frequent and acceptable. This is not to suggest that they are without challenges or that they necessarily evolve into committed and stable romantic relationships. They simply represent alternative pathways to the same possible outcome, although the probability of romantic relationships arising from online contact is more likely than from hookups.

As indicated throughout this chapter, sequential patterns are the most obvious distinction between the online profiles and casual sex profiles. Online relationships move from assessment of romantic relationship potential based on intentional accumulation of information to subsequent physical contact, possibly including sexual involvement. Hookups and other types of sexual relationships move from sexual involvement to an assessment of whether romantic relationship potential is possible and/or desirable and then move to accumulation of information relevant to relationship formation.

Moreover, inherent within these sequential patterns are differences in uncertainty-reduction strategies, which distinguish each type of relationship and distinguish both from more traditional dating sequences. That is, in a traditional dating sequence, when two people first meet in person, often in a classroom, social gathering, or at work, they have opportunities to use active, passive, and interactive strategies to reduce initial uncertainty (Berger, 1987). They can ask friends and acquaintances for information about the other (active); they can also observe him or her in various situations to evaluate responsiveness, physical attractiveness, and interaction style (passive). Finally, they can engage in conversation during which they ask questions and self-disclose personal information (interactive) as a means to judge compatibility. When meeting online, potential partners rely primarily on interactive strategies and occasionally active strategies through links to social networking sites, but cannot employ passive strategies until FtF encounters occur. Such a limitation combined with the not uncommon use of deception about one's physical appearance and age online (Cornwell & Lundgren, 2001) may lead to a certain level of disillusionment when a potential partner is finally observed in real time within a social context (Stieger, Eichinger, & Honeder, 2009). For hookup relationships, the use of uncertainty-reduction strategies is even more complicated. With the possible exception of friends with benefits, there are few opportunities to use passive, active, or interactive strategies because of the somewhat clandestine nature of the relationship. The more open communication necessary to renegotiate the relationship's definition and the opportunity to observe a potential romantic partner in public or social settings may reveal areas of incompatibility not evident when the relationship focused only on sexual gratification.

Despite the distinctions that can be drawn between online relationships and casual sex relationships, the two venues intersect in some circumstances. For example, sexual hookups also occur online, and there is a small literature that has developed on this topic. Research indicates that partner-seeking activities on websites designed to facilitate sexual contacts between interested parties sometimes lead to sexual encounters offline as well as online (Sevcikova & Daneback, 2011). Whether these offline encounters lead to committed romantic relationships has yet to be determined. Relevant also is the use of online sexual activities by a couple in an established relationship. In much the same way that participants in casual sexual relationships and friends-with-benefits relationships experience both positive and negative outcomes, couples who use online sexual exploration report positive outcomes, such as being able to talk more openly about what they want sexually, but also negative outcomes, such as less frequent and less arousing real sex within their intimate relationship or feeling threatened by a partner's "chats" with a member of the opposite sex online (Grov, Gillespie, Royce, & Lever, 2011).

In summary, the traditional pathway from a first meeting, to a dating relationship, to marriage is undergoing noteworthy and rapid variations. We have yet to explore the long-term consequences of these alternative pathways through longitudinal data. Future research that assesses relationships as they develop, rather than as they are recollected and reassessed in ways consistent with the status and emotional quality of the current (or failed) relationship, is warranted. Until such longitudinal data are available, it is difficult to determine whether "love at first sight" was actually "sex at first meeting" that happened to evolve into an affectionate relationship, or whether a friends-with-benefits relationship was actually a predating relationship that finally emerged after exclusivity was established. That no single origin guarantees the development of a committed romantic relationship is not surprising. However, the fact that not all early childhood acquaintances, not all lab partners, not all bar hookups, and not all dating site matches develop into a relationship underscores the timeless presence of romantic attraction as a motivational force in the process of relationship formation.

REFERENCES

Afifi, W., & Faulkner, S. L. (2000). On being 'just friends': The frequency and impact of sexual activity in cross-sex friendships. *Journal of Social and Personal Relationships, 17,* 205–222.

Ahuvia, A., Adelman, M., & Izberk-Bilgin, E. (2009). Commercial channels for mate seeking. In H. Reis & S. Sprecher (Eds.), *Encyclopedia of human relationships* (Vol. 1, pp. 237–240). Newbury Park, CA: Sage.

Baker, A. (1998, July). Cyberspace couples finding romance online then meeting for the first time in real life. *CMC Magazine.* Retrieved June 1, 2007, from *www.december.com/cmc/mag/1998/jul/baker.html.*

Baker, L. R., & Oswald, D. L. (2010). Shyness and online social networking services. *Journal of Social and Personal Relationships, 27,* 873–889.

Bargh, J. A., McKenna, K. Y. A., & Fitzsimons, G. M. (2002). Can you see the real me? Activation and expression of the 'true self' on the Internet. *Journal of Social Issues, 58,* 33–48.

Bartoli, A. M., & Clark, M. D. (2006). The dating game: Similarities and differences in dating scripts among college students. *Sexuality and Culture, 10,* 54–80.

Baxter, L. A., & Pittman, G. (2001). Communicatively remembering turning points of relational development in heterosexual romantic relationships. *Communication Reports, 14,* 1–17.

Ben-Ze'ev, A. (2004). *Love online: Emotions on the Internet.* New York: Cambridge University Press.

Berger, C. R. (1987). Communicating under uncertainty. In M. E. Roloff & G. R. Miller (Eds.), *Interpersonal processes: New directions in communication research* (pp. 39–62). Beverly Hills, CA: Sage.

Berscheid, E., & Reis, H. T. (1998). Attraction and close relationships. In D. T. Gilbert, S. T. Fiske, & G. Lindzey (Eds.), *The handbook of social psychology* (Vol. 2, 4th ed., pp. 193–281). New York: McGraw-Hill.

Bisson, M. A., & Levine, T. R. (2009). Negotiating a friends with benefits relationship. *Archives of Sexual Behavior, 38,* 66–73.

Bogle, K. A. (2008). *Hooking up: Sex, dating, and relationships on campus.* New York: New York University Press.

Bonds-Raacke, J., & Raacke, J. (2010). Myspace and Facebook: Identifying dimensions of users and gratifications for friend network sites. *Individual Differences Research, 8,* 27–33.

Boyd, D., & Ellison, N. (2007). Social network sites: Definition, history, and scholarship. *Journal of Computer-Mediated Communication, 13,* 210–230.

Bradac, J. J. (2001). Theory comparison: Uncertainty reduction, problematic integration, uncertainty management, and other curious constructs. *Journal of Communication, 51,* 456–476.

Bradshaw, C., Kahn, A. S., & Seville, B. K. (2010). To hook up or date: Which gender benefits? *Sex Roles, 62,* 661–669.

Bredow, C. A., Cate, R. M., & Huston, T. L. (2008). Have we met before? A conceptual model of first encounters. In S. Sprecher, A. Wenzel, & J. Harvey

(Eds.), *Handbook of relationship initiation* (pp. 3–28). New York: Psychology Press.

Bryant, E. M., Marmo, J., & Ramirez, A. (2011). A functional approach to social networking sites. In K. B. Wright & L. M. Webb (Eds.), *Computer-mediated communication in personal relationships* (pp. 3–20). New York: Peter Lang.

Cate, R. M., & Lloyd, S. A. (1992). *Courtship*. Newbury Park, CA: Sage.

Cho, S. H. (2007). Effects of motivations and gender on adolescents' self-disclosure in online chatting. *CyberPsychology and Behavior, 10*, 339–345.

Cocks, H. G. (2009). *Classified: The history of the personal column*. London: Random House.

Cohen, L. L., & Shotland, R. L. (1996). Timing of first sexual intercourse in a relationship: Expectations, experiences, and perceptions of others. *Journal of Sex Research, 33*, 291–299.

Cooper, A., & Sportolari, L. (1997). Romance in cyberspace: Understanding online attraction. *Journal of Sex Education and Therapy, 22*, 7–14.

Cornwell, B., & Lundgren, D. C. (2001). Love on the Internet: Involvement and misrepresentation in romantic relationships in cyberspace vs. realspace. *Computers in Human Behavior, 17*, 197–211.

Culnan, M. J., & Markus, M. L. (1987). Information technologies. In F. M. Jablin, L. L. Putnam, K. H. Roberts, & L. W. Porter (Eds.), *Handbook of organizational communication: An interdisciplinary perspective* (pp. 420–443). Newbury Park, CA: Sage.

Derlega, V. J., Winstead, B. A., & Greene, K. (2008). Self-disclosure and starting a close relationship. In S. Sprecher, A. Wenzel, & J. Harvey (Eds.), *Handbook of relationship initiation* (pp. 153–174). New York: Psychology Press.

Dutton, W. H., Helsper, E. J., Whitty, M. T., Li, N., Buckwalter, J. G., & Lee, E. (2009). The role of the Internet in reconfiguring marriages: A cross-national study. *Interpersona, 3*, 3–18.

Eastwick, P. W., & Finkel, E. J. (2008). Sex differences in mate preferences revisited: Do people know what they initially desire in a romantic partner? *Journal of Personality and Social Psychology, 94*, 245–264.

Eaton, A. A., & Rose, S. (2011). Has dating become more egalitarian?: A 35-year review using *Sex Roles*. *Sex Roles, 64*, 843–862.

Ellison, N. B., Steinfield, C., & Lampe, C. (2007). The benefits of Facebook "friends": Social capital and college students' use of online social network sites. *Journal of Computer-Mediated Communication, 12*, 1143–1168.

Epstein, M., Calzo, J. P., Smiler, A. P., & Ward, L. M. (2009). "Anything from making out to having sex": Men's negotiations of hooking up and friends with benefits scripts. *Journal of Sex Research, 46*, 414–424.

Finkel, E. J., Eastwick, P. W., Karney, B. R., Reis, H. T., & Sprecher, S. (2012). Online dating: A critical analysis from the perspective of psychological science. *Psychological Science in the Public Interest, 13*, 3–66.

Fiore, A. T., & Donath, J. S. (2004). *Online personals: An overview*. Paper presented at the meeting of ACM Computer-Human Interaction, Vienna, Austria.

Frost, J. H., Chance, Z., Norton, M. I., & Ariely, D. (2008). People are experience goods: Improving online dating with virtual dates. *Journal of Interactive Marketing, 22,* 51–61.

Giordano, P. C., Manning, W. D., & Longmore, M. A. (2009). Dating relationships in adolescence and young adulthood. In H. Reis & S. Sprecher (Eds.), *Encyclopedia of human relationships* (Vol. 1, pp. 386–390). Newbury Park, CA: Sage.

Glenn, N., & Marquardt, E. (2001). *Hooking up, hanging out, and hoping for Mr. Right: College women on dating and mating today.* New York: Institute for American Values.

Gottlieb, L. (2006, March). How do I love thee? *The Atlantic Monthly,* pp. 58–70. Retrieved June 14, 2009, from *www.theatlantic.com/magazine/ archive/2006/03/how-do-i-love-thee/304602/.*

Grello, C. M., Welsh, D. P., & Harper, M. S. (2006). No strings attached: The nature of casual sex in college students. *Journal of Sex Research, 43,* 255–267.

Grov, C., Gillespie, B. J., Royce, T., & Lever, J. (2011). Perceived consequences of casual online sexual activities on heterosexual relationship: A U.S. online survey. *Archives of Sexual Behavior, 40,* 429–439.

Heino, R., Ellison, N., & Gibbs, J. (2010). Relationshopping: Investigating the market metaphor in online dating. *Journal of Social and Personal Relationships, 27,* 427–447.

Hitsch, G. J., Hortaçsu, A., & Ariely, D. (2010a). Matching and sorting in online dating. *American Economic Review, 100,* 130–163.

Hitsch, G. J., Hortaçsu, A., & Ariely, D. (2010b). What makes you click? Mate preferences in online dating. *Quantitative Marketing and Economics, 8,* 393–427.

Hogan, B., Li, N., & Dutton, W. H. (2011, February 14). *A global shift in the social relationships of networked individuals: Meeting and dating online comes of age.* Retrieved from *http://papers.ssrn.com/sol3/papers.cfm?_id=1763884.*

Hughes, M., Morrison, K., & Asada, K. J. K. (2005). What's love got to do with it? Exploring the impact of maintenance rules, love attitudes, and network support on friends with benefits relationships. *Western Journal of Communication, 69,* 49–66.

Humphries, C. (2010, December 27). Dating sites try adaptive matchmaking. *MIT Technology Review.* Retrieved August 7, 2011, from *www.technologyreview. com/printer_friendly_article.aspx?id=26805.*

Jiang, L., Bazarova, N. N., & Hancock, J. T. (2011). The disclosure–intimacy link in computer mediated communication: An attributional extension of the hyperpersonal model. *Human Communication Research, 37,* 58–77.

Joinson, A. N. (2001). Self disclosure in computer mediated communication: The role of self awareness and visual anonymity. *European Journal of Social Psychology, 31,* 177–192.

Joinson, A. N. (2008). Looking at, looking up or keeping up with people? Motives and use of Facebook. In *Proceedings of the SIGCHI Conference on Human Factors in Computing Systems* (pp. 1027–1036). New York: ACM Press.

Jonason, P. K., Li, N. P., & Cason, M. J. (2009). The "booty call": A compromise between men's and women's ideal mating strategies. *Journal of Sex Research, 46*, 460–470.

Jonason, P. K., Li, N. P., & Richardson, J. (2010). Positioning the booty-call relationship on the spectrum of relationships: Sexual but more emotional than one-night stands. *Journal of Sex Research, 47*, 1–10.

Kim, J., & Dindia, K. (2011). Online self-disclosure: A review of research. In K. B. Wright & L. M. Webb (Eds.), *Computer-mediated communication in personal relationships* (pp. 156–179). New York: Peter Lang.

Lampe, C., Ellison, N., & Steinfield, C. (2006). A Face(book) in the crowd: Social searching vs. social browsing. In *Proceedings of the 2006 20th Anniversary Conference on Computer Supported Cooperative Work* (pp. 167–170). New York: ACM Press.

Laner, M. R., & Ventrone, N. A. (2000). Dating scripts revisited. *Journal of Family Issues, 21*, 488–500.

Laumann, E. O., Gagnon, J. H., Michael, R. T., & Michaels, S. (1994). *The social organization of sexuality: Sexual practices in the United States*. Chicago: University of Chicago Press.

Lawson, H. M., & Leck, K. (2006). Dynamics of Internet dating. *Social Science Computer Review, 24*, 189–208.

Lehmiller, J. J., VanderDrift, L. E., & Kelly, J. R. (2011). Sex differences in approaching friends with benefits relationships. *Journal of Sex Research, 48*, 275–284.

Lenhart, A., & Madden, M. (2007). *Teens, privacy and online social networks*. Washington, DC: Pew Internet & American Life Project.

Lenton, A. P., Fasolo, B., & Todd, P. M. (2008). "Shopping" for a mate: Expected vs. experienced preferences in online mate choice. *IEEE Transactions on Professional Communication, 51*, 169–182.

Lenton, A. P., & Stewart, A. (2008). Changing her ways: Number of options and mate standard strength impact mate choice strategy and satisfaction. *Judgment and Decision Making, 3*, 501–511.

Levinger, G. (1974). A three-level approach to attraction: Toward an understanding of pair relatedness. In T. L. Huston (Ed.), *Foundations of interpersonal attraction* (pp. 99–120). New York: Academic Press.

Long, B. L. (2010). *Scripts for online dating: A model and theory of online romantic relationship initiation*. Unpublished doctoral dissertation, Bowling Green State University. Retrieved April 10, 2011, from *http://rave.ohiolink.edu/etdc/view?acc_num=bgsu1268852623*.

Madden, M., & Lenhart, A. (2006). *Online dating*. Washington, DC: Pew Internet & American Life Project. Retrieved April 30, 2011, from *www.pewinternet.org/Reports/2006/Online-Dating.aspx*.

Madden, M., & Zickuhr, K. (2011). *65% of online adults use social networking sites*. Retrieved November 22, 2011, from *www.pewinternet.org/Reports/2011/Social-Networking-Sites.aspx*.

McClintock, E. A. (2010). When does race matter? Race, sex, and dating at an elite university. *Journal of Marriage and Family, 72*, 45–72.

McGinty, K., Knox, D., & Zusman, M. E. (2007). Friends with benefits: Women want "friends," men want "benefits." *College Student Journal, 41*, 1128–1131.

McKenna, K. Y. A. (2007). A progressive affair: Online dating to real world mating. In M. T. Whitty, A. J. Baker, & J. A. Inman (Eds.), *Online matchmaking* (pp. 112–124). Hampshire, UK: Palgrave Macmillan.

McKenna, K. Y. A. (2008). Myspace or your place: Relationship initiation and development in the wire and wireless world. In S. Sprecher, A. Wenzel, & J. Harvey (Eds.), *Handbook of relationship initiation* (pp. 235–248). New York: Psychology Press.

McKenna, K. Y. A., Green, A. S., & Gleason, M. E. J. (2002). Relationship formation on the Internet: What's the big attraction? *Journal of Social Issues, 58*, 9–31.

Merkle, E. R., & Richardson, R.A. (2000). Digital dating and virtual relating: Conceptualizing computer mediated romantic relationships. *Family Relations, 490*, 187–192.

Metts, S. (2004). First sexual involvement in romantic relationships: An empirical investigation of communicative framing, romantic beliefs, and attachment orientation in the passion turning point. In J. Harvey, A. Wenzel, & S. Sprecher (Eds.), *Handbook of sexuality in close relationships* (pp. 135–158). Mahwah, NJ: Erlbaum.

Mongeau, P. A., & Johnson, K. L. (1995). Predicting cross-sex first-date sexual expectations and involvement: Contextual and individual difference factors. *Personal Relationships, 2*, 301–312.

Mongeau, P. A., Morr Serewicz, M. C., & Therrien, L. F. (2004). Goals for cross-sex first dates: Identification, measurement, and the influence of contextual factors. *Communication Monographs, 71*, 121–147.

Owen, J., & Fincham, F. (2011a). Effects of gender and psychosocial factors on "friends with benefits" relationships among young adults. *Archives of Sexual Behavior, 40*, 311–320.

Owen, J., & Fincham, F. (2011b). Young adults' emotional reactions after hooking up encounters. *Archives of Sexual Behavior, 40*, 321–330.

Parks, M. R. (2007). *Personal relationships and personal networks*. Mahwah, NJ: Erlbuam.

Parks, M. R., & Floyd, K. (1996). Making friends in cyberspace. *Journal of Communication, 46*, 80–97.

Parks, M. R., & Roberts, L. D. (1998). "Making MOOsic": The development of personal relationships online and a comparison to their off-line counterparts. *Journal of Social and Personal Relationships, 15*, 517–537.

Paul, E. L., & Hayes, K. A. (2002). The casualties of 'casual' sex: A qualitative exploration of the phenomenology of college students' hookups. *Journal of Social and Personal Relationships, 19*, 639–661.

Paul, E. L., McManus, B., & Hayes, K. A. (2000). "Hookups": Characteristics and correlates of college students' spontaneous and anonymous sexual experiences. *Journal of Sex Research, 37*, 76–88.

Paul, E. L., Wenzel, A., & Harvey, J. (2008). Hookups: A facilitator or a barrier to relationship initiation and intimacy development? In S. Sprecher, A. Wenzel,

& J. Harvey (Eds.), *Handbook of relationship initiation* (pp. 375–390). New York: Psychology Press.

Perlman, D., & Sprecher, S. (2012). Sex, intimacy, and dating in college. In R. McAnulty (Ed.), *Sex in college: The things they don't write home about* (pp. 91–118). Santa Barbara, CA: Praeger.

Raacke, J., & Bonds-Raacke, J. (2008). MySpace and Facebook: Applying the uses and gratifications theory to exploring friend-networking sites. *CyberPsychology and Behavior, 11*, 169–174.

Rabby, M. K., & Walther, J. B. (2003). Computer-mediated communication effects on relationship formation and maintenance. In D. J. Canary & M. Dainton (Eds.), *Maintaining relationships through communication: Relational, contextual, and cultural variations* (pp. 141–162). Mahwah, NJ: Erlbaum.

Ramirez, A., & Wang, Z. (2008). When online meets offline: An expectancy violations theory perspective on modality switching. *Journal of Communication, 58*, 20–39.

Ramirez, A., & Zhang, S. (2007). When online meets offline: The effect of modality switching on relational communication. *Communication Monographs, 74*, 287–310.

Rose, S., & Frieze, I. H. (1993). Young singles' contemporary dating scripts. *Sex Roles, 28*, 499–509.

Rosenfeld, M. J., & Thomas, R. J. (2012). Searching for a mate: The rise of the Internet as a social intermediary. *American Sociological Review, 77*, 523–547.

Sassler, S. (2010). Partnering across the life course: Sex, relationships, and mate selection. *Journal of Marriage and Family, 72*, 557–575.

Schouten, A. P., Valkenburg, P. M., & Peter, J. (2009). An experimental test of processes underlying self-disclosure in computer-mediated communication. *Cyberpsychology: Journal of Psychosocial Research on Cyberspace, 3*, 1–15.

Sevcikova, A., & Daneback, K. (2011). Anyone who wants sex? Seeking sex partners on sex-oriented contact websites. *Sexual and Relationship Therapy, 26*, 170–181.

Shtatfeld, R., & Barak, A. (2009). Factors related to initiating interpersonal contacts on internet dating sites: A view from the social exchange theory. *Interpersona, 3*, 19–37.

Siegel, J., Dubrovsky, V., Kiesler, S., & McGuire, T. W. (1986). Group processes in computer-mediated communication. *Organizational Behavior and Human Decision Processes, 37*, 157–187.

Smith, A. (2011). *Why Americans use social media*. Retrieved November 22, 2011, from *www.pewinternet.org/Reports/2011/Why-Americans-Use-Social-Media.aspx*.

Sprecher, S. (1989). The importance to males and females of physical attractiveness, earning potential and expressiveness in initial attraction. *Sex Roles, 21*, 591–607.

Sprecher, S. (2009). Relationship initiation and formation on the Internet. *Marriage and Family Review, 45*, 1–21.

Sprecher, S. (2011). Relationship compatibility, compatible matches, and compatibility matching. *Psychological Records Journal, 1*, 187–215.

Sprecher, S., Felmlee, D., Orbuch, T. L., & Willetts, M. C. (2002). Social networks and change in personal relationships. In A. L. Vangelisti, H. T. Reis, & M. A. Fitzpatrick (Eds.), *Stability and change in relationships* (pp. 257–284). Cambridge, UK: Cambridge University Press.

Stephure, R. J., Boon, S. D., MacKinnon, S. L., & Deveau, V. L. (2009). Internet initiated relationships: Associations between age and involvement in online dating. *Journal of Computer-Mediated Communication, 14*, 658–681.

Stieger, S., Eichinger, T., & Honeder, B. (2009). Can mate choice strategies explain sex differences? The deceived person's feelings in reaction to revealed online deception of sex, age, and appearance. *Social Psychology, 40*, 16–25.

Toma, C. L., & Hancock, J. T. (2011). A new twist on love's labor: Self-presentation in online dating profiles. In K. B. Wright & L. M. Webb (Eds.), *Computer-mediated communication in personal relationships* (pp. 41–55). New York: Peter Lang.

Townsend, J. M., & Wasserman, T. H. (2011). Sexual hookups among college students: Sex differences in emotional reactions. *Archives of Sexual Behavior, 40*, 1173–1181.

Utz, S. (2000). Social information processing in MUDs: The development of friendships in virtual worlds. *Journal of Online Behavior, 1*(1).

Valkenburg, P. M., Peter, J., & Schouten, A. P. (2006). Friend networking sites and their relationship to adolescents' well-being and social self-esteem. *CyberPsychology and Behavior, 9*, 584–590.

Vasalou, A., & Joinson, A. N. (2009). Me, myself, and I: The role of interactional context of self-presentation through avatars. *Computers in Human Behavior, 25*, 510–520.

Walther, J. B. (1995). Relational aspects of computer-mediated communication: Experimental observations over time. *Organization Science, 6*, 186–203.

Walther, J. B. (1996). Computer-mediated communication: Impersonal, interpersonal, and hyperpersonal interaction. *Communication Research, 23*, 3–43.

Walther, J. B. (2007). Selective self-presentation in computer-mediated communication: Hyperpersonal dimensions of technology, language, and cognition. *Computers in Human Behavior, 23*, 2538–2557.

Walther, J. B., & Parks, M. R. (2002). Cues filtered out, cues filtered in: Computer-mediated communication and relationships. In M. L. Knapp & J. A. Daly (Eds.), *Handbook of interpersonal communication* (3rd ed., pp. 529–563). Thousand Oaks, CA: Sage.

Wellman, B. (2001). Physical place and cyberplace: The rise of personalized networking. *International Journal of Urban and Regional Research, 25*, 227–252.

Wellman, B., Salaff, J., Dimitrova, D., Yuan, Y. C., & Gay, G. (2006). Homophily of network ties and bonding and bridging social capital in computer-mediated distributed teams. *Journal of Computer-Mediated Communication, 11*, 1062–1084.

Whitty, M. T. (2007). Introduction. In M. T. Whitty, A. J. Baker, & J. A. Inman (Eds.), *Online matchmaking* (pp. 1–16). New York: Palgrave.

Wu, P., & Chiou, W. (2009). More options leads to more searching and worse choices in finding partners for romantic relationships online: An experimental study. *CyberPsychology and Behavior, 12*, 315–318.

Yee, N. (2006). The demographics, motivations, and derived experiences of users of massively multi-user online graphical environments. *Presence: Teleoperators and Virtual Environments, 15*, 309–329.

Chapter **8**

Links and Distinctions between Love and Desire

Implications for Same-Sex Sexuality

LISA M. DIAMOND

*H*azan and Shaver's (1987) seminal notion that romantic love is an adult "version" of infant–caregiver attachment radically transformed our understanding of the nature and dynamics of adult intimate pair bonds, and the reverberations of this conceptual turning point continue to shape psychological research on adult romantic relationships. A key component of their theoretical model was the distinction between the evolved social-behavioral systems of *attachment*, *caregiving*, and *sexuality* (Shaver, Hazan, & Bradshaw, 1988). As they maintained, although experiences of adult romantic attachment typically integrate the feelings and behaviors of these systems, the systems themselves have distinct origins, functions, and underpinnings.

This conceptualization of romantic love and sexual desire as fundamentally distinct has profound implications for our understanding of the nature and development of *same-sex* sexuality, and yet these implications have gone largely unappreciated. Specifically, if love and desire are based in independent social-behavioral systems, then one's *sexual* orientation toward same-sex or other-sex partners need not correspond with experiences of *romantic attachment* to same-sex or other-sex partners. This, of course, runs directly counter to the implicit presumption among both scientists and laypeople that heterosexual individuals fall in love only with other-sex partners and lesbian/gay individuals fall in love *only* with same-sex partners.

Despite these presumptions, the last 30 years of social scientific research on same-sex sexuality have converged to indicate that inconsistencies between *sexual* and *affectional* feelings for same-sex versus other-sex partners constitute one of the primary forms of both interindividual and intraindividual variability in same-sex sexuality, both in the contemporary West and in other cultures and historical periods (Blackwood, 1985; Blumstein & Schwartz, 1977; Brown, 1995; Diamond, 2000, 2004; Faderman, 1981). Most notably, some individuals report falling in love with a same-sex friend in the absence of a generalized predisposition for same-sex *sexual* desire; in some cases, these emotional attachments engender situationally specific same-sex desires that remain restricted to the partner in question (reviewed in Diamond, 2003).

In this chapter I review a biobehavioral model of sexuality and attachment that I have advanced elsewhere (Diamond, 2003) to explain such phenomena. Specifically, I argue that the evolved processes underlying sexual desire and affectional bonding are functionally independent. As a result, one can "fall in love" without experiencing sexual desire. Second, the processes underlying affectional bonding are not intrinsically oriented toward one gender or the other. As a result, heterosexual individuals can fall in love with partners of the same gender, and lesbian/gay individuals can fall in love with partners of the other gender. Third, the biobehavioral links between love and desire are bidirectional. As a result, individuals can develop novel sexual desires—even desires that contradict their sexual orientations—as a result of falling in love. For reasons outlined next, there is good reason to believe that this phenomenon is more common among women than among men.

THE FUNCTIONAL INDEPENDENCE OF LOVE AND DESIRE

It is a truism that love and desire are fundamentally distinct, albeit fundamentally related. Sexual desire is typically defined as a "a wish, need, or drive to seek out sexual objects or to engage in sexual activities" (Regan & Berscheid, 1995, p. 346), whereas romantic love is typically defined as "the constellation of behaviors, cognitions, and emotions associated with a desire to enter or maintain a close relationship with a specific other person" (Aron & Aron, 1991). Historically, sexual desire has been considered to be a necessary precursor for romantic love, and particularly for the feelings of intense passion that characterize the earliest and most intense stages of romantic love (reviewed in Diamond, 2003). At the same time, evidence also suggests that love and sexual desire are functionally independent social-behavioral systems with distinct evolutionary functions and neural bases (Fisher, 1998). This is because sexual desire and romantic love are governed by different social-behavioral systems that evolved to serve different goals. As summarized by Fisher (1998), desire is governed by the mating system, the goal of which is sexual union. Romantic love, however, is governed by the attachment or "pair-bonding" system (Hazan & Shaver, 1987; Hazan & Zeifman, 1999), the goal of which is the formation and maintenance of enduring affectional bonds between individuals. Although these systems are often activated in concert, they are functionally independent: that is, humans can experience desire without love *and* love without desire. This functional independence appears to be a relatively recent mammalian adaptation (most pronounced in humans) that may have evolved to facilitate ecologically contingent flexibility in mating strategy (Fisher, 1998). The conditions that *are* necessary for pair bonding include sustained proximity between partners, often in concert with high levels of physical contact. As noted by Hazan and Zeifman (1994), sexual desire is a powerful motivator for both sustained proximity and intimate physical contact and may, therefore, *facilitate* the formation of pair bonds. Yet the processes underlying sexual desire and romantic love are nonetheless fundamentally distinct.

Numerous studies support the notion that individuals can experience romantic and passionate love without experiencing sexual desire. Tennov's (1979) exhaustive study of infatuation found that 61% of women and 35% of men reported experiencing infatuation without feeling "any need for sex" (p. 74). Of course, it is difficult to know whether respondents interpreted "any need for sex" to mean an *absence* of desire or simply a low motivation to *act* on sexual desires. Given this ambiguity, stronger evidence is provided by Hatfield, Schmitz, Cornelius, and Rapson (1988), who hypothesized that if sexual desire was a necessary component of infatuation, the *weakest* experiences of infatuation should be observed among prepubertal children and *the strongest* experiences of infatuation should be observed among postpubertal adolescents, given that the latter have undergone maturational surges in gonadal hormones that produce notable increases in day-to-day sexual desire (Udry & Billy, 1987; Udry, Talbert, & Morris,

1986). To test this hypothesis, they administered a Juvenile Love Scale (based on their well-validated Passionate Love Scale; Hatfield & Sprecher, 1986) to more than 200 children and adolescents between 4 and 18 years of age to measure the intensity of their infatuation experiences. Respondents were asked to think about an other-gender "boyfriend" or "girlfriend" for whom they had intense feelings (respondents were not given the opportunity to nominate a *same-gender* friend) and to rate their agreement with statements such as "I am always thinking about X" or "When X hugs me, my body feels warm all over." The intensity of respondents' infatuation experiences was then correlated with their degree of pubertal maturation (measured with standardized assessments of physical development).

The results were unequivocal: Children of *all* ages were capable of maximally intense infatuations, and the intensity of these experiences was not associated with pubertal maturation. Although the authors appropriately cautioned that their results could not reveal whether the subjective experience of infatuation was fundamentally the same for 4-year-olds as for 18-year-olds, these data nonetheless provide evidence that sexual arousal is not the "spark" that intensifies the preoccupation, separation distress, and longing for physical closeness and affection that characterize infatuation.

THE BIOLOGICAL BASES OF LOVE AND DESIRE

The research just reviewed clearly indicates that love and desire can be experienced independently, supporting the notion of their functional independence. Yet more powerful evidence for functional independence comes from research on the underlying biological substrates of love and desire. Experiences of sexual desire are strongly influenced by gonadal hormone levels: androgens in men and both androgens and estrogen in women (see reviews in Bancroft, 1978; Baumeister, Catanese, & Vohs, 2001; Udry, 1988). Exogenous administration of androgens reliably stimulates sexual urges in both men and women (Alexander & Sherwin, 1993; Arver et al., 1996; O'Carroll, Shapiro, & Bancroft, 1985; Salmimies, Kockott, Pirke, Vogt, & Schill, 1982; Sarrel, Dobay, & Wiita, 1998; Schiavi, White, Mandeli, & Levine, 1997; Sherwin & Gelfand, 1987; Sherwin, Gelfand, & Brender, 1985). Both cross-sectional and longitudinal research studies among adolescents have found that pubertal increases in gonadal and adrenal androgens are associated with increases in sexual desire (Halpern, Udry, Campbell, & Suchindran, 1993; McClintock & Herdt, 1996; Udry & Billy, 1987; Udry et al., 1986). Among women, estrogen plays an additional role: Cyclic fluctuations in estrogen levels are associated with corresponding fluctuations in sexual interest (Adams, Gold, & Burt, 1978; Judd & Yen, 1973; Stanislaw & Rice, 1988), although they are not associated with patterns of sexual behavior, which are regulated instead by social and interactional factors (Palmer, Udry, & Morris, 1982).

Yet gonadal hormones are not necessary for the experience of attachment formation. Rather, the neuropeptide hormone oxytocin plays a critical role in this regard. Oxytocin is produced in the hypothalamus and released into circulation from the posterior pituitary; oxytocin is also released directly into the brain from neurons in the paraventricular nucleus. Brain oxytocin receptors are found throughout the limbic system and in the brain stem, particularly in areas associated with emotion, autonomic control, and reproductive and social behavior. Oxytocin is most well known for stimulating the contractions of labor and facilitating milk let-down in nursing mothers, but it is also involved in multiple processes of mammalian attachment and affiliation over the life course. Studies of animals (typically rats and prairie voles) have identified direct effects of oxytocin on maternal feeding behavior, maternal–infant bonding, and kin recognition (Carter, 1998; Nelson & Panksepp, 1996; Pedersen, Caldwell, Walker, & Ayers, 1994; Uvnäs-Moberg, 1994). Like endogenous opioids, oxytocin has powerful conditioning effects that are implicated in the formation of stable preferences for places, stimuli, and other animals. For example, one study demonstrated that rats that had already been conditioned to prefer one experimental compartment to another were induced to *reverse* this preference by pairing exposure to the "nonpreferred" compartment with central injections of oxytocin (Liberzon, Trujillo, Akil, & Young, 1997). Another study found that when interactions with novel social partners were accompanied by oxytocin infusion, rats showed enhanced social memory for these interaction partners at a subsequent interaction (Popik, Vetulani, & van Ree, 1992).

Such findings have been interpreted to suggest that oxytocin-mediated conditioning effects may be an important mechanism through which mammals form stable, intrinsically rewarding bonds to *specific* social partners, most importantly the mother. Rats, for example, normally show a strong preference for odors associated with their mother (Galef & Kaner, 1980), which is a key indicator of attachment. Moreover, administration of an oxytocin *antagonist* prevented rats from developing selective preferences for maternally associated odors (Nelson & Panksepp, 1996). Oxytocin also facilitates the *mother's* attachment to her infant. Studies have found that centrally administered injections of oxytocin can induce adult ewes to form strong social attachments to unfamiliar lambs (Keverne & Kendrick, 1992), and administration of oxytocin *antagonists* to rats extinguishes certain maternal behaviors such as pup retrieval (Pedersen et al., 1994). The same basic oxytocin and opioid circuits that underlie infant–caregiver attachment also appear to underlie adult pair bonding. Much of this research has focused on prairie voles, which are one of the few species of rodents to form enduring pair bonds. The formation of pair bonds in voles is typically studied by placing two "stranger" voles in an experimental chamber under controlled conditions and later testing whether the voles prefer one another's company to that of *other* voles. Such studies have found that female prairie voles who were exposed to novel males just after receiving a central oxytocin infusion subsequently displayed a preference for these male "partners" over other males (Cho, DeVries, Williams, & Carter, 1999). Moreover, when exposure to a novel male was paired with administration of an oxytocin *antagonist*, voles failed to form such a preference (Insel & Hulihan, 1995; Williams, Insel, Harbaugh, & Carter, 1994).

BRAIN IMAGING RESEARCH ON LOVE

Given that the hormonal substrates that foster sexual desire and romantic attachment appear to be different, it should come as no surprise that recent research has also found compelling evidence that the brain regions involved in sexual desire versus romantic love are also different. The most relevant data on romantic love come from studies conducted by Bartels and Zeki (2000), Aron and colleagues (Acevedo, Aron, Fisher, & Brown, 2011; Aron et al., 2005), and Ortigue, Bianchi-Demicheli, Hamilton, and Grafton (2007). These studies focused on the stage of romantic love that is arguably most similar to sexual desire: "passionate love" or "infatuation," which is typically characterized by heightened preoccupation with the love object, intense feelings of elation, heightened sexual activity and desire, and heightened proximity seeking (Tennov, 1979). The seminal early work of Bartels and Zeki (2000) found that when participants viewed pictures of their loved one (vs. pictures of friends who were comparable to the loved one with respect to age, sex, and familiarity), activation was detected in the middle insula, anterior cingulate cortex (ACC), putamen, retrosplenial cortex, and caudate. In contrast, deactivation was detected in the amygdala. The insula and ACC are typically associated with emotion and attentional states, whereas the retrosplenial cortex is involved in episodic memory recall, imagination, and planning for the future. The putamen and caudate are associated with motivational states and reward, while the amygdala processes fear and experiences of threat as well as some positive emotions.

Aron and colleagues (2005) also focused on early-stage passionate love and found that when participants looked at the face of their partner and thought about pleasurable, nonsexual events involving the partner, activation was detected in the right caudate and the ventral tegmental area (VTA), whereas the amygdala showed deactivation (similar to Bartels and Zeki's findings). Additionally, they found that the more passionately in love people reported feeling (using the Passionate Love Scale; Hatfield & Sprecher, 1986), the greater the level of activation in the caudate. The caudate and the VTA appear to be the most consistent regions associated with romantic love (Acevedo et al., 2011; Aron et al., 2005; Bartels & Zeki, 2000; Ortigue et al., 2007; Xu et al., 2010). A role for the caudate and the VTA in romantic love is consistent with the fact that these dopamine-rich regions are strongly associated with reward and goal-directed behavior, consistent with the intense motivation to seek proximity to the beloved, which is typically associated with romantic love (reviewed by Aron et al., 2005).

Research by Ortigue and colleagues (2007) used *implicit* representations of the beloved (i.e., subliminal priming with the partner's name vs. a friend's name) and found further confirmation of the critical role of the caudate nucleus and VTA. Ortigue et al. also compared brain activation in response to the partner primes with responses to "generalized passion" primes (i.e., primes describing activities about which individuals had reported feeling passionately, such as "dance" or "piano") to allow for the identification of regions specifically associated with *romantic* passion. Results revealed love-specific activation in the bilateral fusiform regions and bilateral angular gyri, which are involved in the integration of abstract representations, particularly abstract representations of the self, and which call upon episodic retrieval processes. Hence, substantial evidence shows that love activates neural dopaminergic-motivation systems as well as regions associated with self-representation (consistent with Aron & Aron's [1986] model of love as the inclusion of the other in the self).

BRAIN IMAGING RESEARCH ON DESIRE

How do the patterns of activation elicited by romantic love compare with the patterns of activation elicited by sexual desire? First, the results of studies of sexual desire show more variability than the results of studies of love, which may be attributable to the fact that studies of desire have used a much broader range of eliciting stimuli. For example, whereas love studies have used pictures or primes of the romantic partner, studies of sexual desire have used a broad range of visual, auditory, and tactile stimuli, including pictures of nude bodies, videos depicting sexual activity, and direct genital stimulation (reviewed in Fonteille & Stoleru, 2010; Maravilla & Yang, 2008; Ortigue, Patel, & Bianchi-Demicheli, 2009; Stoleru & Mouras, 2007). Furthermore, many of these studies focus on generalized sexual *arousal* rather than desire for a specific sexual partner, and inadequately conceptualize (or operationalize) the distinction between them (Ortigue & Bianchi-Demicheli, 2007). Generally, sexual desire is commonly defined as a cognitively mediated motivational state that leads individuals to pursue sexual activity with specific individuals, whereas sexual arousal is a physiological state of readiness for sexual activity, which is often (but not always) accompanied by a subjective perception of sexual excitement. Accordingly, research suggests that there is no single sexual "center" in the brain.

Nonetheless, certain regions do appear to be reliably activated in response to sexual stimuli, such as the orbitofrontal cortex, parietal lobes, ventral striatum, hypothalamus, and amygdala. Notably, a subset of regions activated during sexual arousal overlap with regions activated by romantic love, such as the caudate, insula, putamen, and ACC. Given that the putamen and the caudate are both associated with motivational states and reward, their joint relevance for *both* sexual desire and romantic love makes sense, given that both love and desire involve strong motivation to seek the love object (albeit for different rewards: proximity in the case of romantic love and sexual activity in the case of desire). The joint relevance of the ACC for both love and sexual desire is notable, given that the specific region of the ACC that was found to be activated in Bartels and Zeki's (2000) study of love-specific brain activation (the rostral or perigenual ACC [rACC]) was found by Walter and colleagues (2008) to be particularly sensitive to the *emotional valence* of sexual stimuli. This pattern of findings is consistent with the fact that the rACC is generally considered the "affective" component of the ACC (in contrast to the dorsal ACC, which is more relevant for cognition, attention, and motor control). It is notable that rACC activation has also been found to be related to the personal relevance and self-relatedness of stimuli (Heinzel et al., 2006; Phan, Wager, Taylor, & Liberzon, 2002).

Hence, one possible interpretation of this pattern is that different "types" of sexual desire elicit different patterns of brain activity, depending on the emotional and interpersonal context. In one of the few studies seeking to identify brain activation attributable to the sexual versus emotional features of sexual stimuli (by having participants rate these features of the stimuli after the functional magnetic resonance imaging recordings were complete), Walter and colleagues (2008) found that the hypothalamus and the ventral striatum (VS) were specifically activated by the sexual intensity of the stimuli, independent of their emotional intensity. A fundamental and specific role for the hypothalamus in sexual arousal and desire has consistently emerged across numerous studies (for examples and reviews, see Fonteille & Stoleru, 2010; Hamann, Herman, Nolan, & Wallen, 2004; Karama et al., 2002; Maravilla & Yang, 2008; Redoute et al., 2000), whereas the VS is involved in motivation and predictive reward value (Kelley, 2004; O'Doherty, 2004). Hence, sexual desires for attractive strangers might involve relatively more hypothalamic and VS activity, reflecting more straightforward sexual motivation, whereas sexual desires *targeted to romantic partners* may evoke particularly high levels of rAAC and temporoparietal junction activation (given that such desires are likely to involve a stronger interpersonal component, greater self-relevance, and greater positive emotional activation).

Hence, sexual arousal and desire clearly involve *both* "sex-specific" forms of neurological activity and more complex cognitive-affective activity, and the relative ratio of activation may differ as a function of context (in particular, involving more of the latter when the target of sexual desire is a love partner). Accordingly, one of the most promising areas for future research concerns pinpointing *conditions* under which patterns of sex/love brain activation are relatively more distinct versus overlapping. For example, just as sexual desire for passionate love partners might evoke more rACC activation than desire experienced for strangers, strong feelings of passionate love for individuals who are *not* appraised as potential sex partners might also have a distinct neural signature, perhaps evoking less "sexual" patterns of brain activation (i.e., characterized by less activation in joint love/sex regions such as the caudate, insula, putamen, and ACC and more activation in regions typically associated with nonsexual, familial forms of love). For example, Bartels and Zeki (2004) contrasted brain activation in mothers viewing pictures of their own child versus a child they were well acquainted with, and directly compared the activation patterns with their previous study on romantic love (Bartels & Zeki, 2000). They found overlapping patterns of activation for maternal love and romantic love in the putamen, globus pallidus, caudate nucleus, middle insula, and ACC, suggesting that romantic love and maternal love have a shared dopaminergic-motivational substrate reflecting their shared basis in the social-behavioral system of attachment (reviewed in Diamond, 2003).

Notably, Bartels and Zeki only found hypothalamic and VTA activation for romantic love (consistent with the well-established role of the hypothalamus in sexual arousal and also with the fact that VTA activation has been found to correlate with sexual frequency and feelings of intense passion in long-term couples; Acevedo et al., 2011), and they only found periaqueductal gray matter (PAG) activation in maternal love. Notably, PAG activation has also been found to be associated with feelings of unconditional love (Beauregard, Courtemanche, Paquette, & St. Pierre, 2009), and in long-term couples, PAG activation is correlated with duration of marriage (Acevedo et al., 2011). This suggests a potential role for the PAG in emotionally intense but nonsexual experiences of love. A promising direction for future research on links and distinctions between love and desire is to evaluate *changes* in patterns of neurological activation elicited by romantic partners over time. Both sexual desire and passionate infatuation are known to decline in long-term relationships, and yet, as shown by Acevedo and colleagues (2011), some long-term couples report experiencing—and show patterns of brain activation consistent with—the sort of passionate infatuation more typical of new couples (i.e., greater activation in the VTA, caudate, putamen, and posterior hippocampus). A fascinating direction for future research would be to examine whether longitudinal changes in couples' subjective experiences of their relationship (i.e., a shift from passionate, sexually charged infatuation to companionate, unconditional devotion) correspond to changes in the constellation of brain regions activated by thoughts and feelings regarding the partner (i.e., reductions in VTA, caudate, and putamen activation and increases in PAG activation). Longitudinal changes might also occur in the brain regions activated during sexual desire (and potentially even activity) in long-term relationships, perhaps reflecting a shift toward more emotionally and cognitively mediated forms of sexual response.

THE EVOLUTION OF LOVE AND DESIRE

Given the aforementioned evidence that love and desire are, in fact, fundamentally distinct phenomenon with different (albeit interconnected) neurobiological substrates, a natural question is *why*? After all, most individuals end up falling in love with partners to whom they are sexually drawn, and this seems to make good evolutionary sense given that pair bonding with one's sexual partner is a good way to ensure that the resulting offspring have two dedicated parents instead of just one. This view assumes, however, that the basic biobehavioral mechanisms underlying affectional bonding evolved *for the purpose of* reproductive pair bonding, which does not appear to be the case. Although these processes would clearly have conferred adaptive benefits on early humans, some researchers have argued that they *originally* evolved for an altogether different purpose: infant–caregiver attachment.

Bowlby (1969/1982) conceptualized attachment as an evolved behavioral system designed to regulate infants' proximity to caregivers and thereby maximize chances for survival, given that mammalian (and particularly primate) infants are born in a particularly vulnerable state requiring intensive maternal care. The attachment system is driven by emotions. Specifically, separation from caregivers elicits distress and anxiety, whereas proximity to and contact with caregivers elicits feelings of calm and security. Although Bowlby developed attachment theory on the basis of observations of infant–caregiver behavior, he argued that the attachment system is operative across the entire lifespan. Similarly, other evolutionary theorists have argued that once the "problem" of keeping human reproductive partners together (for the purpose of jointly rearing their children) emerged, the infant–caregiver attachment system was exploited for this purpose (Panksepp, 1998). Natural selection does not generally result in the production of brand-new mechanisms to solve evolutionary problems where existing ones will suffice, and thus adult pair bonding appears to be an *exaptation*—a system that originally evolved for one reason but comes to serve another. The fundamental correspondence between infant–caregiver attachment and adult pair bonding is supported by extensive research documenting that these phenomena share the same core emotional and behavioral dynamics: heightened proximity maintenance, resistance to separation, and utilization of the partner as a preferred target for comfort and security seeking (Hazan & Zeifman, 1999). Even more powerful evidence is provided by the voluminous animal research documenting that these two types of affectional bonding are mediated by the same opioid- and oxytocin-based neural circuitry (Carter, 1998).

This helps to explain the independence between love and desire: Although sexual desire almost always accompanies adult reproductive pair bonding, it is irrelevant to the process of infant–caregiver bonding. Yet even if one grants that affectional bonding and sexual mating are, in fact, fundamentally distinct processes that evolved for fundamentally distinct purposes, the question still remains: Why do the majority of human adults *only* fall in love with partners to whom they are sexually attracted? One reason is obviously cultural: Most human societies have strong and well-established norms regarding what types of feelings and behaviors are appropriate for different types of adult relationships, and they actively channel adults into the "right" types of relationships through a variety of social practices. Additionally, however, both human and animal data suggest that the process of attachment formation is highly proximity dependent. Specifically, it is most likely to occur between individuals who have extensive proximity to and physical contact with one another over a prolonged period of time (reviewed by Hazan & Zeifman, 1999). Hazan and Zeifman (1999), therefore, argued that because sexual desire and activity provide powerful motives for such extended contact, they effectively ensure that the average adult "ends up" bonded to potential or actual reproductive partners rather than platonic friends.

IMPLICATIONS FOR SEXUAL ORIENTATION

The evolved independence of love and desire has important implications for our conceptualizations of sexual orientation. It is commonly assumed that an individual's sexual orientation shapes not only his or her sexual desires but also experiences of romantic love. Tendencies to become romantically attached to same-sex versus other-sex partners are typically assessed as part of the standard measurements of sexual orientation (Kinsey, Pomeroy, & Martin, 1948; Pattatucci & Hamer, 1995; Russell & Consolacion, 2003; Sell & Petrulio, 1996), and in fact, the majority of openly identified lesbian/bisexual individuals report desiring and participating in long-term romantic attachments with same-sex partners (reviewed in Diamond, 2006), whereas heterosexuals typically form romantic attachments exclusively with other-sex partners.

Yet such attachments are not always the case. Anthropologists and historians have documented unusually intimate, passionate, platonic same-gender friendships among otherwise heterosexual individuals in a variety of different cultures and historical periods, dating as far back as ancient Greece (Blackwood, 1985; Brain, 1976; Faderman, 1981; Gay, 1985; Hansen, 1992; Katz, 1976; Richards, 1987; Rotundo, 1989; Smith-Rosenberg, 1975; Williams, 1992). These bonds often inspired their own unique terms, such as *romantic friendships* (Faderman, 1981; Rotundo, 1989), *bond friendships* (Firth, 1967), *mummy–baby friendships* (Gay, 1985), *camaradia* (Reina, 1966), or *smashes* (Sahli, 1979). One 19th-century schoolmistress described smashes as "an extraordinary habit which [schoolgirls] have of falling violently in love with each other, and suffering all the pangs of unrequited attachment, desperate jealousy etc. etc., with as much energy as if one of them were a man. . . . If the 'smash' is mutual, they monopolize each other & 'spoon' continually, & sleep together & lie awake all night talking instead of going to sleep" (Sahli, 1979, p. 22). Williams's (1992) ethnographic research on North American Indians documented similarly intense but nonsexual bonds between men, which he attributed to the fact that marriage was primarily an economic rather than an affectional tie. Thus, men tended to rely on their male friends instead of their wives to meet their primary emotional needs. Williams noted that early Western explorers were surprised by the unusually intense nature of these relationships (e.g., Parkman, 1969), and one 19th-century American officer remarked outright that these men seemed to "fall in love" with one another (Trumbull, 1894).

Because infatuation and sexual desire are typically presumed to be cut from the same cloth, modern observers reading such descriptions often assume that such relationships contained a subverted sexual element, and that if the participants had lived in a more permissive and enlightened environment, they would have pursued an openly sexual relationship. However, those who study and document such relationships have argued against this view, noting that the presumption of a necessary link between same-gender affectional bonds and same-gender sexual desires is historically and culturally specific (see especially D'Emilio & Freedman, 1988; Faderman, 1981, 1993; Nardi, 1992). Although these authors have readily acknowledged that some of these relationships might have involved sexual interest, they maintain that this was not uniformly so. This belief is consistent with the notion that the passion and intensity of such bonds derive from their status as *attachment* relationships, not as sexual ties.

If, as outlined previously, the basic affective, behavioral, and neurobiological dynamics of pair bonding are based in the infant–caregiver attachment system—and, importantly, *not* in the sexual mating system—then there is no reason to expect the orientation of an individual's *sexual* desires to fundamentally circumscribe his or her propensity for romantic attachment. If individuals were endowed with intrinsic affectional "orientations" driving them to form pair bonds *only* with partners of a particular gender, such orientations would have to be coded into the biobehavioral architecture of infant–caregiver attachment. Of course, this is implausible: Infants do not become selectively attached to same-sex versus other-sex caregivers, and it would be maladaptive if they did. Consequently, the same-sex versus other-sex orientation of an individual's *sexual* desires should not extend to his or her capacity for affectional bonding (Diamond, 2003). It should be possible for individuals to "fall in love" with, and become powerfully romantically attached to, *just about anyone*, regardless of gender. Lesbian/gay individuals should be able to fall in love with other-sex partners and heterosexual individuals with same-sex partners, even in the absence of sexual desire.

This idea, of course, runs counter to the conventional wisdom on same-sex sexuality, in which it is commonly assumed that lesbians and gay men are incapable of falling in love with other-sex individuals and that heterosexual individuals are incapable of falling in love with same-sex individuals. Yet this notion is starkly contradicted not only by extensive cross-cultural and historical evidence as reviewed previously but animal research as well. Research on the famously monogamous prairie voles found that, given sufficient cohabitation, both male and female voles could be induced to bond with same-sex partners, although such bonds could be disrupted by the introduction of a novel other-sex vole (DeVries, Johnson, & Carter, 1997).

WHEN LOVE PRECIPITATES DESIRE

Although I have argued that all individuals are capable of forming full-blown romantic attachments that are devoid of sexual attraction, such cases are exceptional. The majority of individuals fall in love with others to whom they are sexually attracted, underscoring the fact that the majority of adults perceive and experience love and desire as powerfully *interconnected*, despite the functional independence between these systems. These interconnections appear to become established during adolescence as part of the overall process of social and sexual maturation, yet the specific underlying processes involved are not clear. Processes of classical conditioning may play a role, as reproductively mature adolescents' increasingly frequent other-gender interactions provide them with opportunities to experience feelings of infatuation in concert with newly urgent sexual desires. Cultural norms also probably support these developments, sending a strong message regarding what types of feelings and behaviors are appropriate with different social partners. Oxytocin, too, may facilitate the connections between love and desire, given that oxytocin release has been found to be associated with both pair bonding *and* sexual activity (Carmichael, Warburton, Dixen, & Davidson, 1994; Carter, 1992, 1998; Keverne, Nevison, & Martel, 1999; Riley, 1988; Uvnäs-Moberg, 2004). Hence, there are numerous psychological, cultural, and biological processes that may render humans particularly likely to become romantically attached to individuals for whom they experience sexually attractions.

Yet importantly, these same psychological, cultural, and biological processes might also work in the opposite direction, making it possible for individuals to *develop* sexual attractions for individuals to whom they have become emotionally attached, *even if such desires contradict their sexual orientation*. Given that these "cross-orientation" desires are dependent on the emotional processes associated with pair bonding, they should be limited to the relationship in question. There is extensive evidence in support of such "relationship-specific" desires. Scientific and popular writings on sexual orientation are replete with accounts of individuals whose same-sex desires revolve around *specific* people they unexpectedly fell in love with rather than same-sex partners "in general" (Golden, 1996; Pillard, 1990; Savin-Williams, 1998; Walsh, 2010; Whisman, 1996). Notably, such reports are often greeted with skepticism. As Blumstein and Schwartz (1990) noted, our conventional understanding of sexual orientation maintains that it is impossible to have "just a few" same-sex attractions for "just a few" special people. Those making such claims are thought to be misperceiving their true sexual natures in order to consciously or unconsciously avoid the stigma of homosexuality. This is certainly likely to be the case for some individuals, but not all of them. Longitudinal research on sexual identity development in women has shown that numerous women report experiencing their first *and only* experiences of same-sex desire in the context of a powerful affectional bond to a specific female friend (Diamond, 2008).

These "relationship-specific" desires appear to be born out of the emotional attachment formed between the two women and to dissipate along with the dissolution of the relationship. Hence, whereas some women who experience sexual desires for their close female friends end up discovering that they are lesbian or bisexual, for other women such desires are truly atypical and do not constitute "secondary indicators" of a same-sex orientation.

These findings suggest that when we examine the overall population of individuals experiencing same-sex desires and participating in same-sex relationships, it is reasonable to consider that this population contains two "subtypes:" a group possessing an enduring sexual predisposition for the same sex (i.e., lesbian/gay/bisexual individuals) and a group that does not. In the former group, same-sex attractions are direct manifestations of their same-sex orientation. In the latter group, same-sex attractions may arise out of the context of an unusually intense same-sex attachment and are *not* manifestations of a same-sex orientation. Notably, the notion of such subtypes has long circulated in the research literature on sexual orientation. As far back as the late 1970s, Blumstein and Schwartz pointed out that traditional models of sexual orientation failed to account for individuals whose same-sex desires appeared to be born out of intense experiences of attachment for specific individuals, noting that "our cultural logic holds that it is almost impossible to have only some homosexual feelings" (1993, p. 177). Numerous scholars of sexual orientation have considered whether there might be a fundamental difference between individuals with long-standing, generalized, "constitutional" same-sex attractions and individuals with "facultative" same-sex desires (i.e., influenced by and limited to specific individuals and contexts, Bell, Weinberg, & Hammersmith, 1981).

This distinction is also reflected in lay conceptions of same-sex sexuality. The lesbian community, for example, has long distinguished between *primary/born* lesbians, whose same-sex sexuality is presumed to be essential and early developing, and *elective/bisexual/political* lesbians, whose same-sex sexuality is presumed to be prompted by specific situations and/or relationships (Burch, 1993; Ettore, 1980; Golden, 1994; Ponse, 1978).

Such distinctions clearly have some validity, given that intense experiences of same-sex emotional attachment can, in fact, give rise to novel, unprecedented experiences of same-sex desire among otherwise heterosexual individuals. Yet we know little about the long-range implications of this distinction. As reviewed earlier, one possibility is that sexual desires that are specifically generated by intense experiences of romantic attachment might be characterized by different patterns of brain activation than desires that directly reflect an underlying same-sex orientation. Another possibility, which has received some suggestive support, is that same-sex desires that reflect an underlying same-sex orientation might be more strongly linked to ovulatory changes in estrogen levels (Diamond & Wallen, 2011). Future research comparing women with generalized versus "relationship-specific" same-sex desires clearly has much to tell us about the underlying nature and dynamics of love, desire, and sexual orientation more generally.

GENDER DIFFERENCES

All of the preceding examples of "relationship-specific" desire concerned women, and this is no accident. Historically, women's sexual feelings have been viewed as more strongly influenced by emotional attachments than men's sexual feelings (Nichols, 1987; Blumstein & Schwartz, 1977). For example, when Regan and Berscheid (1995) asked undergraduate respondents what causes sexual desire in males versus females, the most widely endorsed category for *male* sexual desire was intraindividual factors such as biological processes and physical "need" for sex. In contrast, the most widely endorsed cause for female sexual desire was the interpersonal experience of love. Women are also more likely than men to claim that they fall in love with—and correspondingly become attracted to—"the person rather than the gender" (Blumstein & Schwartz, 1977; Diamond, 2008; Golden, 1987; Weinberg, Williams, & Pryor, 1994). Thus, affectional feelings appear to play a more important role in structuring women's sexual feelings than men's. In the past, this has been attributed to the fact that women have been historically socialized to restrict their sexual feelings and behaviors to intimate emotional relationships—ideally marital ties—whereas males have not (Gagnon & Simon, 1973).

Yet our emerging understanding of the neurochemical substrates of love and desire raises the intriguing possibility that, in addition to these cultural and experiential factors, *biological* factors might contribute to this phenomenon. As noted earlier, the fact that oxytocin plays a critical role in *both* attachment and sexuality might account for the fact that some individuals appear capable of developing novel sexual desires for individuals to whom they have become powerfully attached. Yet importantly, oxytocin's effects on mammalian attachment and affiliation are estrogen dependent and gender specific, and in some species, females have far more extensive oxytocin brain circuits than males, perhaps to facilitate oxytocin-dependent caregiving behaviors (reviewed in Panksepp, 1998). Furthermore, oxytocin *also* shows gender-specific, estrogen-dependent effects on mammalian *sexual* initiation and receptivity (reviewed in Panksepp, 1998). Among humans, the highest circulating levels of oxytocin are detected during sexual activity, and women show higher plasma levels than men under these conditions (Carmichael et al., 1994). The aforementioned study also found that in some women blood levels of oxytocin were associated with subjective orgasm intensity.

Such findings raise the possibility that women's greater emphasis on the relational context of sexuality (i.e., their greater experience of *links* between love and desire) may reflect oxytocin's *joint, gender-specific* role in both processes. This is not to discount the influence of culture and socialization on sexual feelings experienced within relational contexts, but rather to suggest that sociocultural influences might be facilitated by gender-differentiated biobehavioral processes. Hence, although "relationship-specific" desires might be possible for both sexes, they are perhaps more likely for women because of gender-specific oxytocinergic processes *and* the greater cultural permission for women to develop strong affectional bonds with other women (for a similar argument regarding oxytocin, same-sex female bonds, and gender-differentiated patterns of stress response, see Taylor et al., 2000).

Furthermore, clinical research on female sexual function and dysfunction has increasingly demonstrated a distinctive and important role for interpersonal and contextual factors in female sexual desire (Basson, 2000; Brotto, Bitzer, Laan, Leiblum, & Luria, 2010). Traditional, male-based models of sexual arousal have historically posited that the sexual response cycle begins with an experience of innate and automatic desire, which progresses to sexual arousal and motivates subsequent sexual behavior and release (Masters & Johnson, 1966). Yet recent research has found that "automatic" desire is less common among women than men, and that sexual desire in women is a fundamentally *responsive* system that depends more heavily on the overall cognitive, affective, and interpersonal context (Basson, 2000, 2002). Accordingly, the complex constellation of feelings and cognitions brought about by attachment formation—and their associated neurobiological substrates—may prove more influential on women's sexual desire than on men's.

CONCLUSION

Understanding the ways in which love and desire—despite their basic independence—become *interbraided* in women's and men's intimate experiences across the life course, and why they appear to be more closely interconnected for some individuals than for others, remains one of the most fascinating areas for future research on attachment and sexuality. Importantly, research on this topic will make important contributions to our understanding of not only the basic evolved architecture of human attachment but also sexuality and sexual orientation. In particular, the standard practice of classifying individuals into discrete sexual categories solely on the basis of their *physical* attractions for same-sex versus other-sex partners provides an incomplete picture of the complex interconnections between emotional intimacy and physical eroticism that shape individuals' subjective experiences of their sexuality. Research using animal models, neuroimaging, hormonal assays, and phenomenological accounts demonstrates that there are multiple, complex, gender-specific biobehavioral mechanisms through which love and desire may be experienced both concurrently and independently at different stages of the life course, in different contexts, and for both same-sex and other-sex partners. Our task, now, is to build on this body of literature to develop a more comprehensive understanding of our basic sexual and affectional nature.

REFERENCES

Acevedo, B. P., Aron, A., Fisher, H. E., & Brown, L. L. (2011). Neural correlates of long-term intense romantic love. *Social Cognitive and Affective Neuroscience, 7*(2), 145–159.

Adams, D. B., Gold, A. R., & Burt, A. D. (1978). Rise in female-initiated sexual activity at ovulation and its suppression by oral contraceptives. *New England Journal of Medicine, 299,* 1145–1150.

Alexander, G. M., & Sherwin, B. B. (1993). Sex steroids, sexual behavior, and selection attention for erotic stimuli in women using oral contraceptives. *Psychoneuroendocrinology, 18*, 91–102.

Aron, A., Fisher, H., Mashek, D. J., Strong, G., Li, H., & Brown, L. L. (2005). Reward, motivation, and emotion systems associated with early-stage intense romantic love. *Journal of Neurophysiology, 94*, 327–337.

Aron, A. P., & Aron, E. N. (1986). *Love as the expansion of self: Understanding attraction and satisfaction.* New York: Hemisphere.

Aron, A. P., & Aron, E. N. (1991). Love and sexuality. In K. McKinney & S. Sprecher (Eds.), *Sexuality in close relationships* (pp. 25–48). Hillsdale, NJ: Erlbaum.

Arver, S., Dobs, A. S., Meikle, A. W., Allen, R. P., Sanders, S. W., & Mazer, N. A. (1996). Improvement of sexual function in testosterone deficient men treated for 1 year with a permeation enhanced testosterone transdermal system. *Journal of Urology, 155*, 1604–1608.

Bancroft, J. H. (1978). The relationships between hormones and sexual behavior in humans. In J. B. Hutchison (Ed.), *Biological determinants of sexual behavior* (pp. 493–519). Chicester, UK: Wiley.

Bartels, A., & Zeki, S. (2000). The neural basis of romantic love. *NeuroReport, 11*, 3829–3834.

Bartels, A., & Zeki, S. (2004). The neural correlates of maternal and romantic love. *NeuroImage, 21*, 1155–1166.

Basson, R. (2000). The female sexual response: A different model. *Journal of Sex and Marital Therapy, 26*, 51–65.

Basson, R. (2002). Women's sexual desire: Disordered or misunderstood? *Journal of Sex and Marital Therapy, 28*, 17–28.

Baumeister, R. F., Catanese, K. R., & Vohs, K. D. (2001). Is there a gender difference in strength of sex drive? Theoretical views, conceptual distinctions, and a review of relevent evidence. *Personality and Social Psychology Review, 5*, 242–273.

Beauregard, M., Courtemanche, J., Paquette, V., & St. Pierre, E. L. (2009). The neural basis of unconditional love. *Psychiatry Research: Neuroimaging, 172*, 93–98.

Bell, A. P., Weinberg, M. S., & Hammersmith, S. K. (1981). *Sexual preference: Its development in men and women.* Bloomington: Indiana University Press.

Blackwood, E. (1985). Breaking the mirror: The construction of lesbianism and the anthropological discourse on homosexuality. *Journal of Homosexuality, 11*, 1–17.

Blumstein, P., & Schwartz, P. (1990). Intimate relationships and the creation of sexuality. In D. P. McWhirter, S. A. Sanders, & J. M. Reinisch (Eds.), *Homosexuality/heterosexuality: Concepts of sexual orientation* (pp. 307–320). New York: Oxford University Press.

Blumstein, P., & Schwartz, P. (1993). Bisexuality: Some social psychological issues. In L. D. Garnets & D. C. Kimmel (Eds.), *Psychological perspectives on lesbian and gay male experiences* (pp. 168–183). New York: Columbia University Press.

Bowlby, J. (1982). *Attachment and loss: Vol. 1. Attachment* (2nd ed.). New York: Basic Books. (Original work published 1969)

Brain, R. (1976). *Friends and lovers*. New York: Basic Books.

Brotto, L. A., Bitzer, J., Laan, E., Leiblum, S. R., & Luria, M. (2010). Women's sexual desire and arousal disorders. *Journal of Sexual Medicine, 7*, 586–614.

Brown, L. (1995). Lesbian identities: Concepts and issues. In A. R. D'Augelli & C. Patterson (Eds.), *Lesbian, gay, and bisexual identities over the lifespan* (pp. 3–23). New York: Oxford University Press.

Burch, B. (1993). *On intimate terms: The psychology of difference in lesbian relationships*. Chicago: University of Illinois Press.

Carmichael, M. S., Warburton, V. L., Dixen, J., & Davidson, J. M. (1994). Relationships among cardiovascular, muscular, and oxytocin responses during human sexual activity. *Archives of Sexual Behavior, 23*, 59–79.

Carter, C. S. (1992). Oxytocin and sexual behavior. *Neuroscience and Biobehavioral Reviews, 16*, 131–144.

Carter, C. S. (1998). Neuroendocrine perspectives on social attachment and love. *Psychoneuroendocrinology, 23*, 779–818.

Cho, M. M., DeVries, A. C., Williams, J. R., & Carter, C. S. (1999). The effects of oxytocin and vasopressin on partner preferences in male and female prairie voles (*Microtus ochrogaster*). *Behavioral Neuroscience, 113*, 1071–1079.

D'Emilio, J., & Freedman, E. B. (1988). *Intimate matters: A history of sexuality in America*. New York: Harper & Row.

DeVries, A. C., Johnson, C. L., & Carter, C. S. (1997). Familiarity and gender influence social preferences in prairie voles (*Microtus ochrogaster*). *Canadian Journal of Zoology, 75*, 295–301.

Diamond, L. M. (2000). Passionate friendships among adolescent sexual-minority women. *Journal of Research on Adolescence, 10*, 191–209.

Diamond, L. M. (2003). What does sexual orientation orient? A biobehavioral model distinguishing romantic love and sexual desire. *Psychological Review, 110*, 173–192.

Diamond, L. M. (2004). Emerging perspectives on distinctions between romantic love and sexual desire. *Current Directions in Psychological Science, 13*, 116–119.

Diamond, L. M. (2006). The same-sex intimate relationships of sexual minorities. In D. Perlman & A. L. Vangelisti (Eds.), *The Cambridge handbook of personal relationships* (pp. 293–312). New York: Cambridge University Press.

Diamond, L. M. (2008). *Sexual fluidity: Understanding women's love and desire*. Cambridge, MA: Harvard University Press.

Diamond, L. M., & Wallen, K. (2011). Sexual-minority women's sexual motivation around the time of ovulation. *Archives of Sexual Behavior, 40*, 237–246.

Ettore, E. M. (1980). *Lesbians, women, and society*. London: Routledge.

Faderman, L. (1981). *Surpassing the love of men*. New York: William Morrow.

Faderman, L. (1993). Nineteenth-century Boston marriage as a possible lesson for today. In E. D. Rothblum & K. A. Brehony (Eds.), *Boston marriages* (pp. 29–42). Amherst: University of Massachusetts Press.

Fisher, H. E. (1998). Lust, attraction, and attachment in mammalian reproduction. *Human Nature, 9*, 23–52.

Fonteille, V., & Stoleru, S. (2010). The cerebral correlates of sexual desire: Functional neuroimaging approach. *Sexologies, 10*, 1016.

Furth, R. W. (1967). *Tikopia ritual and belief.* Boston: Allen & Unwin.

Gagnon, J. H., & Simon, W. (1973). *Sexual conduct: The social sources of human sexuality.* Chicago: Aldine.

Galef, B. G., & Kaner, H. C. (1980). Establishment and maintenance of preference for natural and artificial olfactory stimuli in juvenile rats. *Journal of Comparative Physiology and Psychology, 4,* 588–595.

Gay, J. (1985). "Mummies and babies" and friends and lovers in Lesotho. *Journal of Homosexuality, 11,* 97–116.

Golden, C. (1987). Diversity and variability in women's sexual identities. In Boston Lesbian Psychologies Collective (Ed.), *Lesbian psychologies: Explorations and challenges* (pp. 19–34). Urbana: University of Illinois Press.

Golden, C. (1994). Our politics and choices: The feminist movement and sexual orientation. In B. Greene & G. M. Herek (Eds.), *Lesbian and gay psychology: Theory, research, and clinical applications* (pp. 54–70). Thousand Oaks, CA: Sage.

Golden, C. (1996). What's in a name? Sexual self-identification among women. In R. C. Savin-Williams & K. M. Cohen (Eds.), *The lives of lesbians, gays, and bisexuals: Children to adults* (pp. 229–249). Fort Worth, TX: Harcourt Brace.

Halpern, C. T., Udry, J. R., Campbell, B., & Suchindran, C. (1993). Testosterone and pubertal development as predictors of sexual activity: A panel analysis of adolescent males. *Psychosomatic Medicine, 55,* 436–447.

Hamann, S., Herman, R. A., Nolan, C. L., & Wallen, K. (2004). Men and women differ in amygdala response to visual sexual stimuli. *Nature Neuroscience, 7,* 411–416.

Hansen, K. V. (1992). "Our eyes behold each other": Masculinity and intimate friendship in antebellum New England. In P. Nardi (Ed.), *Men's friendships* (pp. 35–58). Newbury Park, CA: Sage.

Hatfield, E., Schmitz, E., Cornelius, J., & Rapson, R. L. (1988). Passionate love: How early does it begin? *Journal of Psychology and Human Sexuality, 1,* 35–52.

Hatfield, E., & Sprecher, S. (1986). Measuring passionate love in intimate relationships. *Journal of Adolescence, 9,* 383–410.

Hazan, C., & Shaver, P. R. (1987). Romantic love conceptualized as an attachment process. *Journal of Personality and Social Psychology, 52,* 511–524.

Hazan, C., & Zeifman, D. (1994). Sex and the psychological tether. In D. Perlman & K. Bartholomew (Eds.), *Advances in personal relationships: A research annual* (Vol. 5, pp. 151–177). London: Jessica Kingsley.

Hazan, C., & Zeifman, D. (1999). Pair-bonds as attachments: Evaluating the evidence. In J. Cassidy & P. R. Shaver (Eds.), *Handbook of attachment theory and research* (pp. 336–354). New York: Guilford Press.

Heinzel, A., Walter, M., Schneider, F., Rotte, M., Matthiae, C., Tempelmann, C., et al. (2006). Self-related processing in the sexual domain: Parametric event-related fMRI study reveals neural activity in ventral cortical midline structures. *Social Neuroscience, 1,* 41–51.

Insel, T. R., & Hulihan, T. J. (1995). A gender-specific mechanism for pair bonding: Oxytocin and partner preference formation in monogamous voles. *Behavioral Neuroscience, 109,* 782–789.

Judd, H. L., & Yen, S. S. C. (1973). Serum androstenedione and testosterone levels during the menstrual cycle. *Journal of Clinical Endocrinology and Metabolism, 36*, 475–481.

Karama, S., Lecours, A. R., Leroux, J.-M., Bourgouin, P., Beaudoin, G., Joubert, S., et al. (2002). Areas of brain activation in males and females during viewing of erotic film excerpts. *Human Brain Mapping, 16*, 1–13.

Katz, J. (1976). *Gay American history.* New York: Crowell.

Kelley, A. E. (2004). Ventral striatal control of appetitive motivation: Role in ingestive behavior and reward-related learning. *Neuroscience and Biobehavioral Reviews, 27*, 765–776.

Keverne, E. B., & Kendrick, K. M. (1992). Oxytocin facilitation of maternal behavior in sheep. *Annals of the New York Academy of Sciences, 652*, 83–101.

Keverne, E. B., Nevison, C. M., & Martel, F. L. (1999). Early learning and the social bond. In C. S. Carter, I. I. Lederhendler, & B. Kirkpatrick (Eds.), *The integrative neurobiology of affiliation* (pp. 263–274). Cambridge, MA: MIT Press.

Kinsey, A. C., Pomeroy, W. B., & Martin, C. E. (1948). *Sexual behavior in the human male.* Philadelphia: Saunders.

Liberzon, I., Trujillo, K. A., Akil, H., & Young, E. A. (1997). Motivational properties of oxytocin in the conditioned place preference paradigm. *Neuropsychopharmacology, 17*, 353–359.

Maravilla, K. R., & Yang, C. C. (2008). Magnetic resonance imaging and the female sexual response: Overview of techniques, results, and future directions. *Journal of Sexual Medicine, 5*, 1559–1571.

Masters, W. H., & Johnson, V. E. (1966). *Human sexual response.* Boston: Little, Brown.

McClintock, M. K., & Herdt, G. (1996). Rethinking puberty: The development of sexual attraction. *Current Directions in Psychological Science, 5*, 178–183.

Nardi, P. M. (1992). "Seamless souls": An introduction to men's friendships. In P. Nardi (Ed.), *Men's friendships* (pp. 1–14). Newbury Park, CA: Sage.

Nelson, E. E., & Panksepp, J. (1996). Oxytocin mediates acquisition of maternally associated odor preferences in preweanling rat pups. *Behavioral Neuroscience, 110*, 583–592.

Nichols, M. (1987). Lesbian sexuality: Issues and developing theory. In Boston Lesbian Psychologies Collective (Ed.), *Lesbian psychologies* (pp. 97–125). Urbana: University of Illinois Press.

O'Carroll, R., Shapiro, C., & Bancroft, J. H. (1985). Androgens, behaviour and nocturnal erection in hypogonadal men: The effects of varying the replacement dose. *Clinical Endocrinology, 23*, 527–538.

O'Doherty, J. P. (2004). Reward representations and reward-related learning in the human brain: Insights from neuroimaging. *Current Opinion in Neurobiology, 14*, 769–776.

Ortigue, S., & Bianchi-Demicheli, F. (2007). Interactions between human sexual arousal and sexual desire: A challenge for social neuroscience. *Revue Medicale Suisse, 3*, 809–813.

Ortigue, S., Bianchi-Demicheli, F., Hamilton, A. F., & Grafton, S. T. (2007). The neural basis of love as a subliminal prime: An event-related functional magnetic resonance imaging study. *Journal of Cognitive Neuroscience, 19,* 1218–1230.

Ortigue, S., Patel, N., & Bianchi-Demicheli, F. (2009). New electroencephalogram (EEG) neuroimaging methods of analyzing brain activity applicable to the study of human sexual response. *Journal of Sexual Medicine, 6,* 1830–1845.

Palmer, J. D., Udry, J. R., & Morris, N. M. (1982). Diurnal and weekly, but no lunar rhythms in humans copulation. *Human Biology, 54,* 111–121.

Panksepp, J. (1998). *Affective neuroscience: The foundations of human and animal emotions.* New York: Cambridge University Press.

Parkman, F. (1969). *The Oregon trail.* Madison: University of Wisconsin Press.

Pattatucci, A. M. L., & Hamer, D. H. (1995). Development and familiality of sexual orientation in females. *Behavior Genetics, 25,* 407–420.

Pedersen, C. A., Caldwell, J. D., Walker, C., & Ayers, G. (1994). Oxytocin activates the postpartum onset of rat maternal behavior in the ventral tegmental and medial preoptic areas. *Behavioral Neuroscience, 108,* 1163–1171.

Phan, K. L., Wager, T., Taylor, S. F., & Liberzon, I. (2002). Functional neuroanatomy of emotion: A meta-analysis of emotion activation studies in PET and fMRI. *NeuroImage, 16,* 331–348.

Pillard, R. C. (1990). The Kinsey Scale: Is it familial? In D. P. McWhirter, S. A. Sanders, & J. M. Reinisch (Eds.), *Homosexuality/heterosexuality: Concepts of sexual orientation* (pp. 88–100). New York: Oxford University Press.

Ponse, B. (1978). *Identities in the lesbian world: The social construction of self.* Westport, CT: Greenwood Press.

Popik, P., Vetulani, J., & van Ree, J. M. (1992). Low doses of oxytocin facilitate social recognition in rats. *Psychopharmacology, 106,* 71–74.

Redoute, J., Stoleru, S., Gregoire, M. C., Costes, N., Cinotti, L., Lavenne, F., et al. (2000). Brain processing of visual sexual stimuli in human males. *Human Brain Mapping, 11,* 162–177.

Regan, P. C. (1998). Of lust and love: Beliefs about the role of sexual desire in romantic relationships. *Personal Relationships, 5,* 139–157.

Regan, P. C., & Berscheid, E. (1995). Gender differences in beliefs about the causes of male and female sexual desire. *Personal Relationships, 2,* 345–358.

Reina, R. (1966). *The law of the saints: A Pokoman pueblo and its community culture.* Indianapolis, IN: Bobbs Merrill.

Richards, J. (1987). "Passing the love of women": Manly love and Victorian society. In J. A. Mangan & J. Walvin (Eds.), *Manliness and morality: Middle-class masculinity in Britain and America 1800–1940* (pp. 92–122). Manchester, UK: Manchester University Press.

Riley, A. J. (1988). Oxytocin and coitus. *Sexual and Marital Therapy, 3,* 29–36.

Rotundo, E. A. (1989). Romantic friendships: Male intimacy and middle-class youth in the northern United States, 1800–1900. *Journal of Social History, 23,* 1–25.

Russell, S. T., & Consolacion, T. B. (2003). Adolescent romance and emotional health in the U.S.: Beyond binaries. *Journal of Clinical Child and Adolescent Pschology, 32,* 499–508.

Sahli, N. (1979). Smashing: Women's relationships before the fall. *Chrysalis, 8,* 17–27.

Salmimies, P., Kockott, G., Pirke, K. M., Vogt, H. J., & Schill, W. B. (1982). Effects of testosterone replacement on sexual behavior in hypogonadal men. *Archives of Sexual Behavior, 11,* 345–353.

Sarrel, P., Dobay, B., & Wiita, B. (1998). Estrogen and estrogen-androgen replacement in postmenopausal women dissatisfied with estrogen-only therapy. Sexual behavior and neuroendocrine responses. *Journal of Reproductive Medicine, 43,* 847–856.

Savin-Williams, R. C. (1998). *". . . And then I became gay": Young men's stories.* New York: Routledge.

Schiavi, R. C., White, D., Mandeli, J., & Levine, A. C. (1997). Effect of testosterone administration on sexual behavior and mood in men with erectile dysfunction. *Archives of Sexual Behavior, 26,* 231–241.

Sell, R. L., & Petrulio, C. (1996). Sampling homosexuals, bisexuals, gays, and lesbians for public health research: A review of the literature from 1990 to 1992. *Journal of Homosexuality, 30,* 31–47.

Shaver, P. R., Hazan, C., & Bradshaw, D. (1988). Love as attachment: The integration of three behavioral systems. In J. Sternberg & M. L. Barnes (Eds.), *The psychology of love* (pp. 193–219). New Haven, CT: Yale University Press.

Sherwin, B. B., & Gelfand, M. M. (1987). The role of androgen in the maintenance of sexual functioning in oophorectomized women. *Psychosomatic Medicine, 49,* 397–409.

Sherwin, B. B., Gelfand, M. M., & Brender, W. (1985). Androgen enhances sexual motivation in females: A prospective, crossover study of sex steroid administration in the surgical menopause. *Psychosomatic Medicine, 47,* 339–351.

Smith-Rosenberg, C. (1975). The female world of love and ritual: Relations between women in nineteenth century America. *Signs, 1,* 1–29.

Stanislaw, H., & Rice, F. J. (1988). Correlation between sexual desire and menstrual cycle characteristics. *Archives of Sexual Behavior, 17,* 499–508.

Stoleru, S., & Mouras, H. (2007). Brain functional imaging studies of sexual desire and arousal in human males. In E. Janssen (Ed.), *The psychophysiology of sex* (pp. 3–34). Bloomington: Indiana University Press.

Taylor, S. E., Klein, L. C., Lewis, B. P., Gruenewald, T. L., Gurung, R. A. R., & Updegraff, J. A. (2000). Biobehavioral responses to stress in females: Tend-and-befriend, not fight-or-flight. *Psychological Review, 107,* 411–429.

Tennov, D. (1979). *Love and limerence: The experience of being in love.* New York: Stein and Day.

Trumbull, H. C. (1894). *Friendship the master passion.* Philadelphia: Wattles.

Udry, J. R. (1988). Biological predispositions and social control in adolescent sexual behavior. *American Sociological Review, 53,* 709–722.

Udry, J. R., & Billy, J. O. G. (1987). Initiation of coitus in early adolescence. *American Sociological Review, 52,* 841–855.

Udry, J. R., Talbert, L. M., & Morris, N. M. (1986). Biosocial foundations for adolescent female sexuality. *Demography, 23,* 217–230.

Uvnäs-Moberg, K. (1994). Oxytocin and behaviour. *Annals of Medicine, 26,* 315–317.

Uvnäs-Moberg, K. (2004). *The oxytocin factor: Tapping the hormone of calm, love, and healing* (R. W. Francis, Trans.). Cambridge, MA: Da Capo Press.

Walsh, C. (Ed.). (2010). *Dear John, I love Jane: Women write about leaving men for women*. Berkeley, CA: Seal Press.

Walter, M., Bermpohl, F., Mouras, H., Schiltz, K., Tempelmann, C., Rotte, M., et al. (2008). Distinguishing specific sexual and general emotional effects in fMRI-subcortical and cortical arousal during erotic picture viewing. *Neuro-Image, 40*, 1482–1494.

Weinberg, M. S., Williams, C. J., & Pryor, D. W. (1994). *Dual attraction: Understanding bisexuality*. New York: Oxford University Press.

Whisman, V. (1996). *Queer by choice: Lesbians, gay men, and the politics of identity*. New York: Routledge.

Williams, J. R., Insel, T. R., Harbaugh, C. R., & Carter, C. S. (1994). Oxytocin administered centrally facilitates formation of a partner preference in female prairie voles (*Microtus ochrogaster*). *Journal of Neuroendocrinology, 6*, 247–250.

Williams, W. L. (1992). The relationship between male-male friendship and male-female marriage. In P. Nardi (Ed.), *Men's friendships* (pp. 187–200). Newbury Park, CA: Sage.

Xu, X., Aron, A., Brown, L., Cao, G., Feng, T., & Weng, X. (2010). Reward and motivation systems: A brain mapping study of early-stage intense romantic love in Chinese participants. *Human Brain Mapping, 32*, 249–257.

Chapter **9**

Patterns of Relating
and of Thinking about Relationships

Conceptualizing and Measuring Individual
Differences in the Adult Attachment System

PHILLIP R. SHAVER
MARIO MIKULINCER

When actress Jennifer Aniston was married to actor Brad Pitt, they often had arguments in which she cried and he remained stoic. After the marriage ended, Aniston talked openly about their relationship: "I cried all the time. Brad called me 'the leaker.'" Years before that, when singers Bob Dylan and Joan Baez were a couple, they argued all the time. After the relationship ended, Baez said that, unlike other couples who fight, she and Dylan could not repair their bond when an argument was over. Later, in her song "Diamonds and Rust," she was nostalgic about their relationship, revealing her continuing love for him. The "diamonds" were the beautiful memories and the rust was the corrosion caused by their inability to get along.

Other couples manage to live together and love each other for a life-time. Nobel prize-winning neuroscientist Eric Kandel has been married to his wife, Denise, for decades, and in his 2006 autobiography, *In Search of Memory*, Kandel describes his lasting love for her. In his 2012 book about art and the brain, *The Age of Insight,* Kandel uses a photograph of his wife to support his claim that "there are few more pleasurable sights than a beautiful human face" (p. 378). These individual differences, and differences between couples, have been the focus of adult attachment researchers since 1987 (Hazan & Shaver, 1987; Mikulincer & Shaver, 2007a). The purpose of the present chapter is to explain how these differences arise and how they can be measured.

We begin with a theoretical overview of the attachment system and the ways in which its functioning is shaped by interactions with attachment figures, which influence the formation of what the theory calls "working models" of the self and others, a key component of relatively stable attachment styles, or orientations. We then discuss the measurement of attachment orientations in adulthood and review empirical evidence indicating that these measures are associated in theoretically expected ways with differences in other aspects of the attachment system, such as regulatory or coping strategies and mental representations of the self and others. We aim throughout the chapter to show how individual differences in attachment system functioning in adulthood can be conceptualized and measured.

INDIVIDUAL DIFFERENCES IN ATTACHMENT SYSTEM FUNCTIONING

A basic tenant of attachment theory (Bowlby, 1973, 1980, 1969/1982, 1988) is that human infants are born with an innate psychobiological system (the *attachment behavioral system*) that motivates them to seek proximity to supportive others (*attachment figures*). This is a means of protecting them from physical and psychological threats and a way of acquiring self-regulatory and social skills that eventually result in healthy autonomy and social connectedness.

Besides proposing this behavioral system and showing how it governs the behavior of humans and other animals in close relationships, Bowlby (1973) outlined individual differences in attachment system functioning that develop in response to primary attachment figures' reactions to a child's bids for closeness (or, in his terms, "proximity") and emotional support. According to attachment theory (e.g., Bowlby, 1973, 1969/1982), each person's attachment system operates, as a function of learning, in ways affected by his or her history of interactions with attachment figures, especially during periods of threat, challenge, or need. Although this system is thought to be automatically activated by perceived threats and dangers, its capacity to ensure protection, safety, and comfort in a particular situation depends on the availability and responsiveness of an attachment figure when one is desired and needed. Therefore, several cognitive and behavioral mechanisms have evolved biologically to make the attainment of security in various contexts more likely, including monitoring and appraising the responsiveness of attachment figures, evaluating the effectiveness of one's attachment bids, and adjusting one's attachment bids to the behavior of particular attachment figures (Mikulincer & Shaver, 2007a).

Over time, after gaining experience in a particular social environment—usually one's family of origin—a child adjusts his or her attachment behavior based on expectations regarding possible access routes and barriers to the attainment of safety and security. These expectations, operating sometimes at a conscious and intentional level but often unconsciously as well, become part of the attachment system's programming and are the basis of individual differences in the way people think about relationships and interact with relationship partners across the lifespan. In the following section of the chapter, we explain briefly how interactions with attachment figures result in individual differences in attachment-related regulatory strategies, mental representations of the self and others, and patterns of relating to others.

Attachment Figure Availability, Sense of Security, and Secondary Attachment Strategies

According to Bowlby (1973), variations in attachment figures' responses to one's bids for protection and comfort can alter the "programming" of one's attachment system. When an attachment figure is available and supportive, an inner sense of security develops, based on beliefs that the world is a generally safe and interesting place, worth exploring energetically; that other people are generally well intentioned and helpful when called upon; and that one is valued by others and can feel genuinely proud of oneself. These beliefs and the accompanying sense of security provide a solid foundation for engaging confidently and curiously with the physical and social worlds. Attachment researchers have conceptualized the mental models that underlie security in terms of an if–then, secure-base relational script (e.g., Mikulincer, Shaver, Sapir-Lavid, & Avihou-Kanza, 2009; Waters & Waters, 2006), which can be sketched as follows: "If I encounter an obstacle and/or become distressed, I can approach a significant other for help; he or she is likely to be available and supportive; I will experience relief and comfort as a result of proximity to this person; I can then turn or return to other valuable activities."

However, when an attachment figure is not physically or emotionally available in times of need, not responsive to one's bids for proximity and comfort, or poor at alleviating distress and providing a secure base, the attachment system's natural goal-seeking strategy is disrupted and the system's possessor does not experience comfort, relief, or felt security. Moreover, the distress that initially activates the attachment system is often compounded by doubts about one's safety, others' motives and intentions, and one's own worthiness of love: "Can I trust others in times of need? Do I have any value in others' eyes?" These worries about the self and others can preoccupy a person's mind with worries about fundamental safety and value, which interfere profoundly with relaxed and productive engagement in other activities.

Painful, frustrating interactions with inadequately available or unresponsive attachment figures indicate that one needs to adopt strategies of interaction different from normal proximity seeking. Cassidy and Kobak (1988) and Main (1990) called these alternative strategies *secondary* attachment strategies and emphasized two in particular: *hyperactivation* and *deactivation* of the attachment system.

Hyperactivating strategies are "fight," or pursuit, reactions to frustrated attachment needs (which Bowlby called "protest," a term that aptly captures a combination of anxiety and anger; Ainsworth, Blehar, Waters, & Wall, 1978). These strategies typically develop in response to attachment figures who are sometimes responsive but only unreliably so, placing the anxious individual on a partial reinforcement schedule that seems to him or her to reward vigilant, energetic, strident, and noisy bids for proximity, because they sometimes succeed (Ainsworth et al., 1978). In such cases, people do not easily give up on proximity seeking and, in fact, intensify it as a way of attempting to induce or coerce an attachment figure's love and support. The main goal of these strategies is to cause an attachment figure, viewed as unreliable or insufficiently available and responsive, to pay attention and provide protection and comfort (Cassidy & Kobak, 1988). Unfortunately, the associated distrust, vigilance, and agitation cause the attachment system to function in a continuously activated state. This involves exaggerating appraisals of danger and indications of attachment figure unavailability, which encourages disproportionate demands for attention, affection, and assistance (Mikulincer & Shaver, 2007a). These demands, which seem natural and necessary to an anxious individual, unfortunately can become causes of relational conflict, rejection, and intense emotional distress.

Deactivating strategies, in contrast, can be viewed as "flight" (rather than "fight" or protest) reactions or as reasons for withdrawing from an attachment figure perceived to be cool, distant, or unavailable. The cool, distancing reactions are perceived by the attached individual to be disapproval of his or her vulnerabilities, needs, and bids for support (Ainsworth et al., 1978). From such interactions, an individual learns to expect better outcomes if his or her signs of need and vulnerability are hidden or suppressed, proximity bids are toned down or inhibited, and the attachment system is deactivated despite its goals (safety and security) having not been achieved. This stance leads to a decision, probably not fully conscious, to try to handle threats and difficulties alone, a strategy Bowlby (1982) called "compulsive self-reliance." The primary goal of deactivating strategies is to keep the attachment system down-regulated in order to avoid the frustration and psychological pain caused by attachment figure unavailability or unresponsiveness (Cassidy & Kobak, 1988). This deactivation requires the dismissal of attachment needs, giving up closeness and interdependence in relationships, and distancing oneself from threatening or challenging activities or contexts that might cause unwanted activation of the attachment system (Mikulincer & Shaver, 2007a).

Attachment Working Models

Beyond characterizing how variations in an attachment figure's responses to one's bids for proximity and protection alter attachment strategies in a particular relationship or over a particular stretch of time (e.g., during an attachment figure's illness or preoccupation with work or family pressures), Bowlby (1973) described how such a relationship, if it persists, can produce more enduring and pervasive changes in mental structures and patterns of relating. At the core of these mental structures are what Bowlby (1973) called internal working models of the self, others, and relationships, which summarize and to some extent integrate knowledge accumulated in one's associative memory network through a long series of interactions with one or more attachment figures. This stored knowledge allows a person to predict future interactions with relationship partners and adjust proximity-seeking efforts without having to rethink each one. Of importance to later laboratory research (Mikulincer & Shaver, 2007b) and to clinical interventions (Bowlby, 1988; Obegi & Berant, 2008), Bowlby (1973) emphasized that although repeated attachment-related interactions result in increasingly stable working models, the models are not set in stone and can be revised in line with new social experiences.

Researchers (e.g., Bartholomew & Horowitz, 1991) have focused mainly on two kinds of working models: representations of attachment figures' responses to one's bids for love and support (*working models of others*) and representations of one's own lovability and competence (*working models of self*). Bowlby (1969/1982, p. 112) argued that "if an individual is to draw up a plan to achieve a set-goal not only does he have to have some sort of working model of his environment, but he must have also some working knowledge of his own behavioral skills and potentialities" (1982, p. 112). Thus, the attachment system, once it has been activated repeatedly during interactions with one or more attachment figures, includes representations of the availability, responsiveness, and sensitivity of such figures as well as representations of one's own ability to garner attachment figures' support and, by implication, one's own likelihood of being loved and cared for.

Because working models, at least initially, are based on memories and impressions of particular interactions with particular attachment figures (Main, 1990), a person can hold multiple working models that differ in expected interaction outcomes (e.g., success or failure in attempting to attain security). These different models foster different means of coping with the distress caused by attachment figure unavailability (hyperactivating or deactivating, also called anxious or avoidant, strategies). In this way, a child can develop working models for situations in which the attachment system has to be hyperactivated as well as situations in which the system must be defensively deactivated. Each such model consists of episodic memories of an interaction sequence; declarative knowledge about the partner's responses and the efficacy of ones' own actions; and procedural knowledge about the ways in which one responds to such situations and deals with various kinds and sources of distress.

Like other cognitive representations, working models form excitatory and inhibitory associations with each other, so that the activation of one model primes congruent models while inhibiting incongruent models (Baldwin, 1992). For example, experiencing or thinking about a gratifying interaction with an attachment figure activates memories of congruent episodes of attachment security with this partner and renders memories of attachment figure unavailability less accessible. With the passage of time and the recurrent retrieval of related memories, these associative links are strengthened, thereby favoring the formation of more abstract and generalized representations of gratifying and frustrating interactions with a specific person (Collins & Read, 1994; Shaver, Collins, & Clark, 1996). Moreover, models of interactions with a particular attachment figure (i.e., relationship-specific models) are created, and through excitatory and inhibitory links with models representing interactions with other attachment figures, more generic working models form as ways of summarizing experiences in different kinds of relationships.

The eventual product of this cognitive generalization and integration process is a hierarchical associative memory network that includes episodic memories, relationship-specific models, and generic models of secure and insecure interactions (Collins & Read, 1994; Overall, Fletcher, & Friesen, 2003; Shaver et al., 1996). As a result, with respect to a particular relationship and across different relationships, a person possesses secure and insecure working models and can, therefore, think about interpersonal relations sometimes in gratifying terms and at other times in more negative, threatening terms. However, because of differences in attachment histories, the dominant, or most often activated, working models will differ across individuals.

In a person's associative memory network, working models differ in cognitive accessibility—that is, the ease with which they can be activated and used to guide relational expectations and behavior in a particular social situation (Collins & Read, 1994). As with other cognitive representations, the accessibility of each model is determined by the amount of experience on which it is based, the number of times it has been applied in the past, and the density of its connections with other working models (e.g., Baldwin, 1992; Shaver et al., 1996). At a relationship-specific level, the model representing the typical interaction with an attachment figure has the highest accessibility in subsequent interactions with that person. At a generic level, the model that represents interactions with major attachment figures (e.g., parents and romantic partners) becomes the most chronically accessible working model and has the strongest effect on a person's relational beliefs and behavior across relationships and over time.

Consolidation of a stably accessible working model is the most important psychological process accounting for the enduring, long-term effects on personality functioning of attachment-relevant interactions during infancy, childhood, and adolescence (Bowlby, 1973; Fraley, 2002; Waters, Merrick, Treboux, Crowell, & Albersheim, 2000). Given a fairly consistent pattern of interactions with primary caregivers during childhood, the most representative or prototypical working models of these interactions become part of a person's implicit procedural knowledge, tend to operate automatically and unconsciously, and are resistant to change. Thus, what began as representations of specific interactions with one or more primary caregivers during childhood become core personality characteristics, are applied in new situations and relationships, and shape the functioning of the attachment system in adulthood.

However, it is important to note that features of a current situation can also contribute to the activation of a particular working model. For example, clear-cut contextual cues concerning a particular partner's love, availability, and supportiveness can activate models of security even among people who have a stable history of insecure interactions. Thus, generally accessible, core, or abstract models coexist in everyone's mind with weaker and less personally characteristic working models, and either kind of model can be activated by contextual factors or a person's current state of mind (Mikulincer & Shaver, 2007a). In support of this view, many laboratory experiments indicate that a person's relational cognitions and behaviors can change depending on current context and recent experiences, including subliminal primes (e.g., attachment-related words or pictures; Mikulincer & Shaver, 2007b), making it possible to study the effects of experimentally activated models of security and insecurity.

Attachment Styles

According to attachment theory (Bowlby, 1988; Mikulincer & Shaver, 2007a), a particular history of attachment experiences and the resulting consolidation of chronically accessible working models lead to the formation of relatively stable individual differences in the ways people relate to others. Most of the research examining these individual differences in adolescence and adulthood has focused on a construct called *attachment style*—a person's characteristic pattern of expectations, needs, emotions, and behavior in social interactions and close relationships (Hazan & Shaver, 1987). Depending on how it is measured, attachment style characterizes a person's most chronically accessible working models and his or her typical relational cognitions and behavior in a particular relationship (the person's relationship-specific style) or across relationships (the global attachment style).

The concept of attachment style, although not given that name, was first proposed by Ainsworth (1967; Ainsworth et al., 1978) to describe infants' patterns of responses to separations from and reunions with their mother in a laboratory Strange Situation assessment procedure. On the basis of this procedure, infants were placed into one of three categories: secure, anxious, or avoidant. Main and Solomon (1990) later added a fourth category, "disorganized/disoriented," which included odd, awkward behavior and unusual fluctuations between anxiety and avoidance.

Infants classified as secure seem to possess chronically accessible working models of security-enhancing interactions, and their pattern of responses to separation and reunion reflects their stable sense of attachment security. (That this sense is fairly stable was convincingly demonstrated early on by Waters, 1978.) Specifically, they react to separation from their mother with overt expressions of distress but then recover quickly and continue to explore the environment with interest. When reunited with their mother, they initiate contact with her, greet her with joy and affection, and respond positively to being picked up and held by her (Ainsworth et al., 1978). Avoidant infants seem to harbor readily accessible working models of unsuccessful proximity bids organized around attachment system deactivation. During separation and reunion episodes, they show little distress when separated from their mother and seem actively to avoid her upon reunion (Ainsworth et al., 1978). Anxious infants also seem to have accessible working models of frustrated proximity bids, but these models are organized around unreliable caregiver attention and attachment system hyperactivation. They readily express dismay and despair during separation episodes and conflictual, angry responses toward their mother upon reunion (Ainsworth et al., 1978).

Disorganized/disoriented infants seem to suffer from a breakdown of the choice among the three major organized attachment strategies: primary, hyperactivating, and deactivating. They either oscillate between strategies or exhibit bizarre behavior, such as lying face down on the floor without moving when their mother appears following a separation or sitting passively under a table, evincing no clear proximity-seeking strategy at all (Main & Solomon, 1990). These odd behaviors seem to be due to disorganized, unpredictable, and discomfiting behavior on the part of attachment figures, who, research shows, are likely to be suffering from unresolved losses or unresolved attachment-related traumas (Hesse, 2008; Lyons-Ruth & Jacobvitz, 2008). When their child approaches them for comfort and reassurance, these figures sometimes look frightened, look away, or "space out" in a dissociative way, causing the child who depends on them to stop abruptly, become confused, or adopt whatever momentary strategy seems to reduce discomfort.

In the 1980s, the study of attachment styles was extended into adolescence and adulthood, and new measures were created to tap adult attachment patterns. Based on a developmental and clinical approach following directly from Ainsworth and Main and her colleagues (e.g., George, Kaplan, & Main, 1985; Main, Kaplan, & Cassidy, 1985; see Hesse, 2008, for a review) devised the Adult Attachment Interview (AAI) to study adolescents' and adults' mental representations of attachment to parents during childhood. In the AAI, a person is interviewed about his or her childhood relationships with parents and other caregivers, episodic memories of specific interactions with parents, experiences of attachment figure loss, and the meanings he or she attributes to such experiences (Crowell, Fraley, & Shaver, 2008). Each AAI is electronically recorded and transcribed, and the transcripts are coded by expert judges using a complex scoring system that is meant to capture both the content of the interviewee's comments (e.g., mother was loving, neglectful, or abusive) and unintended qualities of the person's discourse (e.g., incoherence, inconsistency, and emotional disorganization). In Roisman's (2009) view, this scoring system is used to assess "whether adults have come to construct coherent (i.e., internally consistent but not emotionally overwrought) narratives regarding childhood experiences with caregivers" (p. 122).

Judges code narratives with two sets of scales—parental behavior scales and state of mind scales—and use these scales to sort individuals into three categories paralleling Ainsworth's infant typology: "secure" (or free and autonomous with respect to attachment), "dismissing" (of attachment), or "preoccupied" (with attachment). A person is classified as secure if he or she describes parents as available and responsive; if memories of relationships with parents are presented in a clear, convincing, and coherent manner; and if the person has developed a psychologically mature account of childhood attachment experiences. Dismissing individuals play down the importance of attachment relationships and tend to recall few concrete episodes of emotional interactions with parents. Preoccupied individuals seem entangled in worries and angry feelings about parents, and although they can easily retrieve negative memories, they have trouble discussing them coherently without becoming overwhelmed and disorganized.

Interviewees can also be classified as "unresolved" (with respect to losses, traumas, or abuse) in addition to being assigned to one of the other three categories (Hesse, 2008). Unresolved adults report attachment-related traumas of loss and/or abuse and manifest disorganization of thought processes in narratives regarding experiences of loss or abuse (Lyons-Ruth & Jacobvitz, 2008; Main, Goldwyn, & Hesse, 2002). For example, there may be lapses in the monitoring of discourse (e.g., becoming silent in the middle of a sentence, failing to finish a sentence) or lapses in the monitoring of reasoning (e.g., speaking of a deceased person as though he or she is still currently involved in the speaker's daily life). There is also a "cannot classify" category for interviews that shows no consistent pattern warranting placement in one of the other categories.

In a meta-analysis of 10,500 AAI classifications (from 200 different studies), Bakermans-Kranenburg and van IJzendoorn (2009) provided important support for the interview's validity. Whereas most of the participants in community, nonclinical samples were classified as autonomous (secure), most of the participants in clinical and at-risk samples were classified as insecure or unresolved. Moreover, specific insecurities were associated with particular personality disorders: Personality disorders with an internalizing quality (e.g., borderline personality disorder) were associated with more preoccupied and unresolved attachments, and disorders with an externalizing quality (e.g., antisocial personality disorders) were associated with more dismissing and preoccupied attachments. Bakermans-Kranenburg and van IJzendoorn also found a high stability of attachment classifications across time, no consistent gender differences in AAI classifications, and no association between AAI classifications and language or country of origin.

Despite the great value of the AAI as a method of studying adults' orientations to attachment relationships, especially those between children and parents, the interview is difficult to administer and score, and it focuses almost exclusively on an adult's view of early relationships with parents. It was validated initially, and many times subsequently, with respect to its ability to predict the Strange Situation classification of an interviewee's child, and thus has been viewed at times as a measure of caregiving orientation rather than attachment orientation (e.g., Allen & Miga, 2010; Shaver, Belsky, & Brennan, 2000). The interview does not explicitly assess a person's appraisals of current experiences in close relationships with other adults, including romantic or marital partners (although see Crowell & Waters, 2005, for a version of the AAI focused on couple relationships; also Crowell et al., 2008).

Taking a different path into the domain of adult attachment, Hazan and Shaver (1987) applied Bowlby's ideas to the study of romantic relationships using a simple self-report measure of adult attachment style. This measure consisted of three brief descriptions of feelings and behaviors in romantic relationships that were intended to characterize adult analogues of the three infant attachment styles identified by Ainsworth et al. (1978). Participants were asked to read the three descriptions and place themselves into one of the three attachment categories according to their predominant feelings and behavior in romantic relationships. The three descriptions were as follows:

1. *Secure*: "I find it relatively easy to get close to others and am comfortable depending on them and having them depend on me. I don't worry about being abandoned or about someone getting too close to me."
2. *Avoidant*: "I am somewhat uncomfortable being close to others; I find it difficult to trust them completely, difficult to allow myself to depend on them. I am nervous when anyone gets too close and often, others want me to be more intimate than I feel comfortable being."
3. *Anxious*: "I find that others are reluctant to get as close as I would like. I often worry that my partner doesn't really love me or won't

want to stay with me. I want to get very close to my partner and this sometimes scares people away."

Hazan and Shaver's (1987, 1990) initial studies were followed by hundreds of others that used the simple forced-choice self-report measure to examine the interpersonal and intrapersonal correlates of adult attachment style (see Mikulincer & Shaver, 2007a, for a review).

Over time, attachment researchers made methodological and conceptual improvements to the original self-report measure. For example, they asked participants to rate the extent to which each of the three prototypes described their experiences in close relationships rather asking them to classify themselves into one category (e.g., Levy & Davis, 1988). They also split the avoidant category into "dismissing" and "fearful" subtypes, thus moving from a three- to a four-category classification scheme, in line with proposals by Bartholomew and Horowitz (1991). In addition, they decomposed the descriptions into separate items that formed multi-item scales and reworded the instructions and items to examine global attachment style in all close relationships, not only in romantic or marital relationships. As a result, several multi-item adult attachment scales were created over the years, including the Adult Attachment Questionnaire (Simpson, 1990), Adult Attachment Scale (Collins & Read, 1990), Relationship Styles Questionnaire (Griffin & Bartholomew, 1994), and Experiences in Close Relationships (ECR) inventory (Brennan, Clark, & Shaver, 1998). (See the measurement appendix in Mikulincer & Shaver, 2007a, for items and scoring instructions for these scales.) All of these measures are highly reliable in both the internal-consistency and test–retest senses and have high construct, predictive, and discriminant validity (see extensive reviews by Crowell et al., 2008, Mikulincer & Shaver, 2007a; Ravitz, Maunder, Hunter, Sthankiya, & Lancee, 2010).

In 1998, Brennan et al. factor-analyzed the nonredundant items from all of the self-report attachment measures in use by the late 1990s in a large sample of over 900 university students. This factor analysis resulted in two higher order factors (anxiety and avoidance), which paralleled the model-of-self and model-of-others dimensions underlying Bartholomew and Horowitz's (1991) four-category typology. The items on the attachment anxiety factor are reminiscent of Ainsworth et al.'s (1978) coding scales describing anxiously attached infants; they emphasize both fear of abandonment and anger about separations. For example: "I worry about being rejected or abandoned," "I need a lot of reassurance that close relationship partners really care about me," "I get frustrated if relationship partners are not available when I need them." The items on the avoidant attachment scale are, similarly, reminiscent of Ainsworth et al.'s (1978) coding scales describing avoidantly attached infants: distance, independence, and suppression of emotions; for example, "I find it difficult to allow myself to depend on close relationship partners," "I prefer not to show others how I feel deep down." On the basis of their factor analysis, Brennan et al. (1998) proposed two 18-item scales: one to assess attachment anxiety and the other to assess avoidant attachment. People who score low on both dimensions are considered secure with respect to adult attachment and can be said to have a secure attachment style. They enjoy a chronic sense of attachment security, expect and trust in relationship partners' availability and responsiveness, are comfortable with closeness and interdependence, and use constructive ways of coping with threats and stressors. People who score high on both dimensions (labeled "fearfully avoidant" by Bartholomew & Horowitz, 1991) are especially low in trust and seem more likely than others to have been hurt or abused in important relationships (Shaver & Clark, 1994). (In this way they are similar to those classified as disorganized/disoriented in infancy or unresolved with respect to trauma in the AAI.)

The ECR has been used in hundreds of studies since 1998, always with high reliability (the alpha coefficients are always near or above .90, and test–retest coefficients range between .50 and .75, depending on the time span between administrations and the nature of the sample). The correlation between the two scales is often close to zero, but the scales seem to be more highly correlated when they are administered to members of long-term couples (see Mikulincer & Shaver, 2007a, for a review), suggesting that the two dimensions collapse to some extent toward a single secure–insecure dimension. The wording of the ECR items and the instructions can be altered slightly to apply to a particular relationship, to one's general orientation in romantic relationships, or to one's general or global attachment style in various kinds of relationships. This diversity of focus has resulted in several ECR-based scales tapping attachment orientations within a specific kind of relationship (e.g., Experiences in Close Relationships–Relationship Structures; Fraley, Heffernan, Vicary, & Brumbaugh, 2011) and momentary or state-like attachment orientations at a given time (e.g., State Adult Attachment Measure; Gillath, Hart, Noftle, & Stockdale, 2009).

The construct, convergent, discriminant, and predictive validity of the original ECR has been demonstrated in numerous studies, including ones that have included both experimental manipulations and behavioral observations (see Mikulincer & Shaver, 2007a, for a review). The ECR has been translated into many other languages, always producing more than adequate reliability coefficients and good evidence of construct validity.

Because we have used this measure in our own work, it is a benchmark for us when we evaluate other measures and other people's studies. We do not believe, however, that it is the best imaginable self-report attachment measure. For example, the ECR anxiety scale contains only one reverse-scored item, perhaps making it vulnerable to acquiescence response bias. In addition, both scales contain some items that refer to "partners" plural and others that refer to "partner" singular—an accidentalal result of taking items from different scales and accepting whichever ones loaded highly on the two major factors (Brennan et al., 1998).

GENERAL ISSUES CONCERNING MEASUREMENT OF ADULT ATTACHMENT ORIENTATIONS

Several questions and challenges have arisen with respect to the measurement of attachment orientations in adulthood. Here, we address them briefly to give readers and future researchers some perspective on them.

Convergence (or Lack of Convergence) between the AAI and Self-Report Scales

An important question in adult attachment research is whether the AAI and self-report scales converge on the same phenomenon (e.g., Crowell et al., 2008; Roisman, 2009). To date, 15 published studies have examined associations between the AAI and self-report measures of adult attachment (see Roisman, Holland, et al., 2007, for a review and meta-analysis of 10 of these studies). In general, the findings are not consistent. Whereas some studies have found that self-reports of attachment anxiety and avoidance are not significantly associated with AAI classifications (e.g., Simpson, Rholes, Orina, & Grich, 2002), others have found statistically significant but only moderate associations between self-report and interview measures of attachment patterns (e.g., Creasey & Ladd, 2005; Shaver, Belsky, & Brennan, 2000). Moreover, whereas some researchers have found that these associations were significant only for self-reported avoidance (e.g., Bouthillier, Julien, Dube, Belanger & Hamelin, 2002), others have found significant associations only for self-reported anxiety (Creasey & Ladd, 2005).

To deal with these inconsistencies, Roisman, Holland, et al. (2007) conducted a meta-analysis of 10 studies ($N = 1,221$). Although two small but reliable correlations were found between scores on attachment anxiety scales and the unresolved AAI classification and between scores on avoidant attachment scales and the dismissing AAI classification, the associations between self-report scores and AAI secure–insecure classifications were near zero (combined correlation of .09). Five subsequent studies also found that the associations between the two types of instruments were small (Bernier & Matte-Gagné, 2011; Fortuna & Roisman, 2008; Mayseless & Scharf, 2007; Riggs et al., 2007; Roisman, Holland, et al., 2007, Study 3), supporting the conclusion that the AAI and self-report measures tap distinct aspects of attachment orientations.

On the basis of these results, attachment researchers have begun to search for these different aspects and are finding that the AAI and self-report measures of adult attachment orientations exhibit different patterns of associations with personality traits and relationship quality, even though both are related to personality disorders in conceptually similar ways (see Bakermans-Kranenburg & van IJzendoorn, 2009, for studies based on the AAI, and Brennan & Shaver, 1998, and Crawford et al., 2006, for studies based on self-report attachment measures). With respect to differences, Roisman, Holland, et al. (2007, Study 2) found that an AAI secure–insecure distinction was associated with the trait of conscientiousness (one of the so-called Big Five personality traits), whereas self-report scores on anxiety and avoidance scales were associated with neuroticism and low scores on extraversion. Roisman, Holland, et al. (2007, Study 3) found that self-report measures of attachment orientations were strongly associated with participants' appraisals of the quality of their romantic relationships. In contrast, the AAI classifications showed small and trivial associations with measures of relational quality. Fortuna and Roisman (2008) also found that whereas AAI classifications were associated with self-reports of psychopathology only in a high-risk sample, self-reports of attachment anxiety and avoidance were associated with psychopathology even in low-risk groups (i.e., those with low levels of life stress).

In a recent study, Bernier and Matte-Gagné (2011) found that mothers' secure state of mind in the AAI, but not their ECR scores, was associated with maternal sensitivity during in-home mother–infant interactions when the infants were 12 months of age (a finding compatible with the idea that the AAI measures caregiving qualities, especially those that are observable in behavior between a mother and child or a mother and an AAI interviewer).

These findings imply that adult attachment orientations are not simple or unitary constructs (Roisman, 2009), and that the AAI and self-report measures tap different aspects or dimensions of attachment orientations. Whereas the AAI measures the extent to which a person holds "a psychologically mature account of earlier attachment experiences and their ongoing impact on personality" (Roisman, 2009, p. 122), self-report measures assess a person's attachment-related anxieties, worries, defenses, and behavior in current or relatively recent close relationships. Moreover, there are substantial methodological differences between the AAI and self-report measures in targeted relationships (parent–child vs. adult–adult relationships), method (intensively coded interview transcripts vs. brief self-reports), and analytic focus (structural properties of coherence, believability, and vagueness of a person's narrative of attachment experiences vs. content of a person's perceptions, feelings, and self-observed behavior in adolescent or adult relationships).

Future research should include both the AAI and self-report measures and systematically examine why they seem not to be closely related, especially given that both kinds of measures have generated many findings consistent with attachment theory. More analyses could be done at the level of specific coding scales in the AAI and specific items in the self-report measures. Shaver et al. (2000) found that, although the overall relation between AAI types and the dimensions of Collins and Read's (1990) Adult Attachment Scale were weak, self-report items tapping trust in attachment figures were related to key coding scales, including "coherence of mind," from the AAI.

Also, more could be done to conceptualize differences between interviews focused on discourse coherence and self-report items measuring how people feel in close relationships. Ainsworth et al. (1978) began the study of attachment in infancy by, necessarily, focusing on infant behavior rather than preverbal infants' self-reported feelings. They also coded relatively few infants as anxious, perhaps because the behavioral differences between avoidant and nonavoidant (secure) infants were easier to see. When Main and Solomon (1990) began to identify "disorganized/disoriented" infants and link them with maternal AAIs coded as "unresolved with respect to losses and traumas," they may have gotten closer to noticing some of the effects of attachment anxiety. They chose to make the "disorganized" pattern orthogonal to the existing two-dimensional space defined by anxiety and avoidance, but in the AAI there is often an association between being "preoccupied" in a particular way (labeled E3) and being "unresolved." The self-report measures do not have a third dimension, and it seems possible, as mentioned earlier, that people who score high on both anxiety and avoidance on self-report measures have backgrounds similar to those classified as "anxious" and "unresolved" in the AAI (Shaver & Clark, 1994).

Longitudinal studies could examine trajectories of attachment orientations from infancy to adulthood and discover whether a person's scores on the AAI and self-report measures have different roots in childhood experiences and are differentially associated with attachment orientations in childhood (for relevant studies based on self-report measures, see Dinero, Conger, Shaver, Widaman, & Larsen-Rife, 2008; Zayas, Mischel, Shoda, & Aber, 2011). Moreover, cognitive laboratory experiments of the kinds we have conducted (summarized recently in Shaver & Mikulincer, 2011) can indicate how the AAI and self-report attachment scales relate to theoretically predicted conscious and unconscious mental processes.

Categories versus Continuous Scores

Another general issue that has attracted a lot of attention among adult attachment researchers concerns whether adult attachment patterns are best measured in terms of types or dimensions (e.g., Fraley & Waller, 1998). In this case, the debate seems closer to resolution, and the consensus favors a dimensional approach. Two taxometric studies (Fraley & Waller, 1998; Roisman, Fraley, & Belsky, 2007) have shown that adult attachment patterns assessed with either self-report measures or the AAI are best characterized by dimensional measures. For example, Fraley and Waller (1998) revealed that the latent variation reflected in self-report measures of attachment is continuously rather than categorically distributed, and they explained the many problems that arise when categorical models are used to assess what are actually dimensional phenomena. Roisman, Fraley, et al. (2007) taxometrically analyzed the AAI coding scales and found no support that scores on these scales are categorically distributed. Moreover, a factor analysis of the coding scales yielded two main factors that converge with the two dimensions of self-report measures: the degree to which adults discuss their early experiences defensively (attachment-related avoidance) and the degree to which their discourse reflects anxious preoccupation with attachment (attachment-related anxiety).

Optimal Configuration of the Dimensions

A third issue concerns the optimal configuration of the two main dimensions underlying individual differences in attachment. The most frequent practice is to compute two total scores based on multi-item scales reflecting attachment anxiety and avoidance, a practice initiated by Brennan et al. (1998) because it fits well with Bartholomew and Horowitz's (1991) typology based on the model-of-self and model-of-others dimensions. However, other authors have suggested that it would be better to rotate the axes of the measurement space and compute total scores reflecting individual differences in security (a dimension running from insecurity to security) and type of insecurity (a dimension running from anxiety to avoidance) (e.g., Asendorpf, Banse, Wilpers, & Neyer, 1997; Banse, 2004). Rotating the dimensions in this way fits with Fyffe and Waters's (1997) two-dimensional scoring system for the AAI, and Mikulincer and Shaver's model (2007a) of attachment system functioning. In this model, appraisals of attachment figure availability and the feasibility of hyperactivating and deactivating strategies occur in sequence. That is, people first appraise whether there are security providers available, and only when failing to find such providers do they employ a particular secondary strategy.

The problem of orienting the two dimensions conceptually suggests the potential value of creating a measure that validly assesses security, anxiety, and avoidance (e.g., Gillath et al., 2009). Moreover, it calls for multiple kinds of scales. When the focus of research is on variations in perceived attachment figure availability and the associated sense of felt security, it might be useful to have or create a unidimensional measure of felt security. However, when the key issues are the antecedents, correlates, and effects of different kinds of insecurity, researchers could use the ECR or one of the similar measures reviewed earlier that assess attachment anxiety and avoidance. These different kinds of measures would undoubtedly be correlated with each other, but they might be sufficiently different, and sufficiently distinct in their other correlates, to be useful in mapping the full array of attachment orientations. (An early attempt by Klohnen & John, 1998, has been largely ignored by subsequent researchers, perhaps because it was based on adjectives rather than theoretically specific statements, but it is still worth consulting for ideas. It showed how a circumplex model might be created that has all major axes in the two-dimensional space represented psychometrically.)

General and Relationship-Specific Attachment Orientations

Another issue concerns the relationship category targeted by attachment measures. As reviewed earlier, the ECR can be altered slightly to ask about relationships with parents, relationships with romantic partners, a particular relationship with one romantic partner, or all close relationships. Following Collins and Read (1994) and Overall et al. (2003), we view working models as being arranged in a hierarchical network, with episodic memories of interactions with particular relationship partners being nested within representations of kinds of attachment relationships (e.g., child–parent, romantic, close friendship), and those representations being nested within generic representations of attachment relationships. Considered from this perspective, ratings of attachment orientations for a specific relationship, or relationship domain, may reflect more global attachment orientations (Brumbaugh & Fraley, 2006, 2007). However, the lower level representations may also be a product of experiences and beliefs unique to a particular relationship or relationship type, so they may differ somewhat in details, antecedents, and relational consequence (Fraley et al., 2011). Researchers are becoming increasingly aware of the dual nature of relationship-specific attachment orientations (being both a "top-down" result of global attachment orientations and a "bottom-up" product of specific relational experiences). This makes it useful to include both generic and relationship-specific measures of attachment orientations in research studies (e.g., Fraley et al., 2011; Klohnen, Weller, Luo, & Choe, 2005; La Guardia, Ryan, Couchman, & Deci, 2000). La Guardia et al. (2000), for example, found that only 25–35% of the variance in attachment orientations within a particular relationship reflected a person's core orientation across different relationships.

Overall et al. (2003) provided important evidence concerning the cognitive organization of attachment representations. They asked people to complete self-report measures of attachment style for three specific relationships within each of three domains: family, friendships, and romantic relationships. They then examined whether these measures were organized within (1) a single, global working model summarizing attachment orientations across relationships and domains; (2) three independent working models for the domains of family, friendship, and romantic relationships; or (3) a hierarchical arrangement of specific and global working models. Confirmatory factor analyses revealed that the hierarchical model fit the data best, indicating that ratings of attachment orientations for specific relationships are nested within, or organized under, relationship-domain representations, which in turn are nested within, or organized under, a single, global attachment working model.

Subsequent studies provided more information about this hierarchical network by examining the pattern of associations among measures of domain-specific and relationship-specific attachment orientations (Sibley & Overall, 2007, 2008). They examined the extent to which a domain-specific attachment orientation (e.g., in the romantic domain) was more strongly associated with attachment orientations in specific relationships within this domain than with orientations in other relationship domains (e.g., friends). The results indicated that the domain-specific romantic attachment orientation (i.e., how a person usually feels in romantic relationships) was more predictive of attachment orientations toward particular romantic partners than it was of attachment orientations toward nonromantic partners, including family members, friends, and acquaintances. Similar findings were obtained in different samples, different relationship domains, and different specific relationships within each assessed domain.

The realization that attachment measures can be designed to tap different levels in a hierarchy of working models has important implications for measurement (and clinical interventions, which are not our focus here). For example, particular questions and instructions, in either an interview or a self-report questionnaire, can activate different nodes in the hierarchical network and thereby affect a participant's responses. If we ask participants to describe a particular ongoing romantic relationship, we may get different results than if we ask about an ongoing relationship with a same-sex friend. If we ask about adults' relationship with their mother now, we may get different results than if we ask about the earliest memories they have of relating to their mother during childhood. The fact that adult attachment studies have obtained systematic, theory-consistent findings using generic (global) self-report attachment measures indicates that the generic level of measurement is psychologically meaningful. However, this does not mean that generic measures are equivalent to measures of childhood relationships with particular parents or current relationships with particular relationship partners.

ATTACHMENT ORIENTATIONS, WORKING MODELS, AND REGULATORY STRATEGIES

In this section, we review evidence concerning the extent to which measures of adult attachment orientation, especially those assessed with self-report scales such as the ECR, reflect a person's mental representations of the self and others and the strategies he or she habitually uses to regulate distress. According to attachment theory (Bartholomew & Horowitz, 1991; Bowlby, 1969/1982), higher scores on measures of attachment anxiety or avoidance are reflections of chronically accessible negative working models (Mikulincer & Shaver, 2007a), so such scores should be associated with measures indicating more negative representations of the self and others. Moreover, attachment anxiety and avoidance scores should be associated with measures of a person's habitual self-regulatory strategies. Specifically, lower scores on attachment anxiety and avoidance should be associated with comfortable support seeking and higher scores on attachment anxiety should be associated with rumination, obsessive preoccupation with relationships, and emotional flooding, whereas higher scores on avoidant attachment should be associated with measures of defensive suppression of distressing thoughts as well as emotional and behavioral distancing from sources of stress and distress.

There is extensive evidence for the expected relations between self-reported attachment anxiety or avoidance and more negative appraisals of the self and others. More anxious and/or avoidant individuals are more likely to possess a negative view of human nature (e.g., Collins & Read, 1990; Hazan & Shaver, 1987), to describe relationship partners using more negative trait terms (e.g., Levy, Blatt, & Shaver, 1998), and to perceive partners as relatively unsupportive (e.g., Davis, Morris, & Kraus, 1998). In addition, anxious and avoidant people have more negative expectations concerning their partners' behavior (e.g., Baldwin, Fehr, Keedian, Seidel, & Thomson, 1993) and tend to offer more negative explanations of a partner's objectionable behavior (e.g., Collins, 1996). Furthermore, more anxious participants have lower self-esteem (e.g., Bartholomew & Horowitz, 1991; Mickelson, Kessler, & Shaver, 1997), view themselves as less competent and efficacious in various domains (e.g., Cooper, Shaver, & Collins, 1998), and describe themselves with relatively negative trait terms (Mikulincer, 1995). Although avoidant individuals do not tend to report negative self-views, Mikulincer, Dolev, and Shaver (2004) found that they do exhibit negative self-representations when their suppressive defenses are interfered with by heavy cognitive demands.

With regard to regulatory strategies, there is evidence that attachment anxiety and avoidance are associated with deficits in what Waters and Waters (2006) characterized as the relational if–then, secure-base script. For example, Mikulincer et al. (2009) found that people who score lower on the ECR anxiety or avoidance scale (i.e., the more secure participants) were more likely than those who scored higher to include elements of the secure-base script (support seeking, support provision, and distress relief) when writing about projective pictures of a troubled person. Moreover, the two kinds of insecurity—anxiety and avoidance—were associated with different gaps in the script. People who scored relatively high on the ECR anxiety scale tended to omit or deemphasize the final step in the script (relief and return to other activities), whereas those who scored relatively high on the ECR avoidance scale tended to omit the part about seeking and benefiting from others' support. That is, anxious study participants more often wrote about an injured protagonist who was seeking support and not achieving relief, whereas avoidant participants more often wrote about a person achieving relief without seeking or receiving support. (These results were not explained by alternative predictor variables, such as neuroticism, extraversion, or verbal ability.)

There is also considerable evidence for links between the attachment variables and support seeking. Several investigators have reported negative associations between self-reported attachment anxiety or avoidance and global tendencies to seek support in times of need (e.g., Larose, Bernier, Soucy, & Duchesne, 1999). Similar findings have emerged from studies examining self-reported reactions to a specific stressor (e.g., Berant, Mikulincer, & Florian, 2001) and actual support-seeking behavior in stressful naturalistic and laboratory settings (e.g., Fraley & Shaver, 1998; Simpson, Rholes, & Nelligan, 1992).

Attachment anxiety and avoidance scores are differentially associated with particular approaches to coping with stressful events (see Mikulincer & Florian, 1998; Mikulincer & Shaver, 2007a). Avoidance scores are associated with distancing strategies, and attachment anxiety scores are associated with the use of emotion-focused coping. For example, Feeney (1995) found that avoidance was related to behavioral blunting (seeking distractions when dealing with stress), and Mikulincer and Florian (1998) found that people who classified themselves as anxiously attached reported more frequent task-related, ruminative worries after failing cognitive tasks than were reported by self-classified secure and avoidant people.

Attachment anxiety and avoidance are also differentially associated with strategies for coping with specifically attachment-related threats. For example, Fraley and Shaver (1997) found that attachment anxiety was associated with an inability to suppress separation-related thoughts following a mental suppression task in which the issue of separation was to be excluded from conscious consideration; anxiety was also associated with greater skin conductance during the task. In contrast, more avoidant people were better able not only to stop thinking about separation but also to control the intensity of their autonomic responses to these thoughts. In a series of studies examining the experience and management of death anxiety (e.g., Mikulincer & Florian, 2000; Mikulincer, Florian, & Tolmacz, 1990), anxious individuals were found to intensify death concerns and keep death-related thoughts active in memory. In contrast, avoidant individuals tended to suppress death concerns and dissociate their conscious claims from their unconscious anxiety, which was measured projectively. Although avoidance was associated with weaker self-reported fears of death, it was also related to heightened death anxiety in responses to Thematic Apperception Test pictures. Avoidant people's dissociative tendencies have been also documented by Dozier and Kobak (1992), who found that avoidant people (during the AAI) expressed fewer negative feelings but displayed higher levels of physiological arousal (heightened electrodermal activity), a known consequence of emotional suppression (e.g., Dan-Glauser & Gross, 2011).

Recent studies have also shown that attachment-related avoidance is associated with automatic inhibition of attention to threatening stimuli during cognitive tasks. Using a dot-probe task, for example, people scoring higher on avoidance reacted with attentional inhibition to attachment-related threats (attachment-threat words and angry faces; Dewitte & De Houwer, 2008; Dewitte, Koster, De Houwer, & Buysse, 2007). Using an emotional Stroop color-naming task, Edelstein and Gillath (2008) found that ECR avoidance scores were associated with reduced Stroop interference for negative emotional words, which seems to result from avoidant people's ability to steer attention away from potentially threatening information. Dewitte (2011) used a negative affective priming task to measure dis-attention to emotional information and found that ECR avoidance scores were associated with decreased attention to angry and sad, but not to happy, faces.

CONCLUDING REMARKS

The studies reviewed briefly here are just a few examples of the hundreds of studies that support the construct validity of adult attachment classifications and dimensional scores. They indicate that the measures are associated, as theory leads us to expect, with working models of the self and others, with self-regulatory strategies, and, although not reviewed here, with behavior in close relationships and with important relationship outcomes (Mikulincer & Shaver, 2007a; Shaver & Mikulincer, 2011). Despite the enormous growth and increasing complexity of attachment research over the years since the publication of Ainsworth et al.'s (1978) seminal book, there are still many unresolved problems and unanswered questions concerning adult attachment orientations.

We have focused in this chapter on different approaches to measurement and to relations between self-report measures and measures of working models and self-regulatory strategies. Studies on these topics have become increasingly sophisticated, especially since it has become possible to contextually prime people below the level of awareness (Mikulincer & Shaver, 2007b), to measure a variety of responses (cognitive, affective, and behavioral) in the laboratory, and to image people's brains as they respond to consciously and unconsciously received stimuli. There is every indication that research in the adult attachment area will continue to produce rich, provocative findings that will, we hope, contribute to improvements in clinical interventions for individuals, couples, and families (Johnson, 2008; Obegi & Berant, 2008; Steele & Steele, 2008). Perhaps in the future, couples can suffer fewer of the arguments and tears that plagued the relationships of Jennifer Aniston, Brad Pitt, Joan Baez, and Bob Dylan and instead experience more of the decades of love and satisfaction enjoyed by Eric Kandel and his wife, Denise.

ACKNOWLEDGMENT

Preparation of this chapter was facilitated by a grant from the Fetzer Institute.

REFERENCES

Ainsworth, M. D. S. (1967). *Infancy in Uganda: Infant care and the growth of love*. Baltimore: Johns Hopkins University Press.

Ainsworth, M. D. S., Blehar, M. C., Waters, E., & Wall, S. (1978). *Patterns of attachment: Assessed in the Strange Situation and at home*. Hillsdale, NJ: Erlbaum.

Allen, J. P., & Miga, E. M. (2010). Attachment in adolescence: A move to the level of emotion regulation. *Journal of Social and Personal Relationships, 27,* 181–190.

Asendorpf, J. B., Banse, R., Wilpers, S., & Neyer, F. J. (1997). Relationship-specific attachment scales for adults and their validation with network and diary procedures. *Diagnostica, 43,* 289–313.

Bakermans-Kranenburg, M. J., & van IJzendoorn, M. H. (2009). The first 10,000 Adult Attachment Interviews: Distributions of adult attachment representations in clinical and non-clinical groups. *Attachment & Human Development, 11,* 223–263.

Baldwin, M. W. (1992). Relational schemas and the processing of social information. *Psychological Bulletin, 112,* 461–484.

Baldwin, M. W., Fehr, B., Keedian, E., Seidel, M., & Thomson, D. W. (1993). An exploration of the relational schemata underlying attachment styles: Self-report and lexical decision approaches. *Personality and Social Psychology Bulletin, 19,* 746–754.

Banse, R. (2004). Adult attachment and marital satisfaction: Evidence for dyadic configuration effects. *Journal of Social and Personal Relationships, 21,* 273–282.

Bartholomew, K., & Horowitz, L. M. (1991). Attachment styles among young adults: A test of a four-category model. *Journal of Personality and Social Psychology, 61,* 226–244.

Berant, E., Mikulincer, M., & Florian, V. (2001). The association of mothers' attachment style and their psychological reactions to the diagnosis of infant's congenital heart disease. *Journal of Social and Clinical Psychology, 20,* 208–232.

Bernier, A., & Matte-Gagné, C. (2011). More bridges: Investigating the relevance of self-report and interview measures of adult attachment for marital and caregiving relationships. *International Journal of Behavioral Development, 35,* 307–316.

Bouthillier, D., Julien, D., Dube, M., Belanger, I., & Hamelin, M. (2002). Predictive validity of adult attachment measures in relation to emotion regulation behaviors in marital interactions. *Journal of Adult Development, 9*, 291–305.

Bowlby, J. (1973). *Attachment and loss: Vol. 2. Separation: Anxiety and anger.* New York: Basic Books.

Bowlby, J. (1980). *Attachment and loss: Vol. 3. Sadness and depression.* New York: Basic Books.

Bowlby, J. (1969/1982). *Attachment and loss: Vol. 1. Attachment* (2nd ed.). New York: Basic Books. (Original work published 1969)

Bowlby, J. (1988). *A secure base: Clinical applications of attachment theory.* London: Routledge.

Brennan, K. A., Clark, C. L., & Shaver, P. R. (1998). Self-report measurement of adult attachment: An integrative overview. In J. A. Simpson & W. S. Rholes (Eds.), *Attachment theory and close relationships* (pp. 46–76). New York: Guilford Press.

Brennan, K. A., & Shaver, P. R. (1998). Attachment styles and personality disorders: Their connections to each other and to parental divorce, parental death, and perceptions of parental caregiving. *Journal of Personality, 66*, 835–878.

Brumbaugh, C. C., & Fraley, R. C. (2006). Transference and attachment: How do attachment patterns get carried forward from one relationship to the next? *Personality and Social Psychology Bulletin, 32*, 552–560.

Brumbaugh, C. C., & Fraley, R. C. (2007). Transference of attachment patterns: How important relationships influence feelings toward novel people. *Personal Relationships, 14*, 513–530.

Cassidy, J., & Kobak, R. R. (1988). Avoidance and its relationship with other defensive processes. In J. Belsky & T. Nezworski (Eds.), *Clinical implications of attachment* (pp. 300–323). Hillsdale, NJ: Erlbaum.

Collins, N. L. (1996). Working models of attachment: Implications for explanation, emotion, and behavior. *Journal of Personality and Social Psychology, 71*, 810–832.

Collins, N. L., & Read, S. J. (1990). Adult attachment, working models, and relationship quality in dating couples. *Journal of Personality and Social Psychology, 58*, 644–663.

Collins, N. L., & Read, S. J. (1994). Cognitive representations of attachment: The structure and function of working models. In K. Bartholomew & D. Perlman (Eds.), *Advances in personal relationships: Attachment processes in adulthood* (Vol. 5, pp. 53–92). London: Jessica Kingsley.

Cooper, M. L., Shaver, P. R., & Collins, N. L. (1998). Attachment styles, emotion regulation, and adjustment in adolescence. *Journal of Personality and Social Psychology, 74*, 1380–1397.

Crawford, T. N., Shaver, P. R., Cohen, P., Pilkonis, P. A., Gillath, O., & Kasen, S. (2006). Self-reported attachment, interpersonal aggression, and personality disorder in a prospective community sample of adolescents and adults. *Journal of Personality Disorders, 20*, 331–351.

Creasey, G., & Ladd, A. (2005). Generalized and specific attachment representations: Unique and interactive roles in predicting conflict behaviors in close relationships. *Personality and Social Psychology Bulletin, 31*, 1026–1038.

Crowell, J. A., Fraley, R. C., & Shaver, P. R. (2008). Measurement of individual differences in adolescent and adult attachment. In J. Cassidy & P. R. Shaver (Eds.), *Handbook of attachment: Theory, research, and clinical applications* (2nd ed., pp. 599–635). New York: Guilford Press.

Crowell, J. A., & Waters, E. (2005). Attachment representations, secure-base behavior, and the evolution of adult relationships: The Stony Brook Adult Relationship Project. In K. E. Grossmann, K. Grossmann, & E. Waters (Eds.), *Attachment from infancy to adulthood: The major longitudinal studies* (pp. 223–244). New York: Guilford Press.

Dan-Glauser, E. S., & Gross, J. J. (2011). The temporal dynamics of two response-focused forms of emotion regulation: Experiential, expressive, and autonomic consequences. *Psychophysiology, 48*, 1309–1322.

Davis, M. H., Morris, M. M., & Kraus, L. A. (1998). Relationship-specific and global perceptions of social support: Associations with well-being and attachment. *Journal of Personality and Social Psychology, 74*, 468–481.

Dewitte, M. (2011). Adult attachment and attentional inhibition of interpersonal stimuli. *Cognition and Emotion, 25*, 612–625.

Dewitte, M., & De Houwer, J. (2008). Adult attachment and attention to positive and negative emotional face expressions. *Journal of Research in Personality, 42*, 498–505.

Dewitte, M., Koster, E. H. W., De Houwer, J., & Buysse, A. (2007). Attentive processing of threat and adult attachment: A dot-probe study. *Behavior Research and Therapy, 45*, 1307–1317.

Dinero, R. E., Conger, R. D., Shaver, P. R., Widaman, K. F., & Larsen-Rife, D. (2008). Influence of family of origin and adult romantic partners on romantic attachment security. *Journal of Family Psychology, 22*, 622–632.

Dozier, M., & Kobak, R. (1992). Psychophysiology in attachment interviews: Converging evidence for deactivating strategies. *Child Development, 63*, 1473–1480.

Edelstein, R. S., & Gillath, O. (2008). Avoiding interference: Adult attachment and emotional processing biases. *Personality and Social Psychology Bulletin, 34*, 171–181.

Feeney, J. A. (1995). Adult attachment, coping style, and health locus of control as predictors of health behavior. *Australian Journal of Psychology, 47*, 171–177.

Fortuna, K., & Roisman, G. I. (2008). Insecurity, stress, and symptoms of psychopathology: Contrasting results from self-reports versus interviews of adult attachment. *Attachment & Human Development, 10*, 11–28.

Fraley, R. C. (2002). Attachment stability from infancy to adulthood: Meta-analysis and dynamic modeling of developmental mechanisms. *Personality and Social Psychology Review, 6*, 123–151.

Fraley, R. C., Heffernan, M. E., Vicary, A. M., & Brumbaugh, C. C. (2011). The Experiences in Close Relationships—Relationship Structures Questionnaire: A method for assessing attachment orientations across relationships. *Psychological Assessment, 23*, 615–625.

Fraley, R. C., & Shaver, P. R. (1997). Adult attachment and the suppression of unwanted thoughts. *Journal of Personality and Social Psychology, 73*, 1080–1091.

Fraley, R. C., & Shaver, P. R. (1998). Airport separations: A naturalistic study of adult attachment dynamics in separating couples. *Journal of Personality and Social Psychology, 75*, 1198–1212.

Fraley, R. C., & Waller, N. G. (1998). Adult attachment patterns: A test of the typological model. In J. A. Simpson & W. S. Rholes (Eds.), *Attachment theory and close relationships* (pp. 77–114). New York: Guilford Press.

Fyffe, C., & Waters, E. (1997, April). *Empirical classification of adult attachment status: Predicting group membership.* Poster presented at the biennial meeting of the Society for Research in Child Development, Washington, DC.

George, C., Kaplan, N., & Main, M. (1985). *The Adult Attachment Interview.* Unpublished protocol, Department of Psychology, University of California, Berkeley.

Gillath, O., Hart, J., Noftle, E. E., & Stockdale, G. D. (2009). Development and validation of a State Adult Attachment Measure (SAAM). *Journal of Research in Personality, 43*, 362–373.

Griffin, D. W., & Bartholomew, K. (1994). The metaphysics of measurement: The case of adult attachment. In K. Bartholomew & D. Perlman (Eds.), *Advances in personal relationships: Attachment processes in adulthood* (Vol. 5, pp. 17–52). London: Jessica Kingsley.

Hazan, C., & Shaver, P. R. (1987). Romantic love conceptualized as an attachment process. *Journal of Personality and Social Psychology, 52*, 511–524.

Hazan, C., & Shaver, P. R. (1990). Love and work: An attachment-theoretical perspective. *Journal of Personality and Social Psychology, 59*, 270–280.

Hesse, E. (2008). The Adult Attachment Interview: Protocol, method of analysis, and empirical studies. In J. Cassidy & P. R. Shaver (Eds.), *Handbook of attachment: Theory, research, and clinical applications* (2nd ed., pp. 552–598). New York: Guilford Press.

Johnson, S. (2008). *Hold me tight: Seven conversations for a lifetime of love.* New York: Little, Brown.

Kandel, E. R. (2006). *In search of memory: The emergence of a new science of mind.* New York: Norton.

Kandel, E. R. (2012). *The Age of Insight: The quest to understand the unconscious in art, mind, and brain.* New York: Random House.

Klohnen, E. C., & John, O. P. (1998). Working models of attachment: A theory-based prototype approach. In J. A. Simpson & W. S. Rholes (Eds.), *Attachment theory and close relationships* (pp. 115–140). New York: Guilford Press.

Klohnen, E. C., Weller, J. A., Luo, S., & Choe, M. (2005). Organization and predictive power of general and relationship-specific attachment models: One for all, and all for one? *Personality and Social Psychology Bulletin, 31*, 1665–1682.

La Guardia, J. G., Ryan, R. M., Couchman, C. E., & Deci, E. L. (2000). Within-person variation in security of attachment: A self-determination theory perspective on attachment, need fulfillment, and well-being. *Journal of Personality and Social Psychology, 79*, 367–384.

Larose, S., Bernier, A., Soucy, N., & Duchesne, S. (1999). Attachment style dimensions, network orientation, and the process of seeking help from college teachers. *Journal of Social and Personal Relationships, 16*, 225–247.

Levy, K. N., Blatt, S. J., & Shaver, P. R. (1998). Attachment styles and parental representations. *Journal of Personality and Social Psychology, 74*, 407–419.

Levy, M. B., & Davis, K. E. (1988). Love styles and attachment styles compared: Their relations to each other and to various relationship characteristics. *Journal of Social and Personal Relationships, 5*, 439–471.

Lyons-Ruth, K., & Jacobvitz, D. (2008). Attachment disorganization: Genetic factors, parenting contexts, and developmental transformation from infancy to adulthood. In J. Cassidy & P. R. Shaver (Eds.), *Handbook of attachment: Theory, research, and clinical applications* (2nd ed., pp. 666–697). New York: Guilford Press.

Main, M. (1990). Cross-cultural studies of attachment organization: Recent studies, changing methodologies, and the concept of conditional strategies. *Human Development, 33*, 48–61.

Main, M., Goldwyn, R., & Hesse, E. (2002). *Adult attachment scoring and classification system*. Unpublished manuscript, Department of Psychology, University of California, Berkeley.

Main, M., Kaplan, N., & Cassidy, J. (1985). Security in infancy, childhood, and adulthood: A move to the level of representation. *Monographs of the Society for Research in Child Development, 50*, 66–104.

Main, M., & Solomon, J. (1990). Procedures for identifying infants as disorganized/disoriented during the Ainsworth Strange Situation. In M. T. Greenberg, D. Cicchetti, & E. M. Cummings (Eds.), *Attachment in the preschool years: Theory, research, and intervention* (pp. 121–160). Chicago: University of Chicago Press.

Mayseless, O., & Scharf, M. (2007). Adolescents' attachment representations and their capacity for intimacy in close relationships. *Journal of Research on Adolescence, 17*, 23–50.

Mickelson, K. D., Kessler, R. C., & Shaver, P. R. (1997). Adult attachment in a nationally representative sample. *Journal of Personality and Social Psychology, 73*, 1092–1106.

Mikulincer, M. (1995). Attachment style and the mental representation of the self. *Journal of Personality and Social Psychology, 69*, 1203–1215.

Mikulincer, M., Dolev, T., & Shaver, P. R. (2004). Attachment-related strategies during thought suppression: Ironic rebounds and vulnerable self-representations. *Journal of Personality and Social Psychology, 87*, 940–956.

Mikulincer, M., & Florian, V. (1998). The relationship between adult attachment styles and emotional and cognitive reactions to stressful events. In J. A. Simpson & W. S. Rholes (Eds.), *Attachment theory and close relationships* (pp. 143–165). New York: Guilford Press.

Mikulincer, M., & Florian, V. (2000). Exploring individual differences in reactions to mortality salience: Does attachment style regulate terror management mechanisms? *Journal of Personality and Social Psychology, 79*, 260–273.

Mikulincer, M., Florian, V., & Tolmacz, R. (1990). Attachment styles and fear of personal death: A case study of affect regulation. *Journal of Personality and Social Psychology, 58*, 273–280.

Mikulincer, M., & Shaver, P. R. (2007a). *Attachment in adulthood: Structure, dynamics, and change.* New York: Guilford Press.

Mikulincer, M., & Shaver, P. R. (2007b). Boosting attachment security to promote mental health, prosocial values, and inter-group tolerance. *Psychological Inquiry, 18*, 139–156.

Mikulincer, M., Shaver, P. R., Sapir-Lavid, Y., & Avihou-Kanza, N. (2009). What's inside the minds of securely and insecurely attached people? The secure-base script and its associations with attachment-style dimensions. *Journal of Personality and Social Psychology, 97*, 615–633.

Obegi, J. H., & Berant, E. (Eds.). (2008). *Attachment theory and research in clinical work with adults.* New York: Guilford Press.

Overall, N. C., Fletcher, G. J. O., & Friesen, M. D. (2003). Mapping the intimate relationship mind: Comparisons between three models of attachment representations. *Personality and Social Psychology Bulletin, 29*, 1479–1493.

Ravitz, P., Maunder, R., Hunter, J., Sthankiya, B., & Lancee, W. (2010). Adult attachment measures: A 25-year review. *Journal of Psychosomatic Research, 69*, 419–432.

Riggs, S., Paulson, A., Tunnell, E., Sahl, G., Atkison, H., & Ross, C. A. (2007). Attachment, personality, and psychopathology among adult inpatients: Self-reported romantic attachment style versus Adult Attachment Interview states of mind. *Development and Psychopathology, 19*, 263–291.

Roisman, G. I. (2009). Adult attachment: Toward a rapprochement of methodological cultures. *Current Directions in Psychological Science, 18*, 122–126.

Roisman, G. I., Fraley, R. C., & Belsky, J. (2007). A taxometric study of the Adult Attachment Interview. *Developmental Psychology, 43*, 675–686.

Roisman, G. I., Holland, A., Fortuna, K., Fraley, R. C., Clausell, E., & Clarke, A. (2007). The Adult Attachment Interview and self-reports of attachment style: An empirical rapprochement. *Journal of Personality and Social Psychology, 92*, 678–697.

Shaver, P. R., Belsky, J., & Brennan, K. A. (2000). The Adult Attachment Interview and self-reports of romantic attachment: Associations across domains and methods. *Personal Relationships, 7*, 25–43.

Shaver, P. R., & Clark, C. L. (1994). The psychodynamics of adult romantic attachment. In J. M. Masling & R. F. Bornstein (Eds.), *Empirical perspectives on object relations theories* (pp. 105–156). Washington, DC: American Psychological Association.

Shaver, P. R., Collins, N. L., & Clark, C. L. (1996). Attachment styles and internal working models of self and relationship partners. In G. J. O. Fletcher & J. Fitness (Eds.), *Knowledge structures in close relationships: A social psychological approach* (pp. 25–61). Mahwah, NJ: Erlbaum.

Shaver, P. R., & Mikulincer, M. (2011). A general attachment-theoretical framework for conceptualizing interpersonal behavior: Cognitive-motivational predispositions and patterns of social information processing. In L. M. Horowitz & S. Strack (Eds.), *Handbook of interpersonal psychology: Theory, research, assessment, and therapeutic interventions* (pp. 17–35). New York: Wiley.

Sibley, C. G., & Overall, N. C. (2007). The boundaries between attachment and personality: Associations across three levels of the attachment network. *Journal of Research in Personality, 41,* 960–967.

Sibley, C. G., & Overall, N. C. (2008). Modeling the hierarchical structure of attachment representations: A test of domain differentiation. *Personality and Individual Differences, 44,* 238–249.

Simpson, J. A. (1990). Influence of attachment styles on romantic relationships. *Journal of Personality and Social Psychology, 59,* 871–980.

Simpson, J. A., Rholes, W. S., & Nelligan, J. S. (1992). Support seeking and support giving within couples in an anxiety-provoking situation: The role of attachment styles. *Journal of Personality and Social Psychology, 62,* 434–446.

Simpson, J. A., Rholes, W. S., Orina, M. M., & Grich, J. (2002). Working models of attachment, support giving, and support seeking in a stressful situation. *Personality and Social Psychology Bulletin, 28,* 598–608.

Steele, H., & Steele, M. (Eds.). (2008). *Clinical applications of the Adult Attachment Interview.* New York: Guilford Press.

Waters, E. (1978). The reliability and stability of individual differences in infant-mother attachment. *Child Development, 49,* 483–494.

Waters, E., Merrick, S., Treboux, D., Crowell, J., & Albersheim, L. (2000). Attachment security in infancy and early adulthood: A twenty-year longitudinal study. *Child Development, 71,* 684–689.

Waters, H. S., & Waters, E. (2006). The attachment working models concept: Among other things, we build script-like representations of secure base experiences. *Attachment & Human Development, 8,* 185–198.

Zayas, V., Mischel, W., Shoda, Y., & Aber, J. L. (2011). Roots of adult attachment: Maternal caregiving at 18 months predicts adult peer and partner attachment. *Social Psychological and Personality Science, 2,* 289–297.

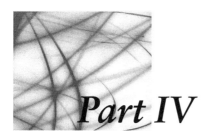

Part IV

RELATIONSHIP EFFECTS
ON MORBIDITY AND MORTALITY

Chapter **10**

Relationship Well-Being

The Central Role of Perceived Partner Responsiveness

HARRY T. REIS

> The greatest happiness of life is the conviction that we are loved—loved for ourselves, or rather, loved in spite of ourselves.
>
> —VICTOR HUGO

Social psychologists often have difficulty explaining to their friends and family just what is "social" about the topics that fill our textbooks. To an outside observer, studies of counterattitudinal advocacy or of implicit motivation, for example, do not map well onto prototypes of what is social about human behavior. Nowhere is this concern more striking than in the study of phenomena that may be loosely grouped under the heading of "Self." Whether the topic is self-efficacy, self-affirmation, self-control, or self-enhancement, most such work rarely adopts an overtly interpersonal perspective. Yet there is a key interpersonal component at the heart of many self-related processes, reflecting the fact that our connections with significant others may substantially affect the way we manage important activities in everyday life. The goal of this chapter is to describe one of the most influential of these processes, perceived partner responsiveness to the self.

Perceived partner responsiveness to the self (which for simplicity I hereafter call *perceived partner responsiveness*) refers to the manner in which significant others are thought to attend to and behaviorally support the self's important needs, goals, and values (Reis & Clark, 2013). This definition is deliberately broad and multifaceted, encompassing many distinct concepts and phenomena. For example, perceived responsiveness touches on such fundamental human concerns as the nature and determinants of felt security; the experience of warmth and caregiving in close relationships; the sense of belonging and connectedness; the ability to give, receive, and recognize the availability of social support; the manner in which people internalize and form mental representations of their experiences in close relationships; and how these representations can provide a useful psychological resource for self-regulation.

Perceived partner responsiveness is not a new topic. Various popular theoretical models have considered the question of what makes a relationship not merely close and warm but responsive—that is, capable of providing psychologically useful supports to the self. These include, for example, attachment theory (Mikulincer & Shaver, 2007a), models of social support (see Cohen, Underwood, & Gottlieb, 2000, for an overview), the risk regulation model (Murray, Holmes, & Collins, 2006), as well as other approaches grounded in interdependence theory, such as the Michelangelo phenomenon (Rusbult, Finkel, & Kumashiro, 2009), trust (Holmes & Rempel, 1989; Simpson, 2007), and interpersonal influence models (Finkel & Fitzsimons, 2011); sociometer theory (Leary & Guadagno, 2011); the communal relationship model (Clark & Mills, 2012); and the construct of autonomy support (Deci & Ryan, 1987). Common to each of these specific theories and models is the general idea that when partners are seen as or expected to be responsive to self-relevant needs, goals, values, or preferences, effective self-regulation and psychological well-being are facilitated. In contrast, when partners are believed to be unresponsive or critical, self-regulation and psychological well-being are hampered. My purpose in this chapter is not to review these theories, which have been well reviewed elsewhere, but rather to take a step back, asking how their varied conceptualizations of responsiveness might be integrated. My premise, as explained later, is that if the same general construct appears in so many discrete theories, then there is value in attempting to identify its common core.

This chapter begins with a general discussion of what is meant by perceived partner responsiveness and how the construct is presumed to operate in personal relationships. Next, to demonstrate its generality, the chapter considers how perceived partner responsiveness is analyzed within several prominent social-psychological theories. The chapter then takes a more empirical turn, reviewing evidence for the impact of perceived responsiveness on two aspects of well-being with particular relevance to self-regulation: psychological openness and relationship health. I conclude the chapter with some general comments about the utility of perceived partner responsiveness as an explanatory construct in the field's understanding of how relationships affect behavior.

WHAT IS MEANT BY PERCEIVED PARTNER RESPONSIVENESS?

Responsiveness, in its most general sense, refers to a relationship partner's supportive reaction to a person's important needs, goals, values, and preferences. When partners are perceived as responsive, individual and relational well-being tends to be enhanced; on the other hand, when partners are perceived to be unresponsive—that is, when they are seen as critical, controlling, or uninterested—individuals and their relationships tend to suffer harm (see Clark & Lemay, 2010; Reis & Clark, 2013, for recent reviews). There is a key distinction here between the partner's actual behavior, as might be appraised by an impartial observer, and the recipient's interpretation of that behavior. Both are meaningful, of course, but as will be discussed later, the impact of responsive behavior depends on how that behavior is experienced.

Figure 10.1 depicts responsiveness as an interaction process. As can be seen, perceived partner responsiveness involves both intrapsychic and interactive elements. The process begins with some sort of eliciting behavior; for example, one person relates a personally meaningful event or goal, expresses a need or wish for help, or discloses something important about the self. These eliciting behaviors provide an opportunity for the partner to respond supportively or unsupportively, contingent on the partner's ability and intention. These responses are, in turn, perceived by the originator as responsive or not. Sometimes the process unfolds straightforwardly: One partner reveals something about the self, to which the other responds supportively. At other times, however, the process may misfire. A request for help may be met with an inappropriate response or no response at all, or a response intended to be supportive may be experienced as intrusive or unhelpful, perhaps reflecting motivated bias. As discussed later in this chapter, there is good reason to believe, and ample evidence to corroborate, that enacted behavior and motivated interpretation both influence perceived partner responsiveness.

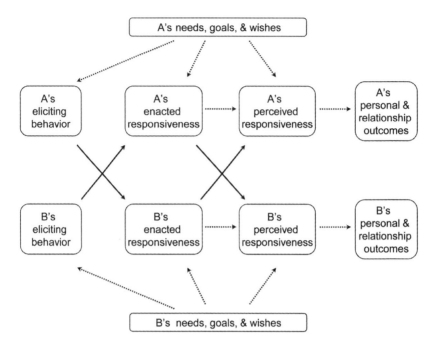

FIGURE 10.1. The interactional model of responsiveness. Interpersonal processes are denoted by solid arrows; intrapersonal processes by dotted arrows. Adapted from Reis and Clark (2013). Copyright by Oxford University Press. Adapted by permission.

Reis and Shaver (1988; see also Reis & Patrick, 1996) proposed that a partner's behavior is likely to be perceived as responsive if it possesses three qualities:

1. *Understanding*, or whether the partner is believed to have accurately "gotten the facts right" about oneself. Understanding matters for several reasons: because it fosters a sense of authenticity and genuineness (Kernis & Goldman, 2006); because it fulfills self-verification needs (Swann, 1990); and, most important, because in its absence, a partner's attempts to show validation and caring would seem misinformed and hence tangential to the self.

2. *Validation*, or the belief that the partner values and appreciates oneself—that is, the abilities, traits, worldviews, and other elements that constitute a person's true inner self (Schlegel, Hicks, Arndt, & King, 2009). Validation matters because it conveys a partner's liking for and acceptance of oneself (Finkenauer & Righetti, 2011),

which reinforces a sense of belongingness and felt security (Leary & Guadagno, 2011; Murray et al., 2006). Validation also facilitates successful adaptation to the demands of living in a social world, as first theorized by Sullivan (1953).

3. *Caring*, or confidence that partners will provide help and support when it is needed. Extensive evidence demonstrates that support availability promotes effective coping with stress and resilience (see Stroebe & Stroebe, 1996, for a review). Expressions of caring reveal partners' concern for each other's well-being, the key attribute of communal relationships (Clark & Mills, 2012).

Responsiveness is an intrinsically interactive process, and because it depends both on enacted behavior and on how those behaviors are experienced, the model depicted in Figure 10.1 explicitly incorporates interpersonal and intrapsychic steps. In my view, focusing exclusively on either set of steps, which some contemporary accounts do, overlooks the dynamic richness of this process; that is, the best way to understand how mental models of the self and relationships, learned through earlier relational experiences (Chen, Boucher, & Tapias, 2006; Mikulincer & Shaver, 2007a), affect later interactions and relationships is to ascertain "what the individual makes of the situation" (Kelley et al., 2003). Thus, although enacted behavior is an essential component of the model, from a theoretical standpoint the end products of responsiveness depend proximally on what has been perceived rather than on what was enacted. In other words, the personal and relational outcomes engendered by this sequential unfolding of self-revelation and response ultimately depend on whether interaction partners feel understood, validated, and cared for or misunderstood, unappreciated, and neglected.

Are Perceptions of a Partner's Responsiveness Veridical?

This analysis suggests an important question: To what extent are perceptions of a partner's responsiveness veridical? By some accounts, accuracy may not matter. As Kelley (1979) first proposed, perceived partner responsiveness signifies an attribution about the intent behind a partner's action: When Jack sets aside his own interests and instead prioritizes Jill's needs or wishes, Jill is logically led to infer Jack's caring and concern, the roots of responsiveness. Attributions are known to be influenced by motivated bias, often strongly so. For example, people with low self-esteem often underestimate or misconstrue their partner's regard and caring (Murray, Rose, Bellavia, Holmes, & Kusche, 2002; Stinson et al., 2010), similar to rejection-sensitive persons' tendency to interpret negatively a partner's ambiguous behaviors (Downey, Freitas, Michaelis, & Khouri, 1998). Also, people with more prominent intimacy goals tend to perceive similar intent in their partner's behavior (Sanderson & Evans, 2001). Even momentarily salient motives and goals can shape people's attributions, both in general (Fiske & Taylor, 2008) and in relationships (Bradbury & Fincham, 1990). It may not be surprising, then, that when the impact on relationship well-being of feeling understood and actually being understood is compared, many studies find stronger evidence for the former (e.g., Finkenauer & Righetti, 2011; Pollmann & Finkenauer, 2009; see Fletcher & Kerr, 2010, for a review).

Nonetheless, there are good reasons to believe that the type of behavior most likely to foster attributions of responsiveness would reflect a partner's accurate understanding of oneself (as the direct link between enacted responsiveness and perceived partner responsiveness in Figure 10.1 indicates). One reason is that many studies show that people who are close tend to perceive each other more accurately than acquaintances or strangers do (see Finkenauer & Righetti, 2011; Fletcher & Kerr, 2010; Reis & Clark, 2013, for recent reviews). (*Accuracy* is defined as the correspondence between judgments about a partner and relevant benchmarks, most commonly the partner's self-ratings.) Other studies have shown that partners' perceptions of support received during a laboratory interaction correlate reasonably well with independent coders' ratings of those same interactions (e.g., Collins & Feeney, 2000; Maisel, Gable, & Strachman, 2008).

Furthermore, because self-verification is an influential goal in self-regulatory striving (Swann, 1990), receiving feedback from relationship partners that matches self-views promotes feeling understood (Swann, Stein-Seroussi, & Giesler, 1992), intimacy (Campbell, Lackenbauer, & Muise, 2006; Lackenbauer, Campbell, Rubin, Fletcher, & Troister, 2010), and positive affect (Campbell et al., 2006; Oishi, Koo, & Akimoto, 2008). Thus, *empathic accuracy*, defined as accurately perceiving a partner's thoughts and feelings, generally predicts relationship well-being (Ickes & Simpson, 1997) and constructive conflict resolution (Bissonnette, Rusbult, & Kilpatrick, 1997). Similarly, understanding a partner's thought process facilitates the development of shared meaning systems, which enhance communication (Sillars & Scott, 1983) and coordination of interdependent activity (Rusbult & Van Lange, 1996). Consistent with this line of reasoning, a daily diary study conducted by Gable, Reis, and Downey (2003) found that daily supportive acts predict relationship well-being best when reported by one partner and detected by the other.

Putting these arguments together suggests that although inferences about a partner's responsiveness may be influenced by motivated bias, they nevertheless have some basis in fact. A functional analysis of social perception implies a similar conclusion—after all, if perceptions of responsiveness were largely out of touch with reality, people would struggle to fulfill their basic relational goals. This is what Bowlby (1973) meant when he observed that "the varied expectations of the accessibility and responsiveness of attachment figures that different individuals develop during the years of immaturity are tolerably accurate reflections of the experiences those individuals have actually had" (p. 202). Some forms of motivated bias may even depend on accuracy. For example, Murray, Holmes, and Griffin (1996) observed that for positive illusions to be effective, they must be grounded in reality—that is, they must represent credible exaggerations of attributes recognized by both partners.

This is not to suggest that perceptions of responsiveness are always linked directly to social reality. Certain dispositions may accentuate the role of motivated bias, which in extreme cases may become dysfunctional. For example, as noted previously, individuals with low self-esteem or high sensitivity to rejection often have difficulty recognizing their partners' attempts to be responsive (Downey et al., 1998; Murray et al., 2002). In this case, the cycle of responsive interaction depicted in Figure 10.1 breaks down, causing relationships to deteriorate over time. For example, Smith and Reis (2012) showed that compared with persons with moderate or high self-esteem, persons with low self-esteem are less likely to benefit following a threat from the sorts of positive relationship-repairing interactions that commonly help partners reestablish intimacy and belongingness. Forest and Wood (2012) documented a similar deficiency in low-self-esteem persons' ability to benefit from their friends' sympathetic responses to distressed self-disclosures on Facebook. I speculate that other personality dispositions, such as narcissism and borderline personality disorder, may also interfere with the link between enacted and perceived responsiveness. Such interference can be expected to be highly problematic for maintaining close relationships.

One type of motivated perception that has recently received considerable attention is projection—the tendency to base perceptions of a partner's motives, intentions, or behavior on one's own motives, intentions, or behavior. The evidence for projection in perceptions of a partner's responsiveness is clear. For example, Lemay and his colleagues (e.g., Lemay & Clark, 2008; Lemay, Clark, & Feeney, 2007) have shown that people tend to describe their partners as more caring when they themselves are more caring toward those partners (controlling for partners' or observers' accounts of the partners' actual care). Other, more indirect evidence that may also be indicative of projection includes findings that perceptions of a partner's behavior are usually less well correlated with that partner's reports of these behaviors than with the perceiver's self-reports. This pattern is commonly observed, for example, in studies of social support (Brunstein, Dangelmayer, & Schultheiss, 1996). Of course, projection can also lead to perceiving partners as less caring and responsive than objectively warranted.

Projection likely reflects several mechanisms. For one, people expect caring and concern in communal relationship to be reciprocated (Clark & Mills, 2012), so that it would be reasonable to assume that a partner's responsiveness is, or will be, similar to one's own. Another explanation is that because people are motivated to see their close relationships as equitable and fair, they tend to perceive reciprocity in uncertain circumstances. Projection may also reflect methodological factors, such as people's tendency to anchor judgments about other people's behavior in self-observation (Biernat, Manis, & Kobrynowicz, 1997).

Whatever the underlying mechanism may be, two points deserve mention here. First, it is interesting to speculate that projected levels of responsiveness may become reality in the manner of a self-fulfilling prophecy. That is, once Jack has assumed on the basis of his own intentions that Jill is behaving responsively, he may behaviorally "reciprocate" that assumed level of responsiveness. Observing and appreciating Jack's kindness, Jill might then respond similarly, yielding enacted levels of responsive behavior comparable to Jack's original projections.

Second, evidence for projection, although clear, does not rule out the possibility that perceptions of responsiveness are simultaneously to some extent accurate, as Lemay and colleagues (Lemay & Clark, 2008; Lemay et al., 2007) acknowledge. For example, in three separate studies using different methods—a short-term longitudinal study, a daily diary study, and a laboratory observation—Rusbult, Kumashiro, and Reis (2009) systematically examined the impact of one partner's enacted responsiveness on the other's perceptions of partner responsiveness. All three studies showed evidence of projection and, after controlling for projection, of accurate perceptions of enacted responsiveness. (Priem, Solomon, & Steuber, 2009, reached a similar conclusion in their laboratory-observational study of support interactions.)

In short, it might be concluded that perceived responsiveness depends on both the head and the hands. Motivated bias (the head) and accuracy (a partner's helping hands) can and should comfortably coexist in models of responsiveness. Indeed, it would seem fruitful for researchers to go beyond the question of "which one" to determining the situational, dispositional, and relational factors that make each type of process more or less influential.

PERCEIVED PARTNER RESPONSIVENESS
IS PROMINENT IN OTHER THEORIES

Responsiveness is a familiar theme in the relationships literature, appearing in many distinct theoretical models of relationship development and maintenance. It is therefore striking that researchers from these varied theoretical approaches rarely consider how their conceptualization of responsiveness compares with other conceptualizations, much less synthesize their differing perspectives into a systematic, coherent account. In an earlier article, I suggested that as relationship science has evolved, so too has its conceptual sprawl: Literally dozens—perhaps hundreds—of phenomena and processes have been identified, all describing something of value about relationships yet remaining vague about their links to one another (Reis, 2007). Furthermore, even when alternative constructs are compared, "scholars typically conclude not that one or another account is better, but rather that they appear to address somewhat different aspects of the phenomenon and therefore are not directly comparable" (Reis, Clark, & Holmes, 2004, p. 202).

Relationship science is still a young discipline, of course, but if it is to become a mature, cumulative science, we will need to do a better job of identifying links among our many strands of research—that is, of articulating "core ideas, the principles that make them cohere, and [thereby providing] an organizational framework for understanding how the many empirical pieces interconnect" (Reis, 2007, p. 9). That is, and notwithstanding the unassailable value of specialization and diversity in research, the field needs models that explain how the diverse constructs we study relate to one another. Models of this sort help establish a nomological network of systematically related constructs and processes, something that characterizes mature sciences (Reis, 2007). Following similar logic, Bradbury and Lavner (2012) argued that integrated models of this sort are necessary for developing effective research-based interventions for the amelioration of relationship distress.

Responsiveness—the tendency of relationship partners to attend to and behaviorally support core features of the self, along with the symbolic representations of this tendency that emerge out of mental life—seems a particularly promising candidate for a core conceptual principle of this sort. Consequently, it will be useful to consider how responsiveness is conceptualized by different theoretical approaches in relationship science. Attachment theory is a good place to start this analysis, in that this theory's account of socioemotional development prominently features caregiver responsiveness to the infant's expressions of need or distress. As Bowlby (1969/1982) first theorized and subsequent research confirmed (Ainsworth, Blehar, Waters, & Wall, 1978; van IJzendoorn, 1995), when caregivers respond sensitively and supportively, infants learn to be confident about their caregiver's availability and likely helpfulness when needed. This internalized sense of confidence, generalized to other caregivers, provides a foundation for secure internal working models throughout life (Hazan & Zeifman, 1999; Mikulincer & Shaver, 2007a). In contrast, insensitivity—either nonresponses or intrusive, noncontingent responses—undermines confidence about caregivers' accessibility and responsiveness, fostering insecure working models of attachment in later childhood and adulthood (Kobak & Madsen, 2008).

Although internal working models are complex and multifaceted (Collins & Read, 1994), in the most general sense they refer to perceived responsiveness of attachment figures. Hazan and Shaver (1994) conceptualized adult working models of attachment in terms of the question, "Will my attachment figure be responsive if I need him/her?" Secure models suggest an affirmative answer. Insecure models, on the other hand, take one of two forms. Anxious–ambivalent models imply uncertainty, fostering anxiety and a hierarchy of behaviors meant to induce caregiving by attachment figures. Avoidant models imply a negative answer, leading to defensiveness, distance, and heightened self-reliance. Scores of studies have shown that these models influence adult behavior across a remarkable range of circumstances, including caregiving, care receiving, bereavement, dating, sex, exploration, and coping with stress, danger, relationship threat, and illness (see Mikulincer & Shaver, 2007a, for a review).

Capturing another side of perceived partner responsiveness, Leary and Baumeister (2000) describe the *sociometer*, which indexes the degree to which individuals believe they are valued and accepted by others as opposed to devalued and likely to be rejected. Because the sociometer "monitors and responds to events that are relevant to interpersonal acceptance and rejection" (Leary & Guadagno, 2011, p. 340), it predicts self-regulatory behavior in a variety of interpersonal settings, including those in which concerns about responsiveness might be activated (e.g., when support is desired or when a partner's commitment is unclear). Perceived acceptance involves all three components of perceived responsiveness: understanding (because the likelihood of acceptance by others is uncertain if those others are not aware of one's true self), validation (because acceptance is more likely when others value the self), and caring (because acceptance is unlikely if others are unconcerned about one's welfare). Thus, the motivational purposes of the sociometer monitoring system reflect core principles of perceived partner responsiveness.

Another prominent theory that has recently broached the concept of responsiveness is interdependence theory (see Van Lange & Rusbult, 2012, for a review). Interdependence theory concerns the manner in which people's outcomes are affected by their interaction with each other. In these terms, responsiveness may be described as a process in which one partner assigns higher priority to the other partner's needs or preferences than to his or her own. To interdependence theorists, this process can only be established in so-called *diagnostic situations*—situations in which partners' personal needs or wishes conflict; after all, if partners want the same thing, one cannot demonstrate that other-interest supersedes self-interest. Thus, perceived partner responsiveness represents an attribution that, at some personal cost, a partner has put aside his or her own preferences and instead prioritized one's own preferences. This sort of inference is fundamental to perceiving that a communal relationship exists (Clark & Mills, 2012). On the other hand, the failure to put a partner's need ahead of one's own frequently leads to the perception of unresponsiveness and can undermine communal relationships. Of course, people do not always accurately perceive their partner's intent. For example, as already mentioned, low self-esteem, anxiously attached, and rejection-sensitive people often misinterpret or fail to notice their partners' genuine attempts to be responsive (Collins & Feeney, 2000; Downey et al., 1998; Murray, Holmes, & Griffin, 2000), a misperception that can instigate conflictual interactions that, in the manner of a self-fulfilling prophecy, confirm the perceived unresponsiveness.

Recent spin-offs of traditional interdependence theory highlight other pivotal instances of responsiveness in close relationships. For example, in their motivation management model of mutual responsiveness, Murray and Holmes (2011) propose that relationship partners work through a series of procedural "If–then" rules to decide whether to engage in or self-protectively withdraw from responsiveness-relevant interactions (e.g., "If partner sacrifices, then trust"). How these rules are applied depends on past experience in similar situations, particularly expectations about whether the partner will reciprocate or exploit one's openness and responsiveness. Another example is Rusbult and colleagues' research on the *Michelangelo phenomenon* (Rusbult, Finkel, & Kumashiro, 2009), which addresses the impact of partner support on individuals' movement toward valued goals. Responsiveness (which in this model is called "affirmation"), both enacted and perceived, facilitates goal-directed progress, whereas unresponsiveness hinders progress.

A final example concerns the concept of autonomy support, which in self-determination theory refers to support of a partner's self-chosen, authentically valued acts (Assor, Kaplan, & Roth, 2002; Deci & Ryan, 1987). Autonomy support is said to be high when partners help each other fulfill basic needs for autonomy (in the sense of freely chosen activity), competence, and relatedness, and is associated with higher levels of satisfaction and commitment in romantic relationships (Patrick, Knee, Canevello, & Lonsbary, 2007) and with similarly positive outcomes in other kinds of relationships (e.g., between patients and their physicians; Williams, Rodin, Ryan, Grolnick, & Deci, 1998). Autonomy support represents a particular kind of responsiveness in the sense that it describes support that attends to and encourages behavior that is central to the recipient's core self (Reis et al., 2004). A key difference, however, is that whereas in self-determination theory the value of autonomy support derives from the motivational significance of autonomy (self-direction), in our formulation the value of responsiveness derives from the motivational significance of forming and maintaining close relationships with others (Reis & Clark, 2013).

In summary, the widespread relevance of responsiveness is apparent; the concept appears repeatedly, albeit expressed in varying terms, across diverse theoretical models of human behavior. Recognizing the complementary role of these varied approaches may allow researchers to weave together a broader, more integrative account of this vital dimension of human bonding—as it were, a spider's web of conceptualization rather than a list.

RESPONSIVENESS AND WELL-BEING

A basic premise behind researchers' interest in responsiveness is the idea that when people feel that their relationship partners are and will continue to be responsive to their needs, their well-being is enhanced. Numerous correlational studies, reviewed elsewhere (e.g., Reis, 2012), show that perceived partner responsiveness is associated with various indicators of well-being. In the remainder of this chapter, I review evidence concerning two types of outcomes with particular relevance to the self and self-regulation: openness/exploration and relationship well-being.

Responsiveness Facilitates Nondefensiveness and Exploration

I group nondefensiveness and exploration together because I see them as exemplars of the same general self-regulatory process. When people are defensive, they engage their environment through the lens of motivated bias—that is, their perceptions, beliefs, emotions, or actions are skewed by self-serving needs and motives, such as to avoid blameworthiness or blows to self-esteem. Although such biases have well-documented self-regulatory benefits, they typically interfere with seeing circumstances for what they are and responding in the most direct, authentic, and effective manner. When people are not being defensive, they deemphasize self-protective motives while being fully open to experience. Exploration similarly implies openness to the environment, either symbolically (as when people are curious about their personal strengths or limitations) or physically (as when people consider unfamiliar places and experiences).

Perceived partner responsiveness may bolster the self-concept in ways that reduce defensiveness and facilitate confident exploration. In attachment theory, the secure base provision describes how individuals feel self-assured dealing with the challenges of everyday life when their attachment figures are believed to be available and responsive if needed (Bowlby, 1973). Perceived unresponsiveness promotes a more defensive orientation, with the underlying (often outside of awareness) intent of either soliciting nurturance or of obviating the need for help through excessive self-reliance. In the Murray and Holmes (2011) motivation management model, motives for self-protection and relationship engagement coexist in a kind of dynamic tension: Uncertainty about a partner's trustworthiness enhances the appeal of self-protection (which includes defensiveness and a reluctance to take risks). In Reis et al.'s (2004) model of responsiveness, perceiving the self as valued and cared for by significant others lessens concerns about acceptance, increasing people's willingness to examine their vulnerabilities. Worry about one's value to a partner, on the other hand, makes doubts about acceptance salient (Leary & Baumeister, 2000), which may motivate strategic attempts to ignore, reject, or minimize personal shortcomings.

Researchers have investigated this process with experimental priming, in which mental representations related to perceived partner responsiveness are temporarily activated. In one such study, Baldwin and Holmes (1987) found that men asked to visualize being liked and accepted by a supportive friend were less likely to blame themselves for failure. Similarly, women subliminally primed with words such as accepting, loving, and supportive evaluated themselves less negatively after imagining an unexpected pregnancy (Pierce & Lydon, 1998). A pair of experiments by Kumashiro and Sedikides (2005) explicitly documented how perceived responsiveness can lessen defensiveness. They gave participants false failure feedback after taking a putative intelligence test. Participants then were asked whether they wanted to receive information about which aspects of their intelligence were weakest, presumably to identify potential areas for improvement. Participants who had earlier visualized close, positive relationships during a supraliminal priming task expressed greater interest in this diagnostic information than participants who had visualized distant–positive or close–negative relationships. Presumably, the latter two groups declined this information for self-esteem protective reasons.

A pair of experiments by Caprariello and Reis (2011) zeroed in on perceived partner responsiveness. In their first study, being subliminally primed with the name of a responsive friend ("someone who knows the real you . . . and esteems you, shortcomings and all") increased the accessibility of words from failed trials on a remote associates task. (Increased accessibility was interpreted as an indication of continued curiosity about the words participants had missed.) Participants primed with the name of an acquaintance, in contrast, were more likely to put these words out of mind, presumably to create mental distance from their failure on the task. Caprariello and Reis's second study examined self-handicapping on a difficult and potentially embarrassing task. *Self-handicapping* refers to the tendency to focus on barriers to success, presumably as a way of protecting self-esteem when failure is anticipated. Compared with participants who wrote about acquaintances or familiar others, participants who felt threatened and wrote for 15 minutes about responsive relationships claimed fewer external factors that might interfere with their performance.

Other studies have illustrated the same process through the lens of attachment theory. Attachment theory posits that a person's sense of security can be temporarily enhanced by activating mental representations of attachment figures in either of two ways: First, priming makes the attachment figure symbolically available as a source of nurturance and support, and second, at least for secure persons, priming activates representations of the self as worthy of love and acceptance (Mikulincer & Shaver, 2007a). Mikulincer, Shaver, and their colleagues have carried out an extensive series of studies using diverse technique to prime attachment security. Their studies show, for example, that security priming lessens defensive biases in social comparison, decreases defensive inflation of self-esteem, reduces symptoms of posttraumatic stress and eating disorders, diminishes hostile perceptions of, and behavior toward, members of outgroups, and promotes nonegoistically motivated altruism (see Mikulincer & Shaver, 2007b, for a review).

Earlier, I suggested that exploration is another side of openness. The role of parental responsiveness in encouraging children's exploratory activities has been studied by developmental attachment theorists (see Grossmann, Grossman, Kindler, & Zimmermann, 2008, for a review). Studies of exploration by adults are more rare. Elliot and Reis (2003) conceptualized adult exploration in terms of effectance motivation. In four studies of academic achievement, they found that more secure college students (i.e., students who felt that their attachment figures were responsive and supportive) viewed their college courses as challenging more than threatening, and exhibited higher achievement motivation, lower fear of failure, and more approach-oriented, rather than avoidance-oriented, motives about school-work. Caprariello and Reis (2006) obtained a similar pattern of findings with regard to college athletes' participation in competitive sports.

Other studies have looked directly at the provision of responsive support. For example, Feeney (2004) found that a partner's responsive support of one's personal goal strivings was associated with greater happiness, self-esteem, and perceived likelihood of attaining those goals. (This result dove-tails with findings from the Michelangelo phenomenon studies by Rusbult, Finkel, et al., 2009, reviewed previously.) Reis et al. (2010) found similar results when partners responded enthusiastically, as opposed to critically or with lack of interest, to each others' disclosures of good news. Finally, using a somewhat different approach, Feeney and Thrush (2010) found that a partner's responsive support—that is, support that was available and encouraging but noninterfering—facilitated creativity on a challenging "brick-by-brick" construction task.

Common to these studies is the idea that when an actual or mental representation of an understanding, validating, and caring partner is more accessible, self-protective motives become less salient. One likely explanation is that a responsive partner's support may inhibit anxieties about acceptance that difficult tasks might otherwise activate ("My part-ner won't want to be with me if she learns that I did poorly"), allowing nondefensive thoughts to gain prominence ("I wonder what I did wrong"). Exploration is similarly facilitated by confidence that others knowledge-ably value the self, are available to provide assistance if needed, and will not be put off by the prospect of failure. These studies provide another reminder that self-regulation is affected by relationships (Finkel & Fitzsi-mons, 2011): Although the behaviors discussed in this section are enacted by individuals, they nevertheless reflect influence by relationship partners.

Responsiveness Contributes to Relationship Well-Being

Scores of studies have shown that responsiveness fosters relationship well-being. Each of the three components of responsiveness is relevant here. For example, understanding enhances trust and empathy (Finkenauer & Righetti, 2011; Simpson, 2007), both of which enhance relationship sat-isfaction and stability. Validation also contributes to positive relationship outcomes, as research on reciprocity of liking (Curtis & Miller, 1986), reflected appraisals (Murray et al., 1996) and feeling appreciated (Gordon, Impett, Kogan, Oveis, & Keltner, 2012) has shown. Caring, or partners' mutual concern for each other's well-being, is the central feature of communal relationships, which tend to be among people's more significant relationships (Clark & Mills, 2012).

How might this process work? To address this question, I draw on the idea of *mutual cyclical growth*, a process by which partners in a close relationship support each other's goals and aspirations, thereby building mutual trust and caring (Wieselquist, Rusbult, Foster, & Agnew, 1999). According to this concept, trust develops when each partner feels confident that the other's motives and behavior are benevolent and caring. In turn, this confidence fuels treating partners in a benevolent and caring manner, setting off the chain-like sequence of mutual cyclical growth. Perceiving a lack of benevolence, on the other hand, has the opposite effect, shutting down any latent desire to contribute to the partner's well-being.

It is instructive to consider how the elements of perceived partner responsiveness contribute to this process. Feeling understood matters, because if the partner's caring appears to target needs that are not consonant with self-perceived needs and preferences, it probably will be experienced as inappropriate or useless. For example, vegans would be unlikely to feel gratitude for a birthday present of six Kansas City steaks. Misdirected expressions of caring denote empathic inaccuracy, perhaps because the donor has not put in the time or effort to discover what one needs. Validation matters for related reasons. Gifts that show little valuing of the self—for example, holiday fruitcakes or hand-me-downs—are unlikely to inspire attributions of benevolence. Even worse, support that implies the donor's belief that one is incompetent or otherwise unable to cope with existing circumstances may superficially suggest caring but nevertheless be experienced as invalidating—for example, offering to pay for a tutoring session that one hadn't wanted. In short, reciprocal concern for each other's well-being is most likely when supportive responses imply understanding and valuing of oneself and one's abilities.

This analysis brings to mind the distinction between visible and invisible support, proposed by Bolger and his colleagues (e.g., Bolger & Amarel, 2007; Bolger, Zuckerman, & Kessler, 2000). Their research demonstrated increased distress following the receipt of *visible support*—support of which recipients are aware—along with lessened distress following the receipt of *invisible support*—support that providers report giving but recipients do not report receiving. These results are typically explained by recourse to the self-esteem threat that receiving help may create (Bolger et al., 2000; Rafaeli & Gleason, 2009), and by the possibility that help recipients may feel indebted to help donors. Our model, in seeming contrast, suggests that the relationship-enhancing effects of support depend on the perception of partner responsiveness, which is more likely when support is visible than when it is invisible.

Reis and Clark (2013) discuss in some detail three reasons why visible, responsive support may not undermine relationship well-being. First, although visible support may have enhanced distress in Bolger et al.'s studies, at the same time it was associated with relationship benefits (e.g., Iida, Seidman, Shrout, Fujita, & Bolger, 2008), particularly among those individuals who showed relatively less mood impairment (Gleason, Iida, Shrout, & Bolger, 2008). Second, support is unlikely to undercut self-efficacy when it is delivered in a skillful (responsive) manner—that is, when it takes the needs, preferences, and self-perception of the recipient into account (Burleson & MacGeorge, 2002). Consistent with this logic, Maisel and Gable (2009) found that "visible support was associated with neutral or even positive outcomes when it was high in responsiveness, and invisible support was associated with negative outcomes if it was low in responsiveness" (p. 931). Third, visible support seems likely to imply indebtedness when it makes salient exchange norms rather than communal norms (Clark & Mills, 2012). Skillful provision of support, in the context of an ongoing communal relationship, is more likely to signal concern for the other's welfare.

Reis (2012) provided additional evidence of the beneficial relationship effects of visible support. These analyses asked whether the relationship-enhancing benefits of positive illusions—people's tendency to see their partners in a more positive light than the partners see themselves (Murray et al., 1996)—depend on awareness: that is, being aware that one's partner has a somewhat idealistic view of oneself. I investigated this question by asking a sample of 88 spouses to describe themselves, their partners, and how they thought their partners saw them. This last question, a measure of perceived partner regard (which conceptually is part of perceived partner responsiveness; Reis et al., 2004), substantially mediated the positive illusions effect. In other words, positive illusions were beneficial primarily when they were visible to spouses.

The impact of responsiveness on relationship well-being is studied primarily in the context of aversive situations and interactions—for example, how partners respond to need or distress, how they contend with conflicts of interest, their willingness to sacrifice and forgive, and their communication about problems. Yet responsiveness may also benefit relationships under happy circumstances. For example, responsive support of personal goal striving, discussed earlier, facilitates progress toward those goals while simultaneously promoting relationship well-being (Rusbult, Finkel, et al., 2009; Rusbult, Kumashiro, et al., 2009). Studies of capitalization examine responsiveness in conversations about one partner's personal good fortune or the "best thing that happened today" (see Gable & Reis, 2010, for a review). These studies show that enthusiastic responses, as opposed to indifferent or critical responses, are associated with greater relationship well-being (Gable, Reis, Impett, & Asher, 2004; Gable, Gonzaga, & Strachman, 2006), higher levels of daily marital satisfaction and intimacy (Gable et al., 2004), and more trust and a generous prosocial orientation toward the responsive partner (Reis et al., 2010). As Gable and Reis (2010) theorize, celebrating a partner's good news conveys genuine concern for the other's well-being and success as well as understanding and appreciation of the event's meaning for the person (consistent with the model reviewed previously).

Of particular interest is the handful of studies that directly compare the relational impact of responsive support for distress with responsive capitalization for good news. Gable et al. (2006) found that responsiveness coded from videotaped discussions of positive events were a better predictor of changes in relationship well-being over 2 months than coded responses to disclosures of negative events. A series of three daily diary studies by Gable, Gosnell, Maisel, and Strachman (2012) reached a similar conclusion. Interestingly, Gable et al. (2012) also found that enacted positive-event support was a better predictor than enacted negative-event support of perceived support availability 2 months later. Taken broadly, these studies indicate that responsiveness is an important contributor to relationship enhancement and not merely a means of preventing distress and conflict from damaging relationships.

CONCLUDING COMMENT: PERCEIVED PARTNER RESPONSIVENESS AS A CORE CONSTRUCT IN RELATIONSHIP SCIENCE

Human bonding, the subject matter of this volume, is one of the most engaging and durable topics in behavioral science. The tendency of humans to bond is universal and innate—arguably, it is the defining characteristic of our species—and it exerts profound, pervasive influence on nearly all aspects of life. It is therefore sensible that the emergence of an interdisciplinary field that concerns itself with describing the nature and impact of human social relations—relationship science—would have the potential to be a "hub science," linking its theories and empirical findings to many other disciplines. This was the tantalizing prospect offered in Berscheid's (1999) famous "Greening of Relationship Science" article, one that many relationship researchers still see as a call to arms.

Relationship science has several promising candidates for core constructs. In this article I have argued for perceived partner responsiveness as one of them. Perceived partner responsiveness integrates elements of intrapsychic processing and interpersonal influence to arrive at a model that has both generality and breadth. Perhaps most important, though, is the idea that the myriad benefits that relationships provide might be understood through a common conceptual core. That core suggests that relationships, and hence individuals, thrive when people feel sensitively and appropriately responded to by the persons with whom their lives are interdependently entwined.

REFERENCES

Ainsworth, M. D. S., Blehar, M. C., Waters, E., & Wall, S. (1978). *Patterns of attachment: A psychological study of the Strange Situation.* Hillsdale, NJ: Erlbaum.

Assor, A., Kaplan, H., & Roth, G. (2002). Choice is good, but relevance is excellent: Autonomy-enhancing and suppressing teacher behaviours in predicting student's engagement in school work. *British Journal of Educational Psychology, 72,* 261–278.

Baldwin, M. W., & Holmes, J. G. (1987). Salient private audiences and awareness of the self. *Journal of Personality and Social Psychology, 53,* 1087–1098.

Berscheid, E. (1999). The greening of relationship science. *American Psychologist, 54,* 260–266.

Biernat, M., Manis, M., & Kobrynowicz, D. (1997). Simultaneous assimilation and contrast effects in judgments of self and others. *Journal of Personality and Social Psychology, 73,* 254–269.

Bissonnette, V. L., Rusbult, C. E., & Kilpatrick, S. D. (1997). Empathic accuracy and marital conflict resolution. In W. Ickes (Ed.), *Empathic accuracy* (pp. 251–281). New York: Guilford Press.

Bolger, N., & Amarel, D. (2007). Effects of social support visibility on adjustment to stress: Experimental evidence. *Journal of Personality and Social Psychology, 92,* 458–475.

Bolger, N., Zuckerman, A., & Kessler, R. C. (2000). Invisible support and adjustment to stress. *Journal of Personality and Social Psychology, 79,* 953–961.

Bowlby, J. (1973). *Attachment and loss: Vol. 2. Separation: Anxiety and anger.* New York: Basic Books.

Bowlby, J. (1982). *Attachment and loss: Vol. 1. Attachment* (2nd ed.). New York: Basic Books. (Original work published 1969)

Bradbury, T. N., & Fincham, F. D. (1990). Attributions in marriage: Review and critique. *Psychological Bulletin, 107,* 3–33.

Bradbury, T. N., & Lavner, J. A. (2012). How can we improve preventive and educational interventions for intimate relationships? *Behavior Therapy, 43,* 113–122.

Brunstein, J. C., Dangelmayer, G., & Schultheiss, O. C. (1996). Personal goals and social support in close relationships: Effects on relationship mood and marital satisfaction. *Journal of Personality and Social Psychology, 71*, 1006–1019.

Burleson, B. R., & MacGeorge, E. L. (2002). Supportive communication. In M. L. Knapp & J. A. Daly (Eds.), *Handbook of interpersonal communication* (3rd ed., pp. 374–424). Thousand Oaks, CA: Sage.

Campbell, L., Lackenbauer, S. D., & Muise, A. (2006). When is being known or adored by romantic partners most beneficial? Self-perceptions, relationship length, and responses to partner's verifying and enhancing appraisals. *Personality and Social Psychology Bulletin, 21*, 1283–1294.

Caprariello, P. A., & Reis, H. T. (2006, January). *Attachment and exploration in the domain of sports achievement.* Poster presented at the meeting of the Society for Personality and Social Psychology, Palm Springs, CA.

Caprariello, P. A., & Reis, H. T. (2011). Perceived partner responsiveness minimizes defensive reactions to failure. *Social Psychological and Personality Science, 2*, 365–372.

Chen, S., Boucher, H. C., & Tapias, M. P. (2006). The relational self revealed: Integrative conceptualization and implications for interpersonal Life. *Psychological Bulletin, 132*, 151–179.

Clark, M. S., & Lemay, E. P., Jr. (2010). Close relationships. In S. T. Fiske, D. T. Gilbert, & G. Lindzey (Eds.), *Handbook of social psychology* (5th ed., Vol. 2, pp. 898–940). New York: Wiley.

Clark, M. S., & Mills, J. (2012). A theory of communal (and exchange) relationships. In P. A. M. Van Lange, A. W. Kruglanski, & E. T. Higgins (Eds.), *Handbook of theories of social psychology* (Vol. 2, pp. 232–250). Thousand Oaks, CA: Sage.

Cohen, S., Underwood, L. G., & Gottlieb, B. H. (2000). *Social support measurement and intervention.* New York: Oxford University Press.

Collins, N., & Feeney, B. (2000). A safe haven: An attachment theory perspective on support seeking and caregiving in intimate relationships. *Journal of Personality and Social Psychology, 78*, 1053–1073.

Collins, N. L., & Read, S. J. (1994). Cognitive representations of attachment: The content and function of working models. In K. Bartholomew & D. Perlman (Eds.), *Advances in personal relationships* (Vol. 5, pp. 53–90). London: Jessica Kingsley.

Curtis, R. C., & Miller, K. (1986). Believing another likes or dislikes you: Behaviors making the beliefs come true. *Journal of Personality and Social Psychology, 51*, 284–290.

Deci, E. L., & Ryan, R. M. (1987). The support of autonomy and the control of behavior. *Journal of Personality and Social Psychology, 53*, 1024–1037.

Downey, G., Freitas, A. L., Michaelis, B., & Khouri, H. (1998). The self-fulfilling prophecy in close relationships: Rejection sensitivity and rejection by romantic partners. *Journal of Personality and Social Psychology, 75*, 545–560.

Elliot, A. J., & Reis, H. T. (2003). Attachment and exploration in adulthood. *Journal of Personality and Social Psychology, 85*, 317–331.

Feeney, B. C. (2004). A secure base: Responsive support of goal strivings and exploration in adult intimate relationships. *Journal of Personality and Social Psychology, 87*, 631–648.

Feeney, B. C., & Thrush, R. L. (2010). Relationship influences on exploration in adulthood: The characteristics and function of a secure base. *Journal of Personality and Social Psychology, 98*, 57–76.

Finkel, E. J., & Fitzsimons, G. M. (2011). The effects of social relationships on self-regulation. In R. F. Baumeister & K. D. Vohs (Eds.), *Handbook of self-regulation: Research, theory, and applications* (2nd ed., pp. 390–406). New York: Guilford Press.

Finkenauer, C., & Righetti, F. (2011). Understanding in close relationships: An interpersonal approach. In W. Stroebe & M. Hewstone (Eds.), *European review of social psychology* (Vol. 22, pp. 316–363). Brighton, UK: Psychology Press.

Fiske, S. T., & Taylor, S. E. (2008). *Social cognition: From brains to culture.* New York: McGraw-Hill.

Fletcher, G. J. O., & Kerr, P. S. G. (2010). Through the eyes of love: Reality and illusion in intimate relationships. *Psychological Bulletin, 136*, 627–658.

Forest, A. L., & Wood, J. V. (2012). When social networking is not working: Individuals with low self-esteem recognize but do not reap the benefits of self-disclosing on Facebook. *Psychological Science, 23*, 295–302.

Gable, S., Gonzaga, G., & Strachman, A. (2006). Will you be there for me when things go right? Supportive responses to positive event disclosures. *Journal of Personality and Social Psychology, 91*, 904–917.

Gable, S. L., Gosnell, C. L., Maisel, N. C., & Strachman, A. (2012). Safely testing the alarm: Close others' responses to personal positive events. *Journal of Personality and Social Psychology, 103*, 963–981.

Gable, S. L., & Reis, H. T. (2010). Good news! Capitalizing on positive events in an interpersonal context. In M. P. Zanna (Ed.), *Advances in experimental social psychology* (Vol. 42, pp. 195–257). San Diego, CA: Elsevier Academic Press.

Gable, S. L., Reis, H. T., & Downey, G. (2003). He said, she said: A quasi-signal detection analysis of daily interactions between close relationship partners. *Psychological Science, 14*, 100–105.

Gable, S. L., Reis, H. T., Impett, E. A., & Asher, E. R. (2004). What do you do when things go right?: The intrapersonal and interpersonal benefits of sharing positive events. *Journal of Personality and Social Psychology, 87*, 228–245.

Gleason, M. E. J., Iida, M., Shrout, P. E., & Bolger, N. (2008). Receiving support as a mixed blessing: Evidence for dual effects of support on psychological outcomes. *Journal of Personality and Social Psychology, 94*, 824–838.

Gordon, A. M., Impett, E. A., Kogan, A., Oveis, C., & Keltner, D. (2012). To have and to hold: Gratitude promotes relationship maintenance in intimate bonds. *Journal of Personality and Social Psychology, 103*(2), 257.

Grossmann, K., Grossman, K. E., Kindler, H., & Zimmermann, P. (2008). A wider view of attachment and exploration: The influence of mothers and fathers on the development of psychological security from infancy to young adulthood. In J. Cassidy & P. R. Shaver (Eds.), *Handbook of attachment* (2nd ed., pp. 857–879). New York: Guilford Press.

Hazan, C., & Shaver, P. R. (1994). Attachment as an organizational framework for research on close relationships. *Psychological Inquiry, 5*, 1–22.

Hazan, C., & Zeifman, D. (1999). Pair bonds as attachments: Evaluating the evidence. In J. Cassidy & P. R. Shaver (Eds.), *Handbook of attachment: Theory, research, and clinical applications* (pp. 336–354). New York: Guilford Press.

Holmes, J. G., & Rempel, J. K. (1989). Trust in close relationships. In C. Hendrick (Ed.), *Review of personality and social psychology: Vol. 10. Close relationships* (pp. 187–220). London: Sage.

Ickes, W., & Simpson, J. A. (1997). Managing empathic accuracy in close relationships. In W. Ickes (Ed.), *Empathic accuracy* (pp. 219–250). New York: Guilford Press.

Iida, M., Seidman, G., Shrout, P. E., Fujita, K., & Bolger, N. (2008). Modeling support provision in intimate relationships. *Journal of Personality and Social Psychology, 94,* 460–478.

Kelley, H. H. (1979). *Personal relationships: Their structures and processes.* Hillsdale, NJ: Erlbaum.

Kelley, H. H., Holmes, J. G., Kerr, N., Reis, H. T., Rusbult, C. E., & Van Lange, P. A. M. (2003). *An atlas of interpersonal situations.* Cambridge, UK: Cambridge University Press.

Kernis, M. H., & Goldman, B. M. (2006). A multicomponent conceptualization of authenticity: Research and theory. In M. P. Zanna (Ed.), *Advances in experimental social psychology* (Vol. 38, pp. 284–357). San Diego, CA: Academic Press.

Kobak, R., & Madsen, S. D. (2008). Disruptions in attachment bonds: Implications for theory, research, and clinical intervention. In J. Cassidy & P. R. Shaver (Eds.), *Handbook of attachment* (pp. 23–47). New York: Guilford Press.

Kumashiro, M., & Sedikides, C. (2005). Taking on board liability-focused information: Close positive relationships as a self-bolstering resource. *Psychological Science, 16,* 732–739.

Lackenbauer, S. D., Campbell, L., Rubin, H., Fletcher, G. J. O., & Troister, T. (2010). The unique and combined benefits of accuracy and positive bias in relationships. *Personal Relationships, 17,* 475–493.

Leary, M. R., & Baumeister, R. F. (2000). The nature and function of self-esteem: Sociometer theory. In M. P. Zanna (Ed.), *Advances in experimental social psychology* (Vol. 32, pp. 1–62). San Diego, CA: Academic Press.

Leary, M. R., & Guadagno, J. (2011). The sociometer, self-esteem, and the regulation of interpersonal behavior. In R. F. Baumeister & K. D. Vohs (Eds.), *Handbook of self-regulation: Research, theory, and applications* (2nd ed., pp. 339–354). New York: Guilford Press.

Lemay, E. P., Jr., & Clark, M. S. (2008). How the head liberates the heart: Projection of communal responsiveness guides relationship promotion. *Journal of Personality and Social Psychology, 94,* 647–671.

Lemay, E. P., Jr., Clark, M. S., & Feeney, B. C. (2007). Projection of responsiveness to needs and the construction of satisfying communal relationships. *Journal of Personality and Social Psychology, 92,* 834–853.

Maisel, N. C., & Gable, S. L. (2009). The paradox of received support: The importance of responsiveness. *Psychological Science, 20,* 928–932.

Maisel, N. C., Gable, S. L., & Strachman, A. (2008). Responsive behaviors in good times and in bad. *Personal Relationships, 15*, 317–338.

Mikulincer, M., & Shaver, P. R. (2007a). *Attachment in adulthood: Structure, dynamics, and change.* New York: Guilford Press.

Mikulincer, M., & Shaver, P. R. (2007b). Boosting attachment security to promote mental health, prosocial values, and inter-group tolerance. *Psychological Inquiry, 18*, 139–156.

Murray, S. L., & Holmes, J. G. (2011). *Interdependent minds.* New York: Guilford Press.

Murray, S. L., Holmes, J. G., & Collins, N. L. (2006). Optimizing assurance: The risk regulation system in relationships. *Psychological Bulletin, 132*, 641–666.

Murray, S. L., Holmes, J. G., & Griffin, D. (1996). The benefits of positive illusions: Idealization and the construction of satisfaction in close relationships. *Journal of Personality and Social Psychology, 70*, 79–98.

Murray, S. L., Holmes, J. G., & Griffin, D. W. (2000). Self-esteem and the quest for felt security: How perceived regard regulates attachment processes. *Journal of Personality and Social Psychology, 78*, 478–498.

Murray, S. L., Rose, P., Bellavia, G. M., Holmes, J. G., & Kusche, A. G. (2002). When rejection stings: How self-esteem constrains relationship-enhancement processes. *Journal of Personality and Social Psychology, 83*, 556–573.

Oishi, S., Koo, M., & Akimoto, S. (2008). Culture, interpersonal perceptions, and happiness in social interactions. *Personality and Social Psychology Bulletin, 34*, 307–320.

Patrick, H., Knee, C. R., Canevello, A., & Lonsbary, C. (2007). The role of need fulfillment in relationship functioning and well-being: A self-determination theory perspective. *Journal of Personality and Social Psychology, 92*, 434–457.

Pierce, T., & Lydon, J. (1998). Priming relational schemas: Effects of contextually activated and chronically accessible interpersonal expectations on responses to a stressful event. *Journal of Personality and Social Psychology, 75*, 1441–1448.

Pollmann, M. M. H., & Finkenauer, C. (2009). Investigating the role of two types of understanding in relationship well-being: Understanding is more important than knowledge. *Personality and Social Psychology Bulletin, 35*, 1512–1527.

Priem, J. S., Solomon, D. H., & Steuber, K. R. (2009). Perceptions of supportive communication in marital interactions: Accuracy, projection, and sentiment override. *Personal Relationships, 16*, 531–552.

Rafaeli, E., & Gleason, M. E. J. (2009). Skilled support within intimate relationships. *Journal of Family Theory and Review, 1*, 20–37.

Reis, H. T. (2007). Steps toward the ripening of relationship science. *Personal Relationships, 14*, 1–23.

Reis, H. T. (2012). Perceived partner responsiveness as an organizing theme for the study of relationships and well-being. In L. Campbell & T. J. Loving (Eds.), *Interdisciplinary research on close relationships* (pp. 27–52). Washington, DC: American Psychological Association.

Reis, H. T., & Clark, M. S. (2013). Responsiveness. In J. A. Simpson & L. Campbell

(Eds.), *The Oxford handbook of close relationships* (pp. 400–423). New York: Oxford University Press.

Reis, H. T., Clark, M. S., & Holmes, J. G. (2004). Perceived partner responsiveness as an organizing construct in the study of intimacy and closeness. In D. Mashek & A. Aron (Eds.), *The handbook of closeness and intimacy* (pp. 201–225). Mahwah, NJ: Erlbaum.

Reis, H. T., & Patrick, B. C. (1996). Attachment and intimacy: Component processes. In E. T. Higgins & A. W. Kruglanski (Eds.), *Social psychology: Handbook of basic principles* (pp. 523–563). New York: Guilford Press.

Reis, H. T., & Shaver, P. R. (1988). Intimacy as an interpersonal process. In S. Duck (Ed.), *Handbook of personal relationships* (pp. 367–389). Chichester, UK: Wiley.

Reis, H. T., Smith, S. M., Carmichael, C. L., Caprariello, P. A., Tsai, F. F., Rodrigues, A., et al. (2010). Are you happy for me? How sharing positive events with others provides personal and interpersonal benefits. *Journal of Personality and Social Psychology, 99,* 311–329.

Rusbult, C. E., Finkel, E. J., & Kumashiro, M. (2009). The Michelangelo phenomenon. *Current Directions in Psychological Science, 18,* 305–309.

Rusbult, C. E., Kumashiro, M., & Reis, H. T. (2009). *Responsiveness and the Michelangelo phenomenon.* Unpublished manuscript, Vrije Universiteit, Amsterdam.

Rusbult, C. E., & Van Lange, P. A. M. (1996). Interdependence processes. In E. T. Higgins & A. W. Kruglanski (Eds.), *Social psychology: Handbook of basic mechanisms and processes* (pp. 564–596). New York: Guilford Press.

Sanderson, C. A., & Evans, S. M. (2001). Seeing one's partner through intimacy-colored glasses: An examination of the processes underlying the intimacy goals-relationship satisfaction link. *Personality and Social Psychology Bulletin, 27,* 461–471.

Schlegel, R. J., Hicks, J. A., Arndt, J., & King, L. A. (2009). Thine own self: True self-concept accessibility and meaning in life. *Journal of Personality and Social Psychology, 96,* 473–490.

Sillars, A. L., & Scott, M. (1983). Interpersonal perception between intimates: An integrative review. *Human Communication Research, 10,* 153–176.

Simpson, J. A. (2007). Foundations of interpersonal trust. In E. T. Higgins & A. W. Kruglanski (Eds.), *Social psychology: Handbook of basic principles* (2nd ed., pp. 587–607). New York: Guilford Press.

Smith, S. M., & Reis, H. T. (2012). Perceived responses to capitalization attempts are influenced by self-esteem and relationship threat. *Personal Relationships, 19,* 367–385.

Stinson, D. A., Logel, C., Holmes, J. G., Wood, J. V., Forest, A. L., Gaucher, D., et al. (2010). The regulatory function of self-esteem: Testing the epistemic and acceptance signaling systems. *Journal of Personality and Social Psychology, 99,* 993–1013.

Stroebe, W., & Stroebe, M. S. (1996). The social psychology of social support. In E. T. Higgins & A. W. Kruglanski (Eds.), *Social psychology: Handbook of basic principles* (pp. 597–621). New York: Guilford Press.

Sullivan, H. S. (1953). *The interpersonal theory of psychiatry.* New York: Norton.

Swann, W. B., Jr. (1990). To be adored or to be known: The interplay of self-enhancement and self-verification. In E. T. Higgins & R. Sorrentino (Eds.), *Handbook of motivation and cognition* (Vol. 2, pp. 408–448). New York: Guilford Press.

Swann, W. B., Jr., Stein-Seroussi, A., & Giesler, R. B. (1992). Why people self-verify. *Journal of Personality and Social Psychology, 62*, 392–401.

van IJzendoorn, M. H. (1995). Adult attachment representations, parental responsiveness, and infant attachment: A meta-analysis on the predictive validity of the Adult Attachment Interview. *Psychological Bulletin, 117*, 387–403.

Van Lange, P. A. M., & Rusbult, C. E. (2012). Interdependence theory. In P.A.M. Van Lange, A. W. Kruglanski, & E.T. Higgins (Eds.), *Handbook of theories of social psychology* (Vol. 2, pp. 251–272). Thousand Oaks, CA: Sage.

Wieselquist, J., Rusbult, C. E., Foster, C. A., & Agnew, C. R. (1999). Commitment, pro-relationship behavior, and trust in close relationships. *Journal of Personality and Social Psychology, 77*, 942–966.

Williams, G. C., Rodin, G. C., Ryan, R. M., Grolnick, W. S., & Deci, E. L. (1998). Autonomous regulation and long-term medication adherence in adult outpatients. *Health Psychology, 17*, 269–276.

Chapter **11**

The Predictors and Consequences of Relationship Dissolution

Breaking Down Silos

LAUREN A. LEE
DAVID A. SBARRA

Nearly 2 million adults are newly impacted by divorce *each year* (Tejada-Vera & Sutton, 2009), and many more nonmarital relationships meet a similar fate, yet relationship science lacks a coherent framework for understanding how the predictors of a separation are associated with adults' responses to the end of their relationship. Over the last 25 years, we have assiduously erected two silos to house the science of romantic loss. The first silo contains research on the predictors of nonmarital breakups and marital separations: *What patterns of marital interaction are most predictive of divorce? Which dating couples are most likely to break up? Why?* The second silo examines the psychological and physical health correlates and consequences of relationship separations: *When relationships end, who fares well or poorly over time? What intrapersonal and interpersonal factors predict successful coping?* Of course, these silos reside in the same general neighborhood of relationship science, but there exists relatively little communication between scientists who conduct the research in each silo. Thus, in the science of romantic breakups, we lack a meaningful integration of the "predictor" and the "consequence" research.

The main goal of this chapter is to review what is known about the predictors and consequences of relationship breakups, with an eye toward fostering greater communication and breaking down the silos that contain each body of research. From the outset, we recognize that this dismantling project is incomplete; in order to cover some of the most fundamental work on these topics, it is important to focus deeply within the given silos. To the extent that we can, this chapter highlights ways to think about integrating the disparate lines of research on romantic breakups. We begin by briefly describing a theoretical framework that can be used to integrate research on both the predictor and consequence sides of a romantic breakup. We then review key findings on the predictors and consequences of romantic breakups,[1] followed by a shift in focus on research using prospective panel designs that span the transition across the end of a relationship to examine consequences of divorce after accounting for the predictors of the separation itself. Finally, we conclude by outlining future directions for a more integrated study of these topics.

GUIDING THEORY: THE SOCIAL BASELINE AND COREGULATION/ DYSREGULATION MODELS

Social baseline theory (SBT; Beckes & Coan, 2011; Coan, 2008) provides a new framework for understanding why and how some relationships succeed or fail as well as the expectable consequences of severing a romantic relationship. At its core, SBT suggests that social proximity and close relationships constitute the *baseline state* for the human brain. Beckes and Coan (2011) write, "In our view, the human brain is designed to *assume* that it is embedded within a relatively predictable social network characterized by familiarity, joint attention, shared goals, and interdependence" (p. 977). Neuroimaging data demonstrate, for example, that brain regions associated with the regulation of emotion are *less active* during social support conditions relative to control conditions (e.g., Coan, Schaefer, &

---

[1]Overall, we make little distinction between romantic breakups and divorce except where the literature indicates this distinction is important. In some instances, there is more work on one topic than another; for example, studies of romantic commitment tend to be located in the nonmarital relationships literature, whereas work on infidelity rests almost entirely in the literature on marriage.

Davidson, 2006). That is, high-quality social relationships permit the brain to address the challenges of the environment in a metabolically efficient way by sharing risk and expended physical effort across the social network (e.g., Fitzsimons & Finkel, 2011).

According to the theory, the brain operates as a "Bayesian bet-making machine" to draw inferences about the risk and load demands in the immediate environment based on one's relationship history (Beckes & Coan, 2011; Coan, 2008). When people have a history of positive social relationships, the brain "bets" that levels of social support will be available in times of need, and thus fewer personal resources are needed to deal with environmental challenges. In contrast, people without a history of positive relationships have relied more on personal resources to face life's challenges, and thus their brains "bet" that social resources are unlikely to be available when needed. This latter strategy is metabolically costly as it forces people to move away from the default, social baseline condition and expend additional resources to cope with environmental demands. This perspective provides a neuroscientific account of some of the core principles in attachment theory (Bowlby, 1969/1982; Mikulincer & Shaver, 2008), including how individual differences in working models of attachment set the stage for detecting threat in the environment and perceptions of threats to felt security within a relationship (see Bretherton, 2005).

In addition to providing a concrete operationalization of how the brain may detect and process environmental threats, the social baseline account is consistent with normative models of adult pair bonding. Sbarra and Hazan (2008) offered a coregulation–dysregulation framework for understanding the potential consequences of relationship loss in terms of the regulatory functions of an attachment relationship. Central to this model is the idea that coregulation is instantiated by a degree of physiological synchrony that helps maintain emotional well-being within intact relationships around a homeostatic set-point. When relationships dissolve, people are faced with many regulatory challenges, and, consistent with SBT, well-being hinges on one's ability to minimize the amount of resources expended to cope with the demands of the loss (Sbarra & Hazan, 2008).

Taken together, SBT and the coregulation–dysregulation framework offer some important ways to think about integrating the predictors and consequences of loss. First, it is reasonable to speculate that when relationships become metabolically costly, we should see an increased likelihood of relationship dissolution. An examination of circulating stress hormones in newlyweds found exactly this: Couples who evidenced increased epinephrine, the primary stress hormone of the sympathetic nervous system, during a conflict task were more likely to divorce over a span of 10 years

(Kiecolt-Glaser et al., 1993). Although this is one of the only studies to demonstrate that direct indicators of the biological stress response increase risk for relationship dissolution, when viewed from the perspective of SBT, these findings suggest that we can view the predictors of romantic break-ups as either (1) indicators or proxies of high effort expenditure within the relationship or (2) variables that increase the likelihood of high effort expenditure (e.g., attachment anxiety).

If effort expenditure within a relationship (or indicators of effort expenditure) increase risk for relationship dissolution, it follows that ending a stressful, conflicted, and unsatisfactory relationship should, under most circumstances, lead to increases in well-being. Recent evidence on the association between relationship quality, divorce, and emotional distress supports this conclusion. When couples in high-conflict marriages divorce, their life happiness increases, whereas adults in low-conflict marriages report decreases in life happiness following a divorce (Amato & Hohmann-Marriott, 2007). Similarly, in the bereavement literature, positive psychological adjustment to widowhood is associated with lower levels of dependence on a spouse prior to his or her death, whereas greater distress is observed among widows who reported a high degree of marital closeness prior to the loss (Carr et al., 2000). Presumably, this latter finding suggests that the loss of a high-quality relationship engenders more regulatory demands and, from an SBT perspective, is more metabolically costly. Using SBT, we can further hypothesize that the greatest risks for poor post-relationship functioning should be observed in instances that increase environmental demands (and thus the corresponding self-regulatory resource expenditures needed to deal with those challenges; see Sbarra & Hazan, 2008) or among people who have a tendency to engage in metabolically costly emotion regulatory and coping strategies (e.g., people high in attachment anxiety; see Lee, Sbarra, Mason & Law, 2011).

Overall, by combining SBT (Beckes & Coan, 2011) with elements of attachment theory (Sbarra & Hazan, 2008), we can begin thinking about the predictors and consequences of relationship breakups in new and more integrated ways. These frameworks underscore the importance of resource expenditure and self-regulatory effort (including emotion regulation) for determining both how well relationships are functioning and how burdensome it may be to end some relationships. Most research on the predictors and consequences of a romantic breakup is not organized in terms of resource savings and expenditures, but this does not preclude recasting what is known about these topics in terms of SBT principles. We should thrive when we end taxing relationships, and run the risk of suffering when we end relationships that provide some net benefit in terms of resource management.

We note that receiving benefits from a relationship does not mean that the relationship is harmonious; rather, we view resource benefit in terms of appraisal theory (Lazarus & Folkman, 1984). In this respect, the central question is whether the demands of staying in a relationship exceed the real or perceived demands of coping with the end of a relationship. This framework provides a parsimonious way of bridging the transition from an intact to a dissolved relationship. Indeed, this "new" perspective on energy savings–expenditures is reminiscent of a much older position, which was first outlined by the psychobiologist Myron Hofer (1984):

> In response to loss, several different processes may be at work having different biological mechanisms. . . . They suggest that we look carefully at the relationship *before* the loss took place and try to understand more precisely who and what has been lost, rather than beginning our investigation with the disruption of the emotional bond or tie between the two individuals, as if bereavement were simply a stress that was suddenly imposed. (p. 194)

THE PREDICTORS OF DIVORCE: WHAT DO WE KNOW?

Nearly everyone who becomes partnered envisions a happy and positive outcome for their relationship, but in many cases this fate is not realized. Among a group of people filing for a first marriage license, 0% estimated that they personally would divorce (Baker & Emery, 1993). This finding illustrates a foundational point: The transition from an optimistic beginning to teetering on the brink of divorce is a developmental process that unfolds over time (Bradbury, 1998). Gottman (1994) referred to this process as the cascade model of marital dissolution. In this section of the chapter, we detail the psychological processes within individuals, interactions between partners, and contextual demands and stressors to understand the cascade toward divorce.

Intrapersonal Predictors

Personality and Individual Differences

The traits or personality characteristics each person brings to their relationship play a pivotal role in its success. People who report low trait levels of positive emotion and high levels of negative emotion and who engage in low-constraint behaviors are more likely to experience the demise and dissolution of their marriage (Kelly & Conley, 1987), and people with greater negative emotionality and neuroticism can engage in interaction patterns that make their dating relationships vulnerable to distress (Karney & Bradbury, 1995). Even a thin-slice indicator of positive emotion—a smile captured during a yearbook photo—can be predictive of the likelihood of marriage (see Ambady, Bernieri, & Richeson, 2000) as well as marital satisfaction and divorce (Harker & Keltner, 2001; Hertenstein, Hansel, Butts, & Hile, 2009).

Longitudinal meta-analyses find that married people who are neurotic and lack both agreeableness and conscientiousness evidence a higher rate of divorce across the lifespan (Roberts, Kuncel, Shiner, Caspi, & Goldberg, 2007). Consistent with this finding, Caspi (1987) reported that tempermentally difficult children—those who displayed bursts of anger and temper tantrums—were twice as likely to divorce later in life relative to more agreeable children. At the extreme, personality disorders also play a role in marital success, with people diagnosed as paranoid, schizoid, antisocial, histrionic, avoidant, dependent, or obsessive–compulsive at greater risk for divorce in epidemiological studies (Whisman, Tolejko, & Chatav, 2007).

Romantic partners are more similar in their affectivity and emotional expression than randomly paired couples, and couples with similar personality traits both report and are judged by others as experiencing greater marital satisfaction (Luo & Klohnen, 2005). People who experience greater negative emotionality tend to enter into and persist in maladaptive relationships (Robins, Caspi, & Moffitt, 2002). Furthermore, personality is enduring and has a transactional effect on a romantic relationship, with more satisfying relationships associated with greater positive emotionality and constraint and poorer relationships with increases in negative emotionality (Robins et al., 2002).

Attachment

Hazan and Shaver (1987) were the first to contend that child–caregiver attachments as conceived of by Bowlby (1969/1982) extend to adult romantic relationships. Attachment style is now widely studied and often cited as a factor in relationship dissolution (Kirkpatrick & Hazan, 1994) and divorce (Kobak, Ruckdeschel, & Hazan, 1994). Attachment style evidences moderate stability across the lifespan and has implications for relationship satisfaction and success (Scharfe & Cole, 2006; see also our closing remarks for the current chapter). Securely attached people are more likely to remain in their romantic relationship across 4 years (Kirkpatrick & Hazan, 1994). Attachment insecurity predicts the likelihood that people remain in unhappy marriages: Newlywed couples who reported greater anxiety related to partner abandonment also reported less marital satisfaction initially and across the first 4 years of their marriage than both their happily married and divorced counterparts (Davila & Bradbury, 2001). Insecurely attached people exhibit a preoccupation with their romantic partner that results in dependence on the relationship for self-validation and a fear of abandonment. Unhappy individuals may persist in a marriage merely to avoid the distress associated with being alone. Futhermore, attachment anxiety appears to moderate the association of partner fulfillment and breakup occurrence (Slotter & Finkel, 2009). People with a high degree of attachment anxiety may feel unworthy of having their needs met and persist in an unfulfilling relationship, whereas an individual low in attachment anxiety would recognize that these needs are unmet and be more likely to terminate the relationship.

Parental Divorce

The intergenerational transmission of divorce theory hypothesizes that marital distress and risk for divorce may be transmitted across generations through both genetic and environmental mechanisms (Amato & Booth, 1996; Pryor & Rodgers, 2001; Wolfinger, 2000). Compared with dizygotic twins, monozygotic twins evidence greater concordance of divorce rates, which points to genetics as a factor in the transmission of marital separation (McGue & Lykken, 1992). A follow-up study demonstrated that between 30% (in women) and 42% (in men) of heritable divorce risk was attributable to personality differences (Jocklin, McGue, & Lykken, 1996). In contrast, other work has shown that the genetic association with controllable life events, such as divorce, is entirely explained by differences in personality (Saudino, Pedersen, Lichtenstein, McClearn, & Plomin, 1997).

Beyond static biological differences, a host of environmental factors may make children who experience the divorce of their parents vulnerable to a relationship breakup in adulthood. Amato and DeBoer (2001) found that parental divorce increased the risk of divorce among children by more than 50%. This increased risk is explained by a lack of commitment to marriage, as opposed to factors such as marital discord and poor communication skills. Other samples find that memories of parental discord, but not parental divorce per se, mediated the association of parental reports of marital distress and reports of distress given by children for their own marriages (Amato & Booth, 2001). Perhaps it is not parental divorce that is most harmful, but acquiring a working model of marriage that does not emphasize commitment through observational learning (see Bandura, 1973).

More recently, D'Onofrio et al. (2007) used a children of twins design (CoT; discussed in greater detail on page 324) to disentangle the genetic and environmental contributions to the intergenerational transmission of divorce. In a study of over 2,300 adult offspring of twins, the authors found that 66% of the variability in risk for divorce among the offspring was accounted for directly by environmental experiences, a finding consistent with a social causation explanation (i.e., divorce among adults operates through environmental processes to increase risk for subsequent divorce among adult offspring), whereas the remaining 34% of risk was due to genetic selection effects (D'Onofrio et al.). What is not yet known is precisely *how* parental divorce increases the risk for divorce in the next generation, but this finding suggests that reducing the stress and strain of marital dissolution among parents may also act to decrease the risk for subsequent divorce by children.

Premarital Cohabitation

The discovery that people who choose to cohabitate prior to marriage are more likely to divorce was surprising and garnered considerable media attention in the 1990s (DeMaris & Rao, 1992; Teachman & Polonko, 1990). It is now clear that people who choose to live together without a marital union may possess certain traits that also make them more likely to divorce (e.g., self-selection; Lillard, Brien, & Waite, 1995). People who cohabitate are also more accepting of divorce and may view marriage with less commitment (Axinn & Thorton, 1992). When analyses correct for these self-selection traits, the chances of marital dissolution are no more likely for couples who lived together prior to marriage.

Cohabitation may result in social pressure to marry because of the "inertia" associated with living together (Stanley, Rhoades & Markman, 2006). Couples are more likely to become married within a year of living together or may dissolve their relationships completely (Bumpass, Sweet & Cherlin, 1991). The reasons people provide for choosing to live together may also be telling of the cohabitation–divorce association. For instance, Rhoades, Stanley, and Markman (2009) identified "testing" of the relationship as a primary factor for both partners in heterosexual relationships, although this was more predominant in men. Testing of the relationship was strongly associated with lower confidence in and less dedication to the relationship, more negative communication and physical aggression, and greater endorsement of depression and anxiety symptoms (Rhoades et al., 2009). Overall, the association between premarital cohabitation and marital dissolution is explained by multiple forces, many of which appear to select people at risk for divorce into cohabitation.

Interpersonal Predictors

Communication Patterns and Marital Interactions

Gottman (1994) described the process by which couples move from a happy union toward dissolution as a cascading event that unfolds over time. Two patterns of interaction between spouses differentially predict the timing of divorce. The *emotionally inexpressive* pattern, characterized by conflict-avoidance behaviors, is associated with divorce later in marriage and the *emotionally volatile attack–defend* pattern, characterized by frequent arguments and makeups, is indicative of divorce earlier in marriage (Gottman & Levenson, 2002). During conflict conversations in the laboratory, levels of husband interest, husband contempt/disgust, wife interest, and wife sadness predicted divorce 4 years later. More surprising, greater wife anger, husband contempt/disgust, and more wife affection during the positive interaction correctly classified later divorce with higher accuracy (Gottman & Levenson, 1992). Couples who demonstrate an emotionally inexpressive pattern have a more difficult time rebounding from the effects of conflict, which results in a spillover effect from the conflict to positive conversations. Wife affection was also greater in these couples, which is counterintuitive. This affection may occur in response to husband contempt, representing a derogation of the wife's emotional response, which, over time, may illustrate an emotionally abusive marriage (Gottman & Levenson, 1992).

Gottman and colleagues have identified four factors, or what he calls the "four horsemen," that, when studied together, can predict a future divorce with a high degree of accuracy: criticism, contempt, defensiveness, and stonewalling (Gottman, 1994). The interaction patterns that define the four horsemen make it difficult to successfully initiate repair attempts during arguments. Repair attempts are those actions that are meant to diffuse the situation and deescalate conflict before couples become emotionally overinvolved. These attempts may or may not be verbal and are characterized by the successful interruption of negativity during an argument.

- *Horseman 1: Criticism* typically occurs in the context of discussing a relationship problem. Criticism takes a complaint about a partner's actions and exaggerates it into a personality or character flaw. Criticism is usually accompanied by a harsh startup, or an introduction to discussing the relationship problem that makes the issue more global than the specific situation at hand.

- *Horseman 2: Contempt*, the expression of disapproval and disgust for a partner, occurs verbally via sarcasm and patronizing or through body language (e.g., rolling eyes and a sneering expression). This horseman is the most predictive of eventual divorce. This interaction style arises out of general negative regard for a spouse. Contempt can also disguise itself in belligerence, which escalates negative regard by direct threatening or challenging of the spouse.

- *Horseman 3: Defensiveness* rears its ugly head when spouses attempt to protect themselves from a real or perceived attack by their spouse. While defending oneself is intended to interrupt the assault, it actually escalates conflict by refusing blame and directing negative emotion back toward the attacking spouse.

- *Horseman 4: Stonewalling* is unresponsiveness to conflict and often follows the three prior horsemen. A stonewaller responds to marital distress by behaviorally disengaging and portraying an air of uncaring. Surprisingly, according to Gottman (1999), stonewalling actually occurs because the stonewaller is so overwhelmed (flooded) by emotional arousal and shock that shutting down feels like the only safe way to escape/negate the attack. This horseman appears more frequently in men, possibly because the male cardiovascular system may be more reactive to stress than the female system (Levenson, Carstensen, & Gottman, 1994). The physical feelings associated with stress may make it virtually impossible for people to engage in productive conversation. Stonewalling is a factor in the well-known demand–withdraw interaction pattern (Christensen & Shenk, 1991), in which wives make increasing demands for husbands' attention or involvement and husbands demonstrate increasing withdrawal, which serves to increase wife demand behavior (the gender roles can be reversed in demand–withdraw, but men are the ones who typically withdraw from marital interactions).

The final sign of a deteriorating relationship, and eventual divorce, is the presence of negative attributions about a partner's behaviors. These negative views develop when spouses interpret bad behavior by their partner as a stable and unchangeable trait (Bradbury & Fincham, 1990; Karney & Bradbury, 1995). Unhappy couples are more likely to rate their relationships/partners as having more negative attributes, to hold unreasonable standards for how their relationships/partners should be, and to expect more negative outcomes for themselves and their relationship than their happy counterparts (Baucom, Epstein, Sayers, & Sher, 1989). Clouded by their relationship's current issues, the view of one's spouse becomes distorted and the optimistic outlook the couple once shared becomes enshrouded in negative expectations (Karney & Bradbury, 1995).

Commitment

A deep level of commitment to a romantic partner and relationship is the foundation of a successful union, and when fluctuations in commitment occur, satisfaction suffers and confidence in the union wanes. From an interdependence framework, greater within-person variability in feelings of satisfaction and dependence are key predictors of the survival of a new romantic relationship (Arriaga, 2001). Satisfaction is measured by balancing expectations and outcomes such that satisfaction will be high in a relationship if interactions between partners yield positive outcomes that exceed either partner's expectations (see Kelley, 1979). Dependence differs from satisfaction in that it is the degree to which a partner believes the most positive outcomes will come from interactions within the relationship as opposed to alternative partners (see Thibaut & Kelley, 1959). The success of a romantic relationship rests on interaction patterns in which people experience the most demonstrable positive outcomes that they believe cannot be replicated with alternative partners.

Using an interdependence framework, Arriaga (2001) examined newly formed romantic relationships over 10 weeks and found greater within-person variability in satisfaction leading to relationship dissolution, which was also associated with waning levels of commitment to the relationship. These fluctuations were most harmful for those people who experienced high initial and increasing levels of satisfaction, which suggests it is the stability of satisfaction and the dependence upon the relationship for positive outcomes that reinforces a pro-relationship interaction style and relationship longevity (Arriaga, 2001).

Perceptions of the partner's commitment to the relationship are just as if not more important to a romantic relationship as one's own feelings (Arriaga, Reed, Goodfriend, & Agnew, 2006). The actions of a romantic partner, especially when considered as a broad-based inference of how invested the partner is in the relationship, can tint the relationship in a less positive light (Kelley, 1979; Wieselquist, Rusbult, Foster, & Agnew, 1999). Arriaga and colleagues (2006) investigated the role of partner perceptions of commitment and found that fluctuations in perceived partner commitment predict whether a relationship will end above and beyond initial levels of commitment, initial perceptions of partner commitment, and fluctuations in reported levels of commitment, satisfaction, and partner's positive behavior.

Inequality in Emotional Experience

As discussed, matching or similarity in positive regard and emotional investment for a partner set the stage for mutuality within the relationship. A recent study examined implicit partner affect (i.e., automatic and spontaneous feelings, thoughts, and emotions about one's romantic partner) in nonmarital romantic relationships by measuring reaction time to preferential choice of letters that included their partner's initials as well as their self-reported ratings of relationship satisfaction and commitment (LeBel & Campbell, 2009). Implicit positive affect was associated with their ratings of relationship satisfaction, but not with levels of commitment. In a follow-up, implicit partner affect was found to have an indirect effect on relationship status through measures of relationship satisfaction (LeBel & Campbell, 2009). In the short term, spontaneous positive feelings for a partner have a direct association with how rewarding a relationship feels but in the long term, and perhaps more importantly, are telling about the likelihood of relationship success.

Imbalances in emotional involvement in the relationship also occur within couples. Sprecher, Schmeeckle, and Felmlee (2006) reported perceptions of inequality in emotional involvement in 76% of the couples studied, which is positively correlated with perceptions of which partner controls the relationship (Sprecher et al., 2006). Greater equality was associated with more relationship satisfaction by both partners. When men experience greater positive and less negative emotion, they report more balanced perceptions of emotional investment within their relationship, while women show more negative emotion if they reported being the more involved partner. Perceptions of greater involvement also predicted significant decreases in relationship satisfaction at follow-up for women, and this inequality further predicted dissolved and intact couples at two other follow-up occasions (Sprecher et al., 2006).

Contextual Factors and Processes

Relationships do not exist in a vacuum, and both day-to-day and chronic stressors can impact relationship quality (Amato, 2010; Amato & Hohmann-Marriott, 2007; Karney & Bradbury, 2005). In this section, we examine how factors outside the marital or romantic relationship impact relationship satisfaction, quality, and longevity.

Economic and Work Strain

Income, spousal employment, job loss, and work stress all play central roles within a marriage, and when these domains of functioning are endangered, a substantial burden is placed on the relationship (Karney & Bradbury, 2005; Lavee, McCubbin, & Olson, 1987). Financial strain is believed to affect marital relations through the family stress model (Conger & Conger, 2002), whereby financial issues alter individual well-being, which, in turn, alters martial satisfaction. Men may be more susceptible to the pressures of financial strain, but the evidence on this topic is mixed. Some findings demonstrate that men instigate more marital disputes relative to finances and are traditionally perceived as the economic provider in the marriage (Crowley, 1998), but more recent evidence shows that financial strain contributes equally to both spouses' reported emotional distress and mediates couples' disagreements and individual judgments of marital instability (Gudmunson, Beutler, Israelsen, McCoy, & Hill, 2007). Further, financial strain also decreases the resources that might help the couple better cope with other contextual stressors such as child care or unemployment (Story & Bradbury, 2004).

Strain can also occur as a result of increased hours spent outside of the home or stressful experiences at work. The negative mood spillover model (Neff & Karney, 2004) theorizes that stress experienced at the workplace carries over into individual's interactions with his or her spouse at home (Story & Repetti, 2006). Daily work-related stressors may precipitate poorer communication, increase hostility, and over time deteriorate marital quality. Alternatively, the social withdrawal model theorizes that occupational stress may cause people to withdraw from spousal interaction in the home (Story & Repetti, 2006). Turning to watching television or surfing the Internet may be an effective emotional coping strategy (for dealing with work demands), but this approach also decreases spousal communication. A formal test of these models found that wives may be more sensitive to these effects. On days when people reported greater workload, they also reported greater marital anger and withdrawal from their spouse, but only wives were able to perceive these behaviors (Story & Repetti, 2006). Negative mood mediated the associations of work strain and both marital anger and social withdrawal, but only for wives.

Transition to Parenthood

One of the most well-studied contextual factors impacting marital satisfaction is the transition to parenthood, especially for couples having their first child (Cowan & Cowan, 2000). Cowan and Cowan (1995) reported that following the birth of a first child about 15% of men and women move above the threshold for clinically significant marital distress on standard self-report assessment instruments. A meta-analysis of the studies on parenthood and marital satisfaction found that parents report lower marital satisfaction compared with nonparents, and that marital satisfaction was negatively correlated with the number of children (Twenge, Campbell, & Foster, 2003). However, the effect sizes obtained from the meta-analysis were small in magnitude and were moderated by individual differences: The effect of parenthood on marital satisfaction was stronger for younger couples and for people from higher socioeconomic groups (also see Mitnick, Heyman, & Smith Slep, 2009).

Stress

The term *stress* reflects an aversive state that is accompanied by diffuse negative affect, and it is well known that stress can encompass financial, familial, and daily (i.e., transient) issues impacting both spouses. As with work strain, spillover processes of external stressors can interfere with the marital relationship. Neff and Karney (2004) assessed 82 newlywed couples every 6 months for the first 4 years of marriage, and found that wives who experienced the highest levels of stress spillover demonstrated the greatest declines in marital satisfaction over the study. Importantly, as reported stress levels increased, wives reported a corresponding increase in perceptions of specific relationship problems, and these negative cognitions mediated the association between stress and relationship quality. Building on this research, Neff and Karney (2007) also found evidence for a dyadic crossover effect, whereby husbands reported lower satisfaction when their wives experienced higher stress. This finding demonstrates that mediating processes linking contextual variables and relationship quality must be considered in terms of moderating processes that include different effects for husbands and wives.

Bodenmann (2000) classified stress along both internal and external dimensions and posited that external stress might be more harmful to marriages because it may not be automatically identified as affecting the relationship. A formal test of this theory used an actor–partner mediation model; findings supported the idea that when either spouse reports external stressors are present, greater tension occurs within the dyad (Bodenmann, Ledermann & Bradbury, 2007). That is, transient relationship annoyances are effectively handled in times of calm but will be more salient during tumult. In terms of gender, women reported greater stress across all domains and were more susceptible to the tension relative to men. This finding suggests that women may be adept at not only providing support but also identifying external stressors as independent of the dyad (Bodenmann et al., 2007).

One specific form of external stress may come from the physical distance that separates romantic partners as a result of occupational and educational pursuits (Guldner, 1996; Guldner & Swensen, 1995). Nonmarital relationships may be vulnerable to this contextual factor, especially as physical separation relates to the transition to college (Van Horn et al., 1997). Several studies have shown that long-distance relationships are no more likely to end than close-proximity relationships (Guldner, 1996; Stafford & Reske, 1990), but those who experience the breakup of a long-distance relationship cite distance as the main cause (Van Horn et al., 1997). Long-distance relationships violate assumptions about what maintains satisfying romantic unions, and less proximity may impact feelings of closeness and intimacy (Pistole & Roberts, 2011). Further, periods of separation may require relationship maintenance behaviors to buffer the added stressor of being apart (Dindia & Emmers-Sommer, 2006; Gilbertson, Dindia, & Allen, 1998). These acts might prepare partners for physical separation, maintain contact during the separation, and reaffirm the relationship when partners are reunited (Pistole, Roberts, & Chapman, 2010).

Infidelity

Commitment plays a central role within a marriage, and when the foundation of commitment is shaken by infidelity, many marriages dissolve (Amato & Previti, 2003; Amato & Rogers, 1997). Although extramarital affairs are rare, they are still cited as the one of most common issues addressed in marital therapy (Whisman, Dixon, & Johnson, 1997). Does infidelity increase the likelihood of divorce, or is it merely an indicator of a failing marriage? To understand this question, Previti and Amato (2003) examined marital happiness and divorce proneness (factors indicative of marital instability and thoughts of divorce) as predictors of infidelity and marital dissolution 17 years later. Marital happiness was negatively correlated with extramarital affairs but did not predict infidelity in a path model, although divorce proneness did predict an affair. The association of marital unhappiness and infidelity appears to be mediated by marital instability (Previti & Amato, 2003). A conceptual replication of this effect found that extramarital affairs were no more likely in high-conflict marriages than low-conflict marriages (Amato & Hohmann-Marriott, 2007). Infidelity increased divorce proneness by .74 and decreased marital happiness by .67 of 1 standard deviation (Previti & Amato, 2003). Proportional hazard analysis also indicated that extramarital affairs double the likelihood of divorce. Taken together, these findings suggest not only that infidelity is an indicator of a declining marriage, but that the event can be predicted by factors indicative of marital instability and thoughts of divorce (Previti & Amato, 2003).

THE CORRELATES/CONSEQUENCES OF ROMANTIC BREAKUPS: WHAT DO WE KNOW?

Although nonmarital breakups and divorce increase risk for a variety of poor outcomes, most people fare well over time following a romantic separation (Mancini, Bonanno, & Clark, 2011), consistent with a general human tendency toward resilience in the face of stressful events (Bonanno, 2004).[2] In this section we review what is known about the correlates and putative consequences of romantic separation.

Mental Health

Romantic breakups in young adulthood are associated with the development of mood disorders as well as increased rates of suicide and substance abuse (Asarnow et al., 2008, Monroe, Rohde, Seeley, & Lewinsohn, 1999; Overbeek, Vollebergh, Engels, & Meeus, 2003; Vajda & Steinbeck, 2000). One large epidemiological study suggests that breakups may increase vulnerability but not cause the onset of a major depressive episode (Monroe et al., 1999). Using a diathesis–stress model, Fordwood, Arsanow, Huizar, and Reise (2007) found that young adults who attempted suicide reported a greater number of stressful life events in the preceding 6 months. The breakup of a romantic relationship evidenced a trend toward significance (p = .08). After controlling for all other stressful events and predisposing pathology, depression severity moderated the association of experiencing a romantic breakup and a later suicide attempt in those with the lowest depression severity (Fordwood et al., 2007).

A great deal of correlational evidence suggests that divorce increases the risk of poor mental health outcomes. For example, using data from the U.S. National Comorbidity Study, Afifi, Cox, and Enns (2006) found that separated or divorced mothers evidenced significantly higher rates of clinically significant major depression and generalized anxiety disorders after

---

[2]A discussion of the consequences of divorce on children is outside the scope of this chapter (but see Amato, 2010, for a review).

controlling for demographic and family variables (also see Aseltine & Kessler, 1993; Bruce & Kim, 1992; Wade & Prevalin, 2004). Other research demonstrates that life satisfaction drops precipitously in the years prior to a divorce and, on average, does not recover to predivorce levels up to 6 years after the divorce (Lucas, 2005). Divorce is also associated with increased rates of psychological distress after accounting for levels of predivorce distress (Johnson & Wu, 2002; Mastekaasa, 1994).

An essential question for this line of research is whether the mental health issues correlated with divorce predate the separation or whether these outcomes constitute a causal consequence of the stress associated with the end of a marriage. Co-twin control designs are especially suited to answer this question because monozygotic (MZ) twins are genetically identical, and when sets of twins who are discordant for divorce (or any life event) are studied, the observed differences in mental health outcomes between twins are presumed to be causal in nature. Osler, McGue, Lund, and Christensen (2008) found significantly higher rates of depression among both male and female MZ twins who experienced divorce or widowhood, suggesting that the end of marriage exerts a causal effect of mood symptom severity (independent of the way mood symptoms may predict the end of marriage). Findings from this study should be interpreted with caution, however, as the process of recovering from widowhood and divorce are assumed to likely be quite different.

Self-Identity Disruptions

An emerging area in the study of separation adjustment is how people reorganize their self-concepts following a breakup. It is well known that romantic relationships provide an important opportunity for self-expansion by exposing us to our partner's knowledge, interests, and resources (Aron, Mashek, & Aron, 2004). Our self-concept becomes defined, in part, by who we are with our partner and in the context of the relationship. This process is often referred to as "including the other in the self" (Aron & Aron, 1997; Aron, Aron, & Norman, 2001).

When love relationships end, people must reorganize their sense of self. Specifically, recent evidence confirms that whereas forming a new relationship is associated with self-expansion, it is posited that terminating a relationship may lead to self-contraction (Lewandowski, Aron, Bassis, & Kunak, 2006). Following a breakup, relationship elements that promote cognitive interdependence, such as greater commitment, cause people both to exhibit greater disruptions in their self-concept and to identify less concrete aspects of their self-concept and ultimately to fare worse (Slotter,

Gardner, & Finkel, 2010). Changes in psychological well-being following divorce result from changes in self-concept clarity (and not the other way around), suggesting that how people think about their self-concept and how certain they are about their self-concept may play a leading role in adjustment to a relationship loss (Mason, Law, Bryan, Portley, & Sbarra, 2011). Consistent with these findings, other research indicates that terminating a low-quality, low-expansion romantic relationship may function to promote identification of "lost" components of the self-concept; in this situation, the breakup precipitates post-relationship growth through self rediscovery (Lewandowski & Bizzoco, 2007).

Mental Health: Mechanisms of Action

One surprising fact about the association between divorce and psychological distress is that almost no studies focus on the mechanisms, or psychological processes, that connect the end of marriage with subsequent emotional distress; mechanistic research of this nature is almost absent in the literature. This lack of empirical research on mechanisms is surprising, given observations that divorce can induce shame, longing, loneliness, humiliation, rumination, identity disruptions, and prolonged anger or grief (Emery, 1994; Weiss, 1975). Presumably, it is these emotional experiences that give rise to, or at least covary with, more severe forms of psychopathology.

Using a dyadic model of child custody disputes, Sbarra and Emery (2008) showed that fathers who reported the greatest levels of conflict were previously married to mothers who reported the greatest acceptance of the separation. Prolonged coparenting conflict following divorce may operate as an attempt to promote a reunion with an ex-partner who is no longer invested in the relationship. In a prospective analysis over 12 years, Sbarra and Emery (2005) also reported that mothers who continued to show regrets about the separation experience (i.e., low levels of acceptance) also reported the highest rates of depression immediately following custody mediation. A potentially adverse effect of helping parents cooperatively renegotiate their separation relationship may be to prolong feelings of grief. Although these studies provide some insight, we still have a great deal to learn about both the mechanisms of recovery (i.e., variables associated with changes in psychological adjustment) and the variables that explain the association between marital status and mental health outcomes.

One inconsistent finding within the divorce and dissolution literature is whether being the person who initiates the end of the relationship alters the course of emotional recovery. Some studies of divorce have found that the emotional trajectories of initiators and noninitiators are similar but vary in timing, with initiators experiencing distress soon after the separation (Buehler, 1987) and entering into subsequent unions more quickly (Sweeney, 2002). Others have found that this relationship is moderated by the number of members in the initiator's social network (Kincaid & Caldwell, 1991). Still other studies found no relationship between initiator status and adjustment to divorce (Sweeney & Horwitz, 2001). For nonmarital romantic breakups, partners are generally in agreement about who was the initiator, although not about wanting the relationship to end or their emotional reactions to the breakup itself (Sprecher, 1994).

Gender Differences

Women, who most frequently initiate divorce (Kincaid & Caldwell, 1995), experience the greatest rates of distress prior to the separation, whereas men report increased distress after the union dissolves (Jacobson, 1977). This observation is bolstered by evidence that women are more adept at assessing and responding to the "emotional pulse" of the marriage (Amato & Rogers, 1997). Women also are more likely to receive custody of children, and, as such, men's distress may follow from changes in family structure and lack of access to their children following the separation (Myers, 1989; Riessman, 1990). Men also may lack an awareness of their emotional dependence on their wives; when the relationship ends, these difficulties may emerge for men because their spouses serve a primary emotion regulatory role (Baum, 2003; Sbarra & Hazan, 2008). The behaviors associated with mourning and grief are also exhibited differently: Women, on average, report more affective responses, and men become more active and self-medicating with substances (Mandell, 1995; Umberson & Williams, 1993) or engage in more sexual relations with new partners (McKenry & Price, 1991). These action-based coping behaviors may occur because of lack of recognition from others (i.e., friends) about the impact of the divorce (Murray, 2001) or constraints associated with male emotional expression. As such, men may feel compelled to alleviate distress in more gender-acceptable ways (Baum, 2003).

Economic strain also differentially affects women and men postdivorce, and research is almost exclusively focused on women (for an exception, see Braver, 1999). Findings are consistent that divorce is associated with anywhere from a 23–40% decrease in financial resources for women in the first year postdivorce (Bianchi, Subaiya, & Khan, 1999; Galarneau & Sturroch, 1997). Results are mixed as to when and if financial strain alleviates; studies find that income generally corrects within 5 years (Galarneau & Sturroch), whereas other research identifies a lifetime trajectory of poverty and hardship (McDonald & Robb, 2004). Recent research also indicates that wives' perceptions of the financial impact associated with divorce mediate the association between their marital satisfaction and the decision to divorce (Dew, 2008), suggesting that the perception of having a less comfortable lifestyle postdivorce may actually prevent the divorce from occurring. While separating from a spouse may lessen relationship distress, the increased likelihood of financial impairment creates a new type of strain. As such, some women may be more motivated to find another partner or to remarry rather than to enter the workforce or increase labor in order to regain financial stability (Jansen, Mortelmans, & Snoeckx, 2008).

Contact with Ex-Partners

Research examining contact between former romantic partners is limited, focusing primarily on post-relationship friendships, and says little about the potential emotional consequences of maintaining contact with one's ex-partner. In the few studies that have addressed this topic, contact with former partners slows the decrease in feelings of love (for one's ex-partner) and sadness (Sbarra, 2006; Sbarra & Emery, 2005) and increases the likelihood of engaging in on-again/off-again relationships (see following section; Dailey, Pfiester, Jin, Beck, & Clark, 2009; Dailey, Rossetto, Pfiester, & Surra, 2009). Much remains to be understood about the mechanisms through which contact causes distress, and two important substantive questions remain to be answered. First, what is the direction of the association between contact and emotional recovery: Does contact lead to distress, or do feelings of sadness (or other forms of psychological distress) drive contact-seeking behavior? Second, what forms of contact are associated with the greatest levels of emotional distress? Is resulting emotional distress affected by the type of contact (i.e., written vs. in-person), valence (positive or negative), presence of sexual intimacy, or duration of contact? If the contact is reciprocal (e.g., having coffee together), is this associated with the same level of distress as nonreciprocal contact (e.g., writing an e-mail and receiving no response)? Future research would benefit from examining these potential associations and including more modern forms of social networking contact (Rhoades, Kamp Dush, Atkins, Stanley, & Markman, 2011).

On-Again/Off-Again

Post-relationship contact research assumes that people are not reestablishing their relationship when contact occurs, and the work of Dailey and colleagues (Dailey, Pfiester, et al., 2009; Dailey, Rossetto, et al., 2009) has started to explore the correlates of on-again/off-again relationships. From a qualitative perspective, partners who eventually rekindle their relationships report similar reasons for the initial dissolution as those who remain uncoupled: conflict, characteristics about the partner or the self, and more attractive alternatives (Dailey, Rossetto, et al., 2009). Among the reasons listed for rekindling the relationship were increased communication skills, renewed effort (e.g., increased time spent together), and intimacy (Dailey, Rossetto, et al.). Contact with an ex-partner was also reported to play a role in returning to the union, with people reporting pursuing postdissolution friendships. In this context, contact may be serving to keep ex-partners attached to each other and prevent them from pursuing alternative novel partners (Dailey, Rossetto, et al.). Follow-up work shows that people in an on–off relationship reported less positive characteristics during the initial phase of their relationship as well as in their current rekindled relationship (Dailey, Pfiester, et al., 2009). Surprisingly, even after rekindling, people also reported less feelings of validation from their partners, relationship satisfaction, and feelings of love for their partner (Dailey, Pfiester, et al.).

Physical Health

Research on the physical health outcomes following divorce is less well developed than the literature on mental health outcomes but is growing rapidly (Sbarra, Law, & Portley, 2011). Given space limitations, we discuss the broad population-level effects, the role of psychological stress on health outcomes, and the mechanisms that potentially explain these effects, but we point the reader to other sources for the most current information on the study of marital status and health.

One of the most consistently replicated effects in the social relationships and health literature is the epidemiological finding that marital status is associated with risk for early death. A recent meta-analysis of 32 prospective studies (involving more than 6.5 million people, 160,000 deaths, and 755,000 divorces in 11 different countries) revealed that, compared with their married counterparts, separated/divorced adults evidenced a significant increase in risk for early death, controlling for age as well as a variety of sociodemographic, health, and health behavior covariates (Sbarra et al., 2011). The effect size estimate is consistent with the magnitude of association observed in other large-scale studies, and divorced men appear to have the highest death rates among unmarried adults (for a review of evidence from 16 developed countries, see Hu & Goldman, 1990).

A more specific literature also focuses on suicide. In a 10-year prospective epidemiological study of mortality risk in 471,922 noninstitutionalized adults living in the United States, Kopsowa (2000) found that men who were separated or divorced at the start of the study were 2.28 times more likely to commit suicide during the follow-up period than their married counterparts, whereas no significant association was found between marital status and suicide for women. In a follow-up analysis, Kopsowa (2003) reported that divorced men were more than nine times as likely to commit suicide as divorced women.

What do we know about the mechanisms linking the end of marriage and risk for poor health outcomes? First, social selection explains some of the physical health outcomes observed following divorce; that is, the variables that increase risk for divorce also appear to increase risk for poor health. Earlier in the chapter we described work by Osler and colleagues (2008), who used a CoT control design to investigate rates of health outcomes between twins who were discordant for widowhood or divorce. The results indicated that depression and greater rates of smoking may follow from the ending of a marriage, but that differences in many other health outcomes (e.g., self-rated health, alcohol use, body mass index) may be due to underlying genetic explanations and not the stress of a relationship transition. In addition, the association between divorce and physical health may be explained by a third variable that both increases the risk for divorce and increases the risk for poor health, such as hostility and neuroticism, but the evidence for this hypothesis is relatively scant. Using data from the Terman Life Cycle study, Tucker, Friedman, Wingard, and Schwartz (1996) reported that the risk associated with having ever experienced a divorce and early mortality could be reduced (by 21% for men and 15% for women) after accounting for childhood conscientiousness and a history of parental divorce.

Beyond social selection processes, separation and divorce can instantiate changes in social resources, health behaviors, and psychological stress that have long-term implications for physical health (for a description of each process, see Sbarra et al., 2011). Only a handful of studies have examined the association between psychological responses to marital separation/divorce and biomarkers that have health implications. The work in this area began in the 1980s with a series of now-seminal studies by Kiecolt-Glaser and colleagues (Kiecolt-Glaser, 1987; Kiecolt-Glaser, Kennedy, Malkoff, & Fisher, 1988). More recently, Sbarra, Law, Lee, and Mason (2009) found that participants who reported greater divorce-related emotional intrusion (e.g., dreaming about the separation, experiencing waves of sudden emotion about the separation) evidenced significantly higher levels of resting systolic and diastolic blood pressure (BP). In addition, during a task in which participants mentally reflected on their separation experience, men who reported that the task required a great deal of emotion regulatory effort (i.e., feeling upset combined with a need to exert control of one's emotions in order to prevent a worsening of distress) evidenced the largest increases in BP, and these effects were in addition to those observed for baseline functioning.

A follow-up to this study also found that the way individuals speak about their marriage and divorce moderates the association of attachment anxiety and BP (Lee et al., 2011). Speaking in a more present-oriented and involved manner, a behavioral measure of a hyperactivating coping strategy, was associated with the highest BP in anxiously attached people who were about to engage in a relationship reflection task (Lee et al., 2011). These findings were interpreted within the capability model of physiological responding (Coan, Allen, & McKnight, 2006); responses to emotionally salient stimuli are the result of the interaction between an individual trait and the evoked emotional state, such that trait-level propensities are best evoked using state manipulations designed to assess the emotional system in question.

In summary, marital separation and divorce are associated with a statistically reliable increase in the probability of early death, yet we still know little about the mechanisms that explain this association. Only a few studies have examined emotional response to divorce and associations with biomarkers that have distinct implications for endpoint health outcomes. Despite the nascent nature of this work, divorce-related subjective emotional experiences are consistently associated with heightened biological stress responses. Future research is needed to see if these emotional responses predict clinically meaningful health outcomes over the long term.

SOCIAL SELECTION AND CAUSATION: THE TRANSITION FROM INTACT TO DISSOLVED RELATIONSHIPS

We began the chapter by noting that very few *psychological* studies span the transition from intact to dissolved relationships. However, a handful of *sociological* studies address this gap in the literature (see Amato, 2010). Most of the work in this area is focused on understanding whether the association between romantic separations and health outcomes are due to social selection or social causation. Social selection process may operate in two primary ways: (1) Mental health problems and psychopathology increase risk for both divorce (e.g., Chatav & Whisman, 2007; Kessler, Walters, & Forthofer, 1998) and poor health outcomes and/or (2) the outcomes of divorce are better explained by marital processes (e.g., large decreases in marital quality) that predate the separation (e.g., Overbeek et al., 2006). Evidence from these large, prospective panel studies provides an excellent illustration of the knowledge to be gained from study designs that span the transition from intact to dissolved relationships. For example, Overbeek and colleagues (2006) found that the association between (1) diagnosed dysthymic disorder based on the *Diagnostic and Statistical Manual of Mental Disorders* (third edition, revised; American Psychiatric Association, 1987) and (2) divorce was entirely eliminated when accounting for marital discord preceding the divorce (a selection effect), whereas the association between divorce and substance abuse problems was not accounted for by marital quality, providing evidence for a causation effect.

Consistent with these findings, Mastekaasa (1994) demonstrated that the effects of psychological well-being on the future likelihood of divorce decrease with time (since the measurement of well-being) but do not go to zero; this observation indicates the presence of both short- and long-term selection, with the former presumably representing distress associated with the end of marriage. In a conceptual replication of this short-term selection effect, Blekesaune (2008) demonstrated that levels of distress decrease prior to divorce but also abate at the same rate postdissolution. Other studies that control for social selection have found the putatively causal effects of divorce to linger over a longer period of time (Johnson & Wu, 2002; Mastekaasa, 1994). Cheung (1998) examined the social class, education, health, and mental health predictors of divorce 10 years later; the significant predictors of divorce were then entered into models examining physical and mental health differences between the divorced and nondivorced. The predictors of divorce eliminated small differences between married and divorced men, but not differences between married and divorced women (Cheung, 1998).

Overall, this literature indicates that while the predictors of romantic separations explain some of the observed correlates/consequences of these separations, they cannot account for the entirety of the association between the experience of marital separation/divorce and increased risk for poor outcomes. Furthermore, because these studies are largely conducted within a sociological framework and tend to include relatively crude predictor and outcome measures, they do not provide information about the continuities and discontinuities of well-being or distress over time. For this, we need psychological research studies to address the transition from intact to dissolved relationships. This review of panel study designs also underscores the fact that the predictors and consequences of a breakup might not be as distinct as current research suggests. One of the best empirical examples of this idea comes from Lucas (2005), who investigated changes in life satisfaction in the years prior to and following divorce. The key finding from this study is that life satisfaction following a divorce is merely a continuation of life satisfaction leading up to the divorce.

FUTURE DIRECTIONS: MORE BRIDGES, FEWER SILOS

The experience of a divorce or relationship breakup does not sentence one to exclusively poor outcomes; a considerable amount of evidence now indicates that even intense emotional reactions can give way to increased well-being and improved future relationships (Amato & Hohmann-Marriott, 2007; Lewandowski & Bizzoco, 2007; Mancini et al., 2011; Tashiro & Frazier, 2003). Precisely how people become resilient in the face of a breakup remains to be discovered, and doing so is an important next step in the research on divorce and relationship breakups. Can we learn more about resilience (the experience of relatively few problems after a breakup), recovery (the experience of moderate to severe problems that abate relatively quickly and steadily over time), and the psychosocial mechanisms that underpin resilience and recovery by building better bridges between studies of the predictors and the consequences of romantic separations?

Not only is it possible to build a better science of romantic loss by breaking down the predictor and consequence silos, but we believe it is imperative to do so. The science of romantic loss needs theory-driven research that studies distressed couples *before* they actually separate. Blending more traditional studies of relationship functioning (e.g., including standardized interaction tasks in the laboratory) with innovative neuroimaging paradigms derived from social baseline theory (e.g., see Coan et al., 2006) would provide insight into the neurophysiogical correlates of relationship distress. In such a "high-risk" sample, it is reasonable to assume that a large percentage of couples will break up over time, and follow-up studies could then map the neurophysiological correlates of relationship dissolution in any participants who have ended their relationship.

Using this approach, we can successfully follow people across the relationship transition using more complete measurement designs. A very important bridge can be created if we conduct more complete and psychologically informed measurements with small samples.

One of the major problems maintaining the silos is that research on the predictors of divorce tends to be very dyadic, whereas, with just a few exceptions (see Sbarra & Emery, 2005), research on the consequences of romantic separation focuses exclusively on intrapersonal processes. Studies that span the transition from intact to dissolved relationships have the potential to be entirely dyadic, both in terms of what we know about the prediction of a separation and the pre- and post-relationship dyadic processes that are associated with better or worse coping following the separation.

Finally, because most marital dissolution studies do not span the separation transition, the field knows much more about the correlates of divorce than about the psychological processes associated with recovering from the end of marriage. Said differently, the field should be studying *marital separation* (i.e., the end of a relationship defined by the people who were in that relationship) instead of divorce (i.e., the formal termination of a legal contract that may occur months or even years after couples' physical separation). Researchers would have the best potential to capture and study how people grieve the end of relationships and the moderators of good or poor outcomes in a recently separated sample. The research design we proposed in this chapter would be an ideal means of staying close enough to participants to capture their lived experiences as they transition out of their relationships. If the field can begin to view this transition period and study the correlates/consequences of romantic breakups as a function of the processes that predicted the end of the relationship, it is only a matter of time before we have more bridges and fewer silos in the study of romantic breakups.

ACKNOWLEDGMENTS

Work on this chapter was supported in part by an F31 National Research Service Award fellowship to Lauren A. Lee (No. HD059396) and an award from National Science Foundation (Division of Behavioral and Cognitive Sciences No. 0919525) to David A. Sbarra.

REFERENCES

Afifi, T. O., Cox, B. J., & Enns, M. W. (2006). Mental health profiles among married, never-married, and separated/divorced mothers in a nationally representative sample. *Social Psychiatry and Psychiatric Epidemiology, 41*(2), 122–129.

Amato, P. R. (2010). Research on divorce: Continuing trends and new developments. *Journal of Marriage and Family, 72*(3), 650–666.

Amato, P. R., & Booth, A. (1996). A prospective study of divorce and parent-child relationships. *Journal of Marriage and the Family, 58*(2), 356–365.

Amato, P. R., & Booth, A. (2001). The legacy of parents' marital discord: Consequences for children's marital quality. *Journal of Personality and Social Psychology, 81*(4), 627–638.

Amato, P. R., & DeBoer, D. D. (2001). The transmission of marital instability across generations: Relationship skills or commitment to marriage? *Journal of Marriage and the Family, 63*(4), 1038–1051.

Amato, P. R., & Hohmann-Marriott, B. (2007). A comparison of high- and low-distress marriages that end in divorce. *Journal of Marriage and Family, 69*(3), 621–638.

Amato, P. R., & Previti, D. (2003). People's reasons for divorcing: Gender, social class, the life course, and adjustment. *Journal of Family Issues, 24*(5), 602–626.

Amato, P. R., & Rogers, S. J. (1997). A longitudinal study of marital problems and subsequent divorce. *Journal of Marriage and the Family, 59*(3), 612–624.

Ambady, N., Bernieri, F. J., & Richeson, J. A. (2000). Toward a histology of social behavior: Judgmental accuracy from thin slices of the behavioral stream. In M. P. Zanna & M. P. Zanna (Eds.), *Advances in experimental social psychology* (Vol. 32, pp. 201–271). San Diego, CA: Academic Press.

American Psychiatric Association. (1987). *Diagnostic and statistical manual of mental disorders* (3rd ed., rev.). Washington, D. C.: Author.

Aron, A., & Aron, E. N. (1997). Self-expansion motivating and including other in the self. In W. Ickes (Section Ed.) & S. Duck (Ed.), *Handbook of personal relationships: Theory, research and interventions* (2nd ed., Vol. 1, pp. 251–270). London: Wiley.

Aron, A., Aron, E. N., & Norman, C. (2001). Self-expansion model of motivation and cognition in close relationships and beyond. In M. Clark & G. Fletcher (Eds.), *Blackwell handbook of social psychology: Interpersonal processes* (pp. 478–501). Oxford, UK: Blackwell.

Aron, A., Mashek, D., & Aron, E. N. (2004). Closeness as including other in the self. In D. Mashek & A. Aron (Eds.), *Handbook of closeness and intimacy* (pp. 27–41). Mahwah, NJ: Erlbaum.

Arriaga, X. B. (2001). The ups and downs of dating: Fluctuations in satisfaction in newly formed romantic relationships. *Journal of Personality and Social Psychology, 80*(5), 754–765.

Arriaga, X. B., Reed, J. T., Goodfriend, W., & Agnew, C. R. (2006). Relationship perceptions and persistence: Do fluctuations in perceived partner commitment undermine dating relationships? *Journal of Personality and Social Psychology, 91*(6), 1045–1065.

Asarnow, J. R., Baraff, L. J., Berk, M., Grob, C., Devich-Navarro, M., Suddath, R., et al. (2008). Pediatric emergency department suicidal patients: Two-site evaluation of suicide ideators, single attempters, and repeat attempters. *Journal of the American Academy of Child & Adolescent Psychiatry, 47*(8), 958–966.

Aseltine, R. H., & Kessler, R. C. (1993). Marital disruption and depression in a community sample. *Journal of Health and Social Behavior, 34*(3), 237–251.

Axinn, W. G., & Thorton, A. (1992). The relationship between cohabitation and divorce: Selectivity or causal influence? *Demography, 29*, 357–374.

Baker, L. A., & Emery, R. E. (1993). When every relationship is above average: Perceptions and expectations of divorce at the time of marriage. *Law and Human Behavior, 17*(4), 439–450.

Bandura, A. (1973). *Aggression: A social learning analysis.* Oxford, UK: Prentice Hall.

Baucom, D. H., Epstein, N., Sayers, S. L., & Sher, T. G. (1989). The role of cognitions in marital relationships: Definitional, methodological, and conceptual issues. *Journal of Consulting and Clinical Psychology, 57*(1), 31–38.

Baum, N. (2003). The male way of mourning divorce: When, what, and how. *Clinical Social Work Journal, 31*(1), 37–50.

Beckes, L., & Coan, J. A. (2011). Social baseline theory: The role of social proximity in emotion and economy of action. *Social and Personality Psychology Compass, 5*, 976–988.

Bianchi, S. M., Subaiya, L. L., Khan, J. R. (1999). The gender gap in the economic well-being of nonresident fathers and custodial mothers. *Demography, 36*, 195–203.

Blekesaune, M. (2008). Partnership transitions and mental distress: Investigating temporal order. *Journal of Marriage and Family, 70*(4), 879–890.

Bodenmann, G. (2000). *Stress und coping bei Paaren.* [Stress and coping in couples]. Göttingen, Germany: Hogrefe.

Bodenmann, G., Ledermann, T., & Bradbury, T. N. (2007). Stress, sex, and satisfaction in marriage. *Personal Relationships, 14*(4), 551–569.

Bonanno, G. A. (2004). Loss, trauma, and human resilience: Have we underestimated the human capacity to thrive after extremely aversive events? *American Psychologist, 59*(1), 20–28.

Bowlby, J. (1982). *Attachment and loss: Vol 1: Attachment* (2nd ed.). New York: Basic Books. (Original work published 1969)

Bradbury, T. N. (1998). Introduction: The developmental course of marital dysfunction. In Bradbury T. N. (Ed.), *The developmental course of marital dysfunction* (pp. 1–10). Cambridge, UK: Cambridge University Press.

Bradbury, T. N., & Fincham, F. D. (1990). Attributions in marriage: Review and critique. *Psychological Bulletin, 107*(1), 3–33.

Braver, S. L. (1999). The gender gap in standard of living after divorce: Vanishingly small? *Family Law Quarterly, 33*, 111.

Bretherton, I. (2005). In pursuit of the internal working model construct and its relevance to attachment relationships. In K. E. Grossmann, K. Grossmann, & E. Waters (Eds.), *Attachment from infancy to adulthood: The major longitudinal studies.* (pp. 13–47). New York: Guilford Press.

Bruce, M. L., & Kim, K. M. (1992). Differences in the effects of divorce on major depression in men and women. *American Journal of Psychiatry, 149*(7), 914–917.

Buehler, C. (1987). Initiator status and the divorce transition. *Family Relations, 36*(1), 82–86.

Bumpass, L. L., Sweet, J. A., Cherlin, A. J. (1991). The role of cohabitation in declining rates of marriage. *Journal of Marriage and the Family, 53*, 913–927.

Carr, D., House, J. S., Kessler, R. C., Nesse, R. M., Sonnega, J., & Wortman, C. (2000). Marital quality and psychological adjustment to widowhood among older adults: A longitudinal analysis. *Journals of Gerontology: Series B. Psychological Sciences and Social Sciences, 55B*(4), S197–S207.

Caspi, A. (1987). Personality in the life course. *Journal of Personality and Social Psychology, 53*(6), 1203–1213.

Chatav, Y., & Whisman, M. A. (2007). Marital dissolution and psychiatric disorders: An investigation of risk factors. *Journal of Divorce and Remarriage, 47*(1–2), 1–13.

Cheung, Y. B. (1998). Can marital selection explain the differences in health between married and divorced people? From a longitudinal study of a British birth cohort. *Public Health, 112*, 113–117.

Christensen, A., & Shenk, J. L. (1991). Communication, conflict, and psychological distance in nondistressed, clinic, and divorcing couples. *Journal of Consulting and Clinical Psychology, 59*(3), 458–463.

Coan, J. A. (2008). Toward a neuroscience of attachment. In J. Cassidy & P. R. Shaver (Eds.), *Handbook of attachment: Theory, research, and clinical applications* (2nd ed., pp. 241–265). New York: Guilford Press.

Coan, J. A., Allen, J. J. B., & McKnight, P. E. (2006). A capability model of individual differences in frontal EEG asymmetry. *Biological Psychology, 72*(2), 198–207.

Coan, J. A., Schaefer, H. S., & Davidson, R. J. (2006). Lending a hand: Social regulation of the neural response to threat. *Psychological Science, 17*(12), 1032–1039.

Conger, R. D., & Conger, K. J. (2002). Resilience in midwestern families: Selected findings from the first decade of a prospective, longitudinal study. *Journal of Marriage and Family, 64*(2), 361–373.

Cowan, C. P., & Cowan, P. A. (1995). Interventions to ease the transition to parenthood: Why they are needed and what they can do. *Family Relations, 44*(4), 412–423.

Cowan, C. P., & Cowan, P. A. (2000). *When partners become parents: The big life change for couples.* Mahwah, NJ: Erlbaum.

Crowley, M. S. (1998). Men's self-perceived adequacy as the family breadwinner: Implications for their psychological, marital and work-family well-being. *Journal of Family and Economic Issues, 19*(1), 7–23.

Dailey, R. M., Pfiester, A., Jin, B., Beck, G., & Clark, G. (2009). On-again/off-again dating relationships: How are they different from other dating relationships? *Personal Relationships, 16*(1), 23–47.

Dailey, R. M., Rossetto, K. R., Pfiester, A., & Surra, C. A. (2009). A qualitative analysis of on-again/off-again romantic relationships: "It's up and down, all around." *Journal of Social and Personal Relationships, 26*(4), 443–466.

Davila, J., & Bradbury, T. N. (2001). Attachment insecurity and the distinction between unhappy spouses who do and do not divorce. *Journal of Family Psychology, 15*(3), 371–393.

DeMaris, A., & Rao, V. (1992). Premarital cohabitation and subsequent marital stability in the United States: A reassessment. *Journal of Marriage and the Family, 54*(1), 178–190.

Dew, J. (2008). Debt change and marital satisfaction change in recently married couples. *Family Relations, 57*(1), 60–71.

Dindia, K., & Emmers-Sommer, T. (2006). What partners do to maintain their close relationships. In P. Noller & J. A. Feeney (Eds.), *Close relationships: Functions, forms and processes* (pp. 305–324). Hove, UK: Psychology Press.

D'Onofrio, B., Turkheimer, E., Emery, R., Maes, H., Silberg, J., & Eaves, L. (2007). A children of twins study of parental divorce and offspring psychopathology. *Journal of Child Psychology and Psychiatry, 48*, 667–675.

Emery, R. E. (1994). *Renegotiating family relationships: Divorce, child custody, and mediation.* New York: Guilford Press.

Fitzsimons, G. M., & Finkel, E. J. (2011). Outsourcing self-regulation. *Psychological Science, 22*(3), 369–375.

Fordwood, S. R., Asarnow, J. R., Huizar, D. P., & Reise, S. P. (2007). Suicide attempts among depressed adolescents in primary care. *Journal of Clinical Child and Adolescent Psychology, 36*(3), 392–404.

Galarneau, D., & Sturroch, J. (1997). Family income after separation. *Perspectives on Labour and Income, 9,* 18–28.

Gilbertson, J., Dindia, K., & Allen, M. (1998). Relational continuity constructional units and the maintenance of relationships. *Journal of Social and Personal Relationships, 15*(6), 774–790.

Gottman, J. M. (1994). *What predicts divorce? The relationship between marital processes and marital outcomes.* Hillsdale, NJ: Lawrence.

Gottman, J. M. (1999). *The marriage clinic: A scientifically based marital therapy.* New York: Norton.

Gottman, J. M., & Levenson, R. W. (1992). Marital processes predictive of later dissolution: Behavior, physiology, and health. *Journal of Personality and Social Psychology, 63,* 221–233.

Gottman, J. M., & Levenson, R. W. (2002). A two-factor model for predicting when a couple will divorce: Exploratory analyses using 14-year longitudinal data. *Family Process, 41*(1), 83–96.

Gudmunson, C. G., Beutler, I. F., Israelsen, C. L., McCoy, J. K., & Hill, E. J. (2007). Linking financial strain to marital instability: Examining the roles of emotional distress and marital interaction. *Journal of Family and Economic Issues, 28*(3), 357–376.

Guldner, G. T. (1996). Long-distance romantic relationships: Prevalence and separation-related symptoms in college students. *Journal of College Student Development, 37*(3), 289–296.

Guldner, G. T., & Swensen, C. H. (1995). Time spent together and relationship quality: Long-distance relationships as a test case. *Journal of Social and Personal Relationships, 12*(2), 313–320.

Harker, L., & Keltner, D. (2001). Expressions of positive emotion in women's college yearbook pictures and their relationship to personality and life outcomes across adulthood. *Journal of Personality and Social Psychology, 80*(1), 112–124.

Hazan, C., & Shaver, P. (1987). Romantic love conceptualized as an attachment process. *Journal of Personality and Social Psychology, 52*(3), 511–524.

Hertenstein, M. J., Hansel, C. A., Butts, A. M., & Hile, S. N. (2009). Smile intensity in photographs predicts divorce later in life. *Motivation and Emotion, 33*(2), 99–105.

Hofer, M. A. (1984). Relationships as regulators: A psychobiologic perspective on bereavement. *Psychosomatic Medicine, 46*(3), 183–197.

Hu, Y., & Goldman, N. (1990). Mortality differentials by marital status: An international comparison. *Demography, 27,* 233.

Jacobson, N. S. (1977). Training couples to solve their marital problems: A behavioral approach to relationship discord: II. intervention strategies. *American Journal of Family Therapy, 5*(2), 20–28.

Jansen, M., Mortelmans, D., & Snoeckx, L. (2009). Repartnering and (re)employment: Strategies to cope with the economic consequences of partnership dissolution. *Journal of Marriage and the Family, 71*(5), 1271–1293.

Jocklin, V., McGue, M., & Lykken, D. T. (1996). Personality and divorce: A genetic analysis. *Journal of Personality and Social Psychology, 71*, 288–299.

Johnson, D. R., & Wu, J. (2002). An empirical test of crisis, social selection, and role explanations of the relationship between marital disruption and psychological distress: A pooled time-series analysis of four-wave panel data. *Journal of Marriage and Family, 64*(1), 211–224.

Karney, B. R., & Bradbury, T. N. (1995). The longitudinal course of marital quality and stability: A review of theory, methods, and research. *Psychological Bulletin, 118*(1), 3–34.

Karney, B. R., & Bradbury, T. N. (2005). Contextual influences on marriage: Implications for policy and intervention. *Current Directions in Psychological Science, 14*(4), 171–174.

Kelley, H. H. (1979). *Personal relationships: Their structures and processes.* Hillsdale, NJ: Erlbaum.

Kelly, E. L., & Conley, J. J. (1987). Personality and compatibility: A prospective analysis of marital stability and marital satisfaction. *Journal of Personality and Social Psychology, 52*(1), 27–40.

Kessler, R. C., Walters, E. E., & Forthofer, M. S. (1998). The social consequences of psychiatric disorders: III. Probability of marital stability. *American Journal of Psychiatry, 155*(8), 1092–1096.

Kiecolt-Glaser, J. (1987). Marital quality, marital disruption, and immune function. *Psychosomatic Medicine, 49*(1), 13–34.

Kiecolt-Glaser, J. K., Kennedy, S., Malkoff, S., & Fisher, L. (1988). Marital discord and immunity in males. *Psychosomatic Medicine, 50*(3), 213–229.

Kiecolt-Glaser, J., Malarkey, W. B., Chee, M., Newton, T., Cacioppo, J., Mao, H., et al. (1993). Negative behavior during marital conflict is associated with immunological down-regulation. *Psychosomatic Medicine, 55*, 395–409.

Kincaid, S. B., & Caldwell, R. A. (1991). Initiator status, family support, and adjustment to marital separation: A test of an interaction hypothesis. *Journal of Community Psychology, 19*(1), 79–88.

Kincaid, S. B., & Caldwell, R. A. (1995). Marital separation: Causes, coping, and consequences. *Journal of Divorce and Remarriage, 22*(3–4), 109–128.

Kirkpatrick, L. A., & Hazan, C. (1994). Attachment styles and close relationships: A four-year prospective study. *Personal Relationships, 1*(2), 123–142.

Kobak, R., Ruckdeschel, K., & Hazan, C. (1994). From symptom to signal: An attachment view of emotion in marital therapy. In S. M. Johnson & L. S. Greenberg (Eds.), *The heart of the matter: Perspectives on emotion in marital therapy.* (pp. 46–71). Philadelphia: Brunner/Mazel.

Kopsawa, A. J. (2000). Marital status and suicide in the National Longitudinal Mortality Study. *Journal of Epidemiology and Community Health, 54*, 254–261.

Kopsowa, A. J. (2003). Divorce and suicide risk. *Journal of Epidemiology and Community Health, 57*, 993.

Lavee, Y., McCubbin, H. I., & Olson, D. H. (1987). The effect of stressful life events and transitions on family functioning and wellbeing. *Journal of Marriage and the Family, 49*(4), 857–873.

Lazarus, R. S., & Folkman, S. (1984). *Stress, appraisal and coping.* New York: Springer.

LeBel, E. P., & Campbell, L. (2009). Implicit partner affect, relationship satisfaction, and the prediction of romantic breakup. *Journal of Experimental Social Psychology, 45*(6), 1291–1294.

Lee, L. A., Sbarra, D. A., Mason, A. E., & Law, R. W. (2011). Attachment anxiety, verbal immediacy, and blood pressure: Results from a laboratory analog study following marital separation. *Personal Relationships, 18*(2), 285–301.

Levenson, R. W., Carstensen, L. L., & Gottman, J. M. (1994). Influence of age and gender on affect, physiology, and their interrelations: A study of long-term marriages. *Journal of Personality and Social Psychology, 67*(1), 56–68.

Lewandowski, G. W., Jr., Aron, A., Bassis, S., & Kunak, J. (2006). Losing a self-expanding relationship: Implications for the self-concept. *Personal Relationships, 13*(3), 317–331.

Lewandowski, G. W., Jr., & Bizzoco, N. M. (2007). Addition through subtraction: Growth following the dissolution of a low quality relationship. *Journal of Positive Psychology, 2*(1), 40–54.

Lillard, L. L., Brien, M. J., & Waite, L. J. (1995). Premarital cohabitation and subsequent marital dissolution: A matter of self-selection? *Demography, 32,* 437–457.

Lucas, R. E. (2005). Time does not heal all wounds: A longitudinal study of reaction and adaptation to divorce. *Psychological Science, 16*(12), 945–950.

Luo, S., & Klohnen, E. C. (2005). Assortative mating and marital quality in newlyweds: A couple-centered approach. *Journal of Personality and Social Psychology, 88*(2), 304–326.

Mancini, A. D., Bonanno, G. A., & Clark, A. E. (2011). Stepping off the hedonic treadmill: Individual differences in response to major life events. *Journal of Individual Differences, 32*(3), 144–152.

Mandell, D. (1995). Fathers who don't pay child support: Hearing their voices. *Journal of Divorce and Remarriage, 23*(1), 85–116.

Mason, A. E., Law, R. W., Bryan, A. E. B., Portley, R. M., & Sbarra, D. A. (2011). Facing a breakup: Electromyographic responses moderate self-concept recovery following a romantic separation. *Personal Relationships, 19,* 551–568.

Mastekaasa, A. (1994). Marital status, distress, and wellbeing: An international comparison. *Journal of Comparative Family Studies, 25*(2), 183–205.

McDonald, L., & Robb, A. L. (2004). The economic legacy of divorce and separation for women in old age. *Canadian Journal on Aging, 23,* S83–S97.

McGue, M., & Lykken, D. T. (1992). Genetic influence on risk of divorce. *Psychological Science, 3,* 368–373.

McKenry, P. C., & Price, S. J. (1991). Alternatives for support: Life after divorce—A literature review. *Journal of Divorce and Remarriage, 15*(3–4), 1–19.

Mikulincer, M., & Shaver, P. R. (2008). Adult attachment and affect regulation. In J. Cassidy & P. R. Shaver (Eds.), *Handbook of attachment: Theory, research, and clinical applications* (2nd ed., pp. 503–531). New York: Guilford Press.

Mitnick, D. M., Heyman, R. E., & Smith Slep, A. M. (2009). Changes in relationship satisfaction across the transition to parenthood: A meta-analysis. *Journal of Family Psychology, 23*(6), 848–852.

Monroe, S. M., Rohde, P., Seeley, J. R., & Lewinsohn, P. M. (1999). Life events and depression in adolescence: Relationship loss as a prospective risk factor for first onset of major depressive disorder. *Journal of Abnormal Psychology, 108*(4), 606–614.

Murray, J. A. (2001). Loss as a universal concept: A review of the literature to identify common aspects of loss in diverse situations. *Journal of Loss and Trauma, 6*, 219–241.

Myers, M. (1989). *Men and divorce.* New York: Guilford Press.

Neff, L. A., & Karney, B. R. (2004). How does context affect intimate relationships? Linking external stress and cognitive processes within marriage. *Personality and Social Psychology Bulletin, 30*(2), 134–148.

Neff, L. A., & Karney, B. R. (2007). Stress crossover in newlywed marriage: A longitudinal and dyadic perspective. *Journal of Marriage and Family, 69*(3), 594–607.

Osler, M., McGue, M., Lund, R., & Christensen, K. (2008). Marital status and twins' health and behavior: An analysis of middle-aged Danish twins. *Psychosomatic Medicine, 70*(4), 482–487.

Overbeek, G., Vollebergh, W., de Graaf, R., Scholte, R., de Kemp, R., & Engels, R. (2006). Longitudinal associations of marital quality and marital dissolution with the incidence of DSM-III-R disorders. *Journal of Family Psychology, 20*(2), 284–291.

Overbeek, G., Vollebergh, W., Engels, R. C., & Meeus, W. (2003). Young adults' relationship transitions and the incidence of mental disorders: A three-wave longitudinal study. *Social Psychiatry and Psychiatric Epidemiology, 38*(12), 669–676.

Pistole, M. C., & Roberts, A. (2011). Measuring long-distance romantic relationships: A validity study. *Measurement and Evaluation in Counseling and Development, 44*(2), 63–76.

Pistole, M. C., Roberts, A., & Chapman, M. L. (2010). Attachment, relationship maintenance, and stress in long distance and geographically close romantic relationships. *Journal of Social and Personal Relationships, 27*(4), 535–552.

Previti, D., & Amato, P. R. (2003). Why stay married? Rewards, barriers, and marital stability. *Journal of Marriage and Family, 65*(3), 561–573.

Pryor, J., & Rodgers, B. (2001). *Children in changing families: Life after parental separation.* Malden, MA: Blackwell.

Rhoades, G. K., Kamp Dush, C. M., Atkins, D. C., Stanley, S. M., & Markman, H. J. (2011). Breaking up is hard to do: The impact of unmarried relationship dissolution on mental health and life satisfaction. *Journal of Family Psychology, 25*(3), 366–374.

Rhoades, G. K., Stanley, S. M., & Markman, H. J. (2009). Couples' reasons for cohabitation: Associations with individual wellbeing and relationship quality. *Journal of Family Issues, 30*(2), 233–258.

Riessman, C. (1990). *Divorce talk: Women and men make sense of personal relationships.* New Brunswick, NJ: Rudgers University Press.

Roberts, B. W., Kuncel, N. R., Shiner, R., Caspi, A., & Goldberg, L. R. (2007). The power of personality: The comparative validity of personality traits, socioeconomic status, and cognitive ability for predicting important life outcomes. *Perspectives on Psychological Science, 2*(4), 313–345.

Robins, R. W., Caspi, A., & Moffitt, T. E. (2002). It's not just who you're with, it's who you are: Personality and relationship experiences across multiple relationships. *Journal of Personality, 70*(6), 925–964.

Saudino, K. J., Pedersen, N. L., Lichtenstein, P., McClearn, G. E., & Plomin, R. (1997). Can personality explain genetic influences on life events? *Journal of Personality and Social Psychology, 72*, 196–206.

Sbarra, D. A. (2006). Predicting the onset of emotional recovery following nonmarital relationship dissolution: Survival analyses of sadness and anger. *Personality and Social Psychology Bulletin, 32*(3), 298–312.

Sbarra, D. A., & Emery, R. E. (2005). The emotional sequelae of nonmarital relationship dissolution: Analysis of change and intraindividual variability over time. *Personal Relationships, 12*(2), 213–232.

Sbarra, D. A., & Emery, R. E. (2008). Deeper into divorce: Using actor–partner analyses to explore systemic differences in coparenting conflict following custody dispute resolution. *Journal of Family Psychology, Vol. 22*(1), 144–152.

Sbarra, D. A., & Hazan, C. (2008). Coregulation, dysregulation, self-regulation: An integrative analysis and empirical agenda for understanding adult attachment, separation, loss, and recovery. *Personality and Social Psychology Review, 12*(2), 141–167.

Sbarra, D. A., Law, R. W., Lee, L. A., & Mason, A. E. (2009). Marital dissolution and blood pressure reactivity: Evidence for the specificity of emotional intrusion-hyperarousal and task-related emotional difficulty. *Psychosomatic Medicine, 71*(5), 532–540.

Sbarra, D. A., Law, R. W., & Portley, R. M. (2011). Divorce and death: A meta-analysis and research agenda for clinical, social, and health psychology. *Perspectives on Psychological Science, 6*, 454–474.

Scharfe, E., & Cole, V. (2006). Stability and change of attachment representations during emerging adulthood: An examination of mediators and moderators of change. *Personal Relationships, 13*(3), 363–374.

Slotter, E. B., & Finkel, E. J. (2009). The strange case of sustained dedication to an unfulfilling relationship: Predicting commitment and breakup from attachment anxiety and need fulfillment within relationships. *Personality and Social Psychology Bulletin, 35*(1), 85–100.

Slotter, E. B., Gardner, W. L., & Finkel, E. J. (2010). Who am I without you? The influence of romantic breakup on the self-concept. *Personality and Social Psychology Bulletin, 36*(2), 147–160.

Sprecher, S. (1994). Two sides to the breakup of dating relationships. *Personal Relationships, 1*(3), 199–222.

Sprecher, S., Schmeeckle, M., & Felmlee, D. (2006). The principle of least interest: Inequality in emotional involvement in romantic relationships. *Journal of Family Issues, 27*(9), 1255–1280.

Stafford, L., & Reske, J. R. (1990). Idealization and communication in long-distance premarital relationships. *Family Relations, 39*(3), 274–279.

Stanley, S. M., Rhoades, G. K., & Markman, H. J. (2006). Sliding versus deciding: Inertia and the premarital cohabitation effect. *Family Relations, 55*(4), 499–509.

Story, L. B., & Bradbury, T. N. (2004). Understanding marriage and stress: Essential questions and challenges. *Clinical Psychology Review, 23*(8), 1139–1162.

Story, L. B., & Repetti, R. (2006). Daily occupational stressors and marital behavior. *Journal of Family Psychology, 20*(4), 690–700.

Sweeney, M. M. (2002). Remarriage and the nature of divorce: Does it matter which spouse chose to leave? *Journal of Family Issues, 23*(3), 410–440.

Sweeney, M. M., & Horwitz, A. V. (2001). Infidelity, initiation, and the emotional climate of divorce: Are there implications for mental health? *Journal of Health and Social Behavior, 42*, 295–309.

Tashiro, T., & Frazier, P. (2003). "I'll never be in a relationship like that again': Personal growth following romantic relationship breakups. *Personal Relationships, 10*(1), 113–128.

Teachman, J. D., & Polonko, K. A. (1990). Cohabitation and marital stability in the United States. *Social Forces, 69*(1), 207–220.

Tejada-Vera, B., & Sutton, P. (2009). Births, marriages, divorces, and deaths: Provisional data for 2008. *National Vital Statistics Reports, 57*(19).

Thibaut, J. W., & Kelley, H.H. (1959). *The social psychology of groups.* Oxford, UK: Wiley.

Tucker, J. S., Friedman, H. S., Wingard, D. L., & Schwartz, J. E. (1996). Marital history at midlife as a predictor of longevity: Alternative explanations to the protective effect of marriage. *Health Psychology, 15*, 94–101.

Twenge, J. M., Campbell, W. K., & Foster, C. A. (2003). Parenthood and marital satisfaction: A meta-analytic review. *Journal of Marriage and Family, 65*(3), 574–583.

Umberson, D., & Williams, C. L. (1993). Divorced fathers: Parental role strain and psychological distress. *Journal of Family Issues, 14*, 378–400.

Vajda, J., & Steinbeck, K. (2000). Factors associated with repeat suicide attempts among adolescents. *Australian and New Zealand Journal of Psychiatry, 34*(3), 437–445.

Van Horn, K. R., Arnone, A., Nesbitt, K., Desilets, L., Sears, T., Giffin, M., et al. (1997). Physical distance and interpersonal characteristics in college students' romantic relationships. *Personal Relationships, 4*, 25–34.

Wade, T. J., & Pevalin, D. J. (2004). Marital transitions and mental health. *Journal of Health and Social Behavior, 45*(2), 155–170.

Weiss, R. S. (1975). *Marital separation.* New York: Basic Books.

Whisman, M. A., Dixon, A. E., & Johnson, B. (1997). Therapists' perspectives of couple problems and treatment issues in couple therapy. *Journal of Family Psychology, 11*(3), 361–366.

Whisman, M. A., Tolejko, N., & Chatav, Y. (2007). Social consequences of personality disorders: Probability and timing of marriage and probability of marital disruption. *Journal of Personality Disorders, 21*(6), 690–695.

Wieselquist, J., Rusbult, C. E., Foster, C. A., & Agnew, C. R. (1999). Commitment, pro-relationship behavior, and trust in close relationships. *Journal of Personality and Social Psychology, 77*(5), 942–966.

Wolfinger, N. H. (2000). Beyond the intergenerational transmission of divorce: Do people replicate the patterns of martial instability they grew up with? *Journal of Family Issues, 21*(8), 1061–1086.

Chapter **12**

Social Connectedness and Health

LOUISE C. HAWKLEY
JOHN T. CACIOPPO

> You can kiss your family and friends good-bye and
> put miles between you, but at the same time you carry
> them with you in your heart, your mind, your stomach,
> because you do not just live in a world but a world lives
> in you.
> —FREDERICK BUECHNER

It is a profound reality: Social relationships and experiences exist not only in the external, easily observable world, but in the internal, largely invisible workings of the brain and body, a reality that has significant implications for our psychological and physical health and well-being. Summarizing the literature published between 1970 and 1998, Seeman (2000) concluded that highly socially integrated individuals (as reflected in a greater number of ties—with a spouse, close friends and relatives, affiliation with religious and other groups) live significantly longer than their less integrated counterparts, and that socially isolated individuals are at greater risk for broad-based morbidity such as incidence of and poor recovery from myocardial infarction and stroke. The detrimental effects of social isolation are similar in magnitude to the effects of well-known health risk factors such as smoking and inactivity and are largely independent of behavioral and biological risk factors in predicting broad-based health outcomes (House, Landis, & Umberson, 1988). These findings have prompted new lines of research that examine psychological and physiological pathways by which social relationships operate to influence health and well-being. A useful inroad into this complexity has been to move beyond the presence and number of social ties to consider how social relationships are perceived and experienced. Perceptions and receipt of social support, for instance, have been shown to contribute to physiological (Uchino, Cacioppo, & Kiecolt-Glaser, 1996) and health (reviewed in Reblin & Uchino, 2008) outcomes. The role of social support in health is just one facet of a more deeply seated role for social connections in human health and flourishing, however (Dunbar & Shultz, 2007). In this chapter, we focus on subjective feelings of social isolation (i.e., loneliness) to highlight the importance of a sense of social connectedness for a healthy and balanced life.

DEFINITION AND CONCEPTUALIZATION OF LONELINESS

Being alone is not synonymous with loneliness, nor does being with others guarantee protection from feelings of loneliness. Rather, loneliness is the distress that occurs when there is a discrepancy between desired and actual social relationships (Peplau & Perlman, 1982). Discrepancies can arise when intimate partners fail to satisfy our need for connectedness and leave us feeling isolated, when the lack of close, confiding friendships leaves us wanting for a sense of relational connectedness, and when social groups or collectives that we value leave us feeling like we don't belong (Hawkley, Browne, & Cacioppo, 2005). Small social network size is associated with loneliness (Hawkley et al., 2008), but perceptions of poor social relationship quality are the most important contributor to feelings of loneliness (de Jong-Gierveld, 1987; Hawkley et al., 2008; Pinquart & Sörensen, 2001; Wheeler, Reis, & Nezlek, 1983). Thus, individuals with insecure attachment styles are lonelier than those with secure attachment styles (DiTommaso, Brannen-McNulty, Ross, & Burgess, 2003), and individuals who perceive inadequate social support are lonelier than those with high levels of social support (Pierce, Sarason, & Sarason, 1991), although it should be noted that loneliness may be as much a cause as a consequence of insecure attachment and poor social support (Cacioppo, Hawkley, et al., 2006). Neither insecure attachment nor poor social support are adequate to explain individual differences in loneliness, however, and the qualities of specific relationships predict loneliness above and beyond what is predicted by general perceptions of social support, for example (Pierce et al., 1991). The importance of good-quality relationships may help explain why the loss of social roles and the increased social isolation that accompany aging in our society (e.g., widowhood, retirement, geographic separation from adult children) do not increase the prevalence or intensity of loneliness among older adults, at least until oldest old age (i.e., > 80 years) (Boomsma, Cacioppo, Muthén, Asparouhov, & Clark, 2007; Pinquart & Sörensen, 2001; Schnittker, 2007). Older adults tend to select and nurture their most valued relationships (Carstensen, Isaacowitz, & Charles, 1999), and good relationship quality may buffer any loneliness effects that result from social losses.

Loneliness is aversive, but, like pain, this aversiveness serves an important purpose for the survival of the species. An evolutionary conceptualization of loneliness holds that the aversive feelings are adaptive because they motivate the protection, repair, and replacement of social connections (Cacioppo, Hawkley, et al., 2006). Human offspring are born to the longest period of utter dependency of any species. Simple reproduction, therefore, is not sufficient to ensure that one's genes make it into the gene pool. For one's genes to make it to the gene pool, these offspring must survive to reproduce. Social connections and the behaviors they engender (e.g., empathy, cooperation, nurturance, altruism, alliances) enhance the survival of the parents, and consequently, their children are more likely to survive to reproduce.

In early human history, members of hunter–gatherer societies who pursued only selfish interests may have survived to reproduce, but their offspring were at risk for not surviving sufficiently long to reproduce. In species whose offspring have long periods of utter dependency, it is the ability of the offspring to reproduce, not one's own ability to reproduce, that determines the constitution of the gene pool. Therefore, genetic mutations that increased the odds of offspring surviving sufficiently long that they, too, reproduced (i.e., long-term fitness), such as those that promoted social connections and collective efforts, conferred an adaptive advantage. In this context, loneliness does for the genes what pain does for an organism: It serves to signal a state of affairs that is dangerous.

The engine of natural selection is individual variation, so one would expect from this evolutionary scenario that there would be heritable individual differences in loneliness. Adoption and twin studies of children and adults support this view. Several studies indicate that as much as 48% of the variability in loneliness levels in the population can be explained by inherited tendencies to experience loneliness (Bartels, Cacioppo, Hudziak,

& Boomsma, 2008; Boomsma, Willemsen, Dolan, Hawkley, & Cacioppo, 2005; McGuire & Clifford, 2000).

Chronic loneliness is the result of an interaction between a genetic predisposition and life circumstances that are in part beyond a person's control. However, once loneliness is triggered, it activates a defensive form of thinking—a "lonely" social cognition—that can perpetuate and exacerbate feelings of loneliness (Cacioppo & Patrick, 2008). Lonely individuals are more likely to construe their world as threatening, hold more negative expectations, and interpret and respond to ambiguous social behavior in a more negative, off-putting fashion, thereby confirming their construal of the world as threatening and beyond their control (Cacioppo & Hawkley, 2005). These cognitions are reflected in distinct patterns of brain activity, particularly in response to social stimuli (Cacioppo, Norris, Decety, Monteleone, & Nusbaum, 2008). Relative to nonlonely participants, lonely participants showed less activation of the ventral striatum and related limbic regions (areas involved in reward) when viewing pleasant pictures of people, possibly explaining why lonely individuals find daily uplifts less heartening (Cacioppo et al., 2000) and positive social interactions less positive (Hawkley, Preacher, & Cacioppo, 2007) than nonlonely individuals. When viewing unpleasant pictures of people, however, lonely participants showed greater activation of the visual cortices, but less activation of bilateral regions of the temporoparietal junction (areas involved in perspective taking and theory of mind) relative to nonlonely participants. These data are consistent with observations that lonely individuals pay more attention to social information (Gardner, Pickett, Jeffries, & Knowles, 2005), but have a more egocentric approach to this information than nonlonely individuals (Pickett & Gardner, 2005). Neural representations of the social cognition suggest that lonely, compared with nonlonely, individuals may be disposed toward the social environment as a generally more threatening context, responding to pleasant social stimuli in a less rewarding fashion and dealing with unpleasant social stimuli in a more threatened, self-protective fashion. In time, these neurobiological differences may take a toll on physical health (Cacioppo, Hawkley, Crawford, et al., 2002; Hawkley & Cacioppo, 2007).

LONELINESS AND HEALTH OUTCOMES

According to this reasoning, chronic loneliness should have a cumulative effect on health that may emerge in early markers of disease processes in young adulthood and in a more rapid progression to clinically relevant disease endpoints in later adulthood. Consistent with this hypothesis, Caspi, Harrington, Moffitt, Milne, and Poulton (2006) reported a dose–response relationship between chronic loneliness from childhood through young adulthood and number of biomarkers of cardiovascular health risk in young adulthood (Caspi et al., 2006). Participants who were lonely at each of three measurement occasions (i.e., childhood, adolescence, and 26 years of age) exhibited a greater number of standard health risks (i.e., body mass index [BMI], systolic blood pressure [SBP], total and high-density lipoprotein [HDL] cholesterol levels, glycated hemoglobin concentration, maximum oxygen consumption) than those who were lonely at only two or one of these occasions. In older adults, loneliness predicts mortality (Holt-Lunstad, Smith, & Layton, 2010; Patterson & Veenstra, 2010; Penninx et al., 1997; Seeman, 2000; Shiovitz-Ezra & Ayalon, 2010; Sugisawa, Liang, & Liu, 1994). For instance, Penninx et al. (1997) showed that loneliness and a low sense of mastery predicted mortality during a 29-month follow-up net of age, sex, chronic diseases, alcohol use, smoking, self-rated health, and functional limitations. Sugisawa et al. (1994) found that the significant effects of loneliness on mortality over a 3-year period were explained by associations between loneliness and chronic diseases, functional status, and self-rated health. Similarly, we observed that poorer physical health (functional limitations, self-rated health) explained the higher risk of loneliness-related mortality in a large population-based sample of adults 50 years of age and older in the U.S. Health and Retirement Study (Luo, Hawkley, Waite, & Cacioppo, 2012). Poor health behaviors (e.g., smoking, lack of physical activity) contributed to greater mortality, but did not explain the effect of loneliness on mortality (Luo et al., 2012). Nor is inadequate health care utilization likely to account for these differences in mortality: Relative to nonlonely individuals, lonely individuals make more visits to their primary physician (Cheng, 1992; Feldman, 2000) and are more likely to make use of hospital emergency departments (Geller, Janson, McGovern, & Valdini, 1999), independent of the presence and intensity of chronic illnesses.

LONELINESS AND PATHWAYS TO DISEASE

Most chronic diseases (e.g., hypertension, coronary artery disease, diabetes) arise out of the interaction of heritable factors, environmental influences, and individual behaviors on physiological functioning. Loneliness may have an effect on some or all of these pathways that contribute to the development of disease (Hawkley & Cacioppo, 2010). For instance, loneliness may have a direct or indirect effect on health behaviors that have recognized consequences for health (e.g., smoking, sedentary lifestyle). In addition, loneliness may operate through any one or more of a family of stress-related processes and outcomes that add wear-and-tear to the body (McEwen & Stellar, 1993). Specifically, loneliness may affect the kinds and quantity of stress to which one is exposed, alter appraisals of and coping responses to stress, and influence physiological responses to stress. In addition, loneliness may disrupt restorative processes that help the organism recover from stress (Cacioppo & Hawkley, 2003). Even genetic factors that play a role in the physiological manifestations of disease may be more likely to be expressed as a result of chronic loneliness (Cole et al., 2007).

In general, the effects of loneliness on psychological well-being (i.e., depressed affect, self-esteem) are relatively immediate. Loneliness and depressive symptoms are conceptually and empirically distinct (Cacioppo, Hawkley, et al., 2006), but levels of loneliness and depressive symptoms covary across the lifespan (Cacioppo, Hughes, Waite, Hawkley, & Thisted, 2006; Nolen-Hoeksema & Ahrens, 2002). Moreover, loneliness has been identified as a risk factor for depressive symptoms in longitudinal studies of older adults (Heikkinen & Kauppinen, 2004). Recent evidence from a nationally representative sample of adults 54 years and older revealed that loneliness was associated with more depressive symptoms independent of demographic factors (age, gender, ethnicity, socioeconomic status, marital status) and related feelings of hostility, perceived stress, and poor social support (Cacioppo, Hughes, et al., 2006). Extending these findings, longitudinal data from a population-based sample of 50- to 67-year-old adults showed that loneliness predicted increases in depressive symptoms over 1-year intervals; the cross-lagged panel model simultaneously showed that depressive symptoms did not predict changes in loneliness over the same interval, again holding constant demographic and psychosocial risk factors (Cacioppo, Hawkley, & Thisted, 2010). Finally, a marginal structural modeling approach to the same data indicated that interventions to lessen loneliness made 1 and 2 years prior to assessing final depressive symptoms would have a cumulative effect on reductions in depressive symptoms (VanderWeele, Hawkley, Thisted, & Cacioppo, 2011).

The effects of loneliness on physiological status and physical health, on the other hand, take a longer time to accrue, and these manifestations are more evident in individuals (e.g., older adults) whose physiological resilience is compromised. Consequently, associations between loneliness and disease pathways may differ between young and older adults (Hawkley & Cacioppo, 2007). Longitudinal and prospective studies are needed to examine the trajectory of behavioral and physiological changes that lead to loneliness differences in disease outcomes in older adulthood. Although most studies are cross-sectional, an increasing number of longitudinal studies support the hypothesis that risk accumulates over time as a function of loneliness.

Health Behaviors

Poor health behaviors are appealing mechanistic candidates for associations between loneliness and health. High-calorie, high-fat diets and sedentary lifestyles, for example, contribute to overweight or obesity, major risk factors for disease in Western society. In a large cross-sectional survey of 1,289 adults 18 years and older (mean age = 46.3 years), the lonely group had a higher mean BMI and a greater proportion of overweight/obese individuals than did the nonlonely group (Lauder, Mummery, Jones, & Caperchione, 2006).

Loneliness differences in physical activity have not been observed in samples that cover a wide age range, from young to elderly adults (Lauder et al., 2006), or in some studies of young adults (Hawkley, Burleson, Berntson, & Cacioppo, 2003). However, loneliness was associated with lower levels of physical activity among grade school, high school, and college students in studies by Page et al. (Page, Frey, Talbert, & Falk, 1992; Page & Tucker, 1994; Page & Hammermeister, 1995) and among middle-age adults (50–68 years) in a population-based community sample (Hawkley, Thisted, & Cacioppo, 2009). In the latter study, individuals with a larger social network were more likely to be physically active, but loneliness effects were not explained by individual differences in network size, suggesting that qualitative aspects of social ties (e.g., feelings of isolation and loneliness) play a unique role in this particular disease pathway. Nor were the loneliness effects explained by social support, hostility, perceived stress, and depressive symptoms, psychosocial characteristics that are related to loneliness and that have also been associated with less physical activity. On the other hand, lonely individuals were poorer at self-regulation, as reflected in a lower tendency to optimize positive emotions, and this tendency explained their lower physical activity. Longitudinal analyses revealed a higher rate of transitioning from physical activity to inactivity among lonely compared with nonlonely individuals, resulting in an even lower likelihood of physical activity in lonely individuals over subsequent years. Physical inactivity could contribute to a shrinking social network and increasing levels of loneliness over time, but this causal direction was not supported by the data. In addition, although health status contributed to the likelihood of becoming inactive across years, the progression of lonely individuals into the physically inactive category was independent of health status (Hawkley et al., 2009).

The Stress Family

Stress Exposure

Surveys of undergraduate students have shown that lonely and nonlonely young adults do not differ in their exposure to major life stressors or in the number of major changes endured in the past 12 months (Cacioppo et al., 2000). A "beeper study," in which undergraduate students were asked to sit down and record their thoughts and experiences at various times during the day, also showed no difference in the reported frequency of hassles or uplifts that the participants experienced on an average day or in the number of minor irritants they were confronting when their beeping wristwatch randomly interrupted them (Hawkley et al., 2003). Among middle-aged adults, however, the number of stressful life events in the past year was greater for lonely compared with nonlonely individuals, and lonely adults also reported more sources of chronic stress such as financial worries, unemployment, family and/or marital problems, and residential concerns (Hawkley et al., 2008). Moreover, stressful life events have been associated prospectively with increases in loneliness (Segrin, 1999), setting up a potential positive feedback loop in which lonely individuals are under the steadily accruing burden of stress and increases in loneliness. Whether differences in acute or chronic stress exposure contribute to loneliness differences in health outcomes is a question for future research, but existing evidence indicates that this disease pathway is plausible.

Stress Perceptions and Coping

A robust finding in studies of loneliness is that lonely individuals, young and old, perceive life as more stressful, even when objective indications are that lonely and nonlonely individuals do not differ in the types of activities and behaviors they engage in on a daily basis (Hawkley et al., 2003). The hassles and stresses of everyday life are more severe and the uplifts less gratifying for socially disconnected individuals (Cacioppo et al., 2000). Even social interactions, which should ameliorate feelings of disconnection and unhappiness, are less efficacious in lonely than nonlonely individuals, in part because the interactions are themselves perceived to be deficient in the positive features (e.g., trust, appropriate disclosure, and affection) that characterize good-quality interactions (Hawkley, Preacher, et al., 2007; Wheeler et al., 1983).

Despite its bad press, stress has the potential for positive outcomes for those who take the opportunity to expand their repertoire of coping behaviors and grow intellectually and emotionally. Lonely individuals, however, show evidence of poorer self-regulation (Cacioppo et al., 2000). Perhaps as a result, they are also more likely than nonlonely individuals to see any given stressor as a threat rather than an invigorating challenge (Cacioppo & Patrick, 2008). Instead of responding with optimism and active engagement, they tend to respond with pessimism and avoidance. Lonely individuals are more likely to withdraw and less likely to seek emotional support when confronted with stress (Cacioppo, Hawkley, Crawford, et al., 2002; Hawkley & Cacioppo, 2007), coping strategies that serve to prolong stress. Passive coping strategies and threat appraisals have also been associated with a pattern of cardiovascular response to acute stress in which increases in blood pressure are driven largely by elevated vascular resistance (Blascovich & Tomaka, 1996; Kasprowicz, Manuck, Malkoff, & Krantz, 1990), a risk factor for the development of hypertension (Franklin et al., 1997).

Cardiovascular Functioning

Elevated SBP is a well-recognized risk factor for cardiovascular disease (Chobanian et al., 2003; Kannel, 1996). SBP is a function of arterial blood volume (i.e., cardiac output) and arterial compliance (i.e., total peripheral resistance [TPR]). TPR, in turn, is influenced by a variety of physiological processes (Sterling, 2004), including activity of the sympathetic nervous system that results in norepinephrine release and binding to alpha-1 adrenergic receptors on vascular smooth muscle cells (Berne & Levy, 1997); local responses to mechanical forces (e.g., shear stress from increased blood flow), including the release from vascular endothelium of substances that mediate vascular relaxation and constriction (e.g., nitric oxide, endothelin-1, prostacyclin) (Spieker, Flammer, & Luscher, 2006); and vascular smooth muscle cell structure and function (Schiffrin, 2004).

In young adults, lonely and nonlonely individuals did not differ in SBP levels, but regulation of blood pressure was attributable to higher TPR among compared with nonlonely individuals (Cacioppo, Hawkley, Crawford, et al., 2002; Hawkley et al., 2003). Results from the Framingham Heart Study indicate that changes in TPR play a dominant role in determining SBP from age 30 until approximately age 50 (Franklin et al., 1997). To the extent loneliness is associated with chronically elevated TPR from early to middle adulthood, elevated blood pressure may subsequently develop during the middle and older age ranges. Consistent with this hypothesis, loneliness was associated with elevated SBP in a convenience sample of

older adults (Cacioppo, Hawkley, Crawford, et al., 2002) and a population-based sample of middle aged adults (50–68 years old) in the Chicago
Health, Aging, and Social Relations Study (Hawkley, Masi, Berry, &
Cacioppo, 2006). This relationship persisted, holding constant the effects
of sociodemographic variables, health behaviors, and psychosocial factors,
including social support, perceived stress, hostility, and depressive symptoms. Moreover, a subsequent prospective study of these same individuals found that loneliness predicted a greater increase in SBP over a 4-year
follow-up (Hawkley, Thisted, Masi, & Cacioppo, 2010), consistent with
our hypothesis that loneliness exacerbates age-related physiological decline
and risk for disease (Hawkley & Cacioppo, 2007). Across the full range
of loneliness scores, the cross-lagged panel model predicted that the most
lonely individuals would exhibit a 14-mm greater increase in SBP than their
least lonely counterparts over the course of 4 years, which translates into
higher rates of hypertension at younger ages in lonely individuals.

The physiological determinants responsible for the cumulative effects
of loneliness on blood pressure have yet to be elucidated. TPR plays a critical role in determining SBP in early to mid-adulthood, but other mechanisms come into play with increasing age (Franklin et al., 1997). Candidate mechanisms through which loneliness may operate involve age-related
changes in vascular physiology, including increased arterial stiffness (Schiffrin, 2004), diminished endothelial cell release of nitric oxide, enhanced
vascular responsivity to endothelial constriction factors, increases in circulating catecholamines, and attenuated vasodilator responses to circulating
epinephrine as a result of decreased beta-adrenergic sensitivity in vascular
smooth muscle (Cheitlin, 2003; Folkow & Svanborg, 1993; Toro et al.,
2002). In turn, many of these mechanisms are influenced by lifestyle factors
such as diet, physical inactivity, and obesity—factors that alter blood lipids
and inflammatory processes that have known consequences for vascular
health and functioning (Danesh et al., 2004; Yusuf et al., 2004).

Hypothalamic–Pituitary–Adrenocortical Axis Functioning

The hypothalamic–pituitary–adrenocortical (HPA) axis is a finely coordinated system of direct and feedback influences that begins with hypothalamic secretion of corticotropin-releasing hormone (CRH), which regulates
the release of adrenocorticotropic hormone (ACTH) from the pituitary
gland, which, in turn, regulates the release of cortisol from the cortex of
the adrenal gland. Glucocorticoids (GCs) such as cortisol liberate stored
energy by increasing glucose availability to peripheral tissues, muscles, and
the brain. GCs are also critical to immune functioning and inflammatory

processes. Under acute stress circumstances, circulating GCs act to reduce or contain inflammation and minimize cellular damage. Chronic stress, however, involves a dysregulation of the HPA axis with elevated circulating GCs but a resistance to their immunosuppressant and anti-inflammatory effects (Avitsur, Stark, & Sheridan, 2001; O'Connor et al., 2003). Poorly regulated inflammation is a trademark of many chronic health conditions, including atherosclerosis and cardiovascular events (Oparil & Oberman, 1999; Paoletti, Gotto, & Hajjar, 2004), diabetes (Qi & Hu, 2007), obesity (Wellen & Hotamisligil, 2005), cancer (Coussens & Werb, 2002), asthma (Vignola et al., 2000), and rheumatoid arthritis (Fox, 2000).

Dysregulation of HPA activity has been associated with loneliness and related psychosocial variables (Hawkley, Bosch, Engeland, Marucha, & Cacioppo, 2007). Evidence for a loneliness difference in activity of the HPA axis was first reported by Kiecolt-Glaser, Ricker, et al. (1984), who observed that lonely, nonpsychotic psychiatric inpatients excreted significantly greater amounts of urinary cortisol than nonlonely inpatients. More recently, Steptoe, Owen, Kunz-Ebrecht, and Brydon (2004) found that lonely middle-aged individuals showed a greater 30-minute post-awakening increase in salivary cortisol. Among young adults, Pressman et al. (2005) found that loneliness was associated with higher early-morning and late-night levels of salivary cortisol. In our study of young adults, we found no loneliness differences in mean daily levels of salivary cortisol, diurnal pattern of cortisol secretion, or cortisol reactivity to acute stressors in lonely and nonlonely individuals (Cacioppo et al., 2000). Among middle-aged adults, however, HPA activity across a 3-day period in participants' everyday lives showed a longitudinal effect consistent with a causal role for loneliness (Adam, Hawkley, Kudielka, & Cacioppo, 2006). Diary reports of daily psychosocial, emotional, and physical states were completed at bedtime on each of 3 consecutive days. Salivary cortisol levels were measured upon waking, 30 minutes after waking, and at bedtime each day. Multilevel models revealed that prior-day feelings of loneliness and related feelings of sadness, threat, and lack of control were associated with a higher cortisol awakening response (CAR) the next day, but the morning CAR did not predict experiences of these psychosocial states later the same day (Adam et al., 2006).

Responsiveness of the HPA axis to daily variations in loneliness and related feelings may be adaptive in matching metabolic energy to anticipated demand and stress, but chronic elevations of the CAR may signal a system that no longer responds to daily variation in need for metabolic support. As noted previously, chronically elevated levels of cortisol have been associated with greater atherosclerosis, higher cholesterol levels, diabetes, decreased immune function, and cognitive impairment (Seeman & Robbins, 1994). These changes typify aging and have also been observed with exposure to chronic stress, leading many of them to become known as forms of "accelerated aging" (Seeman & Robbins, 1994; Fuster, Díez, & Andrés, 2007). To the extent that loneliness contributes to chronic elevation of GCs, a sense of social connectedness stands to play an important role in decelerating the development and progression of age-related chronic conditions.

DNA Transcription and Inflammatory Response

Cortisol can regulate a wide variety of physiological processes via nuclear hormone receptor-mediated control of gene transcription. Cortisol activation of the glucocorticoid receptor (GR) exerts broad anti-inflammatory effects by inhibiting pro-inflammatory signaling pathways. Social isolation, however, is associated with increased risk of inflammation-mediated diseases. One possible explanation for inflammation-related disease in individuals with high cortisol levels involves impaired GR-mediated signal transduction that prevents the cellular genome from effectively "hearing" the anti-inflammatory signal sent by circulating GCs (Cole et al., 2007). Consistent with this hypothesis, a systematic examination of genome-wide transcriptional alterations in circulating leukocytes showed increased expression of genes carrying pro-inflammatory elements and decreased expression of genes carrying anti-inflammatory GC response elements in lonely relative to nonlonely middle-aged adults, despite comparable if not slightly higher levels of circulating cortisol (Cole et al., 2007; Cole, Hawkley, Arevalo, & Cacioppo, 2011). These transcription differences were independent of individual differences in perceived stress, depressive symptoms, and hostility. Impaired transcription of GC response genes and increased activity of pro-inflammatory transcription control pathways provide a functional genomic explanation for elevated risk of inflammatory disease in individuals who experience chronically high levels of loneliness.

The DNA transcription results were obtained using leukocytes, key players in immunity. The up-regulated genes in the leukocytes of lonely individuals included numerous genes indicating immune activation (Cole et al., 2007). Relative to nonlonely individuals, leukocytes from lonely individuals overexpressed genes involved in cell cycling, a process that is critical to immune activation and proliferation in response to antigenic stimulation; pro-inflammatory cytokines (e.g., interleukin [IL]-β, IL-8); receptors for inflammatory mediators (e.g., IL-8 receptor, beta, IL-10 receptor, alpha); immediate-early response gene IER2, which regulates the transcriptional genomic response to antigenic stimuli; and cyclooxygenase-2, which regulates the synthesis of prostaglandins, potent but short-lived molecules that have a number of actions, including the regulation of inflammation.

Up-regulation of immune activation genes may be due to increased activity of the nuclear factor kappa-B (NF-κB) transcription control pathway. In support of this mechanistic pathway, results showed a 2.9-fold greater prevalence of pro-inflammatory NF-κB response elements in genes overexpressed in lonely relative to nonlonely individuals. In addition, up-regulation of immune activation genes may be due to decreased activity of the inhibitory GC transcription control pathway. In support of this mechanistic pathway, the prevalence of GC response elements (GREs) was 63% lower in lonely compared with nonlonely individuals. GRE and NF-κB represent mutually inhibitory transcriptional control pathways, and the fact that NF-κB transcription was five-fold greater than GRE transcription in lonely individuals suggests that the overall pattern is one of poorly regulated immune activation and inflammation (Cole et al., 2007). Together with select underexpression of genes involved in antiviral resistance, antibody production, and mature β lymphocyte function, the transcriptional profile indicates a complex pattern of alterations in immunity in lonely individuals. Additional research is needed to assess the degree to which these transcriptional alterations are reflected in the proteins whose production is regulated by these transcripts.

Immune Functioning

Research on loneliness-related differences in immunity has revealed impaired cellular immunity, as reflected in lower natural killer (NK) cell activity and higher antibody titers to the Epstein–Barr virus and human herpes viruses in high-lonely compared with low-lonely individuals (Dixon et al., 2001; Glaser, Kiecolt-Glaser, Speicher, & Holliday, 1985; Kiecolt-Glaser, Garner, et al., 1984; Kiecolt-Glaser, Ricker, et al., 1984). In addition, under acute stress circumstances (e.g., when performing a Stroop task and a mirror-tracing task), loneliness has been associated with a smaller increase in NK cell numbers among middle-aged adults (Steptoe et al., 2004). The humoral immune response may also be impaired in lonely individuals: Chronic loneliness was associated with poorer antibody response to a component of the flu vaccine in young adults (Pressman et al., 2005). On the other hand, loneliness predicted a slower rate of decline in levels of CD4 T lymphocytes over a 3-year period in HIV-positive men without AIDS (Miller, Kemeny, Taylor, Cole, & Visscher, 1997), suggesting that feelings of loneliness are not uncompromisingly negative. Additional research is needed to examine the role of factors such as age, chronicity of loneliness, life stress context, and genetic predispositions in determining when and how loneliness operates to impair immune functioning. Childhood trauma and early life stress may play a particularly important role in setting a trajectory for loneliness (Wilson et al., 2006), maladaptive immunity (Graham, Christian, & Kiecolt-Glaser, 2006), and poor mental and physical health more generally (Shaw & Krause, 2002).

Cognitive Functioning

The physiological manifestation of a poor sense of social connectedness extends beyond peripheral functioning and includes differences in neural processing and cognitive health (Cacioppo & Hawkley, 2009). For instance, in a 4-year prospective study of initially dementia-free older adults (mean age = 80.7 years), the risk of Alzheimer's disease was more than twice as great in lonely compared with nonlonely individuals (relative risk scores of 3.2 vs. 1.4, respectively), and this effect was independent of functional physical impairments and vascular risk factors and conditions (Wilson et al., 2007). In addition, loneliness was associated with lower cognitive ability at baseline and with a more rapid decline in cognition during the 4-year follow-up (Wilson et al., 2007). In related research, loneliness predicted more rapid cognitive decline over a 10-year period in a Finnish sample of adults 75 years of age and older (Tilvis et al., 2004). Again, we have a reprise on the theme of accelerated aging associated with loneliness.

Sleep Salubrity

Sleep deprivation has been associated with reduced glucose tolerance, elevated evening cortisol levels, and increased sympathetic nervous system activity (Spiegel, Leproult, & Van Cauter, 1999). However, sleep quality is as at least as important as sleep duration in accomplishing its restorative effects. Nonrestorative sleep (i.e., sleep that is non-refreshing despite normal sleep duration) results in daytime impairments such as physical and intellectual fatigue, role impairments, irritability, and cognitive and memory problems (Ohayon, 2005).

Prior research has shown that poor social relations and loneliness are associated with poor sleep quality and daytime dysfunction (Cacioppo, Hawkley, Berntson, et al., 2002; Friedman et al., 2005). In addition, the greater daytime dysfunction reported by lonely young adults is accompanied by more nightly micro-awakenings and not by differential sleep duration (Cacioppo, Hawkley, Berntson, et al., 2002). In an extension of these findings, a 3-day diary study found that loneliness was associated with greater daytime dysfunction in a sample of middle-aged adults, an association that was independent of age, gender, race/ethnicity, household income, health behaviors, BMI, chronic health conditions, daily illness symptom severity, and related feelings of stress, hostility, poor social support, and depressive symptoms. Moreover, cross-lagged panel analyses of daily diary data supported a causal role for loneliness: Lonely feelings one day predicted daytime dysfunction the following day, but daytime dysfunction was not a significant predictor of lonely feelings the following day (Hawkley, Preacher, & Cacioppo, 2010). These results were independent of sleep duration and suggest that the same amount of sleep is less salubrious in individuals who feel more socially isolated.

CONCLUDING REMARKS

Humans are fundamentally social organisms whose survival depends on their collective, not their individual, abilities. In light of the wide-reaching impact of feelings of loneliness on health and well-being, it is clear that a feeling of social connectedness has much to recommend it. Feeling socially connected enriches our lives in ways that include, but also exceed, the support we may feel from close others. To feel socially connected, paraphrasing the opening quote by Frederick Buechner, is to have others live in us. Even in their physical absence, a sense that they are embodied in our thoughts and feelings—and we in theirs—gives us the motivation to engage fully in all that life has to offer and the courage to keep on engaging when life gets tough. The feeling of social connectedness is as vital to our survival as food and drink, yet is so taken for granted that only the absence of that sense has been assigned a unique term: loneliness. All is not lost for the lonely person, however. Understanding that maladaptive social cognitions perpetuate loneliness opens the door to cognitive and behavioral interventions that can ease the emotional suffering and relieve some of the physiological burden of living in felt isolation. Chronic loneliness will not end quickly, nor will the cumulative health burden of having lived a lonely existence be removed, but even small improvements in one's feelings of connectedness can have a dramatic impact on quality of life and might slow down the rate of the physiological decline in the process.

ACKNOWLEDGMENTS

This research was supported by Grant Nos. R01-AG036433 and R01-AG034052 from the National Institute on Aging and by the John Templeton Foundation.

REFERENCES

Adam, E. K., Hawkley, L. C., Kudielka, B. M., & Cacioppo, J. T. (2006). Day-to-day dynamics of experience-cortisol associations in a population-based sample of older adults. *Proceedings of the National Academy of Sciences USA, 103*, 17058–17063.

Avitsur, R., Stark, J. L., & Sheridan, J. F. (2001). Social stress induces glucocorticoid resistance in subordinate animals. *Hormones and Behavior, 39*, 247–257.

Bartels, M., Cacioppo, J. T., Hudziak, J. J., & Boomsma, D. I. (2008). Genetic and environmental contributions to stability in loneliness throughout childhood. *American Journal of Medical Genetics Part B. Neuropsychiatric Genetics, 147B*, 385–391.

Berne, R. M., & Levy, M. N. (1997). *Cardiovascular physiology.* St. Louis, MO: Mosby.

Blascovich, J., & Tomaka, J. (1996). The biopsychosocial model of arousal regulation. In M. P. Zanna (Ed.), *Advances in experimental social psychology* (Vol. 29, pp. 1–51). New York: Academic Press.

Boomsma, D. I., Cacioppo, J. T., Muthén, B., Asparouhov, T., & Clark, S. (2007). Longitudinal genetic analysis for loneliness in Dutch twins. *Twin Research and Human Genetics, 10*, 267–273.

Boomsma, D. I., Willemsen, G., Dolan, C. V., Hawkley, L. C., & Cacioppo, J. T. (2005). Genetic and environmental contributions to loneliness in adults: The Netherlands Twin Register Study. *Behavior Genetics, 35*, 745–752.

Cacioppo, J. T., Ernst, J. M., Burleson, M. H., McClintock, M. K., Malarkey, W. B., Hawkley, L. C., et al. (2000). Lonely traits and concomitant physiological processes: The MacArthur social neuroscience studies. *International Journal of Psychophysiology, 35*, 143–154.

Cacioppo, J. T., & Hawkley, L. C. (2003). Social isolation and health, with an emphasis on underlying mechanisms. *Perspectives in Biology and Medicine, 46*, S39–S52.

Cacioppo, J. T., & Hawkley, L. C. (2005). People thinking about people: The vicious cycle of being a social outcast in one's own mind. In K. D. Williams, J. P. Forgas, & W. von Hippel, W. (Eds.), *The social outcast: Ostracism, social exclusion, rejection, and bullying* (pp. 91–108). New York: Psychology Press.

Cacioppo, J. T., & Hawkley, L. C. (2009). Perceived social isolation and cognition. *Trends in Cognitive Sciences, 13*, 447–454.

Cacioppo, J. T., Hawkley, L. C., Berntson, G. G., Ernst, J. M., Gibbs, A. C., Stickgold, R., et al. (2002). Do lonely days invade the nights? Potential social modulation of sleep efficiency. *Psychological Science, 13*, 385–388.

Cacioppo, J. T., Hawkley, L. C., Crawford, L. E., Ernst, J. M., Burleson, M. H., Kowalewski, R. B., et al. (2002). Loneliness and health: Potential mechanisms. *Psychosomatic Medicine, 64*, 407–417.

Cacioppo, J. T., Hawkley, L. C., Ernst, J. M., Burleson, M. H., Berntson, G. G., Nouriani, B., et al. (2006). Loneliness within a nomological net: An evolutionary perspective. *Journal of Research in Personality, 40*, 1054–1085.

Cacioppo, J. T., Hawkley, L. C., & Thisted, R. A. (2010). Perceived social isolation makes me sad: Five year cross-lagged analysis of loneliness and depressive symptomatology in the Chicago Health, Aging, and Social Relations study. *Psychology and Aging, 25*, 453–463.

Cacioppo, J. T., Hughes, M. E., Waite, L. J., Hawkley, L. C., & Thisted, R. (2006). Loneliness as a specific risk factor for depressive symptoms in older adults: Cross-sectional and longitudinal analyses. *Psychology and Aging, 21*, 140–151.

Cacioppo, J. T., Norris, C. J., Decety, J., Monteleone, G., & Nusbaum, H. (2008). In the eye of the beholder: Individual differences in perceived social isolation predict regional brain activation to social stimuli. *Journal of Cognitive Neuroscience, 21*, 83–92.

Cacioppo, J. T., & Patrick, B. (2008). *Loneliness: Human nature and the need for social connection*. New York: Norton.

Carstensen, L. L., Isaacowitz, D. M., & Charles, S. T. (1999). Taking time seriously: A theory of socioemotional selectivity. *American Psychologist, 54*, 165–181.

Caspi, A., Harrington, H., Moffitt, T. E., Milne, B. J., & Poulton, R. (2006). Socially isolated children 20 years later. *Archives of Pediatric Adolescent Medicine, 160*, 805–811.

Cheitlin, M. D. (2003). Cardiovascular physiology—Changes with aging. *American Journal of Geriatric Cardiology, 12*, 9–13.

Cheng, S. (1992). Loneliness-distress and physician utilization in well-elderly females. *Journal of Community Psychology, 20*, 43–56.

Chobanian, A. V., Bakris, G. L., Black, H. R., Cushman, W. C., Green, L. A., Izzo, J. L., Jr., et al. (2003). The seventh report of the Joint National Committee on Prevention, Detection, Evaluation, and Treatment of High Blood Pressure. *Journal of the American Medical Association, 289*, 2560–2572.

Cole, S. W., Hawkley, L. C., Arevalo, J. M. G., & Cacioppo, J. T. (2011). Transcript origin analysis identifies antigen presenting cells as primary targets of socially regulated leukocyte gene expression. *Proceedings of the National Academy of Sciences USA, 15*, 3080–3085.

Cole, S. W., Hawkley, L. C., Arevalo, J. M., Sung, C. Y., Rose, R. M., & Cacioppo, J. T. (2007). Social regulation of gene expression in humans: Glucocorticoid resistance in the leukocyte transcriptome. *Genome Biology, 8*, R189.1–R189.13.

Coussens, L. M., & Werb, Z. (2002). Inflammation and cancer. *Nature, 420*, 860–867.

Danesh, J., Wheeler, J. G., Hirschfield, G. M., Eda, S., Eiriksdottir, G., Rumley, A., et al. (2004). C-reactive protein and other circulating markers of inflammation in the prediction of coronary heart disease. *New England Journal of Medicine, 350*, 1387–1397.

De Jong-Gierveld, J. (1987). Developing and testing a model of loneliness. *Journal of Personality and Social Psychology, 53*, 119–128.

DiTommaso, E., Brannen-McNulty, C., Ross, L., & Burgess, M. (2003). Attachment styles, social skills and loneliness in young adults. *Personality and Individual Differences, 35*, 303–312.

Dixon, D., Cruess, S., Kilbourn, K., Klimas, N., Fletcher, M. A., Ironson, G., et al. (2001). Social support mediates loneliness and human herpesvirus type 6

(HHV-6) antibody titers. *Journal of Applied Social Psychology, 31,* 1111–1132.

Dunbar, R. I. M., & Shultz, S. (2007). Evolution in the social brain. *Science, 317,* 1344–1347.

Feldman, E. (2000). Loneliness and physician utilization in primary care [Abstract]. *Family Medicine, 32,* 471.

Folkow, B., & Svanborg, A. (1993). Physiology of cardiovascular aging. *Physiological Reviews, 73,* 725–764.

Fox, D. A. (2000). Cytokine blockade as a new strategy to treat rheumatoid arthritis: Inhibition of tumor necrosis factor. *Archives of Internal Medicine, 160,* 437–444.

Franklin, S. S., Gustin, W., IV, Wong, N. D., Larson, M. G., Weber, M. A., Kannel, W. B., et al. (1997). Hemodynamic patterns of age-related changes in blood pressure: The Framingham Heart Study. *Circulation, 96,* 308–315.

Friedman, E. M., Hayney, M. S., Love, G. D., Urry, H. L., Rosenkranz, M. A., Davidson, R. J., et al. (2005). Social relationships, sleep quality, and interleukin-6 in aging women. *Proceedings of the National Academy of Sciences USA, 102,* 18757–18762.

Fuster, J. J., Díez, J., & Andrés, V. (2007). Telomere dysfunction in hypertension. *Journal of Hypertension, 25,* 2185–2192.

Gardner, W. L., Pickett, C. L., Jeffries, V., & Knowles, M. (2005). On the outside looking in: Loneliness and social monitoring. *Personality and Social Psychology Bulletin, 31,* 1549–1560.

Geller, J., Janson, P., McGovern, E., & Valdini, A. (1999). Loneliness as a predictor of hospital emergency department use. *Journal of Family Practice, 48,* 801–804.

Glaser, R., Kiecolt-Glaser, J. K., Speicher, C. E., & Holliday, J. E. (1985). Stress, loneliness, and changes in herpesvirus latency. *Journal of Behavioral Medicine, 8,* 249–260.

Graham, J. E., Christian, L. M., & Kiecolt-Glaser, J. K. (2006). Stress, age, and immune function: Toward a lifespan approach. *Journal of Behavioral Medicine, 29,* 389–400.

Hawkley, L. C., Bosch, J. A., Engeland, C. G., Marucha, P. T., & Cacioppo, J. T. (2007). Loneliness, dysphoria, stress and immunity: A role for cytokines. In N. P. Plotnikoff, R. E. Faith, A. J. Murgo, & R. A. Good (Eds.), *Cytokines: Stress and immunity* (2nd ed., pp. 67–85). Boca Raton, FL: CRC Press.

Hawkley, L. C., Browne, M. W., & Cacioppo, J. T. (2005). How can I connect with thee? Let me count the ways. *Psychological Science, 16,* 798–804.

Hawkley, L. C., Burleson, M. H., Berntson, G. G., & Cacioppo, J. T. (2003). Loneliness in everyday life: Cardiovascular activity, psychosocial context, and health behaviors. *Journal of Personality and Social Psychology, 85,* 105–120.

Hawkley, L. C., & Cacioppo, J. T. (2007). Aging and loneliness: Downhill quickly? *Current Directions in Psychological Science, 16,* 187–191.

Hawkley, L. C., & Cacioppo, J. T. (2010). Loneliness matters: A theoretical and empirical review of consequences and mechanisms. *Annals of Behavioral Medicine, 40,* 218–227.

Hawkley, L. C., Hughes, M. E., Waite, L. J., Masi, C. M., Thisted, R. A., &

Cacioppo, J. T. (2008). From social structural factors to perceptions of relationship quality and loneliness: The Chicago Health, Aging, and Social Relations Study. *Journal of Gerontology: Social Sciences, 63B*, S375–S384.

Hawkley, L. C., Masi, C. M., Berry, J. D., & Cacioppo, J. T. (2006). Loneliness is a unique predictor of age-related differences in systolic blood pressure. *Psychology and Aging, 21*, 152–164.

Hawkley, L. C., Preacher, K. J., & Cacioppo, J. T. (2007). Multilevel modeling of social interactions and mood in lonely and socially connected individuals: The MacArthur Social Neuroscience Studies. In A. D. Ong & M. H. M. van Dulmen (Eds.), *Oxford handbook of methods in positive psychology* (pp. 559–575). New York: Oxford University Press.

Hawkley, L. C., Preacher, K. J., & Cacioppo, J. T. (2010). Loneliness impairs daytime functioning but not sleep duration. *Health Psychology, 29*, 124–129.

Hawkley, L. C., Thisted, R. A., & Cacioppo, J. T. (2009). Loneliness predicts reduced physical activity: Cross-sectional and longitudinal analyses. *Health Psychology, 28*, 354–363.

Hawkley, L. C., Thisted, R. A., Masi, C. M., & Cacioppo, J. T. (2010). Loneliness predicts increased blood pressure: Five-year cross-lagged analyses in middle-aged and older adults. *Psychology and Aging, 25*, 132–141.

Heikkinen, R., & Kauppinen, M. (2004). Depressive symptoms in late life: A 10-year follow-up. *Archives of Gerontology and Geriatrics, 38*, 239–250.

Holt-Lunstad, J., Smith, T. B., & Layton, J. B. (2010). Social relationships and mortality risk: A meta-analytic review. *PLoS Med 7(7)*, e1000316.

House, J. S., Landis, K. R., & Umberson, D. (1988). Social relationships and health. *Science, 241*, 540–545.

Kannel, W. B. (1996). Blood pressure as a cardiovascular risk factor: Prevention and treatment. *Journal of the American Medical Association, 275*, 1571–1576.

Kasprowicz, A. L., Manuck, S. B., Malkoff, S. B., & Krantz, D. S. (1990). Individual differences in behaviorally evoked cardiovascular response: Temporal stability and hemodynamic patterning. *Psychophysiology, 27*, 605–619.

Kiecolt-Glaser, J. K., Garner, W., Speicher, C., Penn, G. M., Holliday, J., & Glaser, R. (1984). Psychosocial modifiers of immunocompetence in medical students. *Psychosomatic Medicine, 46*, 7–14.

Kiecolt-Glaser, J. K., Ricker, D., George, J., Messick, G., Speicher, C. E., Garner, W., et al. (1984). Urinary cortisol levels, cellular immunocompetency and loneliness in psychiatric inpatients. *Psychosomatic Medicine, 46*, 15–23.

Lauder, W., Mummery, K., Jones, M., & Caperchione, C. (2006). A comparison of health behaviours in lonely and non-lonely populations. *Psychology, Health, and Medicine, 11*, 233–245.

Luo, Y., Hawkley, L. C., Waite, L. J., & Cacioppo, J. T. (2012). Loneliness, health, and mortality in old age: A national longitudinal study. *Social Science and Medicine, 74(6)*, 907–914.

McEwen, B. S., & Stellar, E. (1993). Stress and the individuals: Mechanisms leading to disease. *Archives of Internal Medicine, 153*, 2093–2101.

McGuire, S., & Clifford, J. (2000). Genetic and environmental contributions to loneliness in children. *Psychological Science, 11*, 487–491.

Miller, G. E., Kemeny, M. E., Taylor, S. E., Cole, S. W., & Visscher, B. R. (1997).

Social relationships and immune processes in HIV seropositive gay and bisexual men. *Annals of Behavioral Medicine, 19,* 139–151.

Nolen-Hoeksema, S., & Ahrens, C. (2002). Age differences and similarities in the correlates of depressive symptoms. *Psychology and Aging, 17,* 116–124.

O'Connor, K. A., Johnson, J. D., Hammack, S. E., Brooks, L. M., Spencer, R. L., Watkins, L. R., et al. (2003). Inescapable shock induces resistance to the effects of dexamethasone. *Psychoneuroendocrinology, 28,* 481–500.

Ohayon, M. M. (2005). Prevalence and correlates of nonrestorative sleep complaints. *Archives of Internal Medicine, 165,* 35–41.

Oparil, S., & Oberman, A. (1999). Nontraditional cardiovascular risk factors. *American Journal of the Medical Sciences, 317,* 193–207.

Page, R. M., Frey, J., Talbert, R., & Falk, C. (1992). Children's feelings of loneliness and social dissatisfaction: Relationship to measures of physical fitness and activity. *Journal of Teaching in Physical Education, 11,* 211–219.

Page, R. M., & Hammermeister, J. (1995). Shyness and loneliness: Relationship to the exercise frequency of college students. *Psychological Reports, 76,* 395–396.

Page, R. M., & Tucker, L. A. (1994). Psychosocial discomfort and exercise frequency: An epidemiological study of adolescents. *Adolescence, 29,* 183–191.

Paoletti, R., Gotto, A. M., Jr., & Hajjar, D. P. (2004). Inflammation in atherosclerosis and implications for therapy. *Circulation, 109*(23, Suppl. 15), III20–III26.

Patterson, A. C., & Veenstra, G. (2010). Loneliness and risk of mortality: A longitudinal investigation in Alameda County, California. *Social Science & Medicine, 71,* 181–186.

Penninx, B. W. J. H., van Tilburg, T., Kriegsman, D. M. W., Deeg, D. J. H., Boeke, A. J. P., & van Eijk, J. T. M. (1997). Effects of social support and personal coping resources on mortality in older age: The Longitudinal Aging Study Amsterdam. *American Journal of Epidemiology, 146,* 510–519.

Peplau, L. A., & Perlman, D. (1982). Perspectives on loneliness. In L. A. Peplau & D. Perlman (Eds.), *Loneliness: A sourcebook of current theory, research and therapy* (pp. 1–20). New York: Wiley.

Pickett, C. L., & Gardner, W. L. (2005). The social monitoring system: Enhanced sensitivity to social cues as an adaptive response to social exclusion. In K. D. Williams, J. P. Forgas, & W. von Hippel (Eds.), *The social outcast: Ostracism, social exclusion, rejection, and bullying* (pp. 213–226). New York: Psychology Press.

Pierce, G. R., Sarason, I. G., & Sarason, B. R. (1991). General and relationship-based perceptions of social support: Are two constructs better than one? *Journal of Personality and Social Psychology, 61,* 1028–1039.

Pinquart, M., & Sörensen, S. (2001). Influences on loneliness in older adults: A meta-analysis. *Basic and Applied Social Psychology, 23,* 245–266.

Pressman, S. D., Cohen, S., Miller, G. E., Barkin, A., Rabin, B. S., & Treanor, J. J. (2005). Loneliness, social network size, and immune response to influenza vaccination in college freshman. *Health Psychology, 24,* 297–306.

Qi, L., & Hu, F. B. (2007). Dietary glycemic load, whole grains, and systemic inflammation in diabetes: The epidemiological evidence. *Current Opinion in Lipidology, 18*, 3–8.

Reblin, M., & Uchino, B. N. (2008). Social and emotional support and its implication for health. *Current Opinion in Psychiatry, 21*, 201–205.

Schiffrin, E. L. (2004). Vascular stiffening and arterial compliance. *American Journal of Hypertension, 17*, 39S–48S.

Schnittker, J. (2007). Look (closely) at all the lonely people: Age and social psychology of social support. *Journal of Aging and Health, 19*, 659–682.

Seeman, T. E. (2000). Health-promoting effects of friends and family on health outcomes in older adults. *American Journal of Public Health, 14*, 362–370.

Seeman, T. E., & Robbins, R. J. (1994). Aging and hypothalamic-pituitary-adrenal response to challenge in humans. *Endocrine Reviews, 15*, 233–260.

Segrin, C. (1999). Social skills, stressful life events, and the development of psychosocial problems. *Journal of Social and Clinical Psychology, 18*, 14–34.

Shaw, B. A., & Krause, N. (2002). Exposure to physical violence during childhood, aging, and health. *Journal of Aging and Health, 14*, 467–494.

Shiovitz-Ezra, S., & Ayalon, L. (2010). Situational versus chronic loneliness as risk factors for all-cause mortality. *International Psychogeriatrics, 22*, 455–462.

Spiegel, K., Leproult, R., & Van Cauter, E. (1999). Impact of a sleep debt on metabolic and endocrine function. *Lancet, 354*, 1435–1439.

Spieker, L. E., Flammer, A. J., & Luscher, T. F. (2006). The vascular endothelium in hypertension. *Handbook of Experimental Pharmacology, 176*(Pt. 2), 249–283.

Steptoe, A., Owen, N., Kunz-Ebrecht, S. R., & Brydon, L. (2004). Loneliness and neuroendocrine, cardiovascular, and inflammatory stress responses in middle-aged men and women. *Psychoneuroendocrinology, 29*, 593–611.

Sterling, P. (2004). Principles of allostasis: Optimal design, predictive regulation, pathophysiology, and rational therapeutics. In J. Schulkin (Ed.), *Allostasis, homeostasis, and the cost of physiological adaptation* (pp. 17–63). New York: Cambridge University Press.

Sugisawa, H., Liang, J., & Liu, X. (1994). Social networks, social support, and mortality among older people in Japan. *Journal of Gerontology, 49*, S3–13.

Tilvis, R. J., Kähönen-Väre, M. H., Jolkkonen, J., Valvanne, J., Pitkala, K. H., & Strandberg, T. E. (2004). Predictors of cognitive decline and mortality of aged people over a 10-year period. *Journals of Gerontology: Series A. Biological Sciences and Medical Sciences, 59*, M268–M274.

Toro, L., Marijic, J., Nishimaru, K., Tanaka, Y., Song, M., & Stefani, E. (2002). Aging, ion channel expression, and vascular function. *Vascular Pharmacology, 38*, 73–80.

Uchino, B. N., Cacioppo, J. T., & Kiecolt-Glaser, J. K. (1996). The relationship between social support and physiological processes: A review with emphasis on underlying mechanisms and implications for health. *Psychological Bulletin, 119*, 488–531.

VanderWeele, T. J., Hawkley, L. C., Thisted, R. A., & Cacioppo, J. T. (2011). A marginal structural analysis for loneliness: Implications for intervention trials and clinical practice. *Journal of Consulting and Clinical Psychology, 79*, 225–235.

Vignola, A. M., Chiappara, G., Gagliardo, R., Gjomarkaj, M., Merendino, A., Siena, L., et al. (2000). Apoptosis and airway inflammation in asthma. *Apoptosis, 5*, 473–485.

Wellen, K. E., & Hotamisligil, G. S. (2005). Inflammation, stress, and diabetes. *Journal of Clinical Investigation, 115*, 1111–1119.

Wheeler, L., Reis, H., & Nezlek, J. (1983). Loneliness, social interaction, and sex roles. *Journal of Personality and Social Psychology, 45*, 943–953.

Wilson, R. S., Krueger, K. R., Arnold, S. E., Barnes, L. L., de Leon, C. F. M., Bienias, J. L., et al. (2006). Childhood adversity and psychosocial adjustment in old age. *American Journal of Geriatric Psychiatry, 14*, 307–315.

Wilson, R. S., Krueger, K. R., Arnold, S. E., Schneider, J. A., Kelly, J. F., Barnes, L. L., et al. (2007). Loneliness and risk of Alzheimer's disease. *Archives of General Psychiatry, 64*, 234–240.

Yusuf, S., Hawken, S., Ounpan, S., Dans, T., Avezum, A., Lanas, F., et al. (2004). Effect of potentially modifiable risk factors associated with myocardial infarction in 52 countries (The INTERHEART Study): Case–control study. *The Lancet, 364*, 937–952.

Author Index

Subject Index

An *f* following a page number indicates a figure.